CONGREGAT]

This book breaks new ground in the study of hermeneutics. Andrew Rogers has done the Church an incredible service by lifting the veil on how congregations interact with the bible and make sense of it in their everyday lives. This careful and original piece of research builds towards constructive and creative suggestions to help the Christian community as it reads the Bible. It is a must read for anyone interested in qualitative research and the study of the Church.

Pete Ward, Professorial Fellow in Ecclesiology
and Ethnography, Durham University, UK

Andrew Rogers has put us in his debt. His clear and very insightful study of congregational hermeneutics has extended our understanding of how Christian communities actually interpret the Bible in practice. His constructive proposal makes a significant contribution to scholarship in the field. Scholars, students and church leaders interested in practical theology and congregational studies should read this book.

Mark J. Cartledge, Professor of Practical
Theology, Regent University, Virginia, USA

The Bible becomes Scripture as it is read by the community of faith. In telling the tale of two congregations, Andrew Rogers helps us look again at the traditions, practices and epistemologies we inhabit. This is an important ethnographic study in the borderlands between practical theology, biblical studies and congregational studies. The seasoned minister will find a real stimulus to reflective practice. The student will find much they wish to emulate.

Helen Cameron, Ripon College Cuddesdon, UK

Explorations in Practical, Pastoral and Empirical Theology

Series Editors

Leslie J. Francis, University of Warwick, UK
Jeff Astley, St Chad's College, Durham University, UK
Martyn Percy, University of Oxford, UK
Nicola Slee, The Queen's Foundation Birmingham, UK

Theological reflection on the church's practice is now recognized as a significant element in theological studies in the academy and seminary. Ashgate's series in practical, pastoral and empirical theology seeks to foster this resurgence of interest and encourage new developments in practical and applied aspects of theology worldwide. This timely series draws together a wide range of disciplinary approaches and empirical studies to embrace contemporary developments including: the expansion of research in empirical theology, psychological theology, ministry studies, public theology, Christian education and faith development; key issues of contemporary society such as health, ethics and the environment; and more traditional areas of concern such as pastoral care and counselling.

Other titles in the series include:

Sharing Friendship
Exploring Anglican Character, Vocation, Witness and Mission
John B. Thomson

Using the Bible in Practical Theology
Historical and Contemporary Perspectives
Zoë Bennett

The Faith Lives of Women and Girls
Qualitative Research Perspectives
Edited by Nicola Slee, Fran Porter and Anne Phillips

Saving Face
Enfacement, Shame, Theology
Stephen Pattison

Congregational Hermeneutics

How Do We Read?

ANDREW P. ROGERS

University of Roehampton, UK

ASHGATE

Published by
Ashgate Publishing Limited
Wey Court East
Union Road
Farnham
Surrey, GU9 7PT
England

Ashgate Publishing Company
110 Cherry Street
Suite 3–1
Burlington, VT 05401–3818
USA

www.ashgate.com

British Library Cataloguing in Publication Data
A catalogue record for this book is available from the British Library

Library of Congress Cataloging-in-Publication Data
Rogers, Andrew P.
    Congregational hermeneutics : how do we read? / by Andrew P. Rogers.
        pages cm. – (Explorations in practical, pastoral, and empirical theology)
    Includes bibliographical references and index.
    ISBN 978–1–4094–4988–1 (hardcover : alk. paper) – ISBN 978–1–4094–4989–8
    (pbk. : alk. paper) – ISBN 978–1–4094–4990–4 (ebook) – ISBN 978–1–4724–
    0649–1 (epub)
    1. Bible – Hermeneutics. 2. Bible – Study and teaching.
    I. Title.
    BS476.R63 2015
    220.609–dc23   2015016391

ISBN 9781409449881 (hbk)
ISBN 9781409449898 (pbk)
ISBN 9781409449904 (ebk – PDF)
ISBN 9781472406491 (ebk – ePUB)

Printed in the United Kingdom by Henry Ling Limited, at the Dorset Press, Dorchester, DT1 1HD

To Katie, Eden, Rosie and Joel

Contents

List of Figures and Tables

Figures

Tables

Acknowledgements

My heartfelt thanks goes to the pastors and congregants at 'Holder' and 'Fellowship', who welcomed me into their congregations, graciously put up with my scribblings and questions, and without whom there would be no 'Tale of Two Churches'. I am very grateful also to Professors Andy Wright and Brian Street who steered me through this research project when at King's College London, providing much advice, feedback and support along the way. I would like also to thank the Arts and Humanities Research Council who made this project possible through providing the majority of the funding. In addition, I have really appreciated the confidence that the British and Foreign Bible Society placed in this project, and have valued the ways we have worked together on turning recommendations into practice. Particular thanks also to Sarah Lloyd, Jeff Astley, and all at Ashgate who have made this book happen.

Many communities helped this research along the way. Members of the Centre for Theology, Religion and Culture at King's College London provided much insight and guidance. My colleagues at the University of Roehampton, especially in the Research Group in Ministerial Theology, have helped me to think through thorny issues in the later stages of the project. The students of the Congregational Hermeneutics class of Autumn 2011 deserve praise for testing this material out in their own ministry contexts. The Ecclesiology and Ethnography network has challenged me to think through the methodology and structure of the book more rigorously. Special mention must be made of the British and Irish Association of Practical Theology (BIAPT), through whom I have learned most of my practical theology. The special interest group in Bible and Practical Theology has been of particular benefit for thinking clearly and imaginatively about Bible and Practice, which is in no small part due to the influence of my co-convenor, Zoë Bennett. Many thanks also to Richard Briggs for reading through parts of the draft manuscript. Responsibility for the final form of the text is, of course, my own. It would be odd not to recognise the ministers and people of my own congregation who have provided earthed feedback on the outworkings of this research, alongside opportunities to try things out, especially with my wonderful homegroup.

From the long list of acknowledgements here, it will be apparent that this book has been a long time, or even a very long time in the making. My family are the ones for whom this time has been a significant sacrifice. Thanks to my parents-in-law who babysat parts of the book into being. And finally more thanks than I can write to my wife, Katie, and children, Eden, Rosie, and Joel, who let me go to the office when there were other important things to do. This book is dedicated to you all with love.

* * *

List of Abbreviations

Ethnographic Referencing

Details of the ethnographic referencing conventions adopted are given in Chapter 2.

Fellowship	City Reach Christian Fellowship (pseudonym)
Holder	Holder Evangelical Church (pseudonym)
anonH/anonF	Unidentified congregants
SunAM<1–9>h	Sunday morning services (Holder)
SatAM	Saturday morning monthly training sessions (Holder)
S<1–12>h	Sermons (Holder)
SunAM<1–12>f	Sunday morning services (Fellowship)
S<1–13>f	Sermons (Fellowship)
X<1–5>, Y<1–5>	Holder housegroup sessions
WedAM	Wednesday morning Bible study (Holder)
A<1–4>, B<1–4>, C<1–2>	Fellowship housegroup sessions
TuesAM<1–5>	Tuesday morning Bible study (Fellowship)
ThursAM<1–4>	Thursday morning Bible study (Fellowship)
ThursPM<1–3>	Thursday evening Bible study (Fellowship)

Other Abbreviations

Adv. Haer.	Irenaeus, *Adversus Haereses*, Against Heresies
BSG	Bible Study Guide
CBS	Contextual Bible Study
Coll.	John Cassian, *Collationes*, Conferences
Conf.	Augustine, *Confessiones*, Confessions
CSBH	Chicago Statement on Biblical Hermeneutics
CSBI	Chicago Statement on Biblical Inerrancy
Civ. Dei	Augustine, *De Civitate Dei*, The City of God

Gen. Lit.	Augustine, *De Genesi ad Litteram*, The Literal Meaning of Genesis
Mor. Ecc.	Augustine, *De Moribus Ecclesiae Catholicae*, The Catholic (and Manichaean) Ways of Life
Doc. Chr.	Augustine, *De Doctrina Christiana*, On Christian Doctrine
Serv. Arb.	Luther, *De Servito Arbitrio*, On the Bondage of the Will
EA	Evangelical Alliance
FIEC	Fellowship of Independent Evangelical Churches
KJV	King James Version (Bible)
MP	Mission Praise
NE	Aristotle, *Nicomachean Ethics*
NT	New Testament
NIV	New International Version (Bible)
NKJV	New King James Version (Bible)
NRSV	New Revised Standard Version (Bible)
OT	Old Testament
PBR	Personal Bible Reading
Post. Litt.	Nicholas of Lyra, *Postilla litteralis super totam Bibliam*, The Literal Postilla on the Entire Bible
Praesc.	Tertullian, *De Praescriptione Haereticorum*, Prescription against Heretics
SF	Songs of Fellowship
ST	Aquinas, *Summa Theologica*

Chapter 1
How Do We Read?

'How do we read the Bible?' is a deceptively simple question, yet it is really at least two questions in one.

The first question requires a broadly descriptive answer. How is the Bible shaping Christian communities? How are we actually making connections between the text and our context – what processes and starting points are involved? Such a question points to the long overdue expansion of the 'hermeneutics' category towards the descriptive, that builds on the fledgling field of the variously termed congregational/ordinary/empirical hermeneutics.[1]

The second question requires a prescriptive answer which tackles prescriptive hermeneutical matters, in other words, how *should* we read the Bible? This question is related to the first, since we need to know where we are in order to move towards where we want to go. A cursory Google search makes it clear that many church leaders and educators see this second question as primary, with numerous results listed under the heading of 'How to read the Bible'.

Eugene Peterson, translator of *The Message*, considers Jesus' use of the 'how' question in Lk 10:26 when being tested by a religion scholar. Of the law, Jesus asks: 'How do you read it?' Related to this exchange, Peterson warns:

> Reading the Bible, if we do not do it rightly, can get us into a lot of trouble. The Christian community is as concerned with *how* we read the Bible as *that* we read it … An enormous amount of damage is done in the name of Christian living by bad Bible reading (my italics 2006: 81–2).

Peterson is right to identify the importance of the 'how' question, but I am not persuaded that churches demonstrate such a concern for 'how' as he claims. Some have recognised this. The global research project from the worldwide Anglican Communion, 'The Bible in the Life of the Church', drew attention to 'how' in its core message as follows:

> A major finding of these investigations is that how Anglicans engage with the Bible turns out to be just as important as its content. This perhaps unnerving

---

[1]   For congregational see Murray (2000) and Rogers (2013c); for ordinary see Dube and West (1996b), Rogers (2007; 2013c), and Village (2007; 2013); for empirical see de Wit (2012). See extended terminological discussion below.

claim does not contest the unique place and authority which the scriptures have in Anglican life, but it does point up the significance, perhaps thus far overlooked, of the contexts in which and processes by which they are heard and read (2012: 5).

Of an international Baptist colloquium in 2009, the authors of the resulting volume place a similar emphasis on 'how'. So Simon Woodman and Helen Dare argue 'it is crucial for Baptists to devote time to thinking together about *how* we read Scripture: the process is as important as any conclusions we may draw about particular passages' (cited in Goodliff, 2011). 'How do we read?' are questions that deserve attention.

This book addresses both 'How do we read?' questions through paying attention to how Christians actually read the Bible in churches and how that mutually informs theological accounts of how we should read. This is done through drawing on a range of empirical research, from global to national to local, both quantitative and qualitative. The main focus, however, is on two ethnographic accounts of congregations and their biblical hermeneutics – so 'congregational hermeneutics'.[2] Ethnographic accounts allow us to capture something of the everyday, ordinary ways in which the Bible is incorporated into the life of congregations, through personal Bible reading, small group Bible study, formal and informal liturgy, sermons, songs,[3] architecture, and artefacts such as websites and study Bibles. The resonance and dissonance of the voices answering our two questions generates the argument for the book. The core argument, in summary, is that many congregations may need to develop a more intentional, corporate and virtuous hermeneutical apprenticeship as a necessary dimension of being church.

What is Not Being Done

Putting the Bible, church and hermeneutics together tends to bring out the contrarian in Christians. Although not normally recommended, in this case it seems worth making clear in advance what is *not* part of the congregational hermeneutics agenda.

I am not assuming nor arguing for a congregational system of church governance. 'Congregational hermeneutics' here has both descriptive and prescriptive senses, as highlighted above, in that it expands the domain of hermeneutics to the descriptive, but also looks at how churches 'ought' to read.

---

[2]   This book is a substantial development and rewrite of my doctoral thesis (Rogers, 2009).

[3]   'Song' is the generic term used here for all hymns and choruses used by the congregations.

Of the latter, my argument for a more intentional, corporate and virtuous hermeneutical apprenticeship will ask questions of any ecclesiology, but it is not limited to any particular type. Nor is this book aimed at a particular denomination and their hermeneutical characteristics; I would hope that those from all denominations and 'none' might be drawn into this exploration of 'How do we read the Bible?' Congregation(al), then, here has the sense of local church or of that which pertains to a local church.[4]

I am not suggesting that every aspect of the case studies has a direct correspondence to all other churches. Reflecting theologically on ethnographic accounts has become a common approach within the field of practical theology in recent decades, often with the purpose of having something useful to say to the church in its mission. Congregations have their own particularity, which, as Al Dowie comments, 'in certain respects is like that of all others, like some others, and like no other congregation' (2002: 65). Theologically speaking, as Craig Dykstra and Dorothy Bass argue, the 'practices of all Christian congregations are intricately linked to one another' through the unifying power of the Holy Spirit (2002: 27). The particularity of the accounts is held in tension with their capacity for generating theological models, analogies, and imaginative leaps, as well as funding constructive critique of idealised ecclesiologies and ecclesial practices (Fiddes, 2012).

I am not prescribing a narrow hermeneutical blueprint of How-to-Read-the-Bible in six easy steps. There are plenty of these already. Hermeneutics is not taken to be synonymous with interpretation, but rather thinking about *how* we are interpreting Scripture (cf. Thiselton, 2009: 1, 4). Consequently, the discussion here is more 'How?' than 'What?', more process than content, more about developing hermeneutical virtues and skills than specific turn-the-handle hermeneutical programmes. Having said that, I believe that theology, and practical theology in particular, should be transformative, and therefore have no reservations about offering careful proposals for hermeneutical apprenticeship that are drawn from long listening to ethnographic voices, amongst others.[5]

I am not trying to do everything in and with these accounts. They are a focussed study on the hermeneutical discourses, actions, artefacts and mediators within congregations. In other words, the saying, doing, making and learning of biblical hermeneutics in churches (cf. Stringer, 1999: 49f).[6] This is a complex

[4]   The same sense as in the subdiscipline of congregational studies (e.g. Guest et al., 2004; cf. Cameron et al., 2005).

[5]   Cautions about scholars rushing in to help Bible readers in churches are voiced by Andrew Village (2013: 130). I am bound to agree that hasty 'help' is unlikely to be effective, but also think the inevitable risk of proposing and/or enabling revised practices is one worth taking. See examples in Chapter 9.

[6]   As I will discuss in Chapter 2, these all contribute to the category of hermeneutical 'practices'.

enough task in itself. I was not able to consider those under the age of 18.[7] I was not able to observe congregants in settings beyond church and home that might be indicative for hermeneutical choices (perhaps something for a future project). Despite these limitations, the accounts are of sufficient scope to speak to the question 'How do we read?'

I am not wanting to overpower the voices of the churches with theory, yet neither do I want to play at being innocent of prior frames and categories. Indeed, there is an intentional intermingling of theological and ethnographic voices in this book. The discussion is interdisciplinary, drawing mainly on theology/biblical studies and anthropology/sociology of religion, held together within the field of practical theology. Concerns about 'overly cognitive and orthodox definitions of Christian faithfulness' and the theologian's temptation to 'map sense and order onto the worldly' are rightly expressed by Mary McClintock Fulkerson in her own congregational study (2007: 6–7). However, many churches still retain an attachment to cognitive and orthodox definitions of faith alongside more implicit and embodied forms of theological conviction, as these accounts demonstrate, and so need to be engaged with on their own terms.[8]

I am not seeking to replace a theological account of the Bible in the church with a hermeneutical one, largely because I do not see these as mutually exclusive categories. John Webster, in particular, laments the 'underfed theology' that he perceives in accounts of the church's reading of Scripture where hermeneutics is made foundational for theology (2006: esp. chapter 2). While recognising the danger here, it is certainly possible to make a critical appropriation of hermeneutical theory in order to aid a theological construal of the Bible in the church. As Francis Watson has argued, this does not imply a foundational status for hermeneutics, but rather a drawing upon the conceptual resources of hermeneutics, just as in other interdisciplinary theological enterprises.[9] As Watson concludes, it is in this sense that the doctrine of Scripture and hermeneutics need each other (2010).

Defining Congregational Hermeneutics

It would seem appropriate at this point to be a little more precise about some of the concepts, terminology and debates surrounding congregational hermeneutics. The term 'congregational hermeneutics' was coined by the

---

[7]   This was partly due to research ethics limitations at the time, plus the sheer number of youth and their activities in each church, which meant a focus on adults was the appropriate scope.

[8]   This point is expanded in Chapter 3.

[9]   An extended argument is made in Chapter 2 for the validity of theological ethnography.

Anabaptist theologian, Stuart Murray, to describe one component of Anabaptist hermeneutics historically, as well as offering a hermeneutical paradigm for Anabaptists today. Murray sees Anabaptist hermeneutics as having a useful conversation partner role for other hermeneutical traditions (Murray, 2000: esp. chapters 7 and 10; Williams, 2008).[10] By comparison, my usage is also both descriptive and prescriptive, but is concerned with all aspects of contemporary hermeneutics in congregations from potentially any tradition.[11]

Two other related terms are sometimes used in the book, namely 'ordinary hermeneutics' and 'empirical hermeneutics'. Ordinary hermeneutics was inspired by Jeff Astley's work in ordinary theology, and through adapting his definition, I understand ordinary readers[12] of the Bible to be those who have limited or no Bible-related theological education 'of a scholarly, academic or systematic kind' (2002: 56; see also Astley and Francis, 2013). I used ordinary hermeneutics of this research in its earlier forms (Rogers, 2007; 2009) and I have found that people intuitively grasp what is meant. However, not all ordinary readers are in churches, and there is some significant leakage between the categories of ordinary and academic, as Astley acknowledges himself (2002: 57–8, 86).[13] Since the stories here arise from within congregations, and I wanted to include all those engaging with the Bible (ordinary, academic, and those in-between), congregational hermeneutics seemed like an obvious change (Rogers, 2013b; c). Nevertheless, the term 'ordinary' is still useful and will be retained for occasional use. Empirical hermeneutics is a largely descriptive category, coined by Hans de Wit in the Netherlands, and usefully refers to all research based on empirical accounts of hermeneutics (2004: 41; 2012). A more general set of terms that have proved very useful to practical theology are the 'four voices' of the Action, Research, Church and Society (ARCS) project at Heythrop College in London. The espoused voice is what Christians say they believe; the operant voice is what

---

[10]   Indeed, a role his work plays in this book.

[11]   See more occasional uses in Fiddes (2008; cf. Harmon, 2012; also Catholic Church and Baptist World Alliance, 2006–10: §49) and Labanow (2009: 49–50).

[12]   'Reader' is not limited to reading text here, but also listening to the Bible in liturgy and seeing it in artefacts and architecture. In other words, not only do congregants read the Bible as a text, but they also 'read' the Bible through the congregational experience.

[13]   See also Pete Ward's critique (2011). Gerald West's pioneering work in South Africa draws a stronger distinction between ordinary and critical, by defining ordinary readers as all those 'who read the Bible in an untrained or pre-critical way' (1993: 9) as well as being those who are 'poor and marginalised' (1999: 11). Critical readers are those 'who have been trained in the use of the tools and resources of biblical scholarship' (Dube and West, 1996a: 7) as well as being scholars 'who have chosen to collaborate with the poor and marginalised' (1999: 11). In a 2007 discussion, West continues to maintain a distinction between scholar and 'nonscholar' based on 'the kind of interpretive training [these] different sectors have received' (2007a: 2).

their practices 'disclose about our lived out theology'; the normative voice is the theology of their church tradition; and the formal voice is the theology of 'professional' theologians. The four voices intermingle and provide a useful shorthand for congregational hermeneutics (Heythrop College, 2013; cf. Cameron et al., 2010: 53–6).

The standard definition of hermeneutics is 'the science and art of interpretation' (cf. Barton, 1998: xiii–ix; Klein et al., 1993: 5; Marshall, 2004: 11; Gadamer, 2004: 268).[14] Four points about hermeneutics need stressing here, prior to more extended discussion later in the book. *Firstly*, and often omitted, is the importance of the Spirit's role in hermeneutics. We should read with the Spirit however that may be variously construed in different Christian traditions. Such reading is not in opposition to developing hermeneutical skills and virtues if the Spirit is allowed to permeate our faculties and volition. Related to this point, a focus on churchly hermeneutical practices (that I consider long overdue), does not preclude theological reflection upon the place of Scripture in 'the economy of God's communicative grace' (Webster, 2003: 6). Indeed, I will argue that this focus is a necessary part of such reflection. *Secondly*, hermeneutics is not exegesis or interpretation. Rather, it is the 'meta-discipline' that stands back and critically reflects on how we are interpreting the Bible (Thiselton, 1992: 48; 2009: 4; cf. Wood, 2000: 11). In his influential text on hermeneutics, Richard Palmer asserts that, even at the beginning of hermeneutics as a discipline, there was 'a distinction between actual commentary (exegesis) and the rules, methods, or theory governing it (hermeneutics) ... and [this] remains basic to the definition of hermeneutics' (1969: 34). Of course, in 'standing back' we need to apprehend the whole process of interpretation, so hermeneutics in a sense does include exegesis, for example, but only in a second order capacity.[15] Hermeneutics is also distinct from the more general categories of Bible 'use',[16] 'engagement', and 'literacy',[17] although they are valuable for broader discussion of the Bible-in-the-Church, hence I will use them where appropriate. *Thirdly*, it is important to hold the 'science and art' together. A traditional understanding of hermeneutics that persists in some circles tends to emphasise the scientific and rational aspect, where hermeneutics is confined to rules for interpretation (Thiselton, 2009: 2).[18] This is to the detriment of the 'art' aspect, however, as one does not need to spend long in Christian communities to recognise that hermeneutical practices

[14]   Unless quoting someone else, the plural form of hermeneutics will be maintained.

[15]   Consequently, I do not see hermeneutics as a practice that is restricted to textual significance, application or contextualisation (Gadamer, 2004: 307; Thiselton, 1992: 605).

[16]   I take 'use', both noun and verb, to refer to practices that engage with the Bible in some way. See discussion in Chapter 3.

[17]   An interesting parallel study of everyday literacy practices within the field of education has been carried out by David Barton and Mary Hamilton (1998).

[18]   For example, see Klein, Blomberg and Hubbard (1993: 6n4).

include imaginative and intuitive moves between text and context. *Fourthly*, 'hermeneutical apprenticeship' is taken in a broad sense to mean those formal and informal ways in which Christians do and may 'learn how to learn from Scripture' (Stott, 1977: 7). This may well be an apprenticeship through one or more Christian communities rather than one specific apprentice–mentor relationship.

'How Do We Read?' In Context

'How do we read?' is not asked in a theological vacuum. Academics, churches and parachurch organisations have been giving increasing attention to this question. Here I lay out the academic context for congregational hermeneutics, followed by a sample of key surveys from around the world that include questions about the Bible.

The theological ether out of which congregational hermeneutics emerges is the 'turn to context' in the latter half of the twentieth century. Perhaps the most significant factor in this turn was the challenge to traditional theological method from the global south, especially from liberation theology. The 'epistemological break' led to a rejection of a 'theology-from-above' methodology and brought the context of theology into the foreground (Bosch, 1991: 423f). 'Who is theologising, where and with whom?' became more important questions for the theological task. In addition, postmodern currents in the West have led to more attention being paid to the local, and have also generated a critique of the power structures embedded in traditional academic theology. In its modern form, practical theology itself is a child of this turn to context, and biblical studies has also seen a proliferation of books addressing readings of the Bible in specific contexts, especially those from outside the West.[19]

Given the turn to context, and the huge literature on academic biblical hermeneutics, it is surprising how long it has taken the academy to pay attention to the biblical hermeneutics of ordinary Christians.[20] To paraphrase Astley, statistically speaking ordinary hermeneutics are the hermeneutics of God's church (2002: 162). Hans de Wit has described this omission as 'one of the biggest embarrassments and gaps in modern biblical scholarship' (2004:

---

[19] E.g. *Reading from this Place* (Segovia and Tolbert, 1995a; b); *Voices from the Margin* & *Vernacular Hermeneutics* (Sugirtharajah, 1991; 1999); *The Bible in Africa* (Dube and West, 2001), *The Bible in a World Context* (Dietrich and Luz, 2002); *Through the Eyes of Another* (de Wit et al., 2004); *Reading Other-Wise* (West, 2007b).

[20] The turn to context has not always resulted in a focus on ordinary or popular religion. However, one might also speak of a 'turn to the ordinary' in a much smaller sense, especially within practical theology (e.g. Astley, 2002; Village, 2007; Astley and Christie, 2007; Christie, 2012; Astley and Francis, 2013).

10).[21] Generalisations about Bible reading in the church are often made by scholars on the basis of anecdotal evidence or sometimes drawing on the authority of a scholar-practitioner's experience. While such insights can be valuable, they are lacking in empirical substantiation, and are too often cast as a hermeneutics of condescension.

It is true now that the academy has begun to pay attention to congregational and ordinary hermeneutics, especially in biblical studies, practical theology and sociology/anthropology of Christianity. Until relatively recently, such attention has largely been the concern of scholars identifying with a liberation theology/ hermeneutics agenda within biblical studies.[22] So Carlos Mesters has written about the 'popular interpretation' of ordinary Bible readers in Brazil (1980; 1983a; b; 1990), where 'the main concern of the people is not to interpret the Bible, but to interpret their lives with the help of the Bible' (Mesters, 1983a: 86; 1990: 115). In the UK, the series *British Liberation Theology* has been produced by The Urban Theology Unit in Sheffield, with a concern for the ordinary appropriation of the biblical text (particularly Rowland and Vincent, 2001).[23] John Vincent of the Unit refers to this concern variously as 'Use and Influence', 'Outworkings', 'Gospel practice studies' or 'Practice interpretation' (2001; 2002; 2004; 2005; 2011).[24] Gerald West has pioneered reflection on working with marginalised ordinary Bible readers in South Africa since the early 1990s, with a particular interest in what happens when 'critical' and 'ordinary' readers read the Bible together, especially through 'Contextual Bible Study' (e.g. Dube and West, 1996a; b; 2001; West, 1991, 1993, 1999, 2007b). West's work has been a catalyst for many others in the field, and has been developed in the UK by the biblical scholars John Riches (2010) and Louise Lawrence. Lawrence's work analyses and reflects on five Bible reading groups in different contexts in the West of England and proposes a threefold typology for a 'hermeneutics of place', namely allegory, parable, and midrash (2009: 128–9).[25] In the same tradition as West, Hans de Wit in Amsterdam directed a large international study which analysed structured reports of gathered Bible studies on Jn 4:1–41 (The Woman

---

[21]   See also David Clines (1997: 80), Mark Allan Powell (2001: 28–9) and Andrew Village (2007: 2f).

[22]   Exceptions include David Clines's student-led ad hoc survey of Bible use in an English city and Mark Allan Powell's small-scale survey of American laity and clergy (Clines, 1997; Powell, 2001). Powell's results suggested a hermeneutical difference between laity and clergy, in that the 'laity always evinced a reader-oriented hermeneutic' whereas 'clergy tended to evince an author-oriented hermeneutic' (2001: 53).

[23]   Subsumed under 'contextual theology' in the UTU.

[24]   Such work has a forum at the British New Testament Society's 'Use and Influence' seminar group, although it has a strong emphasis on reception history (British New Testament Society, 2013).

[25]   I have drawn on my review of Lawrence here (Rogers, 2011).

at the Well), looking at ordinary reading strategies and comparing cultural approaches (de Wit et al., 2004; de Wit, 2012). The study generated a picture of what ordinary readers 'do with Bible texts and what Bible texts do to readers' (2004: 4).[26] There has also been engagement from the broader discipline of biblical studies through the relatively recent creation of a Bible and Practical Theology section at the *Society for Biblical Literature* annual conference (2013; 2015).

Within sociology and anthropology of religion there has been an upsurge of interest in the use of the Bible over the last few decades. Robert Wuthnow's seminal work on small groups in American religion forms the backdrop to this trend (1994a; b).[27] John Bartkowski's hermeneutical analysis of two popular American evangelical authors led him to call for future research on 'the hermeneutical dynamics of Scripture interpretation in actual communities' using qualitative research methods (1996). Brian Malley undertook an anthropological study of 'evangelical biblicism' within an American congregation. *How the Bible Works* constructs a model of the Bible's function in the church, and includes some analysis of the interaction between tradition, hermeneutics and the congregation (2004).

In relation to congregational hermeneutics, the most substantial work to date from the social sciences is by James Bielo. In his *Words upon the Word*, Bielo argues for the critical significance of small group Bible study within American culture. Using multiple congregational sites, he seeks to develop an ethnography of Bible study life to demonstrate 'the importance of what happens when Evangelicals are "just sitting around talking"' (2009b: 18–19). The broader and more programmatic *The Social Life of the Scriptures* continues to advocate the term 'biblicism' as a 'working analytical framework intended to facilitate comparative research on how Christians interact with their sacred texts'. Biblicism looks for 'identifiable principles and processes' that may describe and explain the interactions between the Bible and its communities. Clearly sharing some common ground with congregational hermeneutics,[28] Bielo's approach aims to 'reimagine the category of scripture' through 'excavating the work ... that we make "scriptures" do for us' (Bielo, 2009a: 2, 9; also citing Wimbush, 2008: 1).

---

[26] This project is on-going, see Intercultural Bible Collective (2015).

[27] There are many social science works that assess the place of the Bible in churches and culture in more general terms (e.g. Ammerman, 1987; Boone, 1989).

[28] However, this social science tradition has a very marked lack of engagement with work in biblical studies and practical theology. Consequently, there seems to be little recognition of the broader descriptive dimension of hermeneutics of other scholars working in the same area. Furthermore, 'biblicism' has been used by some scholars to denote a particular attitude towards the Bible or even specific hermeneutical characteristics. For example, 'biblicism' is one corner of David Bebbington's widely cited historical characterisation of evangelicalism (1989: 3–4), and Christian Smith has argued that biblicism comprises 10 hermeneutical assumptions and critiques them as 'untenable' (2012: 3).

Within practical theology, there has been growing interest in the use of the Bible in church and ministry contexts. Roger Walton in the UK conducted a study of how students in theological institutions used the Bible and Christian tradition in their assignments, reports, and seminars, from which he derived seven distinct types of Bible and tradition use (2003). A significant engagement in the British context was the *Use of the Bible in Pastoral Practice* project,[29] which brought biblical scholars and practical theologians together to talk about some of the critical issues in the Bible/practice interface (Ballard, 2006). A number of publications emerged from this project (Ballard and Holmes, 2005; Oliver, 2006), including a research-based workbook for practitioners (Pattison et al., 2007), as well as a challenging critique of Bible and practice from the initial empirical investigations (Dickson, 2003; 2007). Mary McClintock Fulkerson's *Places of Redemption: Theology for a Worldly Church* is a study of Good Samaritan United Methodist church in Durham, North Carolina. In a chapter on their interpretive practices, Fulkerson constructs a typology of three kinds of Bible study and their 'logics', which she then evaluates according to their contribution to the 'ends of the community' (2007: chapter 6, esp. 188 and 190). Andrew Todd in the UK used discourse analysis to examine the dynamics of biblical interpretation in three Bible study groups. His article draws attention to the 'speech-exchange' patterns in the groups, noting how 'turns of conversation' are significant for projecting a 'preferred response'. Todd argues that traditional and liberal understandings of the Bible co-exist through being 'held in tension within a group's conversation'. He concludes that the groups demonstrate a hermeneutic driven 'not by a quest for knowledge, but rather by relational concerns' where group members together discover 'insight' (2013: 69, 82).[30] Also in the UK, Zoë Bennett's *Using the Bible in Practical Theology* was written out of her conviction that 'one of the deepest needs in the area of public practical theology is a thoughtful, imaginative, persuasive and hermeneutically sophisticated use of the Bible' (2013: 3). Drawing on four diverse case studies,[31] she develops an

---

[29]   A joint partnership between Bible Society and Cardiff University. [Bible Society does not take the definite pronoun]

[30]   While this complementary approach to hermeneutical analysis is to be welcomed, I have a number of concerns with Todd's line of argument. In an engagement with my doctoral research and other writers in the field, Todd objects to my use of categories from theology and philosophical hermeneutics in exploring congregational hermeneutics. As I have argued in this chapter (and develop further in Chapter 3), there cannot be an innocent investigation of Bible practices in churches. It is a false opposition to pit theoretically informed investigations of congregational hermeneutics against 'empirical' ones. The key question is, what helps us to see well?

[31]   John Ruskin's hermeneutic of immediacy/analogy, the resignation of Giles Fraser during the Occupy protests of 2009, the Kairos Palestine document of 2009 and her own experience of running a Professional Doctorate in Practical Theology.

argument for a 'hermeneutic of immediacy' that welcomes a 'more fragmented, sporadic, paradoxical and imaginative "seeing" of connections and analogies rather than a mechanical adherence to models and methods in the "making" of connections' (2013: 73f, 135; Briggs and Bennett, 2014).[32]

The most substantial work to date on ordinary hermeneutics within practical/empirical theology is that of Andrew Village (2007).[33] From a predominantly quantitative perspective,[34] Village analysed how 404 Anglican lay people interpreted the healing story in Mk 9:14–29. He investigated factors affecting interpretation of this passage, such as age, personality type and education across eleven Anglican congregations with differing theological traditions. At the end of each chapter there is a theological reflection upon the statistical analyses presented, addressing matters of hermeneutical significance for theological education in both the church and academy.[35] Village finds that the 'best independent predictors of literalism' for his sample were 'education, university-level theological education, charismatic practice and Bible-reading frequency' (p. 67). Of particular interest was the result that literalism declined with increasing education, especially theological education, *except* amongst evangelicals. For educated evangelicals, literalism appeared to be a deliberate choice. Village also ambitiously measures 'horizon separation' for his sample, and shows again that education shifts interest away from the reader horizon towards the author horizon. Given his results, Village questions models of theological education that move readers towards the author horizon and leaves them there. Such education may destroy our first naïvety, but does it allow a second to flourish? He advances the view that theological education in churches should be 'less about breaking down inherent naivety' and 'more about the ethics of reading' – a 'virtuous way of approaching Scripture' no less (p. 93).[36]

Greater momentum is now evident within practical theology circles for engagement with the Bible, including reflection upon its use. The setting up of a special interest group within the British and Irish Association for Practical Theology (BIAPT) is indicative of this move, as the 2012 symposium illustrates (BIAPT, 2012).[37] The presence of biblical scholars through keynotes and being 'in residence' at conference is a mark of how seriously this is being taken.

---

[32] See discussion of the terminological differences between Bennett and I in Chapter 3.

[33] See also Village (2005a; b; c; d; 2013; Village and Francis, 2005).

[34] A number of survey based articles include congregational Bible use (e.g. Buckler and Astley, 1992; Fisher et al., 1992; Francis, 2000).

[35] Village was also on the steering committee of the 'Bible in the Life of the Church project' discussed later in the chapter.

[36] I have drawn on my review of Village here (Rogers, 2010: esp. 254–5).

[37] The symposium report referenced here is indicative of the range of practical theologians researching in the area of Bible and Practical Theology (e.g. Cameron et al., 2012: chapter 5; Whipp, 2012).

Similarly, the Association of Practical Theology (APT) in the USA themed its 2012 conference 'Practical Theology and Sacred Texts', which included reflecting on 'reading strategies' in American congregations.[38]

The academic context described here provides a growing body of research to draw on in developing an account of congregational hermeneutics. Each disciplinary perspective approaches the role of the Bible in the church with different starting points, questions and audiences in mind. As a theologically framed ethnographic enquiry, this book finds much of value for a critical, robust, yet hospitable engagement with this corpus.

The distinctiveness of congregational hermeneutics in this book arises from a combination of factors. My focus is on the hermeneutical practices of Bible readers in churches, accessing whatever Bible passages they happened to be reading within the various settings of normal congregational life. The research is located within the field of practical theology, using a theological ethnographic approach, which leads to constructive proposals that have been implemented in many English congregations and beyond (Bible Society, 2011a; b).

Surveying 'How Do We Read?'

There is no shortage of surveys regarding how people use the Bible, although most of these are conducted in 'developed' countries, and few address hermeneutics directly. Nevertheless, the selection of surveys that follows provides some broader context for our question 'How do we read?'[39] A suspicious reading would identify the vested interests of those commissioning or conducting the surveys, in that they have a stake in Bible education, literacy and advocacy. Bad news may well be good news for such organisations. Furthermore, some may have constituencies with specific theological traditions. With careful reading, however, there are still insights of value to be gained.

Clive Field has recently completed a meta-study of 158 Bible surveys in Britain since the Second World War, both of the general (123) and religious (35) adult populations. His twelve conclusions make for sobering reading. He claims that 'the decline in Bible-centricism' is 'a manifestation of a wider process of secularisation' both within and without the church (2014: 520). Not surprisingly, 'regular churchgoers are significantly more Bible-centric than adults as a whole', with 'evangelical churchgoers perhaps the most Bible-centric' (p. 518).[40] Churchgoers, however, have not been 'immune from declines in practices,

---

[38] I am grateful to Dr John Falcone for his report on the proceedings of this conference.

[39] Selection of surveys is primarily based on relevance to hermeneutical practices.

[40] Field qualifies this point by noting that some evangelical survey samples tend to be self-selecting. He adds 'evangelical and ethnic minority churchgoers' are now 'the mainstay of Bible-centricism' (2014: 519).

beliefs, and attitudes affecting the Bible' evident in the wider population. Field attributes this decline, particularly amongst 15–24 year olds, to the waning influence of the three traditional instruments of religious socialisation – home, school and church (p. 518). This necessarily macro-level study does not consider the pockets of rapid growth in the UK church, especially in London and amongst ethnic minority churches, and its consequent significance for Bible-centricism (Goodhew, 2012; Rogers, 2013a). Nevertheless, it raises serious questions about Bible trends and religious 'socialisation' in British churches.

In terms of hermeneutical practices, two UK Bible surveys in the past decade have been of particular interest, one surveying Christians and the other the general population. Bible Society commissioned ComRes to survey 3,660 Christians in England and Wales, with the results made available in January 2008 as *Taking the Pulse: Is the Bible Alive and Well in the Church Today?* The sample, which was weighted to be representative of the church population, was also divided into leaders (N=1731) and non-leaders (N=1929), allowing for some interesting comparisons. 47 per cent of leaders were 'very confident' and another 47 per cent 'fairly confident' in their knowledge of the Bible, compared to 14 per cent and 51 per cent of non-leaders respectively. 78 per cent of non-leaders believed 'the Bible is divinely inspired' and 34 per cent free from error, compared to 98 per cent and 47 per cent of leaders respectively. 35 per cent of non-leaders claimed to read the Bible daily, compared to 58 per cent of church leaders (Bible Society, 2008: 5, 7).[41] In response to the question: 'How satisfied or otherwise are you with general levels of Bible knowledge and application in your church?', just 12 per cent of leaders were 'very satisfied', although 45 per cent were fairly satisfied. On the other hand, 34 per cent were 'not particularly satisfied' and 6 per cent 'not at all satisfied'. Methodist, URC, and Anglican church leaders were 'least satisfied with their congregation's Bible knowledge', in contrast to Pentecostal and New Church leaders (p. 86).[42] These levels of dissatisfaction were intensified in focus groups with non-leaders being frustrated with leaders 'going through the motions' rather than 'actually offering an explanation of the underlying message or giving congregation members the tools to discover their own explanation' (p. 126).[43]

---

[41] *21st Century Evangelicals* surveyed 1,159 churchgoers at 35 Evangelical Alliance member churches in 2010. Overall, 55% said they read the Bible daily (Evangelical Alliance and Christian Research, 2011).

[42] 'Not particularly satisfied' was cited by 48% of Methodist leaders, 45% of URC, 44% of Anglicans, compared to 14% of Pentecostals and 22% of New Church leaders.

[43] A later Bible Society survey of over 1,000 members of the public in England and Wales regarding Bible engagement concluded: 'the main issues surrounding readership seem not to be in format, but in accessibility and relevance. Signposting, knowing where to start, and perceptions of formidable language were seen as significant barriers to those who were

Such a survey raises questions about Bible literacy, confidence and 'application'. This resonates with the *National Biblical Literacy Survey* undertaken in 2008 by CODEC at St John's College, Durham University, who conducted nearly 1000 face to face interviews with a wide range of 'ordinary citizens' at nine different locations in England and Wales. A surprisingly large 70 per cent of respondents self-designated as practicing Christians.[44] CODEC found that 75 per cent of respondents owned a Bible and 18 per cent said they had read the Bible in the last week. 47 per cent said that the Bible was never significant for them and this measure reached 70 per cent among 16–24 year olds. As a survey of the general population, the results raise a number of missiological questions. Based on the extensive interview data, Pete Phillips concludes his summary with a touch of preacherly polemic:

> … we have also managed to professionalise (clericalise) the Bible to such an extent that some might argue we are undoing the Reformation by depriving the masses of the very text which we wanted to bring them. We do this by making the Bible the preserve of the clergy or the expert or the religious. We tell people that the Bible needs to be interpreted properly and through quasi-scientific approaches that normal people cannot possibly understand. As such, we might as well as have kept the Bible in Latin and the preserve of the Church. Instead, we have given people their own Bible but persuaded them that they still can't read it – they still need another to interpret the mysteries whether that other is liberal, evangelical, catholic or charismatic (nd).

The paradox of the Bible being for all yet needing interpretation is a theme close to the heart of this book. Here, however, it is argued that interpretative approaches are not beyond the reach of 'normal people'. Indeed, the contention is that hermeneutics is for every Christian.

Surveys that relate to the Bible are especially plentiful in the USA. The Center for Bible Engagement published the *Bible Literacy & Spiritual Growth* survey in 2006 based on over 8,500 Christian respondents from across the United States. The authors acknowledge the limitations of online surveys, but stress the relationships 'uncovered' are still significant. They argue that there is a disconnect between 'respondents' expressed beliefs about the importance of the Bible and their reading habits'. Despite the 'vast majority' indicating the Bible is 'relevant to their everyday lives' only 'one-half read the Bible daily, with another

---

open to encouragement to read the Bible more or indeed start reading it' (Hewitt and Powys-Smith, 2011: 16).

[44]   England has seen a rapid decline in Christian self-identification from 72% to 59% in the 2001 and 2011 censuses respectively (Office for National Statistics, 2013), although there are complex reasons for this (Field, 2012; Day and Lee, 2013).

37% reading it more than once a week, but not daily'. For most respondents, the main hindrance was being 'too busy'. Drawing on the survey findings regarding 'Bible reading habits and associated factors', the authors question church attendance as an 'index of religiosity', arguing that 'the amount of time one actually spends reading the Bible may be a far better indicator of the state of a person's spiritual life' (Center for Bible Engagement, 2006). It is worth noting that how spirituality is measured will be critical for these conclusions.[45]

Other US studies have come to similar conclusions. The Willow Creek REVEAL survey polled over '1,500 churches representing more than 400,000 church attendees at various stages in their spiritual journeys' across a range of congregation sizes, styles and traditions (American Bible Society, 2013b; cf. Hawkins and Parkinson, 2007). Based on analyses of these responses, it is argued that 'nothing has a greater impact on spiritual growth than reflection on Scripture'.[46] Most churches are 'missing the mark' because 'only one out of five congregants reflects on Scripture every day' (Hawkins and Parkinson, 2011: 19). The language of 'scripture reflection' points towards questions about hermeneutics, beyond percentages about Bible reading to how Christians actually engage with Scripture.

American Bible Society have commissioned the Barna Group to survey the 'State of the Bible' in the USA on a number of occasions (e.g. 2011; 2012; 2013a; 2014).[47] Once more, some dissonance was indicated. In the 2013 survey 69 per cent agreed strongly or somewhat that 'the Bible contains everything a person needs to know to live a meaningful life',[48] yet 58 per cent said they did not want 'input and wisdom from the Bible' on topics relating to family and marriage (p. 69).[49] Also in 2013, three out of four adults believed theological education was not a prerequisite for correct interpretation of the Bible (52 per cent strongly disagree, 27 per cent somewhat disagree) (p. 8), in some tension with the British CODEC survey conclusions above.[50]

Barna define Bible readers as those who read the Scriptures 'three or four times a year' or more. By this definition, 53 per cent of American adults read the

---

[45] So in this study it means being less likely to engage in gambling, pornography, getting drunk, and sex outside marriage, and more likely to share one's faith with others.

[46] See also studies by Lifeway Research (2,500 Protestant churches followed for a year) who identified daily Bible engagement as the top 'predictor' of spiritual maturation (cited in American Bible Society, 2013b; cf. Waggoner, 2008; Cole and Ovwigho, 2012). Lifeway also found a disconnect between US churchgoers' attitudes towards the Bible and how often they in fact read it (Rankin, 2012).

[47] Based on a representative sample of the American adult population, with 2,036 responses (telephone and online) in 2014, and a similarly structured 2013 sample of 2,083.

[48] Increased to 69% in 2014 (p. 28).

[49] Not asked in 2014.

[50] Not asked in 2014.

Bible and 15 per cent read it daily in 2014 (p. 11). The amount of time spent reading the Bible is remarkably high – 30 minutes on average for Bible readers (p. 12). The most common reason for reading the Bible was that 'it brings them closer to God' (56 per cent) (p. 14).[51] Moving yet closer to hermeneutics, frustrations in reading the Bible included 'finding the language difficult to relate to' (8 per cent) and 'not understanding the background or history of the Bible' (8 per cent) (p. 15).[52] One in four Bible readers said 'they have no frustrations' in reading the Bible – the inverse therefore is food for hermeneutical thought (p. 15). This should be placed alongside the 57 per cent who said they 'gave a lot of thought to how [the Bible] might apply to their life' and the 37 per cent who gave 'some thought' (p. 16).[53] Regarding the status of the Bible, three in ten adults (30 per cent) said 'the Bible is the inspired word of God and has no errors, although some verses are meant to be symbolic'. 23 per cent viewed the Bible as 'the actual word of God that should be taken literally, word for word' and 15 per cent said it was the 'inspired word of God' but with some 'factual or historical errors' (p. 21).[54] The phrasing and options available to respondents demonstrate the difficulty of measuring these matters quantitatively.

The *Bible Engagement in Canada* survey sampled 4,474 members of the general population (Hiemstra, 2013a; b).[55] Approximately one in seven (14 per cent) Canadian Christians read the Bible at least once a week. Half of Christians 'agree that the Bible has irreconcilable contradictions' and about one in four Christians (23 per cent) 'agree the Bible is relevant to modern life'. The Bible engagement of 'self-identified Christians' was not that different from the Bible engagement of Canadians generally, although evangelicals accounted for 43 per cent of 'frequent Bible readers', despite being only 7 per cent of the study. The conclusion is that 'the Bible is not directly shaping much of the church in Canada', but that 'conversation with others about the meaning of the Bible is the key factor in deepening Bible engagement'.

The *National Church Life Survey* in Australia has been surveying congregations every five years for the last twenty years. The 2006 survey was based on questions to around 400,600 churchgoers from 5,200 local churches in 22

---

[51] Percentages are for 'Bible readers'.

[52] Percentages for those who read the Bible at least once a week.

[53] Percentages for those who had read the Bible in the past week.

[54] Other studies have asked similar questions in the USA, so in 2010 the General Social Survey had 45.5% viewing the Bible as 'the inspired word of God but not everything taken literally' which compares with Barna when both 'inspired' options are added together. 31.2% understood the Bible 'to be taken literally, word for word' (N=4901) (National Opinion Research Center, 2010; cf. Baylor University, 2007).

[55] Research conducted by Vision Critical through forums and qualitative interviews.

denominations.[56] Based on this very large sample, 21 per cent of Australian churchgoers read the Bible daily, but 35 per cent hardly ever or never read their Bibles (Digital Journal, 2008).[57] According to Bible Society Australia, reasons given for not reading were time, uncertainty about the reliability of the Bible, and finding the Bible hard to understand and relate to their lives (Christian Telegraph, 1999–2015). Bible Society in New Zealand conducted a survey of the general population to investigate a perceived 'Bible engagement crisis' (N=3,388). 46 per cent said they were Christian. 5 per cent of respondents and 11 per cent of Christians said they read the Bible daily.[58] 47 per cent of Christian respondents said 'the Bible influences their lives' and 39 per cent said it 'sometimes influences their lives'. Of those that read the Bible daily, 94.6 per cent said it influenced their lives (Opie, 2008). With regard to the Bible, it would appear there is also dissonance down under.

Two multi-country surveys are worth considering. The Catholic Biblical Federation conducted a *Global Survey on the Role of the Bible* spanning twelve countries, namely Argentina, France, Germany, Hong Kong, Italy, Netherlands, Philippines, Poland, Russia, Spain, UK and the USA. Representative samples of the adult population and a sub-sample of largely Roman Catholic churchgoers in each country were generated through nearly 13,000 telephone interviews.[59] Published in 2008, the results show unsurprising divergence between the twelve countries in relation to the Bible on a number of matters. Churchgoers who agreed that the Bible was 'the actual word of God, which must be taken literally word for word' were at their highest proportions in the Philippines, Russia, Poland, and Argentina (between 40–45 per cent). The USA and the UK were lower at 23 per cent and 17 per cent respectively. The highest proportions of those opting for the Bible as 'the inspired word of God, but not everything in the Bible should be taken literally, word for word' were from Netherlands, France, UK, and the USA (65–75 per cent) (Catholic Biblical Federation, 2008a; b). Some of the discrepancies with other surveys here may point to the survey's sampling strategy which was limited to specific denominations in each country. Nevertheless, it provides a perspective on sections of church life in the twelve countries. The most striking result was to the rather simple question asking if 'the contents of the Bible are Easy or Difficult'? Both churchgoing and general samples had a strong 'Difficult' response, with only Hong Kong, Philippines, and Spain having proportions below 50 per cent on this item. Furthermore,

---

[56]   Email from Ruth Powell, director of NCLS Research (17/10/13). Unfortunately, the results of the 2011 survey in relation to the Bible were not available.

[57]   This source was confirmed by Ruth Powell, director of NCLS Research (email, 21/11/13).

[58]   24% read the Bible at least once a week.

[59]   In European Russia the oversample was from the Orthodox church and in the UK from any established Protestant church.

when comparing the churchgoing and general samples, the proportion choosing 'Difficult' in seven of the twelve countries was the same or higher for churchgoers as for the general population. Professor Luca Diotallevi who coordinated the survey working group, underlined the importance of this point: 'the people of God are asking for help reading the Bible' (Wooden, 2008).

The second multi-country 'survey' is the 'Bible in the Life of the Church' (BLC) project, which has already been quoted at the beginning of this chapter. Commissioned by the Anglican Communion in 2009, the report *Deep Engagement, Fresh Discovery* was published in 2012, with perhaps the most explicit focus on hermeneutics of all the Bible surveys encountered. This global and interdisciplinary consultation looked at how Anglicans worldwide actually use the Bible, identifying 'the working principles of Anglican hermeneutics', as well as Bible resources for 'all levels of Christian education' (Anglican Communion, 2012: 3; see also Lyon, 2011). The project sought to build a 'series of snapshots, a collage' of what is happening across the Communion, through a case study approach that drew heavily on qualitative methods.[60] The eight regional groups were in East Africa, North America, the United Kingdom, South Africa, Australia, South Sudan, Cuba, and South East Asia.[61] The key result is to 'mind the gaps' between how Anglicans *should* and *do* interpret the Bible. BLC also identifies gaps between academy and pew or 'scholar' and 'ordinary' Christian, as well as between 'fruits' of biblical engagement and the 'process' of that engagement. There is clearly significant common ground between the exploration of 'How do we read?' here and BLC, not least in evidence through BLC's strong endorsement of a hermeneutics course for churches that drew heavily on this research (see Chapter 9) (Anglican Communion, 2012: 48–9).

From this diverse set of surveys from around the world, repeated concerns can be identified about the 'gap' between Christian's espoused theologies of the Bible and their actual Bible practices. In more nuanced terms, this is a concern about the lack of harmony between the four voices of theology introduced earlier. Even allowing for a suspicious reading of the material presented, this survey of surveys serves to underline the timely nature of the question 'How do we read?' From global and large scale surveys the gaze now shifts to an in-depth study of two contrasting congregations.

---

[60]   A largely online survey was undertaken as part of the project by Andrew Village, with just over 1500 respondents (Anglican Communion, 2012: 43–6). It focussed on biblical interpretation and the conclusions were said to resonate with his previous study in the UK (so 2007), although the bias of the sample was to those who were western, educated and religiously committed.

[61]   Attention to the Bible in Africa is a distinctive of this 'survey' (see also Dube and West, 2001).

The Tale of Two Churches

A tale of two churches and the Bible is narrated in this book (Rogers, 2013b). This tale provided a sufficient thickness and 'this-ness' of description to provoke theological reflection upon congregational hermeneutics (Willis and Trondman, 2001: 394). I trust it will do the same for the reader. The two churches are *Holder Evangelical Church* (Holder) and *City Reach Christian Fellowship* (Fellowship).[62] Both self-designate as evangelical, both are independent,[63] both can be found in London in England, both are roughly the same size, both are 'successful' in their own terms and are influential within their own subtraditions. Neither of the churches is exotic, by which I mean they are not famous, nor do they have outstanding features to attract attention. Holder and Fellowship were deliberately chosen for being ordinary churches that were getting on with worship, ministry and mission in unspectacular ways.

Readers from evangelical traditions may not need the relevance of this tale of church and Bible to be underlined further. For those readers who do not identify with evangelicalism, I maintain there are at least three reasons why it is worth being drawn into this tale. Firstly, it is highly likely that there are overlapping hermeneutical practices between evangelical and non-evangelical congregations.[64] Secondly, that the model of hermeneutical apprenticeship proposed will be valuable for a wide variety of churches. Thirdly, understanding how ordinary evangelicals read the Bible is significant for building the unity of the church, especially given the strength of the tradition globally.[65]

As will become evident throughout the book, congregational hermeneutics are shaped by much more than those factors normally associated with academic biblical hermeneutics. Consequently, something of Holder and Fellowship's broader story needs to be told, given that their demographics, history, structure and identity are thoroughly interconnected with their hermeneutical practices. It will also become apparent that there is a marked contrast between the two churches, which was an intentional part of the research design (detailed further

---

[62]   All names of churches and congregants are pseudonyms. In order to preserve anonymity, it is sometimes necessary to omit Holder and Fellowship details and references.

[63]   Independent churches formed the second largest grouping within the Evangelical Alliance (the largest evangelical umbrella body in the UK) at the time of the research (or the largest depending on how congregational categories are assigned), so 17.1% compared to 23.2% Baptists and 17.0% Church of England (see Rogers, 2009: Appendix A).

[64]   As Village found regarding literalism, discussed above.

[65]   According to the Pew Research Center in 2011, Evangelicals constituted 13.1% of the world's Christian population (285 million), with pentecostals and charismatics together constituting 27% (584 million). The Center also comments that 'many pentecostals and charismatics are also evangelicals' and so the two categories are not mutually exclusive (2011).

in Chapter 2). The introductions below will be expanded in later chapters as the tale develops.

Holder Evangelical Church is situated on the edge of inner London, with a congregation of about 260, which is medium-sized by British standards.[66] 147 congregants had chosen to become members of the church.[67] The church had a mix of working class and middle class congregants, with a male to female ratio of 1:2, and a very small but growing number of ethnic minority congregants.[68] Holder celebrated a significant anniversary during the fieldwork period and had been meeting in its current building since the early twentieth century. The congregation had a long memory, in that over half of my questionnaire sample had been at the church for more than 10 years, and 10 per cent for over 40 years.[69] Such a long history meant there had been much 'natural growth', so many members of the church were related and generations of families attended together. Holder includes 'evangelical' in its name, and is a member of the Fellowship of Independent Evangelical Churches (FIEC, 2011), an affiliation of conservative evangelical churches in the UK,[70] then using the strapline 'Bible Churches Together'.[71] The FIEC itself is the largest corporate member of Affinity,[72] which described itself at the time as a 'Church-centred partnership for Bible-centred Christianity' (Affinity, 2005)[73] – an apt designation for Holder as will be seen. The theological tradition of the church was Reformed with a small 'r', according to Pastor Owen,[74] although there were many congregant memories of Calvinism being very strong in the church's past.

The pastor, Owen, had been at the church for three years, and the associate pastor, Joe, had grown up in the church and had taken on a pastoral role quite

---

[66] Including approximately 60 children and young people.

[67] 'Congregant' is used as the generic term in this book, in preference to 'member', since only Holder operated a membership system.

[68] 38% male to 62% female members (Church office email, 15/3/06). Historically the congregation had been almost entirely white British, but in the last few years a few ethnic minority congregants had become members.

[69] Some of the statistics given here were taken from a questionnaire in both churches – further details are given in Chapter 2. Of questionnaire respondents, 56% had attended for over 10 years, with even a few having attended for over 70 years, N=105.

[70] Approximately 470 churches at the time (Jonathan Stephen, email 8/3/05), also FIEC (2007) and Affinity (2006).

[71] They have since dropped this strapline due to its lack of distinctiveness for FIEC.

[72] Formerly the British Evangelical Council, founded in 1953 (Bebbington, 1989: 265). Affinity said it represented 1200 churches at the time (Jonathan Stephen, email 8/3/05), also Affinity (2006).

[73] Interestingly, they have since changed their strapline to 'Gospel Churches in Partnership' (Affinity, 2013).

[74] All congregant quotes are taken from interviews, unless otherwise stated.

recently. There were also four elders and a number of deacons, all male, which was in keeping with the church's position on gender and leadership. In terms of theological training, Owen had taken a course with the FIEC (2004b), and Joe had attended a mission agency Bible training centre. Strikingly, however, both pastors commented that these courses had not been 'formal theological training', which Joe defined as something like a degree course. Half the congregation sample said they had no Bible-related training, and most of the other half claimed they had taken a church-based course related to the Bible. A small proportion had undertaken Bible-related study at a Higher Education institution.[75]

City Reach Christian Fellowship is geographically not far from Holder, predominantly middle class and located within an inner suburb of London. There were about 230 congregants,[76] with close to a 1:1 male to female ratio[77] and no membership system in operation. There was a sizeable ethnic minority presence of mostly African professionals.[78] Fellowship did not have its own building, but met just once on a Sunday in a local school hall. They also rented a highly visible shop on the local high street, here called the Good News centre, which was used for the church's administration, Bible studies, youth work and various other projects.[79] Fellowship formally split from an established 'new' church known here as Ekklesia during 2003/04,[80] having existed as a congregation in its own right for ten years prior to this. Despite a complex recent history, Fellowship congregants had some longevity in that just under half had been in Fellowship/ Ekklesia for more than 10 years, and 28 per cent for over 20 years.[81] The split led to the formation of a church network known here as Metamorphis, along with other 'splitter' congregations, all roughly within the same area of London. Fellowship opted to set itself up as a limited company, with trustees and a mixed leadership team of eleven people. The latter was deliberately flat in structure as a move away from the perceived hierarchical structure of Ekklesia.

Fellowship was a member of the Evangelical Alliance (EA), an umbrella organisation that represents the largest proportion of British evangelicals,[82] then

---

[75] Of questionnaire respondents at Holder, 50% said they had undertaken no Bible-related training at all, 43% a church-based course, and 8% a certificate/diploma course at a Higher Education institution, N=99. In terms of general educational level, 30% of questionnaire respondents had a degree and 7% a higher degree, N=103.

[76] Including approximately 90 children and young people.

[77] Based on the church address list, although questionnaire respondents split 41% male and 59% female, N=75.

[78] Estimated at 20–30% of the congregation.

[79] After the fieldwork period the church bought the shop.

[80] The provenance of 'new church' is explained in Chapter 3.

[81] Of questionnaire respondents, 44% attended for more than 10 years, N=75.

[82] The Evangelical Alliance then claimed to represent an estimated 1.5 million evangelical Christians in the UK, including approximately 3,200 churches (Maggie Harding,

using the strapline 'Uniting to change society'. The pastor, Derek, told me that congregants knew Fellowship was an EA member, and were aware they were in the 'charismatic evangelical theological camp', although recognition of this evangelical identity was quite muted. Derek added 'we share a lot of values with evangelicals taking the Bible seriously; obviously we react against a type of Calvinist, but would say we fit in with other churches, lots of evangelicals, rather than standing on some extreme edge'. This quote reflects the tensions in Fellowship's identity, in that its estranged parent church was characterised as 'radical Arminian Anabaptist' and had 'a history of being heretics'.

After many years of pastoral experience, Derek had started studying for a diploma part-time at a local theological college. Just under half the congregation sample said they had received no Bible-related training, with 37 per cent saying they had taken a church-based course related to the Bible. A small but significant proportion had undertaken Bible-related study at a Higher Education institution at degree level and beyond.[83] There were also two 'professional' theologians within the congregation.

Where We Are Going

Having headlined the key questions, explained what is and is not being done, introduced key terminology, set out the academic and survey context and begun the tale of two churches, I conclude this chapter with an overview and then a sketch of where we are going.

Chapters 1–3 provide the introduction, methodology and conceptual resources for the book. Chapters 4–7 tell the tale of two churches, particularly addressing the first sense of 'How do we read?', although not exclusively. Chapters 8–9 then move towards the second sense of 'How do we read?' through considering what hermeneutical virtues might look like in practice.

Chapter 2 locates the study in the field of practical theology, and explores what is meant by theological ethnography, particularly the importance of looking theologically at the church in the world. A case is begun for understanding practices within the context of the Christian Story; that is, being eschatological about the empirical. If the reader is tempted to omit methodology, I would urge them not to miss the last section of this short chapter which addresses how the cast of 74 congregants and visitors, 114 distinct songs, 27 public meetings, 33 small

---

email 6/10/04).

[83]   Of questionnaire respondents, 46% said they had received no Bible training, 7% had undertaken certificate/diploma Bible-related study at a Higher Education institution, and 6% had a degree or higher degree of Bible-related study, N=69. In terms of general educational level, 47% of respondents had a degree and 19% a higher degree, N=75.

group sessions, 34 interviews, and 180 questionnaire responses are incorporated into the text of the tale. In addition, there is an initial discussion regarding the relationship between virtue, transformation, Bible and hermeneutics so that it may be developed throughout the rest of the book. Chapter 3 then provides an account of premodern, modern and postmodern biblical hermeneutics (including what can be said about evangelical and charismatic perspectives) in order to aid 'compare and contrast' with congregational hermeneutics. Conceptual resources are drawn on to inform analysis of congregational hermeneutics, especially congregational 'horizons' and 'fusion' processes.

The tale of two churches is addressed through four themes in Chapters 4–7. Tradition in Chapter 4 is understood as primarily congregational tradition and is linked particularly to congregational horizons as the living present of congregational tradition. The focus in the chapter is on how traditions operate within real congregations in relation to Bible and hermeneutics, understood through a number of horizonal starting points and goals (e.g. the address of Scripture, the Bible will be relevant). A reflection on taking tradition seriously considers the place of transformative yet affirmative (of tradition) Scripture reading. Chapter 5 pays attention to practices by characterising the ways in which connections are made between text and congregational horizons ('fusion processes'). Naming the range of Bible uses witnessed across public, small group and personal settings aids a look at overarching fusion strategies, as well as more detailed hermeneutical patterns and processes such as 'text-linking'. The relationship between the operant/espoused and normative/formal processes, including similarities, differences and hybridity, prompts a reflection on what really matters for hermeneutical processes. Epistemology in Chapter 6 returns to matters of horizons, as in Chapter 4, but warrants a chapter of its own, given the significance of epistemology for congregational hermeneutics. Epistemology in this context describes how congregants justified their beliefs and the perceived truth value of those beliefs in relation to the Bible. Central to this discussion is the idea of indeterminacy, indicating the degree to which congregants understood Bible texts to have multiple possible meanings. The implicit epistemologies of the two congregations are compared to well-known positions, and are seen to be strikingly separated by an epistemological 'language barrier'. The charge of fundamentalism, often levelled against evangelical churches, is examined to see if it can be upheld on the epistemological evidence, alongside other considerations. Chapter 7 deals with the mediation of hermeneutics which affects both horizons and processes. Mediators are agents that shape hermeneutical practices and so are important for understanding why such practices are the way they are and how they are learned. They may be internal to the congregation (e.g. housegroups, sermons) or external (e.g. songs, books). The differing ways in which mediation took place at Holder and Fellowship (i.e. their dynamics) are compared, including the degree to which mediation was resisted. This leads to conclusions about the critical role of mediators in achieving a balance between affirmative and disruptive readings of Scripture.

Each of Chapters 4–7 points to hermeneutical virtues emerging from the theme, so of tradition in Chapter 4, honesty and faithfulness; of practices in Chapter 5, all the virtues; of epistemology in Chapter 6, humility and confidence; of mediation in Chapter 7, faithfulness and openness. Virtues are not terribly tidy, however, much like ethnography, hence in Chapter 8 examples of the seven virtues are identified from across the previous four chapters. The purpose of Chapter 8 is to substantially thicken the account of hermeneutical virtue that has begun to take shape. It begins with a selective sketch of the virtue ethics story to provide context and categories for understanding hermeneutical virtue, with extended attention paid to virtue in the Bible and the distinctive story within which Christian virtue is placed. I contend that a reasonable argument can be made for the ongoing importance of virtue today across the Christian traditions. Six hermeneutical virtues are then considered in turn, looking at examples from the tale, as well as hearing from other theological voices about the way that such virtues might shape hermeneutical practices. Drawing the various threads together, a case is then made for why hermeneutical virtue works, addressing questions about the distinction between skills and virtues, the subjectivity of virtue, potential virtuous elitism and the linking of hermeneutics to Christian discipleship. Finally, in Chapter 9, I focus in on the final virtue of community, which provides the context for all the other virtues to flourish. Like Chapter 8, signs of community in the tale of two churches are considered by their chapter themes. Biblical clues pointing to the nature of hermeneutical community are presented, followed by other normative and formal voices advocating hermeneutical community. The implications of community for learning hermeneutics are then developed as hermeneutical apprenticeship, drawing on community of practice thinking. This is made concrete at the end of the book by giving examples of what hermeneutical apprenticeship might look like in churches. Enjoy!

Chapter 2
Exploring

This short chapter sets out the approach taken in this book for exploring congregational hermeneutics. It begins with a discussion of crucial methodological matters associated with analysing the practices of churches, and then leads into a brief summary of the research design and methods employed. The chapter concludes with an initial exploration of hermeneutical virtue and transformation, to allow this theme to be developed further in the rest of the book.

Methodology Matters

Practical theology is a discipline that combines theological reflection with insights and methods from a variety of other disciplines, but especially the social sciences. Consequently it is intrinsically interdisciplinary, and so methodology rightly looms large in its self-understanding. Defining practical theology is not straightforward, as discussions in the guild have indicated,[1] but it is useful to have a starting point. In my view, John Swinton and Harriet Mowatt's provisional definition captures some of the key features (slightly adapted):

> Practical Theology is [constructive], critical, theological reflection on the practices of the Church as they interact with the practices of the world, with a view to ensuring and enabling faithful [and innovative] participation in God's redemptive practices in, to, and for the world (2006: 6).

Seven emphases are prompted by this definition. Practical theology is interested in the *practices* of the Church and world, accessed through some form of contextual analysis. It is *critical*, in that such practices are normed by theological criteria. It is also critical in the sense that it sees practices as generative of theological insight themselves which may challenge existing formulations of the Christian tradition. Consequently, it is suspicious of some 'applied theology' models that fix the direction of critique from context-free theory to practice. The precise revelatory dynamic between practices and Christian tradition is left open in this definition, which allows for the different dynamics in play across the discipline, although it is

---

[1]   See Bonnie Miller-McLemore and responses in the *International Journal of Practical Theology* 16:1, 2012, also Miller-McLemore (2012b).

understood as asymmetric in this study.[2] My additions to the definition underline
the need for practical theology to be *constructive*, so enabling the Church's faithful
and *innovative* participation in the Christian Story. Hence, practical theology
should also be *transformative*. The definition also helpfully implies that practical
theology should be *missional*,[3] not just concerned with the practices of the church,
but also their interaction in the world within the *Missio Dei*. Finally, as the above
and its name indicate, practical theology is *theological*. It is a theological look at
Church and world (cf. Swinton, 2012: 75).

It is worth taking a moment to unpack what is meant by 'Christian Story'
here. In my usage, Christian Story refers to Scripture and subsequent Christian
tradition, although in quite a particular way. I understand the Scriptures to have
an overarching plot of creation, fall and redemption that may be understood as
a drama or theodrama. The principal actor in this drama is the trinitarian God
who invites the church to participate in this drama through its incorporation
into Christ.[4] In this sense, then, the church performs and improvises the script
of the Scriptures.[5] I am aware, however, that the singular use of 'Christian Story'
has been questioned (e.g. Brown, 2009; Sharp, 2004). In response, I would stress
that this is a 'story of stories' that has its tensions, multiple voices, testimony and
counter-testimony. The biblical scholar, Richard Bauckham, draws attention to
the plurality and singularity of Scripture. He recognises the plurality of Scripture
in the 'profusion and sheer untidiness of the narrative materials', 'the ambiguity
of stories', and the place of the non-narrative materials (2003a: 92). At the same
time he observes how the canon 'implicitly gives some nonnarrative books (e.g.,
Psalms, Lamentations) a narrative setting within the story told by the narrative
books'. Books of prophecy and apostolic letters are 'intrinsically related to the
biblical story, to which they constantly refer, even summarizing and retelling
parts of it' (2003b: 39). The biblical texts, to a 'remarkable extent', 'recognise
and assert ... the unity of the story they tell' (2003b: 40). Characterising the
biblical story as a 'nonmodern metanarrative' with a 'noncoercive claim to truth'
(2003b: 53), Bauckham concludes:

> The Bible does, in some sense, tell an overall story that encompasses all its
> other contents, but this story is not a sort of straitjacket that reduces all else to
> a narrowly defined uniformity. It is a story that is hospitable to considerable

---

[2]   As do Swinton and Mowatt, but they take it further by stating that human experience
is *not* 'a locus for fresh revelation' (2006: 7).

[3]   Swinton and Mowatt make this explicit when revisiting their definition of practical
theology (2006: 25), see also Doug Gay (2011: xii–xiii).

[4]   I am drawing here on Kevin Vanhoozer (who draws on Hans Urs von Balthasar)
(2006: 73f) and N. T. Wright (e.g. 1992: 139f).

[5]   Swinton and Mowatt also speak of the church remaining 'faithful to the script of the
gospel' (2006: 9).

diversity and to tensions, challenges, and even seeming contradictions of its own claims (2003a: 93–4).

This nuanced account of the Bible as Story informs my use of 'Christian Story'. Although a brief excursus, it indicates that Story singular does not have to be a problem.

Continuing with the theme of practical theology, theological reflection is at the heart of the discipline. Often described as the pastoral cycle, it classically comprises four stages, namely 1. Experience; 2. Contextual analysis; 3. Reflection (using the resources of the Christian Story); 4. Action (revised practice).[6] This cycle broadly underlies the research process for this book, although the stages are intermingled in the chapters. Identifying these stages is helpful procedurally, as long as the stages are not compartmentalised and the theological nature of the whole cycle is not lost. This last point is particularly critical for stage 2, in that contextual analysis is typically undertaken by engaging with the social sciences. In the case of congregational hermeneutics, that analysis is ethnographic; hence it requires an account of how to be theological about ethnography.

'Theological ethnography' refers to the specific methodology for this book.[7] It allows that the exploration of congregational hermeneutics here is authentically theological *and* ethnographic. This methodological focus has been of growing interest for a group of North American and European scholar-practitioners under the auspices of the *Ecclesiology and Ethnography network* (2013), to which I belong and whose work I draw on here (Scharen, 2012; Ward, 2012b). The proposal of this network is that to understand the church, we need methods that are simultaneously theological and ethnographic,[8] since the church is both a theological and social reality (Ward, 2012a: 2).

Ethnography has its disciplinary home within anthropology, and was traditionally understood as the study of a 'tribe' or cultural 'other', often perceived as exotic, for an extended period of time through the immersion of the researcher within the field. An increase in the interdisciplinary use of ethnography, however, has questioned some of the assumptions in its methods. For example, in the field of education a case has been made for different modes of ethnographic research, especially in relation to time, degree of immersion and focus in the field (Green and Bloome, 1997; Jeffrey and Troman, 2004). As in

---

[6] So Laurie Green's reflective spiral (1990). Swinton and Mowatt's version was particularly influential for this research (2006: 94–8).

[7] When I first used this term in 2009 it was quite rare, with only Lewis Mudge having used this particular term in a programmatic sense previously (Mudge, 1984; Rogers, 2009: §3.2). It has since become more widespread – see Elizabeth Phillips's helpful history of the methodology's development (2012: 99–100, 102–3).

[8] 'Ethnography' is defined broadly in the network to include all forms of qualitative research.

theology, wider trends in academia brought about by the advent of postmodern critique led to anthropology's established positivist epistemology being challenged. One of those challenges was from Clifford Geertz who understood the ethnographic task to be an interpretative one in search of meaning. He argued that 'thick description' of situations is needed,[9] where one moves beyond mere description of cultural signs to understanding their meaning for the actors within a social setting in their own terms. Geertz draws heavily on hermeneutical concepts for his work, and the parallels between reading culture and reading text (or the Bible) are notable (Jackson, 1997: 32f; Willis, 2000: ix–x). A second challenge has come from the hermeneutical insight that the ethnographer's ideological commitments contribute to cultural interpretations, and that such interpretations are therefore not value free. Consequently, there developed a trend for making ethnography explicitly ideologically driven, for example, through Marxist or feminist agendas. Martyn Hammersley and Paul Atkinson describe critical ethnography and emancipatory action research where 'the goal ... is taken to be the transformation of Western societies so as to realize the ideals of freedom, equality and justice' (1995: 15–16).[10] The resonance with theology is remarkable in this explicitly eschatological vision. The converging turns to context and critique in theology and anthropology respectively suggest that theoretical space can be found for a theological ethnography.

I will be carefully appropriating this interpretative and critical tradition within ethnography for exploring congregational hermeneutics. This will therefore entail being hermeneutical about hermeneutics. I must therefore be 'reflexive' about my position as a situated interpreter of congregations who is a co-creator of the tale generated. I do not have 'immaculate perception' (Maanen, 1988: 73). Reflexivity is a move towards greater honesty about the process of knowledge production; hence what I bring to the study is not excluded. The reader may thus be better enabled (it is hoped) to assess the status of the knowledge produced (cf. Johnson and Chambers, 2004: 51–2). Reflexivity also aids greater self-consciousness about the dynamics of co-creation, and can be exploited appropriately. This was indeed the case – alongside the less participatory settings, how congregants responded to me personally also provided valuable insights into their congregational life and practices.

This brings us to the heart of the methodological matter. Underlying any ethnographic exploration are assumptions about the nature of the social setting (ontology) and what can be known about it (epistemology). Consequently,

---

[9]   Borrowed from Gilbert Ryle (1971).

[10]   So Andrew Sayer argued for a social science that is 'critical of the practices which are its objects of study' (2000: 156f). See also Grant Banfield (2004: 62) and Barton and Hamilton (1998: 5).

our ontology and epistemology need to be consistent with our theology.[11] [12] In terms of epistemology, the hermeneutical perspective on ethnography outlined above recognises that what we see is partial, provisional and mediated. I contend that this is entirely consistent with a Christian worldview, which recognises the limitations of our creaturely status, including the impact of sin, upon our knowing.[13] Furthermore, as N.T. Wright argues, such an epistemology finds roots in the biblical concept of stewardship, where knowledge has to do with the 'interrelation of humans and the created world', so:

> To know is to be in a relation with the known, which means that the 'knower' must be open to the possibility of the 'known' being other than had been expected or even desired, and must be prepared to respond accordingly, not merely to observe from a distance (1992: 45).

Such a participatory epistemology seems especially suitable for theological ethnography. In terms of ontology, there should be clarity about the nature of the setting being investigated, in particular, the church. A step back is needed first, to acknowledge that a fundamental element of the Christian Story is that God reveals himself to human beings, climatically in Jesus Christ. A theological ontology therefore includes a commitment to the reality of what is known, albeit only known partially, as something other than the knower (Wright, 1992: 35). Furthermore, an ethnographic look at creation is a look at a created reality that is sustained and grounded in God. So, as John Webster has argued, 'ontological primacy' belongs to God. Therefore ecclesiology cannot be 'only a matter of historical sociology or practical reasoning', as that 'misapprehends the kind of historical society that the church is' (2012: 203–4). In other words, when we take an ethnographic look at the church in the world, it is critical to remember that the 'social-historical' is not all there is to see. The life of the church is moved by God, indwelt by his Spirit, and so the theological ethnographer has the task of reading the signs of God's life in the complex reality that is the church (cf.

---

[11]   In what follows, I am not claiming that all Christians would accept these positions on epistemology and ontology, but rather that a strong case can be made for their theological coherence.

[12]   There is a tradition of angst regarding the incompatibility of theology with the social sciences, the prime representative being John Milbank (1990: 380). Scharen, however, notes Milbank's acknowledgement that his account of church is too idealised and thus develops Milbank's call for ecclesiology requiring 'supplementation by judicious narratives' (2005: 125).

[13]   This relates to the discussion of intellectual virtues and vices in Chapter 8.

Fiddes, 2012: 32; Webster, 2012: 215; Rogers, 2013c: 122).[14] [15] While taking Webster's point that the church is 'in some measure indiscernible', since it is irreducibly 'in the Lord' (Eph 2:21; 2012: 222), I am not as pessimistic about the possibility of this task (cf. Brittain, 2014). A daunting corollary of his argument, however, is that the researcher must discern the signs of where God is at work through 'prayerful reason' and 'contemplative science' (Webster, 2012: 215–16).[16] Requiring such discernment will cause few ripples in the church, but is controversial within the academy where secular norms predominate. I note that both Holder and Fellowship initiated prayer for me and the research, and this trend has been extended in subsequent church research projects.[17] While I am in agreement with the need for spiritual discernment to permeate the ethnographic look, I am aware this raises an issue of authority for such work. A Bible reader may claim their interpretation has been inspired by the Holy Spirit, and this may well be true, but it should be open to testing by various means. Similarly, theological ethnography also needs to be tested by the reader and by communities for whom it is significant.

Alongside the visual metaphor of 'look', the aural metaphor of conversation is also helpful methodologically, given the epistemology and ontology outlined above. Operating within 'the presence of a self-revealing God', the researcher, church-in-the-world and Christian Story are in 'conversation' with one another.[18] I use 'conversation' deliberately, not to imply that the partners are of the same essence or authority, but to indicate the relational and participatory nature of the task. New or revised models, language, categories and connections may (hopefully) emerge from this conversation.

Whether it is expressed as a conversation or a look, a case in point for theological ethnography is the understanding of 'practices'. In this book there is a focus on a variety of hermeneutical practices within two congregations. As introduced in Chapter 1, this is broadly understood as the saying, doing,

---

[14] By this logic, social science accounts of church are likely to be reductionist, as Margaret Archer et al. have argued forcefully (2004a). However, theology has been guilty of reductionism in the opposite direction, by ignoring the empirical in ecclesiology. Such language is rarely helpful in establishing good working relationships between theologians and social scientists who may benefit from mutual collaboration.

[15] ' ... to understand the practices of the church – practices as mundane as reading – we need to see how "God acts in our acts"' (citing Craig Hovey; Paddison, 2009: 22).

[16] A developing theme in theological ethnography, so Swinton (2012: 83–4), but also more generally in Alistair Campbell over a decade ago (2001: 85–6).

[17] Although a small practice, the practice of praying before our research seminar at a leading British University was significant for what it communicated about the nature of research.

[18] The all-encompassing presence of God in this partnership was suggested by Fiddes's model of theological method (2012: 25).

making and learning of biblical hermeneutics. We might characterise this broad diversity of hermeneutical practices as 'hearing God speak through Scripture' – a vital, necessary and constitutive practice of the church.[19] I am not particularly concerned with closely defining the nature of practices, but prefer to let the reader encounter their variety in the tale of two churches.[20] However, it is important to stress that hermeneutical practices, like any practices, have values, ideologies and theologies embedded within them. They are not neutral, but normative, in that they are directed towards certain ends. Bearing in mind the definition of practical theology above, it is important to see practices within the context of the Christian Story which gives them their proper end and meaning. Such a look will suggest transformation of practices that are distorted or misaligned, as Anthony Thiselton argues:

> ... the *present* can be *understood* only in the light of the *past history of traditions* as these move towards the *promised goal of the future* revealed in a provisional and preliminary way in the resurrection of Christ ... the future promise of God may itself bring *transforming discontinuities which transform the meaning of the present in the light of a new future ... divine promise shapes both the nature of reality and how the present is to be understood* (1992: 606).[21]

Without developing this eschatological look, the present practices and situation of the church cannot be understood. Consequently theological ethnography requires being eschatological about the empirical.[22]

Readers may have noticed the resemblance to critical realism in the structuring of the preceding discussion. This is quite intentional, since I contend that critical realism has a valuable role in explicating key aspects of theological ethnography.[23] The three 'pillars' of critical realism are a commitment to *ontological realism,*

---

[19]   This is a fair summary of Holder and Fellowship's goals for reading the Bible. See also John Webster (2012: 216f), Kevin Vanhoozer (2006: 62) and Rowan Williams (Anglican Communion, 2012: 1).

[20]   See Nicholas Healy's concern regarding the 'misplaced concreteness' of some proposed constitutive practices (2003: 290).

[21]   This is in the context of Thiselton critiquing 'pastoral theologians' for their tendency to over-privilege the present.

[22]   Nicholas Adams and Charles Elliott have talked of 'eschatological ethnography', which does not only describe the world merely 'as it is', but also in the light of 'as it shall be'. Such ethnography is then 'for teaching Christians to *see with an eye on transformation*' (2000: 363–4).

[23]   A number of theologians see the explicatory benefits of critical realism. In the preceding discussion I have drawn on N. T. Wright (1992: 32f) and Alister McGrath (2002b: esp. chapter 10). McGrath argues that critical realism is not foundational to the interdisciplinary exercise, but rather 'Christian theology should use or appropriate as many

in conjunction with *epistemic relativism* and *judgemental rationality*.[24] The first two pillars we have addressed. Judgemental rationality means that claims about my perception of reality can be justified by arguments and evaluated against other claims; hence reasoned provisional judgements about reality can therefore be made. For theological ethnographic research this has important implications, since there will be some accounts that can be judged to be better or worse interpretations than others, although such judgement remains provisional (cf. Geertz, 1973: 29). This is reflected in the tale that is to be told where I have a greater degree of confidence in certain conclusions than others. According to critical realism, this is not necessarily a weakness, since it should be expected that judgements will be made with varying degrees of confidence or probability. Allowing for a range of probabilistic judgements enables the creation of a richer account that more faithfully represents the nature of theological ethnographic knowledge.

There is a lot of debate about methodology matters in ecclesiological research, and, because I think it is critical for how we explore congregational hermeneutics, I have given some space to the issues here. Such methodology can itself become idealised and is notoriously difficult to work out in theological ethnographic practice, especially when the researcher faces the widely acknowledged messiness of fieldwork. Nevertheless, I trust that what follows aspires to the ideals outlined above.

Participating Matters

Participating in theological ethnography requires choices. I chose evangelical congregations for two main reasons. Firstly, as an English evangelical insider, I wanted to work out some of the fascination and frustration with the hermeneutical practices of my own tradition. Secondly, evangelicals have been called 'Bible people' (amongst other things) (Stott, 1977: 6, 10). Rather than try to pursue the goal of typicality from the scientific research paradigm, theological ethnography prefers to search for 'telling' cases that are fruitful for exploring a particular research interest (Mitchell, 1984: 238–41). Given the rich tradition of Bible engagement in evangelicalism, it seemed an appropriately telling case for exploring congregational hermeneutics. Furthermore, evangelicalism is a popular movement, inclined to be a religion of the grassroots, which is therefore

---

world-views and forms of language as are appropriate to explicate the truth of God's Word without allowing itself to enter into a relation of dependence upon them' (2002b: 200f).

[24]   I am following the Bhaskar school of critical realism here, especially through its Christian proponents in Archer et al. (2004b). There is not space to develop the value of a stratified or depth ontology for interdisciplinary relations, but the notion of 'emergence' does appear to have significant potential (McGrath, 2002b: 195f; Danermark, 2002).

significant for the largely 'ordinary' aspect of congregational hermeneutics (Noll, 2004: 150f; Tidball, 2005: 259).

Therefore in January 2005 I telephoned the pastor of *City Reach Christian Fellowship*, Derek, and he responded enthusiastically to the proposed research on the Bible. It helped that a renewed emphasis on the Bible for the church had been part of Derek's vision for the year ahead (ThursPM1).[25] I explained that I was from an evangelical background myself, although not from quite the same stable of British evangelicalism as Fellowship. I was what I call a semi-indigenous researcher (cf. Clifford, 1986: 9). Derek agreed that I could join Fellowship for six months immersion.[26] Three weeks later I was standing in a school hall at Fellowship's worship service, participating as I was able, and learning the trick of doing and being many things at the same time. I was shaking hands, being questioned, doing my 'research project' speech, and making church small talk whilst lobbing in the occasional research question. I was standing around looking lonely on purpose, trying to listen very hard, trying to look very hard, checking the recorder, and writing notes in a little black book. In public meetings and small groups I was a participant observer of how the Bible was being used,[27] but kept the gaze broad enough to see how wider patterns of congregational life might be relevant for hermeneutical practices.[28] I also interviewed a range of congregants about their use of the Bible,[29] and towards the end of my time at Fellowship conducted a questionnaire.[30] Throughout this time at Fellowship, I was looking to understand the variety of hermeneutical practices and how they had been mediated. Notes and audio and transcripts and documents and literature made their way into a qualitative software analysis program,[31] which then enabled me to develop a thematic coding system to aid analysis as the fieldwork progressed.

I chose to undertake a second case study after considering the benefits of a contrasting case that would enrich the look at congregational hermeneutics.[32] September 2005 was my first contact with *Holder Evangelical Church*, where

---

[25] Ethnographic referencing conventions in this book are discussed below.

[26] Looking back I realise I attended more church meetings than the pastor or any other congregant in Fellowship. After this burst of ethnographic enthusiasm at Fellowship, some funnelling took place when moving to a second church.

[27] The mix of participation to observation varied according to setting, generally in proportion to the numbers present (Hammersley and Atkinson, 1995: 104).

[28] I attended 14 public meetings, and joined 6 different small groups which led to attending 22 small group settings in total, see Appendices A and B.

[29] 17 congregants across the congregation, see Appendix C.

[30] 140 adult congregants at Fellowship, 122 questionnaires distributed, 75 completed.

[31] Software of this type is referred to as Computer Assisted Qualitative Data Analysis Software or CAQDAS. I used ATLAS.ti.

[32] Robert Yin also cautiously recommends a two case design over a single case, in this instance a two-tail design (1989: 53–4).

I was welcomed by the pastor, Owen, after satisfactory references had been received from my own church. I spent eight months at Holder using the same research methods as at Fellowship.[33] Our look at congregational hermeneutics in the rest of this book is built around these two contrasting cases.[34]

Participating Matters to Me

In a book about hermeneutics, where we come from and what we bring are essential parts of understanding how we read. Therefore, I tell my own (compressed) story here as well.

I approach the task of this book as a practitioner and practical theologian. My own engagement with the Bible has been formed by my family, churches, educational experiences, parachurch agencies and academic institutions/associations – often positively, sometimes less so. I grew up in the Christian Brethren and now have been part of an Anglican church in London for some years, attending a number of independent evangelical churches along the way. I have belonged to conservative, 'open' and charismatic evangelical churches, as well as worked for evangelical mission agencies in Kenya and Ethiopia. Studying at an evangelical theological college and then doing doctoral work and subsequent research at English universities has allowed me to engage with a wide range of approaches to the Bible. More broadly, I recognise that my earlier careers in software engineering[35] and secondary school teaching have also influenced my approach to researching and teaching the Bible.

My own broad hermeneutical practices are similar to many in the evangelical tradition and beyond. I try to read the Bible on my own regularly; I have participated, led, and coordinated small group Bible studies; I enjoy preaching and have done so on an occasional basis over the last thirty years. I have also taught the Bible in theological colleges and universities in the UK and Africa; developed a biblical hermeneutics course for churches with the Bible Society (see Chapter 9) and am currently writing Bible reading notes for the Bible Reading Fellowship. The point of such a list is that the subtitle question is of intense personal *and* academic interest – the 'we' includes me. I have a vivid memory from childhood of a lady breaking down in tears as she 'illegally' (and somewhat shockingly) participated in the morning worship of our Brethren

---

[33]   I attended 13 public meetings, and joined 3 different small groups which led to attending 11 small group settings in total. I conducted 17 interviews with congregants from across the congregation. There were 200 adult congregants at Holder, 200 questionnaires were distributed, 105 completed.

[34]   For a strong argument for the necessity of case-study research, especially the importance of context-dependent knowledge for developing genuine expertise, see Bent Flyvbjerg (2006; cf. Miller-McLemore, 2012a).

[35]   What it was called at the time.

assembly in the Midlands of England. Even then I sensed that how we read the Bible mattered because things like adults crying in public might be the result. More recently, teaching Ministry students from pentecostal backgrounds, I have been made aware that hermeneutics is sometimes a matter of life and death, especially with regard to the question of healing.[36]

In more recent years, I have appreciated learning from a much broader range of Christian traditions, through ecumenical groups, academic communities,[37] and especially the British and Irish Association for Practical Theology (BIAPT) – despite the occasional bout of theological culture shock. As a practical theologian, I am formed by an academic/practitioner community that prizes interdisciplinary study, theological reflection on practice, and a strong tendency to ask 'So what?' This book is intended to sit within this tradition of theological enquiry.

Reading 'The Tale of Two Churches'

The Tale of Two Churches has a total cast of 74 congregants and visitors, singing 114 distinct songs in 27 public meetings, participating in 33 small group sessions and sourced from 34 interviews. To allow the reader to see the interrelations between congregants and settings, a simple form of ethnographic referencing is used. All congregants are given pseudonyms with a suffix of 'H' or 'F' indicating to which congregation they belong, so, for example, the pastors OwenH and DerekF.[38] Services and sermons are numbered, named by day and time, and also have 'h' and 'f' suffixes.[39] Small groups have their own unique pseudonyms,[40] and where the context does not make it clear, the source of congregant excerpts is given, such as 'Conversation'. It may appear at first that congregant excerpts are a little incoherent in places, but I should stress that the effect of transcribing informal speech generates this impression to a large extent.[41] The reader should

---

[36]   Such cases have gained media attention, but are by no means widespread in black majority churches in London (so Lakhani, 2011; but see Rogers, 2013a).

[37]   Especially London School of Theology, Evangelical Theological College (Addis Ababa), King's College London, and the University of Roehampton.

[38]   Those without suffixes are external to the congregations.

[39]   E.g. SunAM1f is the first fieldwork Sunday morning service at Fellowship. S8h is the eighth fieldwork sermon at Holder.

[40]   These do not have suffixes since they are unique. Church-based small groups are named by day and time and numbered by session (e.g. TuesAM3, ThursPM2). Housegroups are named by a letter, so X, Y at Holder, and A, B, C at Fellowship, and also numbered by session.

[41]   Excerpts have been lightly edited, in that some repetitions have been removed and 'ums' and 'ers' have largely been omitted.

therefore calibrate their perception of excerpts accordingly. Fuller details of public meetings, small groups and interviews are given in the Appendices.

As has been noted, the messiness of ethnography is well recognised (e.g. Ward, 2004). The reality of researching in real communities with real people means that excerpts in the accounts, although addressing the theme under consideration, often raise many other issues as well. That is to say that there is a surplus of content even in carefully selected excerpts. It is neither practical nor desirable to comment on every point raised in the accounts. Space precludes the former, and on the latter, the intention in this book is not to overpower the voices of the churches with commentary, as mentioned in Chapter 1. Therefore, within the chapters, there is a progressive distancing of analysis, evaluation and conclusions from the congregational excerpts. To aid a balanced look at Holder and Fellowship, the order of Fellowship and Holder is varied throughout the accounts. In addition, the comparisons of the two churches are structured differently according to the themes being considered, with the rationale given in the relevant chapter.

Virtue and (Trans)formation

The core argument of this book, as has been said, is that many churches may need to develop a more intentional, corporate and virtuous hermeneutical apprenticeship as a necessary dimension of being church. In order to develop this core argument throughout the following chapters, the key ideas of virtue and (trans)formation need some introduction.

The apprenticeship in mind here is one of growth in virtue, specifically, growth in hermeneutical virtue. The contention in this book is that developing a virtuous Christian character has an impact upon how one reads the Bible. Growth in virtue is not only a desired outcome of Scripture engagement, but virtue should also inform that engagement. A virtuous circle is therefore a feature of this hermeneutical apprenticeship. For example, humility is a virtue commended in Scripture, even implied of the reader, yet humility is also critical for understanding and acting upon Scripture. Another way of saying this is that who we are matters for how we read. Hermeneutical practices then hinge on hermeneutical virtues, in the sense that we can make judgements about hermeneutical practices according to their virtue. Indeed, I have noticed how frequently the language of vice and virtue is used by Christian leaders with regard to Bible reading.[42]

---

[42]   Stephen Pardue argues of virtue that 'it gives us a rich vocabulary for assessing the various goals for which we consistently aim when we interpret Scripture' (2010: 304).

As will be seen, virtue hermeneutics thinking has a very long history, reaching back to an implied hermeneutics of love in Augustine (*Doc. Chr.* 1.35–8).[43] In recent decades, a virtue perspective on biblical hermeneutics has been developed more explicitly by a number of scholars, detailed in Table 8.1 in Chapter 8. I will be engaging with many of these existing insights, especially from Richard Briggs (2010), since our approaches have a significant amount in common. What is missing from all these works are contemporary accounts of virtue-in-practice, where we see what hermeneutical virtue looks like in a sustained narrative of practices. This has been noted of virtue ethics more broadly, so Peter Gathje comments: 'What I have found strange in this field of Christian virtue ethics is a lack of sustained attention to the practice of actual communities and how that practice does or does not shape persons in virtues consistent with a community's vision' (2011: 209).[44] Regarding virtuous readers of the Bible, Briggs argues for interpretative[45] virtue based on the implied reader of Scripture, concluding by drawing out the connections between implied and real readers, although 'no blood flows in the veins of implied readers' (2010: 206). It is the hermeneutical virtues and vices of real, blood-filled Bible readers that are largely my concern in this book.

A definition of a hermeneutical virtue is provided by Vanhoozer, which will suffice as a working definition until it is revisited in Chapter 8. 'Interpretive virtue', as Vanhoozer often terms it,[46] is 'a disposition of the mind and heart that arises from the motivation for understanding, for cognitive contact with the meaning of the text' (1998: 376).[47] There are seven particular virtues that are identified and explored within this tale of two churches, namely *honesty*, *faithfulness*, *openness*, *courage, humility*, *confidence* and *community*. These will be developed in subsequent chapters and particularly in Chapter 8. For any Protestant hackles that have been raised in the last few paragraphs, I will be returning to why an emphasis on virtue is not a threat to justification by faith or the disruptive grace of God, drawing on the likes of N. T. Wright and others (e.g. Wright, 2010).

---

[43] See also Alan Jacobs (2001).

[44] See also Ron Beadle and Geoff Moore (2006: 336). Gathje mentions Gloria Albrecht as a notable exception to his point (1995: 52–4, 60–61).

[45] The British English spelling will be used, unless referring to American usage.

[46] I prefer to use 'hermeneutical virtue' as it fits the focus of this study on 'how' congregations read the Bible. Furthermore, virtue pertains to both the first and second order activities of interpretation and hermeneutics respectively. Vanhoozer uses both 'hermeneutical' and 'interpretive' virtue, but the former is rare in his work (1998: 32, 466).

[47] Vanhoozer acknowledges that he develops this definition from Linda Zagzebski's account of intellectual virtue (1996).

Virtue is closely related to the language of Christian formation and transformation.[48] As discussed above, practical theology aims to be a transformative discipline since it fosters *constructive* reflection on the practices of the Church, enabling the Church's *innovative* participation in the Christian Story. In terms of hermeneutical practices, I argued for being eschatological about the empirical, since present practices are shaped by the Christian Story which gives them their proper end and meaning. That end is given in Scripture, where 'transformation' describes God's redemptive practices in bringing about his new creation at the individual, corporate and cosmic levels (so Rom 8:18–25; 2 Cor 5:17f; Gal 6:15; Eph 1:10).

My particular interest is with the biblical sense of individual and corporate transformation, particularly addressed by Paul in 2 Cor 3:16, 18, when talking about the difference that Christ makes to the reading of Scripture, as follows:

> ... but when one turns to the Lord, the veil is removed ... And all of us, with unveiled faces, seeing the glory of the Lord as though reflected in a mirror, are being transformed into the same image, from one degree of glory to another; for this comes from the Lord, the Spirit (NRSV).

The common end for Christians and their communities, especially when encountering Scripture, is to be transformed into the likeness of Christ. Transformation understood within the Christian Story is 'a process by which the transcendent eschatological reality of salvation works determinatively in the earthly lives of Christians'. The transformation envisioned for Christians in 2 Cor 3:18 is 'an unceasing and progressive change into the image of the One whose glory they see' (Behm, 1967: 758–9). Paul uses similar corporate language in Rom 8:29 when he speaks of being 'predestined to be conformed to the image of his Son'. Transformation is an eschatological process that moves individuals and congregations from the 'now' to the 'not yet' of God's future – in doctrinal terms, it describes the process of sanctification. Such transformation cannot occur without the agency of the Holy Spirit, as the text indicates. Commenting on these verses, Richard Hays notes how:

> ... the transformed community reflects the glory of God and thus illuminates the meaning of the text ... the text shapes the community, and the community embodies the meaning of the text. Thus there is a hermeneutical feedback loop

---

[48] Many use 'formation' and 'transformation' without drawing a strong distinction (e.g. Fowl and Jones, 1991). Indeed, Richard Briggs has argued persuasively through an analysis of the relevant New Testament texts that such a distinction would be difficult to justify, and notes that they are also to be understood through the concept of 'conformation' – into the image of God's Son (2007: 177–8). Formation, conformation, transformation, then, are different ways of talking about the same Spirit permeated process.

that generates fresh readings of the New Testament as the community grows in maturity and as it confronts changing situations (1996: 304).

The specific interest in the 'hermeneutical feedback loop' here is the virtuous circle. The connections between transformation and virtue become apparent. To grow in Christian virtue, then, is to be formed, conformed, and transformed into the likeness of Christ.[49] For theological ethnography and congregational hermeneutics, then, this requires being alert to signs of such transformation within the tale of two churches, while recognising the provisionality of those signs. As will be seen in Chapter 3, there is a particular resonance between theological and hermeneutical language regarding transformation (Rogers, 2013c).

Finally, it is important to ask who and what is being transformed? In terms of virtuous hermeneutical apprenticeship, it is a mutual transformation of congregants and congregations through growth in virtue. Indirectly, transformed people may well lead to transformed hermeneutical practices and congregational traditions, although in ethnographic terms it is recognised that evidence of 'change' may not necessarily be of the Spirit (e.g. Browning, 1991: 278). Indeed, the terms *affirmative* and *disruptive* reading of Scripture are used in relation to congregational tradition later in the book, where both modes of reading may be hermeneutically virtuous.

---

[49] Fowl notes the traditional and ongoing nature of this connection between transformation and growth in virtue (1998: 86).

Chapter 3
Hermeneutics

Hermeneutical practices in the church have a history. They come from somewhere. It is likely that such practices will bear some similarity to established hermeneutical categories of the church and academy, although there may be significant variations and some surprises, not least in their mode of expression. As Pete Ward and Sarah Dunlop argue of ordinary theology 'the tradition offers a substantial "bulk" that can be either an obstacle, or a support', so 'ordinary theology is generated in, with, and around this bulk' (2011: 308). The extent to which this is the case for congregational hermeneutics will become apparent as the tale of two churches unfolds.

With congregations improvising, reproducing, ignoring and sometimes resisting this bulk of Christian tradition, understanding normative and formal categories of biblical hermeneutics would seem important for exploring what congregations do with the Bible. A starting point is the distinction developed between special and general hermeneutics in the early nineteenth century by Friedrich Schleiermacher, who then claimed 'at present there is no general hermeneutics as the art of understanding but only a variety of specialised hermeneutics' (1985: 73). By special hermeneutics he was referring to those hermeneutics of the time that focussed on particular texts, such as the Bible. From Schleiermacher onwards, general hermeneutics headed in a more philosophical direction, considering the 'preconditions which make understanding possible' (Lategan, 1992: 149), since 'understanding was a universal process requiring the critical attention of all the disciplines concerned with it' (Jeanrond, 1992: 439). Holding off queries about this distinction for the time being (e.g. Wood, 2000: 20f), it is clear that in subsequent history biblical and general hermeneutics have influenced each other's development significantly (Lategan, 1992: 150). I will be drawing on both biblical and general hermeneutics in this book, as they mutually inform the exploration of congregational hermeneutics. In what follows, I identify key features of three paradigms in biblical hermeneutics, as well as the special case of evangelical and charismatic hermeneutics. Conceptual resources from key twentieth-century thinkers on general hermeneutics are then examined, with these resources then put to work in aiding analysis of congregational hermeneutics.

I have divided biblical hermeneutics into *premodern*, *modern* and *postmodern* paradigms (cf. Thiselton, 1992: 142f). Although these correspond to historical eras, my concern is not primarily with historical development, but with what is distinctive hermeneutically, as recognised in the existing literature. My interest here is therefore with the normative and formal hermeneutics of the church and academy,[1] especially as they relate to Holder and Fellowship. This research confirms that all three of these hermeneutical paradigms are operative in churches today – to paraphrase David Ford, hermeneutics are 'simultaneously premodern, modern and postmodern'.[2] To elucidate the modern and postmodern paradigms further, I will use the well-established metaphors of 'behind the text', 'within the text' and 'in front of the text', which correspond to an emphasis on the author, the text, and the reader respectively (so Gooder, 2008b: xviii).[3] Both these sets of explanatory categories, while tending to sharpen a rather fuzzy picture, are also helpful for that very reason, since they bring into focus significant features of the complex normative/formal hermeneutics landscape for the purposes of understanding congregational hermeneutics.

Premodern

Until we reach the fourth millennium, the premodern paradigm will continue to be the largest period of Christian history, yet it has often been undervalued in biblical studies. There is an assumption that the hermeneutical insights of the modern era onwards have made premodern approaches obsolete.[4] Recent trends in academic hermeneutics, however, have led to a re-evaluation of premodern hermeneutics for the church today. Indeed, there was substantial resonance between the premodern paradigm and the tale of two churches.

Apostolic Hermeneutics

Biblical hermeneutics begins within the Bible itself, with the New Testament providing the very earliest categories of *Christian* biblical hermeneutics. There is a cautious consensus[5] in the literature that Apostolic hermeneutics were in some continuity with Jewish hermeneutics.[6] These may be categorised as

---

[1]   As opposed to the espoused and operant hermeneutics of the two churches that, often by contrast, will be the main focus of this book.

[2]   Ford is speaking more generally of theology, but the point still holds (2005: 761).

[3]   I will return to the origin of these terms with Paul Ricoeur when discussing general hermeneutics below.

[4]   See comments or examples from G. Bray (1996: 45), W.G. Kümmel (1973: 13), J.F.A. Sawyer (1990: 316), D. Tidball (2005: 260).

[5]   Analysing the nature of New Testament hermeneutics is not straightforward (cf. Barrett, 1970: 411) – here my aim is simply to represent a consensus where that is possible.

[6]   E.g. C.K. Barrett (1970: 395), D.S. Dockery (1992: 16), R.P.C. Hanson (1970: 412), R. Longenecker (1975: 207). I am broadly following Longenecker in this section.

literal, midrash, pesher, allegory, and typology (Longenecker, 1975: 28),[7] examples of which can be found in the NT to quite varying degrees. What was *new* in Apostolic hermeneutics was Christ, since for the earliest believers 'upon Jesus converged the whole history of Israel in the past, and from him deployed the whole future of the People of God' (Moule, 1966: 69–70). The Jewish hermeneutical approaches utilised by the New Testament writers were transformed through a new hermeneutical goal: that the Scriptures were about Christ – he was the hermeneutical key (Thiselton, 1992: 150; cf. Dockery, 1992: 24). Paul makes this Christological point explicit in 2 Cor 3:13–16, where he argues that reading the 'old covenant' without Christ is to read as if a veil lies over one's mind. Christ as the fulfilment of the Scriptures was not expressed through just one approach, but rather 'a harmony of notes presented in a variety of ways by different hermeneutical methods' (Dockery, 1992: 34). This emphasis on Christ as the hermeneutical key to Scripture will be referred to as *Christological hermeneutics*, in distinction from the more general term 'Christocentrism'.[8]

Space does not permit an examination of each of these hermeneutical categories, but midrash and pesher are of particular interest. The 'central concept' of rabbinic exegesis was 'midrash',[9] which in one of its senses refers to an interpretative methodology ('midrashic' interpretation) that moves beyond a literal reading (Longenecker, 1975: 32–3). The principle of analogy formed part of midrashic hermeneutics where 'one passage may be explained by another if similar words or phrases are present' (Evans, 1992: 544).[10] An extension of this principle is the practice of 'pearl stringing',[11] where passages from various parts of the Bible are collected together in support of a particular argument (Longenecker, 1975: 115; Bray, 1996: 66).[12] Therefore, as Donald Juel points out, a common feature of midrashic hermeneutics was to treat 'the whole scriptural testimony' as 'part of a single fabric' so 'any verse can be used to interpret any other' (2003: 297). 'Pesher'[13] is associated with the hermeneutics of the Qumran community, who understood interpretation to always have 'a charismatic, revelatory character' (Bray, 1996: 60). In distinction from midrashic hermeneutics which 'spoke of "That has relevance to This"', a *pesher* approach sees the events of one's own day ('this') as being the actual subject matter of biblical prophecy ('that') (Longenecker, 1975: 43). Longenecker argues persuasively

---

[7] Typology is an additional category from Dockery (1992: 27f) not explicitly listed by Longenecker.

[8] Christocentrism is a theological emphasis upon Christ, which may not necessarily be accompanied by Christological hermeneutics.

[9] Meaning 'to investigate' or 'study'.

[10] E.g. Rom 4:1–12, connecting Gen 15:6 and Ps 32:1f.

[11] Longenecker notes that analogy is 'involved' in this practice (1975: 115n27, 116).

[12] E.g. Rom 3:10–18, which 'strings' together Ps 14:1–3; 5:9; 10:7; Isa 59:7, 8; Ps 36:1.

[13] Meaning 'source' or 'interpretation'.

that *pesher* is Jesus' most characteristic use of Scripture through a distinctive 'this is that' fulfilment motif (1975: 70f).[14] Although *pesher* is muted in Paul, within the New Testament *pesher* is distinctive of Jesus and his immediate disciples, who took him as their hermeneutical example (Klein et al., 1993: 29; Longenecker, 1975: 212).[15]

Patristic and Medieval Hermeneutics

A long-lasting development in Patristic hermeneutics was that of tradition and its authority – indeed, it could be considered the distinguishing feature of the premodern paradigm. In the medieval period, broadly speaking, affirmation of the church's theological tradition became the primary form of biblical hermeneutics, where 'exegesis became almost synonymous with tradition, for the good commentator was the scholar who handed on faithfully what he had received' (McNally, 1986: 29).[16]

Given the difficulty inherent in resolving doctrinal issues by appeal to Scripture, the church father Tertullian (ca 155–255) went so far as to advise against such an appeal, since 'victory will either be impossible, or uncertain, or not certain enough' (*Praesc.* 19). Instead, determining the correct interpretation required asking *who* had the authority to interpret the Scriptures. Irenaeus answered 'the presbyters of the church' in succession from the apostles (ca 130–200), and thus he has been described as 'the father of authoritative exegesis in the church' (Grant and Tracy, 1984: 50). The church fathers, such as Irenaeus, formulated the *regula fidei*, the Rule of Faith, which was a creedal prototype that summarised the faith 'received from the apostles' by the Church,[17] both Christological in focus and (some would argue) narrative in style (Wall, 2000: 90; cf. Dockery, 1992: 72).[18] For Tertullian, the Rule of Faith was enough for correct interpretation, since: 'To know nothing in opposition to the rule (of faith), is to know all things' (*Praesc.* 14).

Explicit hermeneutics and hermeneutical self-consciousness found its first full expression in the Patristic period through Origen of Alexandria (ca 185–254), whom Frances Young describes as the first real scholar of the Bible (1990: 10).[19] Origen paid careful attention to the literal sense of the text, but argued that one should also ascend to its spiritual sense, or allegorical meaning.[20]

---

14   E.g. Jesus' reading of Isa 61 in Lk 4.
15   So Jesus' hermeneutics tutorial in Lk 24:25–7, 44–6 and Peter's pesher style formula in Acts 2:16 when quoting Joel 2:28–32.
16   See also B. Smalley (1983: 358) and Thiselton (1980: 315–16).
17   E.g. Irenaeus, *Adv. Haer.*, 1.10; also Tertullian, *Praesc.*, 13.
18   But see N. MacDonald (2009).
19   See also Y. Congar (1968: 42) and K. Froehlich (1984: 16).
20   Allegorical is used broadly in this book to denote any meaning beyond the plain or literal sense of the text.

Origen's influence on later Christian hermeneutics was immense, in that he provided an explicit rationale for allegorisation, which then developed into the 'leading approach to the Bible' in the early Church and beyond (Jeanrond, 1992: 435). The school of Antioch reacted against the allegorical hermeneutics of Alexandria, especially the ways in which they appeared to be 'diverted from the "plain" meaning of the text' and 'the "obvious" narrative sequence' (Young, 2003: 341). The Antiochene school emphasised the historical meaning of texts, and saw this as the primary level of interpretation (Rogerson, 1988: 36), although this was not history in the modern historical critical sense, but rather 'the obvious narrative meaning of the text' (Kugel and Greer, 1986: 195). For example, the hermeneutics of a key Antiochene figure, Theodore of Mopsuestia (ca 350–428), has been characterised as 'anti-allegorical' (Froehlich, 1984: 20; Wiles, 1970: 490, 507).[21] He accepted only four Psalms as messianic (2, 8, 45, 110) and rejected the allegorisation of Song of Songs, instead taking it to be a love poem by Solomon celebrating his marriage to an Egyptian princess (Grant and Tracy, 1984: 66–7). The difference between the two schools should not be over-emphasised, however, since both thought the historical and higher senses important, which suggests caution is needed over co-opting the school of Antioch as a forerunner of modern historical concerns.[22]

Augustine (354–430) was arguably the most significant influence on biblical hermeneutics during this period. In the four books of *De Doctrina Christiana*, Augustine seeks to guide readers of Scripture, as he explains in his preface entitled 'Showing that to teach rules for the interpretation of Scripture is not a superfluous task':

> There are certain rules for the interpretation of Scripture which I think might with great advantage be taught to earnest students of the word, that they may profit not only from reading the works of others who have laid open the secrets of the sacred writings, but also from themselves opening such secrets to others (*Doc. Chr. Pref.* 1).

Augustine also takes to task those who believe all they need for understanding Scripture is 'the unassisted grace of God' and 'divine illumination', which is the 'gift of God' (*Doc. Chr. Pref.* 2, 8). While being led by the Spirit was a critical aspect of hermeneutics for Augustine, it is 'not something that works in spiritual isolation from the shared skills of interpretation and the direction of the church's faith' (Williams, 2005: 64). The striking principle at the heart of Augustine's hermeneutics, however, is that of love:

---

[21] Wiles qualifies this as a 'starting-point'.
[22] See K. Froehlich (1984: 20), H. G. Reventlow (2001: 174), J. Rogerson (1988: 40).

> Whoever, then, thinks that he understands the Holy Scriptures, or any part of them, but puts such an interpretation upon them as does not tend to build up this twofold love of God and our neighbour, does not yet understand them as he ought (*Doc. Chr.* 1.36).

For Augustine, our hermeneutical dispositions matter. This principle, described as the hermeneutics of love in Chapter 2, is evident in his comments on Genesis elsewhere:

> See now, how foolish it is, in the face of so great an abundance of true opinions which can be elicited from these words [Gen 1:2], rashly to affirm that Moses especially intended only one of these interpretations; and then, with destructive contention, to violate love itself, on behalf of which he had said all the things we are endeavouring to explain! (*Conf.* XII.xxv.35)

Like other patristic interpreters that have already been considered, Augustine accepted both literal and figurative senses for the Scriptures. Developing from the time of Augustine and into the medieval period, the fourfold sense of Scripture became an established hermeneutics within the church, particularly as proposed by John Cassian (ca 360–435) and popularised later through a rhyme.[23] Four types of meaning could be sought for every text, namely the letter (historical), the allegory (doctrinal), the moral (tropological), and the anagogy (eschatological). According to Cassian, 'Jerusalem' (cf. Gal 4:22f) was understood to have a fourfold meaning – a characteristic with resonance in Holder and Fellowship.[24]

Further development of the multiple senses of Scripture can be found in the work of Thomas Aquinas (1224–74). In *Summa Theologica*, Aquinas defends the idea that Scripture may have both a literal and spiritual sense, the latter comprising the three traditional senses given above, where the 'spiritual sense' is 'based on the literal, and presupposes it'. The literal sense is 'that which the author intends' where the author is God.[25] There is no confusion between the senses, since 'all the senses are founded on one – the literal – from which alone can any argument be drawn' (*ST* I.1.10). As Healy observes, the literal sense for Aquinas is not historical in modern terms, but 'that which the words of Scripture convey, namely the history of salvation centred upon Jesus Christ' (2005: 16).

---

[23]   Augustine also has this fourfold division in *Gen. Lit.* (1.1). Nicholas of Lyra (1265–1349) included a rhyme about the fourfold sense at the beginning of his *Post. Litt.*

[24]   'Historically as the city of the Jews; allegorically as Church of Christ, anagogically as the heavenly city of God "which is the mother of us all", tropologically, as the soul of man' (*Coll.* 14.8).

[25]   Aquinas understands the literal sense to include metaphor, imagery and parable.

For biblical hermeneutics, then, the key development from Aquinas was the greater primacy given to the literal sense of Scripture (properly understood).

Reformation Hermeneutics

Assisted by the translation of the Scriptures into the vernacular, the Reformation may be described as a 'hermeneutical event' that witnessed a 'fundamental change in hermeneutical thinking' (Jeanrond, 1992: 437; Lategan, 1992: 150). Such a mini-paradigm shift was aided by the resources of the Renaissance, with its emphasis on the literal sense of the text, along with the *ad fontes* ('back to the sources') move towards using the original languages of Scripture (McGrath, 1990: 582; Lindars, 1988: 295f). The crucial change was in the attitude to Scripture, known through the principle of *sola scriptura*. No longer was the tradition and authority of the church to be determinative for Christian faith and practice alongside Scripture, but the Bible alone was to be the Christian's primary authority. For the Magisterial Reformation, their hermeneutics allowed Scripture to challenge the tradition of the church, although such tradition was still held in high regard, especially the Church Fathers.[26] *Sola scriptura* did not mean that an individual interpretation was elevated over the corporate judgement of the church, unless they felt obliged to by 'the latest philological or textual advances' (McGrath, 1990: 584). In short, as expressed by Alexander Jensen, *sola scriptura* meant that 'Scripture, interpreted on the basis of a (purified) tradition, was the basis of Christian faith and theology' (2007: 68). The Reformation was not a monolithic movement, however, with different emphases and approaches evident between representatives such as Luther, Calvin and Zwingli. The Radical Reformation took the *sola scriptura* principle much further, rejecting the tradition and authority of the church from after the apostolic period. McGrath argues that contemporary evangelical attitudes to tradition have been shaped by both the Magisterial and Radical Reformations, and therefore one might expect to encounter tensions arising from these dual influences (2000a: 146).

Closely related to the Reformation principle of *sola scriptura* was that of *claritas scripturae*, also known as the perspicuity of Scripture. Such perspicuity meant that all can read the Scriptures profitably, but not that all Scripture is equally clear or that it does not need explication. Rather, such perspicuity, in Thiselton's appraisal of Luther, means that 'Scripture provides a witness to Christ to which we may confidently respond', but this principle 'in no way offers any short-cut through the problems of interpretation and hermeneutics' (1992: 184–5). Associated with perspicuity was the *analogia fidei* ('analogy of faith')

---

[26]   E.g. McGrath notes that a return to 'the Bible and Augustine' was how Luther styled his reforming programme at Wittenberg (2000a: 143).

principle of *scriptura scripturae interpres* (Scripture interprets Scripture) whereby the Bible was understood to be self-interpreting (within the *claritas scripturae* provisos already given). Echoing Augustine, Luther comments of Scripture:

> But to know that all things in the Scriptures are set in the clearest light, and then, because a few words are obscure, to report that the things are obscure, is absurd and impious. And if the words are obscure in one place, yet they are clear in another (*Serv. Arb.*, 15–16).

The significance of Reformation hermeneutics consists in its challenge to the authority of church tradition, along with an increased emphasis on the literal sense of a clear and accessible text, which some scholars see as opening the way for later hermeneutical paradigms (Grant and Tracy, 1984: 92; Jensen, 2007: 74–5; Lindars, 1988: 316).

Evaluating the Premodern Paradigm

The premodern paradigm is a story of moving from multiple senses of texts towards an emphasis on the text's literal meaning. Hermeneutical playfulness with the text moves towards a more analytical treatment as the critical tools of the Renaissance became available. Not all aspects of these developments have been understood as progress (e.g. Steinmetz, 1997). Thiselton characterises the nature of the premodern hermeneutical paradigm and its resonance with the postmodern, as a joint emphasis upon the individual being part of a community 'in which shared beliefs, practices, conventions, and traditions, decisively shape the individual's understanding' (1992: 143). Premodern hermeneutics operated under a hermeneutics of trust within a theological framework, which reverberates with the explicit postmodern resourcing of theological hermeneutics from the premodern.

Modern

The modern hermeneutical paradigm corresponds to the post-Enlightenment period up until the growing critique of modernity in the later twentieth century.[27] Historical criticisms are the hermeneutical approach most closely associated with this period, which emerged in the eighteenth century,[28] and established supremacy in the academy for nearly two centuries (cf. Grant and Tracy, 1984: 110).

---

[27]   I take this as beginning in the seventeenth century with the classical foundationalism of Cartesian doubt.

[28]   Propagated through largely German scholarship (Harrisville and Sundberg, 1995: 9).

Thiselton detects two paradigm shifts in the history of biblical hermeneutics, where both 'served to break the spell of a prior controlling model'. He argues that the first shift 'threw off dogmatic theology only to sell itself into bondage to history' and the second 'throws off the bondage of history and theology only to find itself captive to politics: to the politics of gender, race, class ... ' (1998: 1570–71). The concern of this section is with the first shift, which was in reaction to the control of the church and its theology over biblical interpretation (cf. Stuhlmacher, 1977: 38). Rogerson captures the nature of this shift to the historical critical method when he observes 'its advent did not mean that scholars began for the first time to ask critical questions' since 'they had been doing this for over a thousand years'. Instead, 'the difference lay in the way the critical questions were answered' (1992: 430). Unlike previous centuries, scholars became increasingly free to say that the Bible might be wrong or inconsistent, particularly regarding its historical accuracy.

Although not a monolithic approach to hermeneutics, certain characteristics of historical criticism can nevertheless be identified (cf. Bartholomew, 2000: 4–5). It is an approach that aims to uncover the historical referents 'behind the text' of the Bible, whereby the text is used as a window onto a world that may be reconstructed through historical investigation. Meaning is found by discovering the original intention of the author in communicating to their audience. Critical tools were developed to aid this historical enterprise, such as source, form, tradition and redaction criticism, so that the text may be 'methodically analysed and subjected to the modern judgment of reason' (Stuhlmacher cited in Piper, 1980: 329).[29] This understanding of criticism in modernity has led a number of biblical scholars to identify the shift to the modern paradigm as moving from a pre-critical to a critical paradigm (cf. Wolters, 2000: 91). Given the contemporary resonances with the 'pre-critical' paradigm evidenced in Holder and Fellowship, then much of contemporary congregational hermeneutics might be described as 'non-critical' from the perspective of academic biblical studies (cf. Barton, 2007a; b).

Historical criticism reflects the worldview of modernity, as Brueggemann has said 'historical criticism is our particular practice of modernity' (1993: viii). Wolfhart Pannenberg characterises this worldview as one where 'supernaturalism' is 'unacceptable to the critical reason of the historian' since 'by asserting transcendental incursions it would cut short historical research into inner-worldly causes and analogies' (1970: 76). In addition to this closed universe, historical criticism emphasised the scientific and objective study of the text, which would yield 'assured results'. Coherent with this approach, meaning was assumed to be monovalent and historical. That is, the biblical scholar's task was to recover what the text *meant* through exegesis, and the

---

[29]   Translated by Piper.

theologian's task was then to decide what it *means* for the life of faith today.[30] Under this scheme, it is possible for the biblical scholar to concern herself only with historical meaning – what I call a one-horizon reading. Moving *from* meant *to* means is the primary function of hermeneutics in this scenario of biblical meaning – what I call a 'one-way' hermeneutics, or more pejoratively, the 'historical two-step' or 'conveyer belt' hermeneutics.[31] Therefore, according to this model of hermeneutics, the context of the interpreter is not germane to the process of understanding.

From its beginning, the results of historical criticism have been in some tension with orthodox Christian faith. Probabilistic judgements about biblical events and history sit uneasily with those who base their lives on the teaching of Scripture. Historical criticism first came to the widespread attention of the British public with the publication of *Essays and Reviews* in 1860. Ordinary orthodox Christians were faced with the question 'Is the Bible to be treated like any other book or not?' (Neill and Wright, 1988: 31, 33). At the time, many thought not, and many have continued to think so (e.g. Moberly, 2010), although Christian biblical scholars came to a measure of accommodation with their faith and academic practice. Westcott, Hort, and Lightfoot were notable in the latter half of the nineteenth century in developing a moderate 'believing criticism' for the New Testament – a tradition that has continued to the present through scholars such as F. F. Bruce, I. H. Marshall, and N. T. Wright (Bartholomew, 2003: 5).[32] Marshall uses the term 'grammatico-historical method', drawing on R. P. Martin, to signify an approach that uses the same tools as the historical critical method, but:

> ... without acceptance of antireligious presuppositions that rule out the possibility of the supernatural from the start. It is possible to do "grammatico-historical" study without accepting the starting point laid down by Troeltsch.[33] Over against the sceptical "historical-critical method" may be placed the approach of "believing criticism" (2004: 16, 20).

The strong form of historical criticism initially described here has therefore evolved and mutated over time and taken less stridently modern forms. The method has also undergone a sustained period of criticism with the emergence of postmodern hermeneutics, which has called for greater acknowledgement of

---

[30]   The meant and means distinction is fundamental according to Krister Stendahl (1962).

[31]   Nicholas Lash refers to this as the 'relay race' model (1986: 79) and Joel Green calls it 'linear hermeneutics' (2002).

[32]   See also Neill and Wright (1988: 35f) and Noll (2004: 62f).

[33]   A key proponent of a strong historical criticism from the late nineteenth century (cf. Abraham, 1982).

the situatedness and subjectivity of our interpretations (e.g. Bultmann, 1964; Wink, 1973). Historical criticism lost its monopoly and has had to take its place in the hermeneutical marketplace. However, its demise is sometimes overstated, as it still enjoys great prestige within the academy, particularly in its modified grammatico-historical form amongst evangelical scholars.

Evaluating the Modern Paradigm

The modern paradigm of hermeneutics brought a number of perceived benefits to study of the Bible. Some scholars have argued that historical meaning can act as a constraint on interpretations, providing a legitimate critique of the relativist excesses of both the premodern and postmodern paradigm. Furthermore, orthodox Christians understand God's acts in history as being indispensable to their faith (to varying degrees), and therefore an emphasis on historical research resonates with this concern. Problems with some species of the historical critical method are found in the assumption that history is the only worthwhile hermeneutical goal, a pretension to scientific objectivity, and an insufficient awareness (ironically) of its own historically conditioned nature. From the perspective of congregational hermeneutics, a striking issue from the modern paradigm onwards is one of expertise and perspicuity. How is the ordinary Christian to interpret the Bible without the critical tools that only an expert few can master? As Joseph Parker of the City Temple in London said in the late nineteenth century: 'Have we to await a communication from Tübingen, or a telegram from Oxford, before we can read the Bible?' (cited in Neil, 1963: 286). For evangelicals, the Bible is a book that ought to be accessible to everyone, and therefore this has led to ongoing suspicion of academic biblical hermeneutics within the tradition.

Postmodern

Zygmunt Bauman characterised postmodernity as modernity coming to terms with its limitations (1991: 272). More specifically, Stanley Grenz and John Franke understand postmodernity at its heart to be a call for a 'chastened rationality' (2001: 22f).[34] In this study 'postmodern' will be used in these senses, that is, as a potentially constructive critique of modernity. The postmodern paradigm for hermeneutics concerns the proliferation of hermeneutical approaches that

---

[34] A number of theologians and philosophers dislike the term 'postmodern' (e.g. Blocher, 2004: 41–2; Collier, 2004: 89n3), due to its imprecision (amongst other reasons), but I will retain it pragmatically since it now has common currency within theological discourse.

began to emerge in the latter half of the twentieth century, which were typically in reaction to features of the modern paradigm. I will characterise the complex nature of postmodern paradigm hermeneutics in three groupings, namely literary, ideological and theological approaches.

Literary Criticism

Literary critique of the Bible is a venerable hermeneutical approach, but the distinctive of the literary turn in hermeneutics was a move away from meaning being located 'behind the text' in history to 'within the text' in its final form and its effects upon readers 'in front of' the text. The initial postmodern impetus in biblical studies came from moves in secular literary studies, which were then incorporated into biblical literary criticism (Bartholomew, 2000: 5). Although literary concerns in their earlier stages may not strictly be considered 'postmodern', there is a broader sense in which literary criticism functioned as a critique of modernity in the form of historical criticism. As C. S. Lewis wryly observed, it is no good claiming to 'read between the lines of the old texts' if there is an 'inability to read ... the lines themselves' (1975: 11).

Literary criticism is a diverse field which does not admit of easy categorisation, but one can divide approaches into those reflecting structuralist and then poststructuralist influences in the wider academy, corresponding to a hermeneutical emphasis on the text and reader respectively. Structuralist analysis, derived from social anthropology (Lévi-Strauss) and structural linguistics (Saussure), seeks to look beyond the surface features of texts to their deep underlying structures that are common to the human condition (Lindars, 1988: 382f). The approach stresses the autonomous nature of texts which should be read synchronically, as opposed to the diachronic reading of historical criticism. Therefore the text is understood according to the interrelations of its parts, rather than by external criterion (Lategan, 1992: 151). Criticism has been directed at structuralist analysis for its 'impenetrable jargon' and small interpretative return for significant methodological effort (Lindars, 1988: 385; Morgan, 1988: 219, 252f). Arising from structuralist concerns, amongst others, narrative criticism focusses on features of the text such as plot, theme, characterisation and symbolism. Interpretative benefits have been notable for narrative criticism in seeking to understand literary works as wholes, thus providing explanations for literary features that may be more satisfactory than purely historical critical approaches (e.g. narrative repetitions, so Alter, 1981: 49–56). Furthermore, such an approach allows for discussion across theological boundaries, due to issues of historical reference being bracketed out of narrative criticism (Klein et al., 1993: 434).

Poststructuralist approaches can be grouped broadly as reader-response criticism and deconstruction. Reader-response criticism focusses on the reader's role in meaning-making when encountering the text. For Wolfgang Iser, readers are co-creators of meaning largely through filling in narrative gaps (1978), whereas more radical critics such as Stanley Fish deny that meaning resides in the text, so:

> ... it is the interpretive communities, rather than the text or the reader, that produce meanings and are responsible for the emergence of formal features ... [interpretative] strategies exist prior to the act of reading and therefore determine the shape of what is read rather than, as is usually assumed, the other way round (1980: 14).

Therefore, meaningful dialogue is most likely to occur between those who belong to the same interpretative community, and critique from outside the community becomes very hard to hear. The reader can judge from the accounts of Holder and Fellowship that follow as to the accuracy of Fish's analysis. Deconstruction, according to Jacques Derrida, is an approach that 'is certainly the undoing of logocentrism' (1976: 74). Logocentrism is, as Thiselton explains, 'seeing a "fixed" or "given" relation between words and meanings' that cannot be altered (2009: 332, 334). Deconstruction rejects the view that language makes present a reality beyond its signs, but rather that words are 'ambiguous, unsteady on their feet, and not to be trusted as dependable representatives of something "out there"' (Anderson, 1996: 82). The purpose of deconstruction is one of 'generating conflicting meanings from the same text, and playing those meanings against each other' (Seung, 1982: 271). Derrida argues in *Limited Inc*, however, that deconstruction does not support total freedom of meaning (1988), despite its anarchic reputation. Through an analysis of biblical scholars employing deconstructive approaches (Moore, 1989; Clines, 1990), Briggs argues for disarming the hermeneutical minefield that is the deconstruction debate, concluding 'deconstruction is less about denying the possibility of communication and rather about making explicit the kind of interpretive stance that any reading betrays' (Briggs, 1995: 30; cf. Klein et al., 1993: 441).

Ideological Criticism

According to Thiselton, the postmodern paradigm attempted to break the spell of the prior controlling model, only to become captive to politics. Whether it is a 'captivity' or not, ideological criticism is the key instance of political hermeneutics. Although hermeneutical theory would recognise that all interpreters bring their ideologies to the text, nevertheless, ideological approaches deliberately foreground a specific context and ideology. Such approaches are rarely a matter of ideological application, but rather an ideological conversation with the text. The worlds 'in front of' the text include liberation (e.g. Rowland

and Corner, 1990; West, 1991), feminist (e.g. Fiorenza, 1983; Trible, 1984), and black contexts (e.g. Mosala, 1989), with these agendas driving the question 'Whose interests do/should biblical interpretations serve?' under a hermeneutic of suspicion. Such contextual approaches make an epistemological break with the modern paradigm since they allow local contexts to shape hermeneutical approaches – a hermeneutics 'from below'. In ideological criticism, the biblical text is read both for that which is emancipatory and oppressive according to one's foregrounded agenda, using a variety of critical tools.

Ideological criticism is important in drawing attention to the Bible's emancipatory themes relating to poverty, justice, and equality, as well as in identifying perceived oppressive interpretations or texts. One of its strands was instrumental in drawing academic attention to ordinary readers of the Bible, as discussed in Chapter 1. A key question facing all ideological criticism is whether the text can be any more than a mirror for the ideological interests of an interpretative community? (Thiselton, 1992: 410). In addition, to speak of oppressive texts (rather than oppressive interpretations) is problematic for Christians with a high view of Scripture.

Theological Hermeneutics and Interpretation

The postmodern paradigm and ideological criticism in particular makes space for bringing any number of ideologies and agenda to the Bible. Reading the Bible theologically then, from a postmodern perspective, is a form of ideological criticism (although not a view necessarily supported by its practitioners). There is some slippage in usage between theological hermeneutics and interpretation, but the difference is clear in the following definitions. Charles Wood explains theological hermeneutics as 'reflection upon the aims and conditions of what may be called the "Christian understanding" of Christian Scripture and tradition ... ' (2000: 21). This is effectively a theological general hermeneutics, to which we shall return. Stephen Fowl more specifically characterises theological interpretation as 'that practice whereby theological concerns and interests inform and are informed by a reading of Scripture' (1997b: xii). Theological interpretation may seem self-evident to the church, and indeed was a common practice within Holder and Fellowship, but it has been controversial within the academy (Bartholomew, 2000: 24f). This is not surprising, given the legacy of historical criticism, where historical reconstruction behind the text was separated from its theological significance in front of the text. Craig Bartholomew notes the oddity of the situation where 'biblical criticism has been philosophically in the extraordinary position of refusing to allow theological / Christian influence on its enterprise while making room for traditions and ideologies often antithetical to Christian belief' (2000: 25).

Theological interpretation has been gaining momentum in the academy in recent decades, through its presence in the *Society of Biblical Literature* and in dictionaries, commentary series, and the launch of the *Journal of Theological Interpretation* in 2007 (Fowl, 2009: ix). Indeed, Miroslav Volf considers the return to 'theological readings of the Bible' as 'the most significant theological development in the last two decades' (2010: 14).[35] Fowl identifies four beneficial characteristics of theological interpretation, namely taking premodern hermeneutics seriously; shaping and being shaped primarily by Christian communities; resisting the fragmentation of theology; and being pluralistic in its methods (1997a: xvi). Theological interpretation is a movement that at least aims to recover practices that have been lost from academic biblical hermeneutics and many forms of theological education (e.g. Treier, 2008). However, the long memory of 'throwing off dogma' from the first hermeneutical paradigm shift informs the key criticism of theological interpretation – how will it escape simply reinforcing the beliefs and practices of the church by imposing a preformed theological framework on the text? The question might be asked of any hermeneutics, of course, given that they all come embedded with particular ideologies, whether explicit or not.

Evaluating the Postmodern Paradigm

The postmodern paradigm has seen a multiplication of hermeneutical approaches,[36] as has been described above. The move towards a hermeneutical emphasis on the text and reader has provided invaluable additional resources for understanding 'how texts work' and the contribution of readers to meaning-making. Resonance with the premodern paradigm is seen in the greater acceptance of multiple senses and an increased emphasis on interpretative communities in some forms of the postmodern paradigm. However, in contrast with the premodern hermeneutics of trust, the postmodern paradigm exalts a hermeneutics of suspicion through ideological criticism and deconstructionism. The bracketing of historical concerns may aid theological ecumenism, but conversely there is a danger of postmodern approaches becoming detached from history, if there is no careful integration of plural hermeneutics. Indeed, Thiselton questions whether hermeneutics can be pluralist if one 'cannot arbitrate between competing goals and interests' (1998: 1571). Of all hermeneutical developments in the modern and postmodern paradigm, one might expect theological hermeneutics and interpretation to be the most fruitful for exploring the church's reading of Scripture. Indeed, the hermeneutical arguments developed in this book would certainly fit well under such headings.

---

[35]   Also cited approvingly by David Fergusson (2013: 25).
[36]   What Vanhoozer refers to as 'hyperactive hermeneutics' (1992).

Characterising Evangelical and Charismatic Hermeneutics

I start here with a focus on evangelical/charismatic hermeneutics and then in Chapter 4 examine briefly the contours of the broader tradition. It is not easy to identify normative and formal evangelical and charismatic hermeneutics and their commonalities across the variety of global evangelicalisms. It is notable that evangelical bases of faith in the UK (e.g. Evangelical Alliance, FIEC, Affinity) tend to avoid issues of hermeneutical method, but rather focus on the status of Scripture. Indeed, this focus appears to be the primary component of wider evangelical self-definition with regard to hermeneutics (Noll, 2004: 142f).[37] This is a little surprising for a tradition that invests so much in seeing the Scriptures 'rightly interpreted' (e.g. London School of Theology, 1998). However, there are North American evangelical statements that have touched upon hermeneutical method, notably *The Chicago Statement on Biblical Hermeneutics* (CSBH) (1982) and to a lesser extent *The Chicago Statement on Biblical Inerrancy* (CSBI) (1978),[38] both of which have had indirect influence on British evangelicals.[39] Christian Smith has also recently identified ten features of American evangelical 'biblicism',[40] most of which are hermeneutical in the broad sense (2012).[41] Like all evangelicals, and in continuity with the Reformation principle of *sola scriptura* (cf. McGrath, 2000b: 29), the British tradition gives a high place to Scripture, variously formulated with the terms inspired, inerrant, infallible, authoritative and trustworthy. Broadly speaking, conservatives have used the language of inerrancy and infallibility, whereas open evangelicals have preferred to speak of Scripture as authoritative and trustworthy (cf. Kings, 2003: 169f). Significantly, inerrancy and infallibility have not been central to evangelical identity in the UK in the same way as in the USA (Holmes, 2009).

Evangelical biblical scholars share certain other commitments in addition to the status of Scripture, some of which are common to other Christian traditions. A belief in an open universe which allows for divine agency (Noll, 2004: 145f), or does not rule it out a priori is key (so Wright, 1992), as is a commitment to some form of ontological realism, critical or otherwise (Noll, 2004: 146). Just these points in themselves put evangelical scholars in conflict

---

[37]   Gabriel Fackre provides a good example of this focus in his article 'Evangelical Hermeneutics' (1989).

[38]   'The leading theologian behind its wording' was James Packer, according to Blocher (1997: 121).

[39]   Commenting on both the US and British scene, Gerald Bray doubts that many evangelical biblical scholars would subscribe to all of the CSBI and CSBH articles (1996: 542, 560). Notably, British scholars James Packer and John Wenham were signatories.

[40]   This is a much more specific sense than used by David Bebbington (see Chapter 4) and a more pejorative usage than that of James Bielo (see Chapter 1).

[41]   In a strong polemic, he argues that such biblicism is 'impossible'.

with the assumptions of many in the wider academy. On epistemology there is less agreement, with conservative scholars emphasising the importance of propositional truth (CSBH Article VI 1982) often within an implicitly foundationalist system. Open evangelical scholars tend to stress the storied and world forming nature of Scripture (Wright, 1992), and may set this within a form of non-foundationalism (Grenz and Franke, 2001).[42]

In terms of hermeneutical method, there does appear to be some limited commonality for evangelical hermeneutics. Within the framework of believing criticism, the grammatico-historical approach predominates (CSBH Article XV 1982; CSBI Article XVIII 1978; Packer, 1990; Stott, 1984: 181), even if multiple hermeneutical methods are accepted. The original setting of the text and the intention of the author are cornerstones of evangelical hermeneutics (Marshall, 2004: 25; Fee, 1990). Often there is also an assumption that the text has a determinate or single meaning (CSBH Article XVIII 1982), even if it is only theoretically recoverable. The default model for understanding texts is 'application' or one-way hermeneutics from text to reader (cf. Warner, 2007: 190), with even some 'pockets of exegetical resistance in the evangelical world to the very notion of hermeneutics' (Vanhoozer, 2004: 83).[43] Beyond this common position, scholarly self-description of evangelical hermeneutics appears to lack consensus with regard to method, as Noll suggests (2004: 142), particularly for less conservative positions that are more inclined to hermeneutical pluralism. It may be that evangelical hermeneutical method is not particularly different to the methods of the wider academy. Although there is a diversity of religious and confessional backgrounds in New Testament study, Neill and Wright perceive a widespread recognition of the propriety of historical critical tools (1988: 360).[44] There is some evidence that theological interpretation of the premodern[45] and the more intentional postmodern variety may have many evangelical adherents (Bartholomew, 2000: 24f; 2003: 10f).

Identifying a charismatic hermeneutics is even more of a challenge than for evangelical hermeneutics. Firstly, the charismatic tradition is much more recent in development than evangelicalism, hence its distinctives have had less time to be characterised. Furthermore, charismatic hermeneutics are frequently subsumed under pentecostal hermeneutics, and the terms 'charismatic' and 'pentecostal' are often used interchangeably in the literature. William Kay distinguishes

---

[42] Epistemology and these terms in particular are discussed in both theoretical and empirical detail in Chapter 6.

[43] Notably, CSBH Article IX excludes from the concept of hermeneutics the idea that 'the message of Scripture derives from, or is dictated by, the interpreter's understanding', and thus the fusion of horizons is also denied.

[44] See the book length discussion of Kenton Sparks (2008).

[45] What Plantinga refers to as 'Traditional Biblical Commentary', following Chrysostom, Augustine, Calvin etc. (2003: 23f).

between classical pentecostals, who look to the Azusa Street revival of 1906 in Los Angeles as the crucial starting point of their story, and the emergence of the charismatic movement in the 1960s, when pentecostal experience spread to the historic churches. Sometimes referred to as the first and second wave respectively, the 'third wave' refers to the establishing of charismatic 'new churches', formed independently of the historic denominations (2004: xxxi). It is this 'third wave' to which Fellowship belongs.

Charismatic hermeneutics, while an intersecting set of evangelical hermeneutics, have their own distinctives according to an influential article by Mark Stibbe,[46] whose portrayal resonates with the tenor of subsequent accounts (e.g. Davies, 2009; Tennison, 2005). Stibbe argues for a 'mediating hermeneutics' that combines the 'historical criticism' of conservative evangelical scholars with a more subjective 'reader response' approach characteristic of the postmodern paradigm, which is 'primarily interested in a prophetic, contemporary reading of a text's significance' (1998: 181). As indicated in Chapter 2, one feature (amongst others) of this charismatic hermeneutics is a *pesher* 'this is that' approach taken as an exemplar from apostolic hermeneutics, in contrast to Longenecker's 'hermeneutical cessationism' (1998: 193). Stibbe identifies one of the major distinctives of charismatic hermeneutics as 'emotional intelligence' which combines the objective and subjective, or cognitive and affective reading of Scripture (1998: 191).[47]

Conceptual Resources from Hermeneutics

The conceptual resources discussed in this section are drawn largely from general hermeneutics, particularly Hans-Georg Gadamer, supplemented by Paul Ricoeur and Jürgen Habermas, as an aid for exploring congregational hermeneutics. As headlined in Chapter 1, some scholars have objected to utilising such resources on the grounds that they are not theological enough (e.g. Paddison, 2009; Webster, 2006). Accepting that this is not a veiled attempt to insist that all must be 'theological' in the same mode, there are some striking parallels here with my earlier arguments regarding theological ethnography. A theological look at the understanding of Scripture (i.e. theological hermeneutics) needs to avoid naïve imports from general hermeneutics, as I also argued for the case of ethnography.

---

[46]   Described as a 'focal theologian' for charismatic evangelicals by Kings (2003: 175). See also Tidball's summary which resonates with Stibbe's account (2005: 260–61).

[47]   Brian Stanley identifies the trend in evangelical hermeneutics of 'an increasingly common appeal to the evidence of personal spiritual experience as a decisive argument in the endeavour to establish how the biblical text should be applied today'. Notably, he identifies this characteristic under the heading of 'evangelical' while observing this appeal is most widely made in pentecostal and charismatic Christianity (2013: 211–12).

With critical appropriation, however, this does not need to be naïve, but instead a pertinent resourcing for the task, as captured by Watson's closely related argument, introduced in Chapter 1 and summarised here:

> ... the doctrine of Scripture 'needs' hermeneutics in the sense that hermeneutics provides conceptual resources for addressing some of the problems that this doctrine has historically encountered – problems with the very idea of a 'Word of God', addressed to us by an Other, together with problems in clarifying the relationship of the written Word of God to temporality and to its communal location (2010: 142).

For congregational hermeneutics, then, my aim is to equip the theological ethnography methodology with the appropriate resources from general hermeneutics. My approach has much in common with J. Todd Billings who sensibly contends:

> ... even in our general hermeneutical reflection on the practice of reading texts in general, we are not in a theology-free zone. As some scholars point out, there are biblical and theological resources that can inform our hermeneutical approach to texts in general. But further, in drawing on broad, human disciplines in understanding the nature of general hermeneutics, we are affirming that the truth that we encounter in general hermeneutical reflection is God's truth. Given the expansive work of God's Spirit in the world, we can affirm that "all truth is God's truth", wherever it may be found. So if truth is found in philosophers such as Hans Georg Gadamer or Jürgen Habermas, Christians should celebrate it (2010: 33–4).[48]

This is what I shall do now, albeit the celebration will be brief. General or philosophical hermeneutics includes reflection on the very conditions that make it possible for us to understand texts (Thiselton, 1992: 48). The tenor of philosophical hermeneutics is quite abstract and as noted above, includes positions that are not always consistent with the approach developed in this book. Nevertheless, biblical scholars, theologians[49] and many others have found much of value in philosophical hermeneutics, not least Thiselton who has productively drawn on the field for the enrichment of biblical studies and

---

[48] For a very similar argument based on Augustine as a dialogue partner, see James A. Andrews's *Hermeneutics and the Church* (2012: 213–14).

[49] Don Browning sees his argument for a fundamental practical theology as a consequence of taking Gadamer, Ricoeur and Habermas (amongst others) to their logical conclusion (1991: 8).

theology (so 1980; 1992; 2007).[50] Building on the definition in Chapter 1 and above, it has been said that hermeneutics is more than rules for interpreting the Bible. Such an approach only recognises the historical conditioning of *the text*, whereas the larger sense of hermeneutics acknowledges that historical conditioning is two-sided – 'the modern interpreter, no less than the text, stands in a given historical context and tradition' (Thiselton, 1980: 11). Gadamer's theory of textual understanding examines the situation of the interpreter who brings their traditions and context to a text. In his seminal work, *Truth and Method*,[51] Gadamer asks 'how we can break the spell of our own fore-meanings' and answers that a hermeneutically trained person must be open to the text's otherness. This does not require 'neutrality' nor 'the extinction of oneself', but rather that we remain 'open to the meaning of the other person or text', which includes 'situating the other meaning [of the text] in relation to the whole of our own meanings or ourselves in relation to it'. That is, our fore-meanings or 'prejudices', as Gadamer confusingly refers to them (for English speakers), are necessary for situating our understanding in relation to the otherness of the text (quotations from Gadamer, 2004: 270–71). So, in an uncharacteristically clear summary, Gadamer states: 'The important thing is to be aware of one's own bias, so that the text can present itself in all its otherness and thus assert its own truth against one's own fore-meanings' (2004: 271–2). Therefore the key insight that 'gives the hermeneutical problem its thrust' is that 'all understanding inevitably involves some prejudice'. This leads to one of Gadamer's best known lines – 'there is one prejudice of the Enlightenment that defines its essence: the fundamental prejudice of the Enlightenment is the prejudice against prejudice itself, which denies tradition its power' (2004: 272–3).

Of particular interest for this book is the metaphor of 'horizon'. Encompassing talk of 'prejudice', 'fore-meanings' or 'presuppositions', Gadamer explains horizon as 'a standpoint that limits the possibility of vision' and 'the range of vision that includes everything that can be seen from a particular vantage point' (2004: 301). With particular resonance for a theological and thus transformative understanding of Bible reading, Gadamer explains:

> ... we speak of narrowness of horizon, of the possible expansion of horizon, of the opening up of new horizons ...

> A person who has no horizon does not see far enough and hence over-values what is nearest to him. On the other hand, "to have a horizon" means not being limited to what is nearby but being able to see beyond it. A person who has an horizon

---

[50]   The 'Two Horizons' series of theological commentaries is a notable example (2015a; b).

[51]   First published in 1960 (German), 1975 (English).

knows the relative significance of everything within this horizon, whether it is near or far, great or small. Similarly, working out the hermeneutical situation means acquiring the right horizon of inquiry for the questions evoked by the encounter with tradition (2004: 301–2).

Understanding occurs through a 'fusion' of horizons. So in congregations, this might mean fusing the horizon of the interpreter/Bible setting with the horizon of the biblical text. Fusion begins with the distancing of horizons, so as to allow the 'indissoluble individuality' of each horizon to be established (Gadamer, 2004: 304–5). In the 'fusion of horizons', the reader's understandings of the world are enriched and broadened 'by the understanding of the world contained in the text' (Jensen, 2007: 141). Although this is provocative language theologically speaking, it need not be so. While not a problem for Holder and Fellowship, the distancing of horizons should not be overplayed for the church, as Robert Jenson argues: 'The community from which Scripture comes and which is its immediate community of interpretation is simply the same community, the church, that we are' (1995: 104; cf. Paddison, 2009: 31). In addition, the language of 'fusion' can be misleading. Gadamer is careful not to imply that complete fusion can occur between horizons, since in every horizonal encounter there is 'the experience of a tension between the text and the present'. The task of hermeneutics is not to cover up this tension 'by attempting a naïve assimilation', but to 'consciously bring it out' (2004: 305; cf. Thiselton, 1980: 307–8). This language of horizon and fusion of horizons will serve our exploration of congregational hermeneutics. To this end, Ellen Charry's assessment of Gadamer is instructive, where she argues that:

> ... he reintroduced the interpreter into the interpretive process in what he described as the principle of effective-history, the interpretation of a historical text by someone addressed by the text, someone whose own historicity is taken up in the interpretive act. By admitting the subjectivity of the interpreter into the interpretive process, Gadamer opened a space for the reclamation of sapiential knowledge, as theology understood itself in the premodern period (1997: 16–17).

Such an assessment is promising for the employment of Gadamerian categories in this book, which interact with the tale of two churches to produce an account of hermeneutical virtue. Before proceeding further, however, there are some remaining qualifications to consider from Gadamer's critics.

Jürgen Habermas brought a critique formed by the Frankfurt School. Employing a particular Marxist understanding of society, its proponents seek to unmask the 'false consciousness' of society by exposing its oppressive ideologies (Jensen, 2007: 192–3). Consequently, in developing his own critical hermeneutical theory, Habermas attacked Gadamer's lack of critique (1971; 1985; 1988). That is, Gadamer is too uncritical with regard to tradition, since he fails to identify the potential of ideologies embedded within tradition and its language to prohibit human emancipation. Habermas and others have a point, particularly given the critical nature of practical theology outlined above (cf. Browning, 1991: 52). However, theological hermeneutics pivots its critique through the shape of the Christian Story, rather than what might be described as Habermas's over-realised secular eschatology.

This leads to the work of the French philosopher, Paul Ricoeur, whose writings on general hermeneutics include implications for understanding the Bible (e.g. Ricoeur and Mudge, 1981).[52] Ricoeur engages with both Habermas and Gadamer in his writing, and commends the fruitfulness of the two horizons metaphor, although not without reservations (1981: 62). Ricoeur is also critical of Gadamer's apparent absence of critique, through emphasising the need for *explanation* as well as *understanding* of texts. It has been said that Gadamer's masterpiece, *Truth and Method*, might better be named *Truth or Method*, given his principled rejection of method (e.g. Bartholomew, 2005: 137). As Thiselton summarises, Gadamer left 'no metacritical or even critical procedure for testing the validity of traditions', whereas for Ricoeur, hermeneutics 'embodies both the unmasking function of explanation and the creative function of understanding' (1992: 344).

Following Jensen's admirable summary of Ricoeur's difficult writing (2007: 145f), the notion of 'second naïvety' links together a number of key ideas for exploring congregational hermeneutics. An initial reading of a text is superficial or naïve in Ricoeur's thinking, hence a critical explanation is needed. This requires moving from 'in front of the text' to 'behind the text' using a range of critical tools available from the modern and postmodern paradigm. In particular, Ricoeur wanted to 'do away with idols' in our explanations through filtering texts through the ideological critiques of Marx, Nietzsche, and Freud, the modern 'masters of suspicion' (Ricoeur, 1970: 27–8). But the interpreter(s) must not become stuck in this critical place. In Ricoeur's memorable words that pull at the heartstrings of many Christian theologians, 'beyond the desert of criticism, we wish to be called again' (1969: 349). The interpreter(s) need to return 'in front of the text' to read it again, but to read with a second naïvety that is critically informed. Such a naïvety may need further critical moments, meaning there may be a third, fourth, fifth etc. naïvety, which also underlines the circular nature of understanding (Ricoeur, 1981: 178). Ricoeur's hermeneutical approach may be captured partially in his saying: 'Hermeneutics seems to me to be animated by this double motivation: willingness to suspect, willingness to listen; vow of rigour, vow of obedience' (1970: 27). I will consider the role of suspicion in this 'double motivation' in the explorations to follow, but consider the emphasis on

---

[52]   Jeanrond claims that Ricoeur is the philosopher whose work has exerted the greatest influence on the development of biblical hermeneutics (1992: 440).

critical explanation in Ricoeur a valuable corrective to Gadamer. Having now received qualifications to Gadamer's conceptual resources from both Habermas and Ricoeur, it is time to return to the congregations.

Congregational Hermeneutics in Holder and Fellowship

Hermeneutical practices occur in a context, hence hermeneutics itself is contextual. I hope that a contribution of congregational hermeneutics will be to put some flesh on this idea. You do not need to spend much time in a church to notice that hermeneutical practices are embedded within the warp and weft of congregational life in complex, conflicting and sometimes unexpected ways.[53] In Holder and Fellowship, hermeneutical practices shaped and were shaped by a host of mediators including items such as sermons, housegroups, church interior design, motto text cards, other congregants, worship songs, liturgy, prayers, Christian publications, news media and Christian events (developed further in Chapter 7). Despite the complexity and potential for what one anthropologist has called 'ethnographic dazzle' (Fox, 1991: 272), it was possible to detect certain patterns of hermeneutical practice within the two churches. These overall patterns I will refer to (not very often) as 'configurations' of hermeneutics. Drawing on the conceptual resources from Gadamer et al. above, it became apparent after some time in the field that 'horizon' and 'fusion' would be fruitful and large initial categories for analysing hermeneutical practices in the congregations (cf. Dowie, 2002: 113).[54]

I recognise there are other practical theologians who appear to be more pessimistic than I about the possibility of detecting or identifying or describing or analysing practices in congregations. In an article by Sally A. Brown, this pessimism, or more positively, modesty, specifically relates to hermeneutical practices (2009). The critical realist framework outlined in Chapter 2 assists in responding with a 'Yes' and a 'No' to Brown's position. Firstly, a critical realist approach has a commitment to epistemological relativism (carefully defined), hence it is never appropriate to claim that a practice and its logic has been mastered (2009: 291). Throughout the accounts that follow there are many exceptions and counter-examples, as well as the 'althoughs', 'buts', and 'howevers' of ethnographic writing. 'Humility' is a virtue that emerges from the accounts, similar to modesty, and must surely be appropriate for theological ethnography also. In this respect, I have to say 'Yes' to cautions about what can

---

[53]   I am developing material from two previous articles in this section, so Rogers (2013b; c).

[54]   Sally A. Brown describes Gadamer as introducing concepts that 'have proved richly informative for practical theology', particularly horizon and fusion (2011: 114).

be claimed for accounts of practice. Secondly, however, a critical realist also holds to judgemental rationality, which allows for making reasoned provisional judgements about practices with varying degrees of confidence. It is apparent in the tale that some practices are relatively clear and others much less so. While aspects of a practices' inner logic may always be hidden from researchers and even practitioners, sometimes many of its contours can be established. It is possible to both overestimate and underestimate the mystery of practices. This pillar of critical realism accounts for the varying tones of the accounts, including that of confidence. I offer therefore a hesitant 'No' to being too modest. Of course, no-one wants to be 'over-confident' regarding 'hermeneutical moves and norms' of 'biblical reading', nor 'project our own sense of hermeneutical logic on the communities we are reading' (2009: 293), yet neither should the practical theologian lose the confidence to contribute careful judgements about hermeneutical practices.

On this latter point, also raised in Chapter 1, and so continuing my response to Fulkerson, it is recognised that theologians may be tempted to map too much 'sense and order' onto ethnographic accounts. It may also be possible to map too little. We all bring theoretical apparatus to our stories and analysis, and it is better that they are made explicit at the outset. What matters is that the categories we bring help us to see well. In addition, the conviction that some sense and order will be found is underwritten by the church being indwelt by the Spirit of God. Ultimately the church reflects who God is, albeit in convoluted and broken ways.

Bible Settings and Horizons

For both Holder and Fellowship, it became apparent that there were three key settings where congregants used Scripture, each with their own unique combination of Bible uses and hermeneutical practices (cf. Gillett, 1993: 157). These were public settings (Sunday services and other congregational meetings), small group settings (housegroups and Bible studies), and personal settings (personal Bible reading and mediators accessed personally). The language of 'setting' indicates the importance of understanding hermeneutical practices in their context, especially the traditions that have led to that context (MacIntyre, 1985: 206). As was evident in the two congregations, each Bible setting has its own distinctiveness that is not straightforwardly transferable to other settings. So, to use the hermeneutical language, there are horizons of individual congregants, of small groups and of public settings. There are strong interconnections between these horizons, but they are not reducible to each other (cf. Steven, 2002: 49). Consequently the 'congregational horizon' is at least the product of a complex interaction between these three 'reader' horizons.

Horizonal Beliefs and Fusion Processes

There were a number of horizonal beliefs in both congregations that were significant for hermeneutics. These divided into *starting points* and *goals* for engagement with Scripture. Key starting points in formal terms included the place of Scripture, assumptions about the individual or corporate address of Scripture, implicit epistemologies, and distinctive theological positions ingrained in the tradition of the congregations. Goals shared by both churches were to hear God speak through the Bible and that engagement with the Bible should be relevant to life today. A focus on the individual address of Scripture was especially notable in Fellowship. Since these horizonal features are part of Holder and Fellowship's tradition, I will continue to develop their congregational substance, including their shaping of fusion processes, in Chapter 4 on Tradition and Chapter 6 on Epistemology.

The fusion of horizons, as used in the rest of this book, refers to the encounter between the horizons of the biblical text and the horizons of a congregation – thus the importance of looking at horizons before fusion. I will include under 'fusion' all those processes in the congregations that made connections between text and congregational horizons, where 'making connections' refers to both the art and science of hermeneutics, including the spontaneous, imaginative, chaotic *and* methodical.[55] This is examined at length in Chapter 5 on Practices.

---

[55] So 'making connections' in my usage includes both 'seeing' and 'making' connections in Zoë Bennett's work, discussed in Chapter 1 (2013: 73f, 135).

Chapter 4

Tradition

My contention in this chapter is that thinking carefully about congregational hermeneutics and the Bible requires taking tradition very seriously. Drawing on the analytical framework in Chapter 3, the significance of tradition for congregational hermeneutics in the two churches will be explored.[1] In particular, the hermeneutical starting points and goals of Holder and Fellowship's congregational horizons will be examined. To place all of this in context, an explanation of the much misunderstood term 'tradition' is given, as well as a brief account of evangelical distinctives.

The term 'tradition' is used in multiple senses in theology, so it is important to clarify how it is being used in this book. In the New Testament, tradition in its positive sense refers to both the core apostolic content of the Gospel *and* the process of handing it on (so McGrath, 2000a: 141; Walker, 2007a: 65f). Developing out of this early sense of tradition (of which the New Testament became the written form), many scholars continue to speak of Tradition or the Great Tradition as 'the core teaching and preaching of the early church which has bequeathed to us the fundamentals of what it is to think and believe Christianly' (Williams, 1999: 6; cf. McGrath, 2000a: 142f).[2] The primary senses of tradition in this book are derived from this Great Tradition, so the various ecclesial traditions that have developed over the centuries (e.g. evangelicalism, pentecostalism, etc.) and especially the expression of those ecclesial traditions in local congregations.[3] *Congregational* tradition, then, is the primary sense used here and is explicated in theological ethnographic terms. Such a tradition, seen through a theological lens, consists of patterns of discourses, actions, artefacts and mediators over time.[4] The focus of this chapter is with the contemporary tradition of the congregations in relation to hermeneutics, whereas the process of mediating tradition (and practices) is addressed in Chapter 7. A distinction

---

[1]   In the 'tale' section of this chapter, the two churches are treated individually to allow for their traditions to be told as a whole.

[2]   One must surely add 'behave'.

[3]   Gordon Fee offers five senses of 'tradition' although curiously ignores congregational tradition, moving from ecclesial tradition to personal traditions (1991: 422f). See also the distinction between Tradition and tradition of the Faith and Order Commission, §39 (Ford et al., 2012: 338).

[4]   From a systematic theology perspective, Stephen Holmes has a similarly broad and inclusive definition of tradition (2002: 5n9).

is also made between the general tradition of the congregations and particular hermeneutical traditions,[5] as seen in their horizons and fusion processes.

Building on the conceptual resources introduced in Chapter 3, the notion of 'tradition' is also key in Gadamer's use of horizon language. As he argues, 'a hermeneutical situation is determined by the prejudices[6] we bring with us' which 'constitute ... the horizon of a particular present'. Horizons are dynamic since 'the horizon of the present is continually in the process of being formed' since congregations (in this case) are continually in the process of negotiating their horizons and history (albeit often implicitly) (2004: 304–5). To put this another way, congregational horizons together form the living present of congregational tradition.

Tradition sometimes provokes hostile reactions within evangelicalism, either through its perceived threat to the authority of scripture, or through a confusion with 'traditionalism' (McGrath, 2000a: 141–2). As the discussion above and in the rest of this chapter indicates, such concerns should not preclude evangelicals from taking tradition seriously. Here, the reader is invited to consider how traditions actually operate within congregations in relation to Bible and hermeneutics, and how that may contribute to our theological understanding of tradition.

Characterising English Evangelicalism

This book is primarily focussed on congregational hermeneutics, rather than the blessings and woes of evangelicalism. Nevertheless, characterising evangelicalism briefly will provide a formal account of the tradition that may enrich understanding of Holder and Fellowship's hermeneutical practices. There are a number of competing schemas for defining evangelicalism,[7] which is not surprising given the diversity within even the UK, as the phrases '57 varieties of evangelicals'[8] and 'the twelve tribes of evangelicalism'[9] would suggest. It has become an essentially contested tradition (Warner, 2007: 4f).[10] David Bebbington's fourfold historical characterisation has been something of an industry standard, so:

---

[5]   Although the dividing line is inevitably fuzzy.

[6]   In the non-pejorative Gadamerian sense.

[7]   E.g. Alister McGrath (1995: 51), James Packer (1978), John Stott (1977, 2003), Derek Tidball (1994), Robert Warner (2007).

[8]   From the Church of England Newspaper April 1998, cited by John Stott (2003: 21).

[9]   Former head of the Evangelical Alliance, Clive Calver (Calver and Warner, 1996: 128–30).

[10]   Mark Smith, under the heading 'A Movement in Search of Definitions', claims that: 'Evangelicalism is probably the most over-defined religious movement in the world' (2008: 1).

There are the four qualities that have been the special marks of Evangelical religion; *conversionism*, the belief that lives need to be changed; *activism*, the expression of the gospel in effort; *biblicism*, a particular regard for the Bible; and what may be called *crucicentrism*, a stress on the sacrifice of Christ on the cross (italics original, 1989: 2–3).

These qualities or 'quadrilateral of priorities' have been the constants of the tradition since the eighteenth century, albeit with some varying emphases over time (1989: 3–4). More recent definitions tend to take Bebbington as a point of departure, such as Robert Warner's modification that proposes two rival axes within the contemporary English tradition, namely conversionist-activist and Biblicist-crucicentric (2007: 20, 247). Fellowship and Holder might be placed under the former and latter axes respectively, although one objective of ethnographic study is to interrogate such macro categories.

Although the particularities of English evangelicalism are in view here, it is not possible to disentangle local from global evangelicalisms, especially in relation to the USA and Australia in the case of Holder and Fellowship. Bebbington argues that the relationship between US-UK evangelicalisms is somewhat symbiotic, albeit with more traffic from North America to the UK (1994: 368–9), and concludes that the separate contexts have produced variant forms of evangelicalism on either side of the Atlantic (1994: 382; cf. Holmes, 2007). Such influences will become apparent when considering mediation in Chapter 7.

Given that Fellowship is a charismatic evangelical congregation, the characterisation of evangelical and charismatic hermeneutics in Chapter 3 included a short summary of charismatic origins. There has been a measure of agreement for some time now amongst British commentators regarding the significant overlap or even inclusion of charismatics within evangelicalism. Derek Tidball concludes that 'the evangelical tent is being enlarged to embrace charismatics as true members of the family' (1994: 28)[11] and Dave Tomlinson speaks of 'the "charismaticizing" of mainstream evangelicalism' (1995: 15–16; cf. Stanley, 2013: 181f).[12] Indeed, this study shows evidence of this latter influence in the worship songs of the two congregations.

---

[11]   Bebbington cautiously makes a similar case (1989: 268).

[12]   Notably, the English church statistician, Peter Brierley, classifies evangelicals in the English Church Census according to the categories Broad, Mainstream, and Charismatic (2006: 50).

Tradition in Holder and Fellowship

In Chapter 1, the traditions of Holder and Fellowship were introduced in a tale of two churches. After briefly considering here congregational attitudes to tradition, the focus narrows to the linkages between tradition and hermeneutics, through examining the horizons of each congregation. As introduced in Chapter 3, the type of starting points considered here are *the place of Scripture*, *the address of Scripture*, and the *distinctive theological traditions* of the congregations. The hermeneutical goals examined common to both congregations are that *God will speak through the Bible* and that *the Bible will be relevant*. The special and highly significant case of epistemology has been reserved for Chapter 6.

There was some contrast in Holder and Fellowship's attitude to tradition, encapsulated in the prevalence of the terms 'faithful' at Holder and 'radical' at Fellowship, although neither congregation were without their exceptions. The housegroup leader, PaulH, spoke of how Holder had become 'more biblical' in recent years in terms of its church governance, adding that he chooses Scripture over tradition. Examples of such changes were plural leadership and discontinuing female housegroup leaders (Conversation, Y3). As RodneyH put it, 'I think we're always reviewing what we do, biblically, and making changes where we feel we need to, to get back to what Scripture would intend'. In this quote and elsewhere, there was a suspicion of 'tradition' as something that was likely to be a deviation from Scripture. When discussing this research project in terms of Bible, hermeneutics, and tradition, PaulH commented that they were trying to get rid of tradition at Holder, although the sense of 'tradition' was not entirely clear (Conversation, Y5). With a little contrast, in another Holder housegroup discussion on Mal 1:6–14, KateH talked about how tradition was not necessarily a bad thing (X2). ThelmaH and KarlH then posed the problem of some Holder traditions getting in the way, such as 'Reformedness', as JustinH also makes clear later in this chapter.

There was more explicit awareness of tradition at Fellowship, possibly because change was a feature of their current congregational life, and so they were more conscious of what they were changing (and leaving behind). Indeed, it had been said of Ekklesia (the church Fellowship had split from) that the leader, Charles, had 'institutionalised change'.[13] Inevitably, Fellowship tradition was formed by Ekklesia tradition, as GordonF aphorised: 'You can take the church out of [Ekklesia], but you can't take [Ekklesia] out of the church' (Conversation, SunAM1f). The dynamic nature of Fellowship tradition in relation to leaving Ekklesia was well illustrated by 'a Word'[14] from BruceF during SunAM9f

---

13   From an internal Ekklesia report produced in the mid 1980s.
14   Details of this practice are given in Chapter 5.

regarding 'issues of healing in our congregation as a whole'. Addressing the fallout from the split with Ekklesia, an abbreviated version of the Word follows:

> ... we thought a little bit about the history the fellowship's been through in the last couple of years, and we know, for many, it's been a difficult time and there have been many challenges and many struggles.

> ... we have had many wonderful things happen to us over our lives together, those who have been part of this community for many years will know that we've seen wonderful things happen. We've seen the Lord break out and we've seen healings and we've seen marvellous works of the Lord. My sense of it was that we understand that work of God, some of us, still ... in terms of people and labels, and a history which the Lord now wishes to replace, He wants to give these understandings new words for us.

This corporate Word delivered as from God to the whole congregation was sweeping in its intent for God to reshape their horizons through a redemptive retelling of their congregational story.

The discourse of radicalism was marked within Fellowship, and the name of Fellowship's network, Metamorphis,[15] reinforced this emphasis. DerekF referred to 'traditional churches' which follow church calendars and how Fellowship 'didn't want to be locked into that' (S10f). Such an attitude was heightened by Dan, a visiting speaker, who, in advocating the importance of 'prayer and fasting', felt it was important not to exclude those from 'traditional church streams' who 'may not understand the concept of prayer and fasting' (S9f). When asked how he would describe Fellowship, SteveF responded:

SteveF: I'd say it was a Bible-believing ...

Andrew: And charismatic?

SteveF: What's that? I would just say, you know, we just worship Jesus. We believe in the Bible, we're up for Jesus, I would say we're free from any kind of title denomination thing.

One of the most explicit instances of tradition and congregational hermeneutics was evident in Housegroup C's study on 'The Exegesis and Hermeneutics of the Epistles'. The detailed study guidance written by the leader, ReneeF, included

---

[15] A dynamic equivalent pseudonym.

the statement 'Ask what the texts mean, not how to make them fit your views/ culture/church tradition'.[16]

Both churches were wary of tradition and mirrored the two reasons offered by McGrath above, namely the challenge to the authority of Scripture (Holder) and the perceived dangers of historic church traditions, which Fellowship were consciously attempting to escape.

Place of Scripture

The place of Scripture at Holder was evident in their own term 'Bible-centredness'. A striking degree of Bible-centredness permeated Holder's congregational life, and as such framed Holder's public horizon with regard to the Bible's role and status. The associate pastor, JoeH, described the tradition of the church as one where 'the Word of God has always featured very, very highly'. The pastor, OwenH, said that historically the church had been known for 'wanting to get the Bible into every aspect of ministry' since 'we want everything to be Bible based'. Holder artefacts reinforced this Bible-centredness, such as the extent of Bible verses on display through a range of media (described in Chapter 5) and the sea of open Bibles on laps during service Scripture readings. Even the church's interior architecture pointed to Bible-centredness, since the pulpit was the focal point of the main hall – a physical embodiment of the church's theological priorities (cf. Oliver, 2006: 117f).

The centrality of the Bible was also reflected in the church's Basis of Faith, which was that of the FIEC. This was reproduced on the church website as follows:

> God has revealed himself in the Bible, which consists of the Old and New Testaments alone. Every word was inspired by God through human authors, so that the Bible as originally given is in its entirety the Word of God, without error and fully reliable in fact and doctrine. The Bible alone speaks with final authority and is always sufficient for all matters of belief and practice (FIEC, 2004a).

The FIEC and Affinity respective strapline phrases of 'Bible Churches Together' and 'Bible-centred Christianity' captured this horizonal distinctive of the congregation. Affinity's doctrinal basis was yet more specific than the FIEC's, in that it affirmed:

> The inerrancy of the Holy Scriptures as originally given, their verbal inspiration by God and their supreme authority as the only rule of faith and practice (Affinity, 2006–07).

---

[16]   This occurred after the fieldwork period (email, 22/1/06).

Significantly, Affinity placed this doctrine of Scripture first, before that of the Trinity, further emphasising their 'Bible-centred Christianity' and, by implication, Holder's. The 'sufficient' and 'only' in both these statements also matched Holder's aspiration to order church practice on their understanding of a biblical model. There was a clear concern that Holder practices and traditions should be Bible-centred or the basis of 'direction for Church matters' (Anniversary booklet), as well as a perception that this was also generally the case. A Bible basis was understood to inform male-only leadership, as well as the institutions of elders and deacons (Anniversary booklet), which was a distinction 'from conviction' that it was 'more of a biblical structure' (OwenH). Regarding liturgical use of the Bible, JoeH liked to 'use the Psalm as almost a call to worship, really', because:

> ... what we're doing, why we're doing it, often the Bible almost just confirms that what we're doing is what God wants us to do. So, I found the Psalms are the best for almost saying ... this is what we're doing, singing and praying, is what God wants us to do. It's not just a tradition, it's not just good, it's actually what God's called us to do.

The status of Scripture was expressed in more formal terms by the pastor and some elders, who described the Scriptures as 'infallible' and 'inerrant'. The elder, JustinH, thought these terms important because:

> **JustinH:** I believe that it is God's Word to us, and I don't believe that we have the right to fiddle, change, adapt, adjust or whatever.
>
> **Andrew:** Would you say that's a view that's common at [Holder]?
>
> **JustinH:** Yes. I mean, it's the general view that we would take from an eldership point of view, and it is a view that we would expect people to adopt, because ... it's part of our basis of faith, anyway. So, people coming into membership would be expected to take that sort of a view as well.
>
> **Andrew:** And that position is taught in the church explicitly?
>
> **JustinH:** It has been from time to time, yes. It's always part ... of this sort of subculture of expectation ... But we have, within the housegroups, actually looked at the doctrine, the basis of faith, and we've actually worked through that ... And certainly those within a leadership role within the church would be expected to take that view ...

Key to this excerpt is the 'subculture of expectation' that church members will share these public views about the status of Scripture, which interviewee responses suggested was largely the case. This position on the inerrancy and infallibility of Scripture appeared to have been well mediated internally, as only one (fringe) interviewee wanted to 'fight shy' of such a term (KarlH). Indeed, HarryH commented on the internal mediation of this doctrinal point, saying 'we're well taught at [Holder]'. For example, DorisH expressed her view of the Bible in terms of 'all or nothing' as follows:

> **Andrew:** Is it important to define the Bible as being without error, do you think?

> **DorisH:** I do, because if it has got an error, then the whole of our faith and what we believe is, is not sound and concrete, and we can't take one thing without the other. So, it's either all the truth, and nothing but the truth, or else it's nothing at all.

Interviewees in leadership did qualify their inerrancy, so the associate pastor, JoeH, did not see the term applying to 'the NIV or the King James, but about the Scriptures that were originally penned down in Hebrew and Greek'. This qualification sees inerrancy applying only to the 'original autographs', a view well established in conservative evangelical scholarship (e.g. Article X, CSBI). RodneyH thought inerrancy 'absolutely vital', but opted for a limited inerrancy (cf. Erickson, 1983: 222f) where 'minor details' such as 'historical dates and facts and whatever' were 'not important to me', rather his inerrancy applied to 'the major things'.

The twin of inerrancy was a view of genre as defaulting to the historical, which was associated with a 'literal' reading, although there was some very limited recognition of apocalyptic, prophecy, and poetry by interviewees.[17] This is a common equation for many inerrantists, particularly with regard to creation (e.g. Article XXII, CSBH). For example, JoeH accounted for their six-day creation position as 'based on our interpretation of Scripture as literal, other than if it's indicated'. 'Believing in the Bible' and its truth was strongly associated with historicity, as JoeH remembered:

> ... the Sunday school teacher I had really did install in us, you know, biblical Christianity, creation, Noah, there was no doubt, Moses, all these things really happened. And so, from the age I can remember, there was no doubt in my mind, the Bible's true.

---

[17]   Genre is an aspect of congregational hermeneutics that works as both a starting point and a process, hence its inclusion in Chapter 5 as well. It is the historical assumptions about genre that constitute horizonal starting points that then shape processes.

The only (strong) critique of such an assumption was (again) from KarlH, who was 'ill at ease' with these aspects of Holder's hermeneutics which he described as 'positivist, at its worst, just flat, literalist'. Here 'literalist' is used pejoratively, as in much academic writing, in contrast to the approving sense of 'literal' used by other Holder interviewees.

Public discourse amplified Holder's Bible-centredness further. In performing rites of passage, a few selected verses of Scripture were always read out and given to the participants, underscoring the Holder attitude that no event was complete without the Bible. Bible-centredness was also reinforced through children's songs in services, notably in one of the most popular songs during the fieldwork, *As For Me And My House* (SF1175; Kingsway Music, 2003).[18] This took its title from Josh 24:15 and contained the lines: 'In this family we'll do things properly / Read God's Word every day and then we'll try to pray'.[19] 68 per cent of Holder's songs included Scripture either directly or in reconstructed form.[20] Service leaders made very frequent reference to the supreme status of the Bible, most often described as 'God's Word'. This was well captured in OwenH's opening comments at their Anniversary service, an occasion which celebrated Holder's history and distinctives:

> ... what we're going to do in a moment is we're going to read God's Word, for a 125 years God's Word has been proclaimed from this church, [DeborahH] is going to come now, she is going to read God's Word, Psalm 100, and if we could stand as we read God's Word ...

The guest speaker at this service, John, who knew the church well, gave the following impassioned exhortation regarding the Bible:

> Are you a Bible Christian? Are you superglued to God's Word? Are you hungry to know more of God's revelation? Do you read that Word? Are you eager to be present when that Word is preached? And not just in the morning, but in the evening as well? (S6h)

Being Bible Christians and a 'Bible believing church' (OwenH, S10h) was the fundamental element of Holder's self-understanding (Rogers, 2013b: 491). One's attitude to the Bible, therefore, was the key criterion for further involvement in the church, as OwenH stated 'if a person wants to serve, the first

---

[18]   All song references in this book, unless otherwise referenced, are taken from *Songs of Fellowship* (SF) (Kingsway Music, 2003) or *Mission Praise* (MP) (Horrobin and Leavers, 1990).

[19]   Extract taken from 'As for me and my house' by Jim Bailey, Copyright © 1997 Thankyou Music*.

[20]   A formal typology for a song's relation to Scripture is given in Chapter 5.

question is: Do you love God's Word? Do you take God's Word seriously? Do you know God's Word?' (S10h).

At times there was a sense that Holder considered itself to take the Bible more seriously than other churches. This was hinted at by OwenH in a sermon when he spoke of wanting to ' ... be the best, we want to teach God's Word in the best way possible' (S1h). Such a view was made more explicit by interviewees, so LucyH stated 'we have the deep teaching at [Holder]'. If LucyH was 'ever querying anything' she would 'go to the Bible and say "Is that right, what he's just said?"' – but at Holder the result was to 'find the answer that they've said, exactly in the Word of God'. In a telling interview excerpt, JoeH, who grew up in Holder, reflected thoughtfully on this aspect of Holder's tradition:

> ... this feeling was often, people who don't believe in some of the things we believe at this church, believe it because they don't take Scripture as seriously as we do. I'm not saying that was ever said but that's the impression I got as a kid.

Preaching was treated as the primary vehicle of Bible-centredness at Holder. The Anniversary service showcased what Holder particularly wanted to celebrate, namely their history of preaching God's Word, as JoeH prayed:

> ... we thank you that you used this place to let people know about your word and Lord we pray your word would continue to be preached in this place, we thank you for those people who have faithfully preached your word and taught it, Lord we give you thanks for that, we give you thanks ... that it has changed many of our lives, it has been used to bring glory to your name ... we pray that that would continue for many years to come that your word would be preached in this place and taught to many people ...

Notably, JoeH understands preaching in this prayer to have been transformative for 'many of our lives'. Sermon outlines were often distributed in the weekly newsletter, which might have encouraged congregants to take notes during the sermon, and so reinforced the importance of the sermon further (OwenH, interview). The sermon Bible reading was treated as a formal liturgical event, usually by someone other than the preacher or service leader, and was nearly always prefaced by a statement such as 'X is now going to read God's Word to us'. Prayers said before the sermon Bible reading or the sermon nearly always expressed the desire for God to speak through the preacher.[21]

The focus of Holder's preaching seemed to be Bible-centredness itself. This was sometimes a rather reflexive preaching about 'preaching about the Bible', and often about the importance and role of the Bible. For example, a striking 'Bible-centred'

---

21   Further detail about the structure of the services is given in Chapter 5.

impulse was observed towards the end of the sermon on Ezra 5:1–5, which closely followed the sermon outline given in Figure 4.1 (S11h). A reading of Ezra 5:1–2 highlights the force of this core horizonal conviction for hermeneutical practice. Coherent with this core was the occasional habit of preachers to switch between 'God', 'Jesus', and 'the Bible' as if they were virtually synonyms.

Ezra 5
From Failure to Success

Introduction
What is your guide in life?
Recap, the story so far

1) God intervenes v1
2) God sends prophets v1
3) God's truths are declared v1
4) God's people obey God's word v2

Concluding lessons
You must read the bible every day.
You must pray that the bible will change you.
You must pray for all bible teachers.
You must turn to the bible when trouble strikes.
You must expect the bible to change you.
You must believe the bible will save people.
You must expect the bible to encourage you.
You must expect the bible to break and humble you.
You must pray that you or others will go full-time!

Figure 4.1   Holder Sermon Handout on Ezra 5:1–5

Source: Rogers (2013b). This figure is taken from my article published in *Journal of Contemporary Religion* on October 2013, available online: http://www.tandfonline.com/10.1080/13537903.2013.831657

Bible passion refers to the particular place of the Bible within Fellowship's horizons, evident through activism during the fieldwork period that sought to increase congregational exposure and 'passion' for the Bible in all Fellowship settings. The church website, written by the pastor, was Fellowship's most public 'artefact' regarding the place of the Bible in their church. Sunday morning services were described as 'contemporary' and 'Bible-based', with the Bible discussed in more detail on the 'Vision' page, here in summary:

> We believe that the Bible is inspired by God and reveals to us God's Word on how to live our lives and how to be church together. The Bible is taught in our meetings and is the basis for our activities. We have 3 foundational verses which help to shape and define who we are as a church. Each one gives us one of our key words: LOVE: John 13:34–35; DEVOTION: Acts 2:42; ACTION: Matthew 28:18–20
>
> ... We want to emulate the devotion of the first Christians and have a passion for the Bible ...
>
> ... God has given us the Bible and we can look into it and see how Jesus began to train men and women to follow him. The important keys are there to be discovered and put into practice in our lives.
>
> [One area is] DYNAMIC DEVOTION Bible reading – reading the Bible regularly, growing in understanding, application, and ability to teach others (accessed 25/2/06).

The 'passion for the Bible' or Bible passion referred to here was a striking aspect of Fellowship during the fieldwork. This was expressed through the Bible's increased profile in Sunday services, as well as the sheer number of opportunities to 'get into the Word' across Fellowship settings (DerekF, SunAM8f). On the first Sunday I attended Fellowship, the principal of the local evangelical Bible college was preaching on 'How to read the Bible', which included a good deal of academic hermeneutical material. At the beginning of this service, DerekF roved around the congregation, asking for members' favourite Bible verses (SunAM1f). Strategies for encouraging personal Bible reading were also floated in the services (detailed in Chapter 5). Church Bible studies, mostly led by DerekF, also reflected this passion – indeed, DerekF was the key mediator of Bible passion, and he saw it as self-evident that his job was 'to inspire a greater love for the Word'. That this was a change for Fellowship was indicated by DerekF when he spoke of his fourfold vision for the year, one aspect of which was an emphasis on 'the Word' (ThursPM1f).

It was notable that such Bible passion did not result in a focus upon the precise nature of Scripture. As a member of the Evangelical Alliance (EA), Fellowship were required to agree with its Basis of Faith, revised in 2005. Regarding the Bible it states: 'We believe in ... The divine inspiration and supreme authority of the Old and New Testament Scriptures, which are the written Word of God – fully trustworthy for faith and conduct' (2005). Notably this statement avoids such terms as 'infallible' or 'inerrant', which may be a diplomatic necessity for an organisation that aims to represent British pan-evangelicalism (Warner, 2007: 218f). Such terms were also absent from Fellowship's public settings, although the status of Scripture was addressed through various other terms in services. That the EA Basis of Faith had a low profile in the congregation may also point to Fellowship's lack of concern with defining Scripture's status. DerekF clarified this further when I asked him to describe the Bible:

> **DerekF:** God's book, inspired or breathed out by God, the ultimate reference point in life, faithful, authoritative ... source of spiritual food and life ... not dictated from heaven and to be slavishly obeyed, but a treasure house of God's truth to be engaged with, and to shape one's life and thought. I'd steer away from the kind of inerrancy, extreme positions, but want to put sufficiency and reliability and authoritative.

> **Andrew:** ... would you use the term 'infallible' of the Bible?

> **DerekF:** No. I think ... Tom Wright, he seems to be the popular one, you take it and you use it today, you must be faithful to it, but God needs to interpret it to you, in our own day and age and culture. I think 'infallible' – 'this must be exactly right, I'm going to hit you over the head with it', seems a wrong kind of flavour of things, I think you do theology by thinking and engaging with culture, and not just slavishly following the black and white words of the Bible. I think 'infallible' emphasises that too much, and any version you have is fallible ...

> ...

> The primary thing, the Bible interprets itself, Holy Spirit is given us to interpret the Bible, we need to come with our own cultural perspective, we will always skew things because we can never have a completely impartial God-given perspective ourselves ...

DerekF's avoidance of the concepts inerrant and infallible is notable here, particularly in relation to the diversity of interviewee responses on this point. All interviewees made some comment which placed a high value on Scripture, even when current difficulties with the Bible were included. On a simple notion of (in)errancy (usually expressed as 'Are there any errors in the Bible?'), interviewees expressed a wide range of views from yes to no. Some took a 'yes and no' view, such as SteveF who said of the Bible 'I believe everything in it to be true', then continued 'it wasn't written by God, it was written by people, there's a flawing already'. SarahF concurred with this latter point in rejecting inerrancy:

I don't know that I would take it word to word, everything is written, because it was done by human beings and it is written a certain part of time, which is very different from now, isn't it? ... No, I wouldn't take it word by word ...

GordonF, however, affirmed the infallibility of the Bible,[22] in that 'I don't think the Bible makes mistakes or is contradictory', although he added 'what's often important is people's interpretation of what the Bible says, and our interpretation is not infallible'.

The spectrum of views expressed by interviewees on the status of the Bible, some in contrast with the pastor's position, strongly suggested a lack of doctrinal uniformity regarding Scripture within Fellowship and the lack of its internal mediation. This was also indicative of the somewhat pragmatic attitude to Scripture that emphasised its value and purpose over its doctrinal status. Indeed, as will be seen in Chapter 6, there was a certain freedom at Fellowship to raise questions about the Bible.

Like many aspects of Fellowship, Bible passion was not uniform in all settings. 20 per cent of questionnaire respondents said they read the Bible at least once a day,[23] which is not particularly high for an evangelical church, especially in the light of the broader UK Bible engagement statistics discussed in Chapter 1. However, a striking 60 per cent of respondents said they had read the whole Bible,[24] perhaps pointing to a latent Bible passion within the congregation.

Further Bible passion tensions within Fellowship were expressed by some small group leaders who noted its lack, such as NadineF, who was from a minority ethnic background and different evangelical subculture:

Well, to be honest, what I have found in the housegroups is people don't want ... Bible studies so much anymore ... it's been a bit of a surprise to me ...

... people like a lot of worship ... which is good ... but ... maybe ... it was just ... the way we were brought up differently, but I really think housegroups should have Bible study as well, should be based on what the apostles' did in Acts, you know, Bible study, prayer, breaking of bread and all that.

... I think people feel Bible study is something you do on your own, private, independent, we've had some ... impressions from that, but we do have Bible study, and some people in the group are very enthusiastic.

---

[22]   His unprompted choice of term.
[23]   N=71.
[24]   N=72.

... really what we thought was British Christianity ... one of the housegroups we were in before this one ... it was worship *every time* ... I don't think we ever had a Bible study ... every meeting someone would play music and sing and prayer and then that would be it.

Notably, both TomF and SteveF said in interview they had stopped attending housegroup due to the lack of Bible study. DerekF located this lack of Bible passion somewhere between the two poles of 'lifestyle and the demands of job' and 'insufficient hunger for the Word'. He saw 'something solid' as 'an ideal' for housegroups but recognised 'we're not always delivering that'.

Address of Scripture

Scripture addresses us both individually and corporately. For Holder, two distinctive and related aspects of Holder's public horizon was a particular corporate emphasis in their hermeneutics along with a concern for maintaining congregational boundaries. When compared to Fellowship, analysis of Holder songs showed a marked preference for objective over subjective and reflexive songs.[25] This was further borne out by Holder's lower use of intimacy songs and proportionately more 'We' songs (i.e. the congregation) than 'I' songs (i.e. the individual).[26]

Although much of preached Scripture was designed to pose an existential challenge to individual congregants, there was also a strong corporate dimension to sermons, as has already been seen. This hermeneutical factor was made explicit in a notable excursus during a sermon by JustinH, who contrasted Judas' perceived isolation in Mark 14 with the benefits of belonging to a Christian community:

> ... We read God's Word, we spend time with him in prayer. We meet with God's people who follow him, we wouldn't be out on a limb, or with those who are not involved, because if we are by ourselves we can think our own thoughts in our own way, even when we are reading Scripture sometimes, and when we're praying, sometimes we can even deceive ourselves, it's good to be with God's people ... we need the fellowship and support of others – we need their constraint – we need the challenge of good Christian company (S4h).

---

[25] These categories are applied to songs as a specific typology in Chapter 5, see Appendix D.

[26] Based on an analysis of total songs sung, where 'I' type pronouns were compared against 'We' type pronouns, see Appendix D.

The community here is valued for its role as constraint on understanding of the Bible. This particular form of corporate emphasis in hermeneutics appeared to be linked to a strong sense of corporate identity, which included a concern to protect the boundaries of that identity. A key instance of this in Holder public discourse was the distinction between church and world, which was often expressed through prayer, as OwenH prayed in the Anniversary service 'come and remind us that there is so much to do, remind us of this dark community round and about us, lonely, scarred, upset, grieving, lost, oh, hurtling on their way to a lost eternity'. When referring to Rev 2:13 during a sermon, OwenH declared that 'Satan lives in [this area]' (S1h), and, in another service, JoeH prayed about being 'surrounded by a godless society' (SunAM1h), amongst many other examples. More generally, the protection of the church's identity was strikingly addressed in the following sermon excerpt:

> ... maybe some of you have come into membership recently and you might think its like the Spanish Inquisition joining [Holder], but we have a responsibility as leaders here at the church to do things wisely, to do things carefully.

> ... Bird Flu ... what happens with those infected chickens and birds, and people who've got that awful illness – they're isolated. Why? Because they're in danger of spreading things. As a church, as leaders, we have a responsibility, to make sure God's house, God's people are protected, that everything we do here is to honour him and glorify him ... (OwenH, S10h)

Scripture was understood to have the crucial role in defining congregational boundaries, so OwenH spoke of 'how we should guard very carefully the preaching and teaching in this church', adding that 'we've said it again and again, I'll say it again this morning' (S11h; also RodneyH, interview). OwenH illustrated his sermon on 'Deadly Compromise' with the following hypothetical example:

> ... no, you can't take the Bible study this week, I haven't heard you, I don't really know, and have a conversation with you, I'm not really sure that you're a thorough evangelical, and that you believe all of God's Word to be true and only sufficient ... (S1h)

The target of these frequent polemics was unclear, as it seemed unlikely that any 'false teacher' would ever have the opportunity of infiltrating Holder. Congregational boundaries were most frequently addressed in the context of talking about the children and youth of the church, underscoring an implicit concern for preserving the identity of the church across the generations – i.e. their tradition.

As will be seen below and also in Chapter 7, personal Bible reading had a high profile at Holder. Despite the inevitable emphasis on the individual in this Bible use, it was within the context of more overt corporate language used in other Holder settings.

Fellowship had a tendency to emphasise the individual in their public hermeneutics, although this was not the strongest of Fellowship traits, since there were also corporate elements in their hermeneutics. However, their tendency was to understand the address of Scripture as being to the individual, and this was particularly evident in songs. Based on an analysis of their song words during the fieldwork, 'I' language (i.e. the individual) was approximately four times more common than 'We' language (i.e. the congregation). In addition, there was a marked preference for subjective (80 per cent) over objective songs (46 per cent), a focus on the individual that was reinforced by 28 per cent of songs using the language of intimacy. Such a focus resonates with Ward's view that songs in charismatic 'liturgy' function as a 'means to a personal encounter with God' (2005: 198; cf. Walker, 2007b: 25n27). This individual tendency in songs was also significant for hermeneutics, since 77 per cent of Fellowship songs incorporated the Bible in some way.[27]

Sermons also exhibited individual hermeneutics, although to varying degrees. The most telling example was found at the Metamorphis celebration, which was based on what is sometimes called Jesus' Nazareth manifesto in Lk 4. The visiting speaker, Walter, commented of Jesus' words: 'What he's announcing is what he's on the planet for' and continued: 'This is the dream that wakes him up Monday morning, this is the dream that sends him into the week' (S8f). Implicitly taking the words of Jesus in Luke 4 as a 'mission statement', Walter and Daphne[28] then asked congregants to individually create their own mission statements based on 'what ... God [has] been saying to you as you've been reading the Scriptures'. A less sustained but similarly individual emphasis was observed in Derek's Pentecost sermon on Acts 2:1–4. He concluded by stating that 'we need that personal Pentecost' and then asked congregants 'if you feel empty and want a personal Pentecost' to respond by coming to the front for prayer (S10f). An implicit individual hermeneutics was also conveyed by a number of testimony slots in services and one sermon, where speakers spoke of how Scripture had been meaningful in their own experience (S11f).

Given that I was asking interviewees about their own Bible reading practice, it was partially understandable that responses were often couched in individualistic terms. Even taking this into account, the emphasis on the individual being the addressee of Scripture was quite marked, resonating with the same theme observed in public settings. So MattF spoke of the 'many

---

[27] N=62, see Appendix D for all these statistics.
[28] International charismatic evangelical writers and speakers.

pervading messages' in the Bible that 'you can just pick up and apply to your own life'. Hermeneutical indeterminacy regarding the book of Revelation led him to comment 'so many people have come up to different responses I think it almost has to be a purely individual response, in a way'. GordonF summarised his hermeneutical programme (revisited in Chapter 5) with 'two questions' for the text which were 'What does it say? And what does it say to me?' As has been seen above, there was criticism from NadineF of this focus on the individual and its perceived adverse impact on enthusiasm for small group Bible study.[29] A more radical self-critique was given by TomF of his 'me-centred' reading perspective:

> ... I think my understanding of the Bible ... I think that's changed a lot ... the way that I perceive the Bible has changed a lot over the last few years ... when I read it now, I try more and more to not ... for a lot of years, I ... read the Bible from a very me-centred perspective, and how does this passage relate to me, what's God saying to me about this? And I think, in doing that, I think I've weakened the message of the Bible, very significantly. And I think that when you read the Bible, it's almost like you kind of have to ... read it and then ... think about, well, how does this actually apply to me, how does it apply to our society in England, how does it apply to broader society around the world? And when you read passages about suffering or about protection, it's very tempting for me to sort of say, "Well, that's" – you're almost saying, "How is God going to protect my economic status?" or whatever, when clearly ... it was written two thousand years ago when people were more concerned about dying of famine or in wars and things, which are still very real issues today, in other parts of the world. It's something which, on the whole, we're distanced from.

TomF ascribed his slow hermeneutical change to being 'becoming more aware ... of what's going on in the world' through the media, in conjunction with reflection on what he had heard in church. These internal critiques were typical of Fellowship's multiple tensions within its configuration of congregational hermeneutics. Unsurprisingly, there are further significant counter-examples emphasising God's corporate address through Scripture in subsequent chapters. Horizons are dynamic and while the individualist starting point was predominant at Fellowship, there was an observable degree of flux.

---

[29]   A handout sheet in a Fellowship small group explicitly recognised this emphasis upon the individual as a feature of the wider tradition, as it noted the 'tendency amongst evangelical Christians to prize the one-on-one relationship with Jesus above all else' (B2).

Distinctive Theological Traditions

Most of the congregational hermeneutics characterised in this book would come under the broad heading of 'theological tradition', but here there is an interest in distinctive theological traditions evidenced in Holder's horizons.[30] Bible-centredness is, of course, a special case of a distinctive theological tradition.

Holder's encounter with Scripture did appear to be informed by their theological tradition – an approach that is often termed 'theological interpretation', as discussed in Chapter 3.[31] Some theological positions were used as boundaries on interpretation, as in one small group where a literal understanding of the LORD having 'hated' Esau in Mal 1:3 was rejected by JamesH (X1), and in another group the mediated idea of God being on trial in Job 1 was also rejected by PatriciaH since it 'makes God too small' (Y2). Bible-centredness was the most distinctive emphasis within the congregational tradition, and this has already been seen to shape Holder's understanding of Scripture. There were a number of other distinctive theological emphases within Holder's tradition that were significant for encounters with Scripture, namely Calvinism, Christ, the cross/atonement and hell.[32] Notably Theo accurately captured some of these emphases in his sermon, despite being a visitor, when he stated 'the Christian faith is being saved, let's get this clear, from hell, through the cross, for heaven, that's the Christian faith' (S9h). Theo's influential position within English conservative evangelicalism suggests these distinctives were common to a wider constituency. Such atonement theology was evident in a small group when JamesH explained the 'covenant' of Mal 3:1 as 'the eternal covenant [which] is Jesus' death for us, which allows us to be acceptable to God and to know Him, in turn' (X4).

Songs also carried Holder's theological distinctives, as has been seen already regarding Bible-centredness, but in addition the cross was a key theme in Holder songs;[33] they were largely Christocentric;[34] and Calvinistic readings were also evident. So the song *Jesus, King of Kings* (SF295) incorporated a reworked segment of the Lord's Prayer at the end of each stanza, including the adapted

---

[30]   Francis Watson argues that Christian doctrine has a hermeneutical function, in that 'hermeneutics, theology, and exegesis flow into and out of each other with no fixed dividing lines' (1994: 241).

[31]   In its academic usage, theological interpretation has a degree of intentionality about it that may be much less marked in congregational hermeneutics.

[32]   Some of these emphases reflect the influence of wider evangelicalism (e.g. Warner, 2007: 17f).

[33]   28%, N=65.

[34]   In songs, 'Father' was over eight times less frequent than 'Jesus' (and equivalents) at Holder, and 'Spirit' was only found in their song lyrics twice, N=65, see Appendix D.

line 'Your *sovereign* will be done'.[35] Indeed, Calvinism was the most distinctive of these theological emphases after Bible-centredness, as OwenH commented:

> I would describe it as 'reformed' with a small 'r'. The people would probably be Calvinistic but without knowing, really, the five points of Calvinism and the whole of Reformed theology, really. The ministers have definitely all been Reformed, going back as far as I know, fifty-odd years, but the people have been more diverse in their views. It wouldn't be a classically Reformed church.

The elder, JustinH, who had been at the church much longer than Owen,[36] thought that 'Calvinism was very strong' when he was younger, to the extent that 'Calvinism was the doctrine, rather than what Christian truth was'. He added that Calvinistic teaching was less strongly mediated now than it had been in the past. Certain points of Calvinistic doctrine, particularly relating to predestination and God's sovereignty were clearly in evidence across all Bible settings at Holder. Perhaps the most memorable example came during the Anniversary service when an ex-Pastor's stroke was attributed by his interviewer (TimH) to God having 'struck you down'. Such a stark expression of God's sovereignty was characteristic of Holder's embrace and acceptance of difficult doctrines. Small groups saw some striking references to Calvinist doctrine, many of which functioned as 'full stops' to particular units of discourse, so PaulH commented of Abraham's lying episode in Gen 20:

> ... every decision you make, in weakness or in strength, Abraham's example for us is that the outcome remains the same, we are still saved and nothing can take our salvation from us. And that's such an encouragement, I think, in this passage, don't you? (Y3)

When talking about the flood, LucyH made a similar move, but with less of a full stop:

> I find it difficult when God – we know about the flood, but then when you read about "and God destroyed all the people" and I think, I wonder if they ever had a chance, the children, whether they ever had the chance to know about these things, and what will happen to them? But then I say, "But you are sovereign". But, humanly speaking, it's hard when you think, "But they weren't the ones that caused the trouble ... "

---

[35]   Extract taken from 'Jesus, King of Kings' by Chris Rolinson, Copyright © 1988 Thankyou Music*.

[36]   'it would be almost fifty years'.

This Calvinist tradition was also mediated through commentaries, so RodneyH quoted Warren Wiersbe regarding the story of Job, saying: 'Nothing can come to your life that is outside His will' (Y2).

Fellowship's encounter with Scripture was certainly informed by their theological tradition, which was partially shaped by Ekklesia, as discussed above and in Chapter 1. There were instances of theological positions acting as boundaries on interpretation. In Housegroup B, for example, FrancisF's strong commitment to conditional immortality[37] saw the group's occasionally detailed engagement with the biblical text heavily informed by this doctrinal stance. However, this and other examples of bounded interpretation were often specific to individuals or housegroups, rather than cohering with an overarching theological tradition.

Bible passion was an emerging distinctive of the congregation, but was hardly traditional by the time of the fieldwork, although it did illustrate the dynamic nature of Fellowship tradition. Fellowship's most distinctive theological emphasis was Christocentrism with a particular focus on the atonement. There was a conspicuous tradition in Fellowship public settings of inserting into many sermons and other public discourse highly compressed accounts of Jesus' atoning death on the cross, often without much connection to what came before or after.[38] As at Holder, songs also reflected their Christocentrism and its emphasis in wider evangelicalism (Warner, 2007: 17f).[39] DerekF spoke of their history of Christocentrism, recalling:

> I've brought a Benedictine monk ... to a celebration, and the songs focus on Jesus, Jesus reigning, Jesus coming to people, and the preacher's very much, you know, Jesus loves you, Jesus can heal you, and he turned to me and said, 'Are you Trinitarian in [Ekklesia]?', because there was such a focus on Jesus, obviously are Trinitarian, but there, there was this Jesus centredness, give maximum honour to Jesus, find Christ in all the Scriptures, a very strong theme.

DerekF did note a 'swing back' towards being 'more explicitly Trinitarian' now, although the Christocentric emphasis was still clear during the fieldwork. Such Christocentrism also elides into Fellowship's 'Jesus hermeneutics' or Christological approach to hermeneutics, discussed further below and in Chapter 5.

---

[37]   The view that immortality is only for those who are in Christ.

[38]   E.g. DerekF in S3f and TheresinaF in SunAM9f. The cross was also a theme in 21% of Fellowship songs, N=62.

[39]   'Father' and 'Spirit' were both more than ten times less frequent than 'Jesus' (and equivalents) at Fellowship, N=62, see Appendix D.

Theological distinctives at Fellowship were less marked and uniform than at Holder, which meant that examples of such distinctives shaping encounter with Scripture were less striking as well. Fellowship's more recent and dynamic tradition may have militated against such distinctives being established, and it is also likely that their focus on activism and experience led to downplaying the priority of doctrinal concerns.

Hermeneutical Goals

Hermeneutical goals were quite explicit at both Holder and Fellowship. Indeed, as discussed in Chapter 2, the broad diversity of hermeneutical practices in the congregations might be characterised by their overriding goal of 'hearing God speak through Scripture'.

The practice of personal Bible reading at Holder, discussed more fully in Chapter 5, was considered very important by interviewees. The necessity of personal Bible reading arose from the desire 'to know what the Lord wants to say to me ... every day' (DennisH), a point repeated or implied by most interviewees. Embedded in this goal was the view that the Bible should be relevant for life today. So JustinH wanted sermons that were 'purposeful for life ... not just abstractly "this is what the Bible says", but "this is how it impacts in life today"'. Holder's website encapsulated their horizonal goals, which identified relevant and understandable teaching of the Bible as being central to their activities. 'God's voice is heard' when the Bible is explained.[40] This goal of hearing God speak in a relevant way through encounter with Scripture was a key shaper of hermeneutical practices.

The goal of 'hearing God speak through Scripture' was similarly explicit at Fellowship. The visiting speaker, Ian, who knew the church well, stressed of the Bible that 'in this book, we hear God, and that's the crucial thing ... God speaks' (S1f) – a point echoed in other sermons and also particularly by interviewees. Fellowship congregants talked about their motivation for reading the Bible as wanting to hear God speak. The intensity of this goal for Fellowship was captured by BruceF:

> I want to hear from God, in my life. I want to hear what he's saying about what's relevant to what's happening in my life today, like *today*, not just generally in this period of my life, but today, what's going on.

Such an existentially urgent expression of their key hermeneutical goal recurred in many Fellowship settings. It may also have been shaped by the practice of giving 'Words' from God to the congregation, heightening expectations of

---

[40]   I have paraphrased this in order to maintain anonymity.

relevance in relation to Scripture. A corollary of Words is that it appeared to relativise the status of Scripture for Fellowship, as there were other practices, not necessarily involving Scripture, that enabled the congregation to hear from God.

Taking Tradition Seriously

From this focussed tale of two churches and their multiple horizons, it should be clear that congregational tradition has significant potential for shaping how churches engage with Scripture. This shaping might be in terms of guiding one's interpretation, of providing interpretative emphases, or through providing boundaries to possible interpretations. The extent of this shaping upon hermeneutical practices is elaborated further in Chapter 5. Although such a conclusion may not be news for all churches, the manner of such shaping may well be.

Tradition can have a bad name for many reasons, as has been seen at Holder and Fellowship earlier in the chapter. Taking tradition seriously means acknowledging that congregations cannot be tradition free when reading Scripture, and therefore that a critical embrace of tradition is needed.[41] Plenty of criticism has been directed at hermeneutical practices with an overly traditioned reading of Scripture. Ian Dickson's research for the *Use of the Bible in Pastoral Practice* project generated responses from 64 UK 'Bible practitioners'.[42] He concluded that the use of the Bible in pastoral ministry was 'largely for pragmatic purposes' where the Bible was a 'product' suitable for 'reinforcing particular pre-existing stances and ministries'. This is Bible use with 'a consumerist edge' where texts are used for 'purposes of comfort or challenge without imposing hermeneutic controls' (2007: 109). Using more explicitly hermeneutical language, Thiselton expressed his concern that the premature fusion of horizons will lead to an interaction with Scripture that is 'uneventful, bland, routine, and entirely unremarkable'. He launches the following broadside regarding his perception of hermeneutical practices in the church:

> Within the Christian community the reading of the biblical texts often takes this uneventful and bland form. For the nature of the reading-process is governed by horizons of expectation already pre-formed by the community of readers or by the individual. Preachers often draw from texts what they had already decided to say; congregations sometimes look to biblical readings only to affirm the community-identity and life-style which they already enjoy. The biblical writings in such a situation become assimilated into the function of creeds: they become

---

[41]   This section develops an argument in an earlier publication (Rogers, 2007: 96f).
[42]   Largely those engaged in pastoral ministry.

primarily institutional mechanisms to ensure continuity of corporate belief and
identity (1992: 8).

Thiselton does qualify this negative portrayal of congregational hermeneutics
when he adds that not all Bible reading should be iconoclastic, since Scripture
can have an 'affirming function in relation to prior tradition'.[43] Such 'affirmative
reading' has a partial fit with Holder and Fellowship, but this tale of two
churches suggests that the picture is more nuanced than Thiselton's portrait.
Churches like Holder and Fellowship are swimming in a stream of biblical
language, metaphors and ideas, hence their traditions have been shaped by
their hermeneutical practices over decades and even centuries. Hearing God
speak through Scripture has been preserved to an extent in their congregational
traditions. Therefore, while agreeing that the disruptive power of Scripture
engagement is too often missed in churches, there is nevertheless a place for a
reading of Scripture that affirms congregational tradition.[44] Both affirmative and
disruptive modes of reading may be theologically transformative in ways already
discussed in Chapter 2.[45]

Tradition, therefore, is a theological, ethnographic and hermeneutical fact
of life for congregations. Rather than solely seeing tradition as something to
be eliminated or at least minimised in congregational hermeneutics, tradition
has something valuable to offer churches in their engagement with Scripture.
Thus speaking of a critical 'embrace' of tradition is quite deliberate. A number
of scholars have argued for a retrieval of tradition in recent decades, particularly
aimed at 'suspicious protestants' and evangelicals, for whom tradition, as has been
seen, is sometimes problematic (Williams, 1999: title page; 2005; Evans, 2003;
Holmes, 2002; Walker, 2007a).[46] For example, Stephen Holmes argues that
taking tradition seriously is a theological necessity. He points to the doctrine of
creation in order to develop a 'theology of the goodness of historical locatedness'
(2002: 5). Drawing on a Christological argument, Holmes contends that Christ
existing in a 'particular historical location' is not problematic, but 'is a necessary,
and so good, implication of his being human'. Consequently history is:

> ... part of the good ordering of creation in which God was pleased to place us. Just
> so, it is proper to human reception of the apostolic witness that it is mediated
> through a process of tradition, of handing on. We should not attempt to escape

---

[43]   Thiselton cites the intra-biblical example of Deut 6:4.

[44]   Walter Brueggemann uses similar language, so 'equilibrium' and 'transformation',
noting, as Thiselton, that both these tendencies are present in Scripture as well as in the
church (2009: 20f).

[45]   Which is why I distinguish between affirmative, disruptive and transformative readings.

[46]   It is recognised that some churches might say they never 'lost' tradition in the first
place.

from our embeddedness in the Christian tradition, but should rather celebrate it. To attempt to engage with the scriptural witness in any other way than as that which has been handed on is simply theologically improper, a refusal to accept the way in which God has created us (2002: 13).

In addition to embracing our historical locatedness, Holmes makes an ecclesiological case for a 'proper doctrine of church' that 'requires us to acknowledge both the communal nature of the work of theology, and that that community is not limited to the living, but encompasses those who have gone before as well' (2002: 5). Such an argument has strong resonance with the congregational hermeneutics agenda of this book, which will be developed further in Chapter 9 particularly. Holmes's arguments are focussed on church and tradition in the broadest sense, but they also have validity at the level of congregational tradition. As one tributary of the larger Christian tradition, one can embrace and celebrate congregational tradition in reading Scripture.

But. In order to do so, it is critical for churches to know their tradition, to be aware of their congregational horizons. It is all too easy for churches to ignore their influence in engaging with Scripture, perhaps instead claiming to 'just read' the Bible. Such a move collapses the distinction between congregational horizons and the Scriptures (cf. Wall, 2000: 99), rendering their horizons invisible, thus making the fusion of horizons impossible. As a practical theologian, this underlines for me the importance of inculcating habits of theological reflection in the church, so to aid churches in being honest about their horizons – honest about where they are coming from.[47] This double edge to tradition and hermeneutics is captured by Gordon Fee, who acknowledges that 'the effect of tradition on hermeneutics in itself is not necessarily a bad thing', but adds that 'tradition may be fully affirmed and appreciated, on the one hand, but not allowed totally to skew our hermeneutics, on the other' (1991: 424).

In demonstrating the manner of tradition's interaction with hermeneutics, the tale of Holder and Fellowship points to the need for congregations to be self-aware in their reading of Scripture. As was seen in Chapter 3, Gadamer argued that 'working out the hermeneutical situation means acquiring the right horizon of inquiry for the questions evoked by the encounter with tradition' (2004: 302). Congregational horizons are the present of their tradition, so by foregrounding their horizons they make plain the tradition which informs their reading of Scripture. An analogy may be drawn here between a congregational tradition being made explicit, and the *regula fidei* or Rule of Faith from the early church period (also discussed in Chapter 3) as both have the function of informing the conversation between horizons. The purpose of the Rule was to provide a minimal response to the question 'What sort of horizon is appropriate

---

47 Honesty, amongst other hermeneutical virtues, will be considered further in Chapter 8.

for a Christian reading of Scripture?' (Rogers, 2007: 99–100), through a theological and hermeneutical framework that preserved the apostolic tradition and limited indeterminacy. The Rule was not thought separate from Scripture, but was understood as the Church's summary of the apostolic faith. Evangelical congregations would similarly want to stress that such explicit rules were derived from Scripture, as the practice of citing biblical references on some rules makes plain. Ruled reading was also evident in both congregations through statements of faith, oral traditions distinguishing between salvation and secondary issues (see Chapter 6), and through horizontal convictions that were more or less explicit, as has been seen. The localised and therefore elastic nature of the ancient Rule (Williams, 2005: 117f; Wall, 2000: 102) also corresponds to the great variety of rules found just within English evangelicalism, to which this study alludes. The difference between contemporary rules and the *regula fidei*, according to this study, lies in how self-conscious evangelical churches are regarding the intentional contribution of rules to hermeneutical encounter.

Ruled reading was seen in the fieldwork to encourage affirmative encounter with Scripture, which I want to stress is an important aspect of congregational scriptural encounter. If congregational horizons are shaped by an accumulation of past encounters with Scripture, then affirming these horizons can be a matter of celebrating the truths of the faith carried by congregational tradition.[48] Therefore such affirmation does not necessarily imply hermeneutical dishonesty. Indeed, affirmative reading might sometimes be the more virtuous option, since it may be more faithful to the Christian Story than the apparently transformative readings of 'maverick preachers and writers' (McGrath, 2000a: 157).[49] Relative hermeneutical stability is necessary for congregational hermeneutics, since 'lives and behaviour are at stake' for congregants (Jenson, 1995: 94).[50] Ruled reading therefore contributes to this stability. It was noticeable in the fieldwork, however, that rules for reading, both formal and informal, varied in their size and specificity. Too large a rule for reading fixes too many horizontal points for hermeneutical encounter, which can drastically reduce the disruptive potential of Scripture. While hermeneutical stability is valuable, too much of it is not desirable. Overly large rules correspond to the situation described by Malley, where Scripture engagement largely consists of knowing how to connect beliefs to biblical texts that affirm those beliefs (2004: 73f).

In this reflection on tradition, the focus has been on the aspects of congregational horizons that were especially significant for their hermeneutical practices. In recognising the importance of affirmative reading of Scripture, it

---

[48] Leonora Tubbs Tisdale makes a similar point in relation to preaching, which can 'affirm and confirm the right imaginings of the congregational heart' (1997: 111f).

[49] Faithfulness as a hermeneutical virtue will be explored further in Chapter 8.

[50] See also Fee (1991: 435) and McGrath (2000a: 157).

has been argued that this must be done self-consciously and honestly. However, this is not to say that affirmative reading is enough. As Thiselton was arguing in the quote above, Scriptural encounter should also be disruptive. I have argued previously:

> ... tradition has a habit of becoming fossilised, of ceasing to be a dynamic expression of the Story that ruled reading should encapsulate. There needs to be a means of breaking open a church's ... tradition so that the Christian story is faithfully improvised in its contemporary context (2007: 101).

It is too easy for the more explicit aspects of congregational horizons and thus tradition to become fixed and overwhelm more implicit hermeneutical practices, swallowing up their potential for disrupting congregational tradition in transformative ways. How such 'breaking open' of tradition might happen is developed in subsequent chapters.

Chapter 5
Practices

Hermeneutical practices have been introduced in earlier chapters as the saying, doing, making and learning of biblical hermeneutics. Whether explicit or implicit, this cluster of practices comes under the insider heading of 'hearing God speak through Scripture'. 'Horizon' and 'fusion' are the particular conceptual resources that have been utilised for understanding congregational hermeneutics within Holder and Fellowship. In the previous chapter I examined the significance of congregational horizons for hermeneutical practice across three Bible settings. In this chapter I turn to consider fusion, which, as has been said, refers to all those processes in the churches that sought to make connections between text and congregational horizons. Although I am using 'practices' as the broad term for all facets of congregational hermeneutics, fusion processes constitute the most substantive part of those practices, thus the approximate equivalence of terms.

In order to properly set fusion processes within their congregational context, I will drill down from more general Bible practices (relatively speaking) to the particular. I begin by considering Bible uses in the two congregations, then look at overarching fusion strategies, then come to consider in detail fusion processes across the three Bible settings in both churches. All this leads into a reflection on the degree of dissonance between the 'given' categories from the three paradigms outlined in Chapter 3, and whether such dissonance matters.

Bible Uses in Holder and Fellowship

Before delving into the Bible uses of Holder and Fellowship, I should say first that I do not consider Bible 'use' necessarily a theologically deficient or pejorative term. Angus Paddison rightly draws attention to some of the dangers that Bible 'use' terminology might represent under the heading of 'Why Christians Don't "Use" Scripture' (2009: 38f), but there is more than a whiff of theological pedantry here. Just as practical theologians have to deal with the fact that 'application' language is often used in ways that do not imply a solely theory-to-practice mentality,[1] so too, the detractors of 'use' need to recognise

---

[1]   I speak from personal experience.

its common and mundane reference that carries very little systematic baggage.[2] By 'Bible use', then, I mean the way in which the Bible was incorporated into a particular setting within the congregations. That this is a more general ecclesial practice is evident when we consider that a Bible use does not necessarily specify particular fusion processes.

Public Bible Uses

Four Bible uses could be identified in Holder public settings, namely sermons, songs, bible display and liturgical. Bible display was typified by the selection of a 'motto text' annually, which was then printed onto cards for display in the church and homes of the congregation. The weekly newsletter always had at least a phrase from Scripture on the front, which was sometimes referred to by service leaders and preachers. Two Bible verses were also on permanent display on the outside wall of the building by the entrance. Bible display was also evident in virtual space on the church website. Each subject page had a sidebar containing a related Bible verse – so 'Where to find us' was accompanied by 'I am the way ... ' (Jn 14:6) and ' ... a highway will be there' (Isa 35:8–10).[3] In liturgical use, Scripture was incorporated into services predominantly through worship-orientated Bible readings, prayers, occasional communion services and rites of passage such as thanksgivings/dedications for babies,[4] adult baptisms, and entering into church membership. It is important to note that there was an order and pattern to services in both churches, but in a more implicit mode than liturgy in other Christian traditions. Songs were a specific and popular form of liturgy for Holder, embedding the Bible in their lyrics in various ways as will be seen shortly.

Sunday services incorporated these Bible uses through the classic non-conformist pattern of a 'Hymn-prayer sandwich'. In a relatively structured manner, service leaders would intersperse songs, prayers and Scripture readings with each other, as well as allowing time for congregational rites of passage. Within this service structure, songs acted 'as a kind of glue joining the different parts of worship together' (Ward, 2005: 198). Given their convention of standing to sing, an average of 7 songs per service during the fieldwork meant a good deal of standing up and sitting down. Sermons averaged 28 minutes during the fieldwork, and were largely based on the New Testament. The sermon was the clearly defined climax of the service, evident in formal liturgical markers such as the sermon Bible reading and prayer for the preacher.

---

2   The *Use of the Bible in Pastoral Practice* project is a key example of 'use' in this theologically mundane sense. See discussion in Chapter 1.

3   Complete verses were given.

4   The alternative to infant baptism.

Fellowship shared three of these public Bible uses, namely sermons, songs and liturgical use. Liturgical use was similar to Holder in terms of Scripture being incorporated into worship-orientated Bible readings, prayers and just the occasional rite of passage, but there was little interest in Bible display. The distinctively charismatic practice of giving 'Words' was an additional liturgical use at Fellowship and a key element of their spirituality. A Word was sometimes literally a word or phrase, or a Bible verse/passage, or message which was understood to be from God specifically for the congregation, or a group, or an individual *here* and *now*. Individuals would come to the front of the, service usually during the worship time and explain, the Word to DerekF or the service leader, whereupon they would normally be asked to share it with the congregation. Songs also formed a substantial part of the congregation's liturgy and exposure to Scripture, although functioning somewhat differently to songs at Holder.

Sunday services usually began with a welcome and a prayer and possibly a reading from Scripture. This was always followed by a shorter period of singing, involving two or three songs, after which notices were given and other short items included. A block worship session came next (cf. Steven, 2002: 92f; Ward, 2005: 199), which would last for up to 30 minutes, led by a music group headed by a worship leader ('the band') using about five songs.[5] The convention, for those who were able, was to stand for a good part of this period. With varying degrees of spontaneity, service leaders and members of the congregation would intersperse the songs with prayers, Bible readings, or a 'Word' from God, usually from the front of the meeting. This was followed by a sermon of about 40 minutes on average during the fieldwork, sometimes with an opportunity to respond to the message (usually through prayer). All sermons during the fieldwork were based on the New Testament, which included a series on the Sermon on the Mount for 7 out of the 12 Sundays, drawing on Nicky Gumbel's book *Challenging Lifestyle* (1996). The service structure appeared to have a double climax, in that both the block worship time *and* the sermon were liturgical high points.

Small Group Bible Uses

Small groups were a key Bible use in both congregations. According to questionnaire respondents, 77 per cent at Holder and 85 per cent at Fellowship attended housegroups.[6] Holder's small groups were fairly uniform in their Bible

---

[5]   So there was an average of seven songs per service during the fieldwork, each of which could be repeated up to four times.

[6]   This is likely to be a maximum figure, N=105 and 75 respectively. The *21st Century Evangelicals* survey found that 77% of respondents said they had attended a small group at least once a fortnight (Evangelical Alliance and Christian Research, 2011) (see also Chapter 1).

use.[7] Normally small groups prayed, read a passage of Scripture, questions were then asked by the leader(s) either from a handout sheet or Bible Study Guide, whereupon members would make short contributions to a discussion of the questions and biblical text. Of the small groups I attended, Housegroup X were studying Malachi using questions supplied and written by the housegroup organiser, JustinH. Housegroup Y were doing a thematic study on Integrity using a Bible Study Guide (Nystrom, 2000), and the women's group 'Growing Together' were using a Bible Study Guide on women of the Bible (Vander Velde, 2000).

Fellowship small groups had greater variation in their Bible use, given their broader aims for meeting. Church-based Bible study groups were primarily for studying the Bible, similar in format to Holder small groups. There was more latitude, however, regarding the role of the Bible in housegroups – pastoral support and learning through sharing experiences together were highly valued. Of the groups I attended, Housegroup A largely studied Mark's Gospel using a Bible Study Guide (Bolt and Payne, 1997); Housegroup B drew on a variety of themed studies generated by group members; Housegroup C made brief and occasional use of Scripture; Tuesday AM was an open group working through the Pauline epistles led by the pastor DerekF; Thursday AM was for church staff and was working through 2 Corinthians, again led by the pastor; and Thursday PM was working through James, once again, led by the pastor.[8]

Personal Bible Use

Personal Bible reading, sometimes called the 'Quiet Time', has long been an ideal of evangelical spirituality (Tidball, 2005: 265f; cf. Randall, 2005: 45f). It was certainly a widespread practice in the two churches and intensely so at Holder. Congregants spoke to me about their personal Bible reading in interview, which was complemented by their responses on the questionnaire. 54 per cent of respondents at Holder said they read the Bible at least once a day, rising to 96 per cent that read once a week or more. 42 per cent of Holder respondents said they had read the whole Bible.[9] [10] For the majority of Holder congregants, then, personal Bible reading constituted their most frequent encounter with Scripture. Indeed, it was the pre-eminent Bible use within Holder spirituality.

---

[7]   There were six housegroups which all met on Tuesdays and were centrally organised by the elder, JustinH. There was also a monthly Saturday morning training session for men and a weekly women's Bible study.

[8]   I will refer to these latter three groups as 'church-based'.

[9]   N=105.

[10]   67% of Holder respondents read four or more times a week for more than 10 minutes, N=97.

Personal Bible reading was less common at Fellowship, so 20 per cent of respondents said they read the Bible at least once a day, rising to 85 per cent that read once a week or more. A striking 60 per cent of Fellowship respondents said they had read the whole Bible.[11] [12] The relative difference between the two churches should be understood in the context of the national and global surveys reviewed in Chapter 1.

Reading the Bible 'every day' was described by Holder's pastor, OwenH, as 'vitally important' although 'not in a legalistic way'. As seen in Chapter 4, the children's song, *As for Me and My House* (SF1175), which was very popular in services during the fieldwork, emphasised this point as well. The associate pastor, JoeH, also commented on Holder's 'every day' Bible reading tradition:

> ... it seems to be a tradition of this church to really emphasise that. I mean, occasionally you'll get whole sermons, almost, on that. Just the Bible, reading the Bible and prayer has been the most important things we could be doing, essential ... I think ... it's like eating, it's just good to keep doing it, every day.

Metaphors of necessity, often featuring food, were common, as LucyH explained: 'It's like food to me. If I didn't read the Bible, I would starve ... And unless you do, you will not grow. And, to me, it's vital'.[13] Similar sentiments were expressed by some at Fellowship, so NadineF said:

> I can honestly say now that I read it because I want to read it. I genuinely feel that it's really the only way I can live as a Christian ... I can't do without it ... I want to make sure I'm doing what I should be doing ... I've seen the way the Bible has ... changed me, so I feel that I want to keep reading it to keep changing ...

Fellowship's 'Bible passion' considered in Chapter 4 included congregants' personal Bible reading. Early in the fieldwork period the 'City Reach challenge' was launched by BobF during a sermon (apparently spontaneously), offering £10 per Testament to those who could read them all by the end of the year (S2f). In response, an accompanying website was set up by TomF which kept a record of how much of the Bible had been read and also suggested future reading plans.

Describing what we do with the Bible in churches, even at this general level, is probably not something many of us will have done. We just do it. The act of looking at our Bible use in this way, however apparently familiar and mundane, is

---

[11]   N=75.

[12]   33% of Fellowship respondents read four or more times a week for more than 10 minutes, N=66.

[13]   The biblical use of food metaphors relating to Christian growth may have accounted for this metaphor's popularity – a link made explicitly by WendyH, so 1 Cor 3:1–2; Heb 5:12–14; 1 Pe 2:2–3. See also Simon Coleman (2006: 163).

a move towards aiding reflection on how and why we do what we do. These Bible uses might be found in many evangelical, charismatic and pentecostal churches, and a number will overlap with Bible uses in churches more broadly. Reiterating the point made in Chapter 1, Holder and Fellowship are in certain respects like all other churches, like some other churches and like no other churches. We now delve deeper to uncover the fusion processes linked to these various Bible uses.

Fusion Processes

The first thing to say about fusion processes is that they were largely implicit.[14] That is, congregants rarely talked about or indicated that they were reflecting on the processes of biblical interpretation. Horizonal beliefs were sometimes made explicit, in some instances quite loudly as Chapter 4 has shown, but fusion processes lay largely beneath the surface of congregational life. This is a critical point of dissonance for the argument in this book, especially given the broader context of similar hermeneutical dissonance in national and global surveys.

Overarching Fusion Processes

Certain overarching strategies for fusion processes were noted in sermons, small groups and songs. Consequently I generated some typologies from the accounts to identify the emphases of such strategies. Sermons incorporated the Bible in four main ways at Holder, namely *textual, thematic, narrative* and *springboard*. Fellowship added *testimony* as a fifth type.[15] Textual sermons were driven by a biblical passage, whereas thematic sermons were shaped around a (possibly biblical/theological) theme, although many sermons had elements of both approaches. Narrative preaching moved between the stories of Scripture and of the congregation, although this was quite rare in both churches. My dictionary defines a springboard figuratively as 'a thing that lends impetus to a particular action, enterprise, or development' (Pearsall, 1998: 1801) – so in this study, how the biblical text gives an initial impetus to a sermon. 'Initial' because once contact has been made with the springboard, it was usually left behind. Such minimal engagement with Scripture would not be acceptable for Holder sermons, but

---

[14]   Somewhat contra Tidball's over-optimistic account of evangelical hermeneutics where he claims: 'Basic hermeneutical skills are taught, at least implicitly, in most evangelical churches where people gain an understanding of the need to consider the genre of a passage they are reading, where it comes in the unfolding plan of God, how to read it in context and relate it to other parts of Scripture, and make the connection between the Bible's own time and our own' (2005: 271).

[15]   Broader homiletical types are proposed by a number of scholars, including Michael Quicke (2005) and Leonora Tubbs Tisdale (1997: 136f).

a multiple springboard variant was evident where a number of texts in a given passage were utilised to then launch a number of (not necessarily related) points. Fellowship sermons employed a greater variety of these strategies and spent substantial time in the horizon of the speaker/congregation. The extreme example of this was a testimony sermon which largely inhabited the horizon of the speakers, with incidental use of the biblical text.

Textual, thematic and springboard strategy types were also evident in small groups. Holder small groups largely followed a textual approach, with discussion being driven by the text and questions that stepped through the passages, although a theme may have been associated with the study (so Integrity in Housegroup Y and Women of the Bible in WedAM). Fellowship small groups were more varied in their strategies, with church Bible studies all working in a 'just the text' mode,[16] and housegroups varying their approaches even during the fieldwork. Housegroup B notably used all three types, with some ambitious member-generated thematic studies such as 'Hell' and 'The Idolatry of Materialism and Narcissism'.

Songs incorporated Scripture in a fascinating variety of ways. I identified four types in the study, so *dependent*, *quotation*, *reconstructive* and *referential*. In contrast to sermons, the use of Scripture in worship songs does not appear to have received much analytical attention. Dependent songs are largely based on a specific biblical passage,[17] whereas quotation songs include one or more distinct biblical quotations,[18] sometimes in composite form. Reconstructive songs exhibited greater freedom with the use of the text, combining rewordings of biblical phrases and scriptural allusions, demonstrating a certain hermeneutical playfulness (cf. Stackhouse, 2004: 44; Troeger, 1998).[19] The language of Scripture is eschewed in Referential songs, which instead use their own terms to refer to significant biblical events and ideas – a type common in more traditional style hymns.[20] There were quite a few songs that did not incorporate Scripture at all. A number of these sounded like they were from the Bible, but closer analysis found no matches. Nevertheless, the majority of songs in both churches used Scripture in dependent, quotation or reconstructive ways.[21] A further useful typology is employed by Ward for assessing the nature of songs and will be referred to as the Ward typology. Songs are classed as objective (songs which

---

[16]   In ThursAM, the text was made available to members on handouts with the verses deliberately formatted individually by the youth leader.

[17]   E.g. *To Him Who Loves Us And Freed Us* taken from Rev 1:5b–6 (SF1068).

[18]   E.g. *For This Purpose Christ Was Revealed* quoting 1 Jn 3:8 (MP155).

[19]   E.g. *Who Paints the Skies Into Glorious Day?* alludes to Isa 61:10 (possibly); Ezek 36, 37; Dan 7:10; and Mi 4 (SF1118).

[20]   E.g. *Name Of All Majesty* (MP481).

[21]   So, during the fieldwork, 68% and 77% of songs at Holder and Fellowship respectively were dependent, quotation or reconstructive types, N=65/62.

give 'an account of a theological theme or biblical event'), subjective (songs with theological or biblical content but include implications for the worshipper), and reflexive (songs which focus on 'the act of worship itself') (2005: 206–7).[22]

Public Processes

A strong emphasis on the importance of preaching at Holder meant that sermons were (potentially) the most significant example of horizon fusion in public settings. Most sermons included some exploration of the text horizon through including matters of grammar, historical and literary context.[23] Indeed, OwenH thought it important to be 'faithful to the original text' by setting it 'completely in its context, in the situation when it was first written and who it was first written for'. Such mentions were mostly brief, however, so when the visiting speaker John made five references to the Greek, this stood out as unusual (S6h). Exegetical material was sprinkled lightly throughout sermons followed by such hermeneutical pivots as 'so what can we learn from X?' (S2h) or 'what is the lesson for us regarding X?' (S10h). Sermon structure was generally quite formal, with a number cycling through a few phases of (brief) exegesis then application.[24] The predominant hermeneutical concern of Holder sermon recipients was for horizons to be fused ('two horizon reading'). Cohering with Holder's goal of relevance, WendyH commented:

> To listen to sermons that are just about thousands of years ago, as much as it's really interesting, I'd find that a little bit like a history book, whereas to actually apply it today, that really brings things to life, and it's challenging.

Not unlike Holder, sermons were the most developed form of horizon fusion in Fellowship public settings. Unlike Holder, they displayed a marked range of approaches to incorporating Scripture, which was no doubt affected by the variety of speakers from within and without the church.[25] DerekF preferred to speak on a biblical passage, moving from text to theme and then to (frequently) numerous contemporary anecdotes and stories. Text horizon engagement veered from close readings that took in grammar, historical and literary context (e.g. S1f, S3f, S10f) to those where such features hardly mattered at all (e.g. S4f, S8f, S11f). Sermons were therefore notable for their attention *and* lack of attention

---

[22]   Ward is following hymnologist Lionel Adey. In my analysis, following Ward, I have allowed for songs to belong to more than one category.
[23]   8 out of 12 fieldwork sermons were of the textual or textual/thematic mix.
[24]   Thus the potential for multiple springboard sermons characterised above.
[25]   Out of 12 fieldwork sermons, DerekF gave 4, other members of the congregation gave 4, and outside speakers gave 4.

to the text. Sermon structure was similarly varied, tending to default towards an informal and unstructured style, often with some congregational interaction.

A key feature of Fellowship sermons was occasional explicit hermeneutical content (mainly S1f, but also briefly in S7f and S13f). This content was notable beyond itself, in that it indicated what was acceptable for public Fellowship discourse. A visiting professional theologian, Ian, with close links to the church, encouraged the congregation to read the text closely in S1f because: 'the Bible is a book to be read very, very carefully ... there are some books it takes a lifetime to understand, and the Bible is one of those books'. Ian then expanded on the storied and Christological nature of Scripture. The latter in particular resonated with an explicit Ekklesia-derived Fellowship hermeneutical tradition of 'Jesus hermeneutics', as DerekF named it. One report described this tradition as 'a salient aspect of Ekklesia's approach to theology', namely 'their Christ-centred method of interpreting and applying Scripture to the life and mission of the church'.[26] DerekF explained this hermeneutical approach as follows:

> **DerekF:** I think, in the [Ekklesia] tradition ... and I think applies to lots of people in [my college] as well, the idea of Jesus hermeneutic, or Jesus-centred hermeneutics, so Jesus is God's answer, Word to us, and so we interpret the written Word in the light of who Jesus is, and we look back at the Old Testament in the light of who Jesus is, I think that's the goal, obviously there are sub-goals of what did the author mean to say in that culture and time, I think that's useful to not take fanciful leaps, I think that being grounded with some of those disciplines is helpful. I think we want to find Jesus in the Word, and we want the use of the Word to be helpful, and feeding people spiritually, rather than a dry and dusty intellectual exercise.

> **Andrew:** You mentioned the Jesus hermeneutic ... was that explicitly taught or at least demonstrated in [Ekklesia]?

> **DerekF:** Both explicitly taught and demonstrated, so Christ in all Scriptures, how can I find Jesus in Deuteronomy 24, was [Charles's] passion, that came across explicitly, not just implicitly ... [27]

The 'Jesus hermeneutics' here described was an instance of Ekklesia's normative appeal to the early church, given that a Christological hermeneutics was their

---

[26] This was an internal Ekklesia report, hence for reasons of anonymity, no reference can be given.

[27] While recognising that such an approach might come under all three of starting point, goal and process, in the tale it most closely resembles a process.

key distinctive (so Chapter 3). Despite public recommendation[28] and a few examples of Jesus hermeneutics, the approach was often aspirational, since there were limited opportunities to practice such hermeneutics due to the infrequent use of the Old Testament at Fellowship.[29]

Fellowship sermons made much use of biblical characters and events as examples for Christians and the church today. Due to the specific sermon series during the fieldwork, this was largely restricted to the life of Christ, with more extended comparisons tending towards allegory. So in S12f, five points from the story of Jesus' baptism in Matt 3:13–17 were seen as exemplary for a baptismal candidate. Exemplar hermeneutics were one of the commonest means of fusion in Holder sermons. A particularly telling instance was in S6h where John spoke on Acts 2:36–47:

> The Bible gives us five marks of a true spirit-filled church and they are contained in Acts chapter 2 verses 42 to 47 ... and I just want to bring out ... those five marks of a true, spirit-filled church ... and let's use them as bench marks ... let's hold them up here against [Holder] ... does this church meet these criteria?

Exemplar hermeneutics often took text and congregational horizons to be proximate, that is, to have little hermeneutical distance between them. Such proximate fusion was a notable feature of Holder sermons, so, for example, OwenH understood Christ's warning in Rev 2:16 for the church in Pergamum to directly apply to Holder. He declared 'we at [Holder] have been warned, the promises, the rewards are ours, or we face the sword' (S1h).

A widespread fusion practice in both churches was the juxtaposition and linking of biblical texts in many different Bible uses. This was the most distinctive 'ordinary' practice in the congregations, although it was not named, hence I refer to it as 'text-linking'.[30] In some continuity with the Reformation principle of 'Scripture interprets Scripture', text-linking was especially pronounced in the congregation's sermons and songs. JoeH was the main exponent of the practice in Holder sermons, explicitly linking eleven additional passages to his given text of Mk 11:1–19 in S2h. Dan at Fellowship managed to incorporate 19 separate passages into S9f, moving from one text to another, showing how they related to the theme of prayer. This premodern 'pearl-stringing' (introduced in Chapter 3) was evident in quite raw form in a thematic sermon on the crucifixion by BillF, in that ten passages were read one after another with little comment (S6f).

---

[28]   A clear statement of Christological hermeneutics was also given during ThursPM1, in an unexpected 'preach' from Martyn, who had been closely associated with Ekklesia.

[29]   During the Fellowship fieldwork, over 80% of passages were from the NT and so under 20 per cent from the OT.

[30]   This is more than the insider term 'cross-referencing', although it includes it.

The most intense text-linking, however, was found in songs.[31] One of the most popular songs at Fellowship during the fieldwork was *These are the Days of Elijah* (SF1047), which quoted, reconstructed, and referred to biblical texts from Dan 7:13, possibly Psa 14 and 15, Zec 9:9, and Jn 4:35 (KJV) amongst many others.[32] This song also was a prime example of 'this is that' or pesher hermeneutics which may be characteristic of charismatic hermeneutics, in that numerous connections are made between 'these … days' (this) and events cited from biblical history (that). Text-linking in Holder songs was also marked,[33] especially in comparison to the style of other hermeneutical practices in the congregation. Text-linking was a form of recontextualisation allowing for new understandings of text, although this could also have unintended deconstructive effects.

Allegorical hermeneutics, a venerable tradition from the premodern era (see Chapter 3), were not especially prominent in the congregations.[34] Songs, however, invited allegorical understandings more than other Bible uses, especially with regard to Old Testament terms such as enemies, city, Zion, Jerusalem, and love language from the Song of Songs. *The King of Love is My Delight* (SF1025) was an example of the latter at Fellowship, which drew on Song of Songs in the line 'My lover's breath is sweetest wine / I am His prize, and He is mine' (so Song 2:16, 6:3, 7:8–9).[35]

Much Bible use in public settings left fusion processes largely for congregants to see for themselves. Such 'minimalist' hermeneutics were most commonly seen in Bible display, liturgical uses and some songs. Biblical texts at Holder were presented as standalone in Bible display, leaving congregants open to decide on their sense. Both congregations favoured a Scripture reading at the start of a service as a prelude to worship, with the Psalms being a favourite. Sometimes a comment was made, so HarryH said of Psa 146: 'Let's stand and worship that Lord in song', and of Psa 96 MelissaF exclaimed: 'Isn't that wonderful? That's our God that we come to worship this morning', but on other occasions no comment was made. Minimalist hermeneutics particularly applied to some songs, especially dependent songs which function in a similarly minimalist way as liturgical readings.[36] The physical, virtual or liturgical context and congregational tradition had the potential to do partial hermeneutical work, underlining that

---

[31] 62% of Fellowship fieldwork songs were reconstructive, N=62.

[32] The music edition of *Songs of Fellowship* lists 19 Scripture references for this song (cited in Page, 2004: 89).

[33] 55% of Holder fieldwork songs were reconstructive, N=65.

[34] Two 'Words' at Fellowship made use of allegorical hermeneutics when drawing on Psa 123 (SunAM8f) and 1 Sam 17 (David and Goliath) (SunAM2f). One sermon at Holder paralleled the return of the exiles in Ezra 2 with the congregation's situation (S10h).

[35] Extract taken from 'The King of Love is My Delight' by Stuart Townend and J. K. Jamieson, Copyright © 1997 Thankyou Music*.

[36] E.g. *Lord Let Your Glory Fall* (SF1430).

'just the text' in a service is never 'just the text' hermeneutically. Nevertheless, there was ambiguity for congregants, as Chapter 7 explores further.

Small Group Processes

Fusion processes were notably diverse in Fellowship small groups, due to their variety of Bible uses and reasons for meeting. TuesAM was representative of the textual usage type observed in all Fellowship church Bible studies. DerekF addressed issues of authorship, audience, genre, literary structure, historical/ cultural context, brief references to the Greek and thematic emphases in the text. In short, this was a grammatico-historical approach with a few extras. Much of the exegetical work was done by questioning the group on these issues listed (along with some comprehension style questions), then steering them towards an answer, or in some cases providing explanatory information (e.g. the cultural situation of women addressed in Eph 5, TuesAM1). Attention to the text horizon was also attempted in Housegroup A, which aspired to a closer narrative reading of Mark's Gospel, mediated by a Bible Study Guide. Housegroup B was distinctively characterised by short intense bursts of text horizon engagement on matters of grammar and historical context from their professional theologian leader FrancisF.

Holder small groups had a sustained and more consistent degree of engagement with the text horizon than Fellowship. Closer readings of the text were prompted through comprehension-style questions in handout sheets and other aids, and group leaders frequently brought participants back to the text during the sessions. So AnnaH thought small groups 'different from going to church' as 'it's more to depth ... really, deep down in the Bible' so 'you learn more in housegroup' because 'we break it down'. There were regular references to a passage's context, aided partly by regular references to Study Bibles which provided some historical or literary information pertinent to the text. Attention to genre was marked by a default historicity, as in all Holder settings – so historical reference was made to Adam and Eve, Noah, Job, Jonah, Dorcas, and even the wife of noble character. Consideration of genre varied across Holder small groups, with the naming of narrative and their narrative 'gaps' occurring in Housegroup Y relatively often. Literary devices were occasionally perceived in the text, so, in Y3, Abimelech's words about Sarah's brother in Gen 20:16 were thought to be ironic. More daringly, in Y5, RodneyH tentatively spoke of Jas 3:1–12 as hyperbolic (esp. v6f) since it was 'passionate', 'emotive', and 'exaggerated' in order to 'evoke a suitable response'. Uncertainty about genre was also evident when RodneyH read the following 'fantastic' cross-referenced proverb in relation to Joseph (Gen 39) in Y4:

> Do you see a man who excels in his work?

He will stand before kings;
He will not stand before unknown men.[37]

In the short subsequent discussion regarding this proverb, there appeared to be some uncertainty as to whether this should be understood propositionally (and so a universal truth) or in some other way.[38]

Text-linking appeared to be the most distinctive hermeneutical practice within Holder small groups. It was more marked than in public liturgy and sermons, and more active than the passive variety experienced through songs. Indeed, text-linking seemed to be an instinctive practice for many group members, and was probably viewed as an important aspect of small group discipleship. A significant number of these biblical connections were mediated through cross-referenced Bibles and commentaries, as I will explore further in Chapter 7. Some text-linking followed the grain of the Bible's own self-interpretation, such as Mal 3:1 being used messianically within Mk 1:2–3 in X4. However, the practice was not always helpful, so the WedAM session based on a connection between Prov 31 (wife of noble character) and Acts 9 (story of Dorcas) provoked some difficulty for members as to how they informed each other. Most text-linking practice served to complement understanding of the text, but occasional reference was made to conflicting texts. The prevalence of text-linking at Holder required a high level of biblical knowledge within their small groups, a point reinforced by the language of many group members being permeated with strong scriptural echoes (cf. Hays, 1989).

Text-linking varied across Fellowship small groups. The practice was common enough in church Bible studies but was restrained by attention being focussed on particular passages of Scripture. In Housegroup A, their Bible Study Guide tried to mediate the Bible's internal text-linking, except in A4 when SteveF visited and linked eleven passages of Scripture on the theme of mission. Text-linking was not an instinctive fusion practice across all Fellowship small groups, which may have reflected their differing levels of biblical knowledge, evident in the perceived need for greater 'Bible passion'.

In a somewhat complex tension, the horizons of small groups and the biblical text were treated as distant *and* proximate by small groups in both congregations. The 'first pass' tendency for TuesAM at Fellowship was to make direct connections between text and context, minimising the distance between horizons. A telling example of this was during a discussion in TuesAM2 regarding slaves in Eph 6:5–9, as follows:

JasonF (leader): Anything strike anyone about … the next part of the passage?

---

[37] Prov 22:29 (NKJV).

[38] WedAM were also uncertain about the genre of Prov 31, regarding the 'noble wife'.

anonF: Well, slaves – just slaves, you can change it to servants ... I mean, people – people in employment, you know, rather than slaves.

This proximate and rapid fusion co-existed with some awareness of horizon separation in most TuesAM sessions. Such awareness was evident in group discussion which uncovered tensions between the participants' Christian experience and the text, as well as DerekF's mediated hermeneutics which contributed to disrupting the 'first pass' tendency. On relations between children and parents in Eph 6:1–4 there was a discussion, again in TuesAM2, where MaryF commented:

> It always seems very clear cut, doesn't it? Whereas today it's all the psychological stuff ... all to do with counselling and psychology, whereas that doesn't come into it here, it's that you do as you're told and you respect each other.

This complex tension was similar in other church Bible studies at Fellowship, although horizon distance had a greater stress by DerekF's deliberate design. Housegroups varied on this point, so apart from FrancisF's detailed grammatico-historical bolts from the blue, Housegroup B often took the text horizon to be particularly proximate to the group's experience. For example, after an impromptu reading of Psa 46 in B3, God 'making wars cease' in v9 was applied to a person in ill health and incorporated into prayer.

Holder small groups shared this complex tension, sometimes in quite explicit ways. HarryH prayed at the beginning of X3 regarding Mal 2:10–17:

> Lord God, I really do pray that you will open up new truths to us, help us to think about what the passage means to us, how we can apply the lessons that we learned to our lives, Lord God, what to mean to us as 21st century Christians in London, Lord God. Laws written so many thousands of years ago and yet still as relevant today as they were when they were written.

Here HarryH acknowledges the distance between horizons while also expressing confidence about the possibility of fusing horizons. RodneyH was more cautious at the beginning of a study on Job 1:1–2:10 in Y2. He warned 'we need to be on our guard since it is a familiar passage and we think we know what it means'. Some questions on handout sheets also recognised this potential distance, so in X5 groups were asked of Mal 3:6–12, 'How relevant do you feel this is to us today both personally and as a church?' On the other side of the tension, and driven by a hermeneutical goal of relevance, the rapid fusion of horizons was commonplace within Holder small groups. In its more pronounced form, this was evident through a 'multiple springboard' style of hermeneutics, similar to that practiced in Holder sermons. Such an approach touched upon the text briefly to bounce back into the group horizon, so a handout sheet in X1 pivoted on Mal 1 by asking '1a) Verse 2 tells us that the Lord was speaking directly to and specifically to Israel. How directly does the Lord speak to us today?' The ensuing discussion took the form of catechetical style exchanges regarding the group's own spirituality.

Exemplar hermeneutics were similarly held within this tension in small groups at both churches. Participants at Holder looked to the lives of biblical characters, such as Jesus, Job, Abraham, Joseph and Dorcas. The default move was to hold them up as examples and/or cautions, with some group discussion treating them in quite contemporary categories, so in Y2 Job was described as 'elder material' by RodneyH (cf. Job 1:5) and Potiphar's wife was said to be a 'bored housewife' by AngelaH in Y4. Some distance between these characters and group horizons were recognised, however, a point more to the fore in Fellowship, where David, Christ, and Paul in TuesAM were all seen as ideals to be imitated, where the ideal itself created distance.

There was some evidence that a Christological hermeneutics may contribute to slowing fusion down. In Holder small groups this fusion strategy was more explicit than in public settings. In Y2, for example, where Job sitting in the ashes (Job 2:8) was understood to point to Christ's sufferings, RodneyH explained that you 'have to train yourself to keep coming back to Christ'. Since the Christological move was rarely the first, it added a second potential move to the group's reading of the text. At Fellowship, with its more explicit Christological tradition, its operation was less clear in small groups, since the vast majority of hermeneutical work moved directly from Old Testament texts to the present.

There were some striking examples of one horizon readings that tended towards non-fusion, although this was limited to Fellowship. In their three studies using a Bible Study Guide on Mark's gospel, Housegroup A spent most of their time in the horizon of the text and made relatively few connections to the life experience of their members. The guide directed the group towards a closer reading of the text, through a relatively detailed focus on the narrative and theological framework of Mark's gospel. The one horizon reading that resulted was amplified by the group's adaptive use of the guide, which meant there was insufficient time to dwell in the group horizon. The opposite (and lesser) one horizon tendency was found in Housegroups B and C, with their strong emphases on the group horizon. The thematic use of Scripture in B meant that the Bible was taken as a series of reference points for framing their discussion. So in the B2 session on 'The Idolatry of Materialism and Narcissism', the tension between self-love and self-denial was explored through reading out sets of contrasting verses,[39] which then led to wide-ranging discussion in

---

[39] E.g. Matt 22:37–40 'You shall love your neighbour as yourself' vs Jn 12:25 'Those who love their life lose it, and those who hate their life in this world will keep it for eternal life' (NRSV).

the group's own horizon. Such springboard use also facilitated an emphasis on the group horizon. For example, in Housegroup C, Jesus' saying about faith that moves mountains (Matt 21:21) prompted a discussion in C1 as to its meaning for problems faced by some group members. One horizon reading was not particularly evident in church Bible studies, probably due to the pastor's influence, as one of the members, SteveF, explained:

> I do like ... the style that [DerekF] does, where you read through the Bible, Scripture, and you just go through it, bit by bit, looking at what it means, what the implication is of that. I love Bible studies where there's application, where there's learning, and you're learning about what it's saying ... and maybe even going back to the original stuff. And obviously, the culture content ... but I think it's key to have application, because otherwise you just go away going, "Oh, that was interesting". You forget it ...

In terms of direction of fusion, TuesAM and the other church-based Bible studies at Fellowship were largely one way, with a proclivity for starting with questions of exegesis then moving to points of application. In other words, it was akin to the classic hermeneutical 'two-step' with a linear movement from the text to group horizon. The final stage of the fusion process was prayer, described as 'praying this into our lives' – a practice that was common after Bible use in many Fellowship settings. The apparent intention was to make the results of the fusion process a spiritual reality for the group participants. The confident thematic use of the Bible in Housegroup B potentially allowed for more explicit two way fusion however.

Holder small groups were more intentional about fusing horizons, as seen in the prayers at the beginning of studies, in the frequent language of 'application', and in the fairly standard small group pedagogy observed. The pedagogical process took the form of multiple short discourse units which moved from the text to reader horizon, often prompted by hermeneutical 'pivot' questions. The process was even more marked in Housegroup Y, since 'application' was also a formal stage at the end of the session, with RodneyH talking of 'moving towards ... the application we take away' (Y4). Although there were sometimes initial discussion questions that prompted a light examination of the group horizon, fusion processes were intended to be largely one way in Holder small groups.

Personal Processes

Accessing fusion processes for personal Bible reading was necessarily different to public and small group settings. I did not go to congregants' homes and observe them reading the Bible on their own – not much would have been gained by this approach if I had. Instead, congregants were interviewed about their own Bible reading practices, and fusion processes were part of this.

Unsurprisingly, interviews elicited more explicit reflections on hermeneutical practice than in observing public and small group settings.[40] At Holder, context was raised as key for understanding Scripture by a number of church leaders. RodneyH stated: 'I think context is the number one thing'. HarryH held the conviction that 'the background and history' would 'enhance ... your understanding' and 'make it more real' and thus 'strengthen and deepen your faith'. HarryH also understood the context to 'guard against misinterpretation', which was a theme that framed the comments of five interviewees who critiqued Scripture being used out of context. JustinH gave what might have been an internal hermeneutical critique:

> So ... there are certain promises ... in Scripture, which I think can be taken quite
> out of context ... because they were relevant to the people at the time but can be
> seen to be one line catchphrases which Christians can perhaps take, but, actually,
> it's not so relevant for us today in that way. Yes, they are relevant, but not taken
> sort of literally, as maybe a short, out of context phrase might be considered.

For Fellowship interviewees, their more explicit accounts of fusion processes included context as a key feature. Its importance was raised by both leaders and non-leaders, who referred to literary, historical and cultural aspects of context. This sometimes had a Fellowship twist, as in BruceF's comments regarding his generally conservative views on homosexuality and the Bible:

> ... you've got to look at sources, you've got to try and take a view about whether
> cultural things have been added into this book that may or may not be what God
> is saying, because I do believe that this isn't a perfect ... it's a historical book, as
> well, that men have copied ... But, in the heart of it, there's enough to find out
> what God's saying.

Regarding what might be called 'theological context', some Fellowship interviewees such as SarahF thought it important to 'know the whole'. GordonF similarly thought interpretation was aided by 'having an overview of what God's about, what God's character [is] like, or how he reveals himself in the Bible'. However, this aspect of context was quite understated compared to Story references in public settings. Developing an overview of Scripture was a practice held in high esteem by leaders at Holder, with 'overview' being the deliberate

---

[40] Astley has underscored the importance of listening to ordinary theologians' accounts of their practice, not just observing practice (2013).

term, in contrast to 'story'. JustinH thought having an 'overview of the Bible' important because 'for some people in the church' the 'chronology of the Scripture and the events of the Bible are not always fully understood'. 'Story' was only used by KarlH who sat on the very edge of Holder tradition.

It was notable that just a few leaders at Holder referred to the practice of text-linking, so JoeH thought it important to 'allow Scripture to interpret Scripture'. Given the ubiquity of text-linking at Holder, particularly in small groups, there was very little explicit comment about the practice. This suggests that it was an intuitive and implicit practice rather than being known as a formal principle. This was also true of Fellowship interviewees, for whom text-linking hardly registered.

Christological hermeneutics were much more pronounced, both implicitly and explicitly in interviewees' comments at Fellowship, so reflecting their public hermeneutics and those of Ekklesia. Having learnt such hermeneutics on an Ekklesia course, TomF expressed it as: 'when we read the Bible, even the Old Testament, it's important to look at it in terms of Jesus being at the centre of the Bible and, really, the whole thing is about Jesus'. Despite the aspirational nature of Fellowship 'Jesus hermeneutics' discussed previously, their spread throughout Fellowship settings suggests that it was nevertheless a genuine hermeneutical tradition with the potential to impinge on fusion processes. For Holder interviewees, Christological hermeneutics were lacking in their accounts, matching their rarity in observed Holder settings.

Explicit reflection on fusion processes themselves was limited at Holder. In response to a question about interpreting Scripture, JustinH prioritised an examination of the text horizon in terms of 'the real essence of the communication at the time'. He continued by explaining 'to then draw from that, well, if that was what was happening then and that was relevant at that time, how can this potentially apply to us in our situation today? So, that there's a measure of consistency'. Given this excerpt was the most explicit characterisation of the fusion process I heard in any Holder setting, it may be argued that the fuller two horizon fusion process remained largely at the level of the intuitive and implicit.

There was more explicit discussion of fusion processes amongst interviewees at Fellowship, such as GordonF's 'two question' hermeneutical programme, namely 'What does it say? And what does it say to me?', which he expanded as follows:

> ... the "What does it say?" was because – and I've seen it demonstrated very usefully on a number of occasions – we so often come to the Bible with preconceptions and we don't actually read what's there, or we read the first half of a sentence and forget the second bit, especially when we remember it. So, the first thing is, "What does it actually say? What do the words mean?" Rather than what overlay we've put on them. And the second was, "What does it say to me?" If it's not relevant, then what am I reading it for? So, I've got to approach the Bible saying, "God,

show me how this is relevant to me". So, it's a very simple approach but one that I've found very useful.

Here GordonF addresses issues of context, grammar, relevance, as well as the danger of premature fusion in his language of 'preconceptions' and 'overlay'. In more sophisticated language, ReneeF distinguished between exegesis and hermeneutics as follows:

> My understanding is that "Exegesis" is looking at, you know, who wrote it and when they wrote it and who they were writing it to and what issues they might have been addressing and the culture of the people that it was addressed to ... And then "Hermeneutics" is saying, "OK, here are we now, in our culture, and everything that surrounds us, how do we apply it?" Is it the literal – what seems on the face of it, the literal meaning? Are there some deeper truths? Is it, in fact, not relevant to us in this culture today, but it might be to somebody else in another culture, or somebody else in another time?

In this excerpt, ReneeF underlines the importance of text horizon engagement as well as 'How do we apply it?', reflecting the two-step process observed in church-based Bible studies discussed previously. The importance of applying the Bible was a strong theme amongst interviewees, and interestingly was often spoken of in terms broader than the individual (e.g. situations, housegroup, society, life today). It may be that the idea of 'application' in the Fellowship context was the closest ordinary equivalent to the theoretical notion of 'fusion'. Notably, one response to the open-ended 'further comments' page in the questionnaire perceived a need for help with application, so:

> We need more help with practical application of the vast knowledge we have – not theoretical application! How does my Bible knowledge help others discover and follow Jesus for themselves? Understanding without practical application = boredom!

This might be understood as a plea for a more substantial hermeneutical tradition within Fellowship that would enable moving beyond one horizon readings to fusing the horizons of text and reader(s).

Interviewees in both congregations spoke strongly about the significance of being a Christian and the role of the Spirit when it comes to understanding the Bible. At Fellowship, MichelleF explained:

> ... before I become a Christian, there was lots of [the Bible], it was a big issue for me, and then when I became a Christian, they weren't an issue anymore. So, I

had lots of questions about [the Bible] prior to becoming a Christian and not so many afterwards.

The difference that a faith relationship made to hermeneutics was brought out further by GordonF when reflecting on a remembered saying regarding the need for both the Word and the Spirit in hermeneutics – a popular point across Fellowship settings. He continued:

> ... in terms of interpretation of the Bible, I take that to mean that if you want to understand it properly, then you have to ask God to help you. Maybe it's the end of second Corinthians,[41] where Paul talks about truth being spiritually understood, and that's clearly true in many cases. And I guess I've certainly found the longer I've been a Christian, the more I've read the Bible, and I hope the more I've asked God to help me understand that some things which twenty, thirty years ago, I found very difficult to read or didn't understand, now seem obvious. And it's not necessarily that someone has told me what it means, or that I understand English better, it's just that it takes time to understand God better and allow Him to speak through the Word.

Here a relationship with God and spiritual discernment is considered indispensable for understanding the text, beyond hermeneutical mediators and grammatical issues. Holder interviewees had strong and similar views on this point, as DennisH expressed it:

> ... the Bible will only speak to people who are open, who the Holy Spirit has actually opened their eyes ... because my eyes weren't open to what the Bible says, I didn't understand a word of it ... Until the Holy Spirit comes and, as the Lord says, "Take the scales away from your eyes" you'll never ever see what you're reading, you'll never understand it, until you become a child of God, where he's going to put the Holy Spirit in you and let you know about how he is and what his Word says and to understand it, it will never happen.

Here the action of the Holy Spirit is understood as a necessary requirement for fusing the text and reader horizons. Other interviewees also talked about the Holy Spirit as guiding, instructing, and speaking to them when reading Scripture. Being a Christian also made it possible to believe things in the Bible, so for DotH's husband: 'Even with creation, like with Darwin, he had to find out for himself that it was God that created it, and it was only like when you're a Christian that you really believe that'. This Spirit-enabled fusion might reduce the number of interpretations of a passage as well. When the issue of multiple (and

---

41   Probably 1 Cor 2:14.

possibly conflicting) interpretations was posed to MossH, he responded ' ... but what does your heart say? ... what is God's Spirit saying to me?' DennisH perceived such Holy Spirit fusion to result in interpretative uniformity at Holder, adding 'we're all part of the same wavelength' and 'think the same thing' – a perception that ties in with the significant degree of doctrinal homogeneity within the church.

Reflecting on Fusion Processes

Where does this tale of hermeneutical practices in congregations take us? Such a tale has rarely been told, hence there is value in telling the tale for its own sake. In addition, it is hoped that the particularities (and peculiarities) of practice described may prompt other congregations to reflect on their own practices through 'compare and contrast'. Indeed, the benefit of compare and contrast is already evident in telling Holder and Fellowship's story side by side. However, this tale also stirs up two larger questions about congregational hermeneutics. Firstly, 'How do such practices relate to normative and formal accounts of biblical hermeneutics?' and secondly, 'If there are differences, does it matter?' The second question might be formalised as 'On what basis do we assess congregational hermeneutics?'[42]

In response to the first question, posed initially in Chapter 3, hermeneutical traditions carried by church and academy through history have clearly had an influence on hermeneutical practices at Holder and Fellowship. Premodern practices especially had their counterparts in the two congregations, such as Christological readings, text linking (pearl-stringing/scripture interprets scripture), 'this is that' (pesher), and allegory. For Fellowship, this hermeneutical 'looking back' was quite intentional. Modern hermeneutical practices were also evident in adapted form through the grammatico-historical method and historical 'two-step' as described. Postmodern influences on hermeneutical practice were less obvious. They were mainly seen through Fellowship epistemology (so Chapter 6) and to a lesser extent through flashes of literary critique, the occasional voice that raised questions about interpretative interests and the somewhat tenuous sense of theological interpretation being both premodern and postmodern (so Chapter 3). Intentional ideological hermeneutics were interesting by their near absence from the congregations. It is important to observe, however, that hermeneutical practices in the congregations were not always straightforwardly derived from normative or formal hermeneutical traditions. Most practices had their own particular development set within specific Bible uses and settings that gave them their own hybrid distinctiveness, despite it being possible to trace connections to the larger tradition (albeit some traces were fainter than others).

---

[42] Or normative/formal hermeneutics for that matter.

This account of congregational hermeneutics clearly counters Brian Malley's work on evangelical hermeneutics and tradition in the United States (introduced in Chapter 1). Malley presents two theses, as follows:

> 1. Evangelicals are inheritors of an *interpretive* tradition, a species of belief-tradition in which a set of beliefs is transmitted along with the attribution of those beliefs to a text, the Bible. The tradition presents the text as an object for hermeneutic activity, but the goal of that hermeneutic activity is not so much to establish the meaning of the text as to establish transitivity between the text and beliefs. The tradition emphasizes the *fact* of connection more than of particular connections. And thus a great deal of "what the Bible says" may be transmitted quite apart from actual exegesis.
>
> 2. Evangelicals are not inheritors of a *hermeneutic* tradition, a socially transmitted set of methods for reading the Bible ... Rather, in each generation, the interpretive tradition mobilizes hermeneutic imaginations anew (2004: 73f).

According to Malley, the 'interpretive' tradition of (American) evangelical congregations consists of beliefs and their traditional connection to the Bible, without needing to engage with the particularity of the text itself, so there is no need for a 'hermeneutic' tradition. Although these points find some targets at Holder and Fellowship, they are insufficiently nuanced to account for the complexity of congregational hermeneutics. Firstly, such a characterisation employs too stark a distinction between 'interpretive' (belief) tradition and 'hermeneutic' tradition, and thus works with too narrow a definition of hermeneutics. Horizonal convictions, as has been seen, play a key role in shaping hermeneutical practices, such as horizonal starting points and goals. Secondly, his 'interpretive' tradition is overly cognitive in emphasis and underplays the way that beliefs are embedded in congregational discourses, actions, artefacts and mediators. The account here demonstrates that hermeneutical traditions can exist in evangelical congregations in terms of starting points, goals and processes. They did not conform to academic categories in every respect, nor were they especially explicit, particularly when considering processes, but there were patterns of hermeneutical practice within and across Holder and Fellowship that enabled congregants to make connections between text and context.

The second question extends debates about evaluating hermeneutics to congregations. As argued in previous chapters, the evaluative move is in keeping with the nature of practical theology study. The initial form of the second question is to ask whether it matters that congregations develop their own hybrid hermeneutical practices apart from the academy. Does it matter if congregants move between text and context rapidly, treating text horizons as being only minimally distant from the twenty-first century? Does it matter that congregants look for examples to follow or avoid in biblical characters? Does it matter if hermeneutical practices are largely implicit? Does it matter that Christ is taken as the key to reading Scripture? Does it matter if churches link texts from multiple Bible genres together? Does the Spirit not move in such hermeneutical practices?

Breaking the second question down further includes asking if hermeneutical practices from church history and the academy are models for the church today? If so, why? There is a common discourse expressed by those involved in theological education (especially ministerial formation), which tells how poorly churches read the Bible, measured against a benchmark of academic hermeneutical practice (i.e. how the experts do it). This discourse hits the mark in places, but what is missing is that it lacks nuance with regard to congregational practices, fails to address why such academic practices are the gold standard, and fails to adequately explain why congregational practices are lacking. In particular, the discourse often omits to clarify how academic hermeneutical practices are accounted for theologically within the church. How are behind/within/in front of the text approaches to be justified theologically? What is the place of premodern approaches in the church theologically speaking?

There are too many questions prompted by this tale to respond adequately to them all. I can, however, offer a partial response to what I consider to be the underlying question identified above as the question of hermeneutical criteria. There is no magic bullet which will provide objective criteria, as centuries of Christian history and academic effort have testified. The subjective criteria offered in this study emerge from both within and without the tale – that of virtue. As introduced in Chapter 2, the contention in this book is that virtue provides a theologically appropriate evaluative language for guiding both congregations and Christian scholars in their hermeneutical practices.

A recurring theme in this chapter is that hermeneutical practices were largely implicit. There was no silence of the Bible in Holder and Fellowship, but there was a strange silence of hermeneutics in terms of fusion processes (Smart, 1970). Such an exploration of congregational hermeneutics supports my claim in Chapter 1 that Peterson and others overstate the concern of Christian communities for *how* we read the Bible (2006: 81). This lack of explicit hermeneutics in the congregational accounts may be a particular instance of a general pattern within at least independent English evangelicalism. This is not to decry the more implicit patterns of hermeneutics observed in both churches, such as the mediation of a grammatico-historical-literary approach by the pastor at Fellowship, or the practice of text-linking within small groups at Holder. However, without naming and justifying some of these hermeneutical characteristics, such implicit hermeneutics are easily overwhelmed by more explicit aspects of congregational horizons.[43] Following on from Chapter 4, an explicit hermeneutical tradition could be built into explicit 'ruled readings' of Scripture. It is notable, within evangelicalism at least, that hermeneutical practices are rarely to be found in contemporary 'ruled readings', as has been discussed in Chapter 3. Developing a more explicit hermeneutical tradition within congregations would also allow for the growth of hermeneutical virtues aided by hermeneutical apprenticeship – points that will be developed in subsequent chapters.

---

[43] I am not suggesting that all things hermeneutical should be made explicit, as there is much that is intuitive and imaginative in fusion processes that cannot be expressed.

Chapter 6
Epistemology

If there is a word used less in congregations than 'hermeneutics', then 'epistemology' may well be a good contender. The 'E' word is not being used here for the sake of multiplying academic terminology, but because it was a highly significant category for congregational hermeneutics. Epistemology was not looked for in the churches, but it was found to be a key feature of their horizons that shaped hermeneutical practice. This resonates with Richard Palmer's assessment of epistemology (and ontology) for hermeneutics, when he observes: 'We ... see how decisive is our underlying theory of knowledge and our theory of the ontological status of a work, for they determine in advance the shape of our theory and practice in literary interpretation' (1969: 81). Similarly for theology, Alexander Jensen argues:

> One's epistemology will then shape one's hermeneutics, because what one believes to be the nature of religious knowledge will shape the way in which one sees religious knowledge understood and communicated (2007: 5).[1]

Epistemology is the study of knowledge which asks 'How do we know what we know?' (Wood, 1998). It is not confined to academic theorising, but, in Mary Healy and Robin Parry's words, 'it deals with matters at the heart of all our human engagement with the world, with other people, and with God' (2007: xi). In terms of congregational hermeneutics, epistemology describes[2] how congregants justified their beliefs and the perceived truth value of those beliefs, where those beliefs were linked to the Bible in some way. Such congregational or ordinary epistemologies were almost entirely implicit, even more so than their hermeneutics.

This chapter proceeds by first furnishing the discussion with some epistemological concepts, and then turns to examine the implicit epistemologies of Fellowship and Holder separately. Public, small group, and personal encounters with Scripture are recounted through the lens of epistemology for

---

[1]   William J. Abraham argues similarly for the importance of epistemology when he proposes a new subdiscipline called 'epistemology of theology' (2003: 66).

[2]   As per congregational hermeneutics, congregational epistemology is an expansion of the traditionally normative use of epistemology to the descriptive.

each congregation, leading into a reflection on what the tale of two churches illuminates for 'knowing the Bible'.

Speaking of Epistemology

There are a few epistemological ideas that will be helpful for speaking of epistemology in Holder and Fellowship. 'Critical realism' has already been identified as a particular epistemological stance (and more) in Chapter 2, summarised through its three pillars of ontological realism, epistemic relativism and judgemental rationality. In terms of epistemology, then, a critical realist stance sees our knowing as partial, provisional and mediated. Consequently, such a position is sometimes described as being subjective (to varying degrees). 'Direct realism', or 'common sense realism', or more pejoratively, 'naïve realism', is in some contrast to this position, in that our knowledge of the world around us, including texts such as the Bible, is known more or less directly and unmediated by other agents (Dretske, 1995: 202, 602). Therefore, such a stance is sometimes described as objective.

In terms of justifying our beliefs, 'foundationalism' is understood through a building metaphor. The foundations of our belief system are a set of basic beliefs which in themselves require no justification. These basic beliefs provide support to all of our other non-basic beliefs or 'noetic structure' and offer a sure foundation for knowledge, as well as eliminating any infinite regress of justification (Plantinga, 1983; Wolterstorff, 1984; Wood, 1998: 77f). Candidates for basic beliefs have classically been those that are 'self-evident', 'evident to the senses' or 'incorrigible' (Plantinga, 1983: 59).[3] In theology, basic beliefs have often been rooted in religious experience for those towards the liberal end of the spectrum and in an inerrant Bible for those towards the conservative end of the spectrum (Grenz and Franke, 2001: 23–4). By contrast, 'coherentism', as the name suggests, sees our beliefs as justified to the extent that they cohere with our existing beliefs. The asymmetry of justification in foundationalism is eschewed in coherentism for a 'noetic network' where beliefs may mutually justify each other (Wood, 1998: 114f; Grenz and Franke, 2001: 38f). These theoretical epistemological positions function as ideal types in relation to the implicit epistemologies of the two churches. Their fit to any of these positions is inexact, but they provide us with a map to navigate the epistemological terrain.

A language is also needed to speak of the multiple interpretations of the same Bible passages observed in the churches. As has been seen in Chapter 3, the polyvalency or indeterminacy of Scripture has been a matter for serious

---

[3]   'A belief is incorrigible if and only if no one could ever be in a position to correct it' (Dancy, 1985: 64).

attention throughout the history of the church.[4] Holder and Fellowship were no exception. Malley also refers in his study to the phenomenon of the Bible's 'indefinite interpretability' in small group Bible settings, also identifying relevance and group dynamics as factors. However, his distinction between the 'meaning of the passage' and 'what impressed' participants does not capture the nuances of hermeneutical practice found in the tale told here (2004: 125f). There is no consensus on preferred terminology,[5] so to aid clarity within congregational hermeneutics, I have made a distinction between *textual* and *reader* indeterminacy.[6] Textual indeterminacy is where readers perceive multiple interpretations as being a property of the text, whereas reader indeterminacy is understood to be produced by multiple reader perspectives.

Fellowship Epistemology

Fellowship's public epistemology might be described as subjectivist in orientation, with a reasonably good match to an implicit critical realism. A nexus of congregational characteristics shaped Fellowship's public epistemology, namely a *low authority emphasis*, *marked informality* and *epistemic caution*. These characteristics were also aligned with the Bible passion explored in Chapter 4. A low authority emphasis was noticeably evident in their leadership style and flat leadership structure, in a deliberate break from the reported high authority approach of Ekklesia. The low authority emphasis also contributed to the autonomy of their housegroups, a lack of concern for doctrinal boundaries, disavowal of interpretative certainty and particularly the cautious language of preaching.

A most striking aspect of Fellowship identity was a pronounced informality that pervaded the congregation to the extent that it might almost be described

---

4   Christian Smith has placed indeterminacy at the heart of his critique of American evangelical 'biblicism', where he argues that 'pervasive interpretive pluralism' fatally undermines inerrancy and associated biblicist assumptions (2012).

5   A. K. Adam distinguishes between 'integral' and 'differential' hermeneutics, where the former seeks a 'legitimate path to correct interpretation' and he argues for the latter which 'permits [academic] practitioners to see in interpretive variety a sign of the variety in human imagination' (2004: 25, 29). Stephen Fowl distinguishes between 'determinate', 'anti-determinate', and 'underdetermined', and argues for the latter (1998). David Clines has argued that the varieties of indeterminacy he has encountered in different contexts leads him to conclude that there is an indeterminacy of indeterminacies (1995: 17).

6   The notion of distinguishing between types of indeterminacy is drawn from Charles Cosgrove's work in this area (2004: 5–6), but the ethnographic accounts did not require nor fit the particular types he proposed.

as ruled informality.[7] For example, although the main Sunday service started at 10.30am officially, I soon discovered that almost nothing started at its advertised time in Fellowship. There were many other indicators of informality: the congregation often continued talking when the leader had started the service;[8] the collection was taken with very little ceremony; preachers and speakers used a hand-held microphone enabling them to move around when leading and especially when preaching; the language of service leaders and preachers was notably colloquial; everyone dressed casually for church; formal liturgy was used infrequently; the school hall in which they met had no traditional Christian symbolism or artefacts; and a certain form of spontaneity in congregational services appeared to be prized. Synonyms for 'informal' include casual, colloquial, relaxed, simple, unceremonious, unconstrained and unofficial (McCleod, 1986: 269), and all these terms resonated with the practices observed at Fellowship, and not just in public settings. This informality was also coherent with the low authority nature of the congregation, both of which were consistent with a tendency to epistemic caution at the church.

Epistemic caution was evident in the notable freedom in Fellowship public discourse to raise questions about the status, value or coherence of the biblical text.[9] In Ian's words 'when we are dealing with the Bible, we are not dealing with an easy book, we're not dealing with a book that we don't have to wrestle with' (S1f). Caution was expressed by BobF, amongst others, when preaching on Matt 5:25f, since 'there may be lots of ways of understanding this' (S2f). However, epistemic caution was most evident in the language of some speakers through the use of terms such as 'may(be)', 'possibly', 'perhaps', 'seem(ed)', and 'think' in relation to the Bible, with statements of certainty being quite rare. The sermonic exception that provided a stark contrast to this tendency was the visiting speaker Dan who spoke with an unusual degree of certainty for Fellowship, both linguistically and hermeneutically (S9f). In conversation with BobF afterwards, he commented obliquely that sometimes teachers talk at people rather than to them and can be very authoritative (SunAM8f). Many songs, however, were in tension with the prevailing epistemic caution of Fellowship public horizons, being a genre that deals mainly in epistemic confidence, and some Words also had a strong note of confidence.[10] Nevertheless, epistemic caution was a significant aspect of Fellowship's public horizon, and as such, allowed for a certain indeterminacy in their public hermeneutics.

----

[7]   The wider cultural influences that may have occasioned such a congregational subculture have been addressed by David Bebbington (2007: 12f).

[8]   E.g. SunAM1f, SunAM2f, SunAM8f.

[9]   E.g. S1f, S2f, S3f, S6f.

[10]   Although it was noticeable that such confidence was expressed in the language of 'feeling'. So AnneF gave a Word on Psa 123, framed with the phrases 'I really felt some of [Psalm 123] laid on my heart … ' and 'the bit that I felt really challenged about' (SunAM8f).

Small groups exhibited an intensification of Fellowship's implicit epistemology, where an operant epistemic relativism appeared to obtain. Key characteristics contributing to this intensification were *group dynamics*, *informality* and *low authority*, which in turn allowed for greater *questioning of the Bible* and *hermeneutical indeterminacy*.

Group dynamics were a particularly important characteristic of Fellowship small groups,[11] as FrancisF explained of Housegroup B:

> I like to have an open style of discussion but, at the same time, I do have a clear sense in my mind of where the discussion ought to be headed, and I like to give everybody an opportunity ... to contribute freely ... I tend to ... a fairly open agenda.

His wife and co-leader, SarahF, amplified this point by commenting 'that's why we have a housegroup that's a free for all, and people say outrageous things, sometimes, but it's almost, I going to throw this bomb in ... better to let them have a freedom rather than rein them in'.

Small group leaders thought it important for group discussion to be open-ended and free, even in the more structured church Bible studies. For example, DerekF explained his perception of the TuesAM Bible study format to a newcomer, by saying: 'We usually just pick out things that strike us and talk about them for a while before we pray' (TuesAM4).[12] The opening gambit of 'Anything strike you about that passage?' or some such equivalent was quite common in Fellowship small groups,[13] and could facilitate open-ended discussion. One leader of Housegroup C, GordonF, saw such freedom as crucial for building community, which could be gained through:

> ... people just chatting together, to some extent, it's gained more significantly if people share on a spiritual basis, and a Bible study by people where it seemed worthwhile for anyone to say, "This is what I think", or, "This is how I understand it", can build that sense of community, whereas, teaching, of itself, I don't think does. I guess it could if you had a very strong teaching, if people felt they were all followers of a particular teaching ... but it doesn't build the same intra-relations.

Here the building of group relationships through discussion appears to be of greater importance than arriving at a particular understanding of Scripture (cf. Bielo, 2009b; Todd, 2013). Notably, GordonF also implies a diversity

---

[11] On the significance of group dynamics for small group hermeneutics, see Lanser-van der Velde (2004).

[12] But this perception did not appear to match practice, as was seen in Chapter 5.

[13] E.g. JaneF in A3 and SarahF in B3.

of theological positions within small groups in this excerpt, itself a wider characteristic of Fellowship.

The informality of public settings was also evident in all small groups through their flexible attitude to time and relaxed social dynamic, although this characteristic was more pronounced in housegroups.[14] Informality elided into a low authority approach, seen in the leading of Bible studies being shared out amongst group members,[15] sometimes as an explicit discipleship strategy.[16] This resonated with the informality and low authority of Fellowship's public horizon, although there may have been some internal mediation *from* small group *to* public horizons, due to their autonomy and greater longevity than the congregation in some cases.[17] These interconnected characteristics of Fellowship small groups (group dynamics, informality, low authority) meant that insisting on particular interpretations or confronting the interpretations of others was uncommon, since it would be out of step with group identity (cf. Stackhouse, 2004: 23f). Contributions to group discussion were given with a degree of epistemic caution, although this was not as distinctive as in public settings, particularly in the church Bible studies.

These small group characteristics also allowed for more directly epistemological characteristics, such as the respectful questioning of the text seen in Housegroups A and C. PenelopeF, one of the leaders of Housegroup A, wanted the group to 'feel they can ask questions' and the members of A concurred, so RossF said: 'It's a place where you can question things and get some answers ... or people offer answers'. According to the other group leader, GrahamF, this questioning characteristic may have been heightened, since 'what's good is that we've got some really bright people in the housegroup, I don't mean one or two, I mean, across the range'.[18] Furthermore, PenelopeF saw this questioning characteristic as distinctive of the Ekklesia tradition in interview:

> ... I think that's one of the things we liked about [Ekklesia], that there was more encouraging people to use their brains, to think things through, to question and to view the other end ...

> I don't know if it was a clear picture but there just seemed an atmosphere of more, you could ask questions and if you had problems with something, that was OK, you could voice them.[19]

---

[14] In Housegroup A, the 'formal' proceedings began up to 1¼ hours after the official start time. All housegroups allowed for lengthy periods of social interaction.
[15] E.g. Housegroups A and B, ThursAM.
[16] MichelleF, conversation, 13/3/05.
[17] So Housegroups B and C, both FrancisF and GordonF in interview.
[18] See educational level statistics in Chapter 1.
[19] Note the assumption that this Ekklesia tradition was also Fellowship's.

Such questioning was evident in Housegroup A's study of Mark's Gospel, where the logic of the narrative provoked questions somewhat independently of their Bible Study Guide. For example, FlorenceF asked, 'How was Jesus managing to sleep?', given the waves breaking over the boat in the storm in Mk 4:37–8. No explanation was offered that was thought satisfactory (A1). Theological 'knots' in the text also prompted questioning, such as in Mk 6:52, where it refers to the disciples' hearts being 'hardened' (A3). This text provoked some fascination for JasonF since he could not decide what it meant – a knot that may have been exacerbated by the inherited Arminian stance of Fellowship. His response was to search out other occurrences of 'hardening' in the Bible, but neither this strategy nor my tentative suggestion of a narrative explanation for the verse[20] removed the difficulty for JasonF, and thus the knot was left unresolved in the session. Other examples reinforced the questioning characteristic, such as Jesus' commands 'not to let anyone know' in Mk 5:43 and similarly in 8:26, with group members commenting that this was very strange and that it doesn't make any sense. Speaking of a non-fieldwork session in Housegroup A, RossF had asked 'Why did Jesus need to be baptised?' and although 'we didn't really get an answer on it', he was sure there was one (interview). The questioning characteristic of Housegroup A and other Fellowship small groups indicated a view of Scripture that permitted some critical examination and yet expected the text to be coherent, as the examples above imply.

Closely connected to the characteristics described above, a significant degree of hermeneutical indeterminacy and its concomitant reduced concern for resolving textual meaning was observed throughout Fellowship small group settings. The most frequently mentioned benefit of small groups in interviews was exposure to multiple understandings of Scripture. NinaF explained 'I do like when [Bible study] was opened up for everyone to say what they think, because we all understand very differently, it doesn't mean they're wrong or right, but understanding' so 'it's like each time when we read, we understand something very different'. Others wanted to reserve more judgement, so SteveF thought it 'good to hear other people's opinions' as they may 'say stuff that is completely what you don't think' which is a 'challenging thing'. Although it was not made explicit whether interviewees were referring to textual or reader indeterminacy, the latter was implied by most interviewees, as one of Housegroup A's leaders, GrahamF, explained:

... you do see a wide variety of interpretation, and often, I don't think there's necessarily one understanding for one particular point. Sometimes there's more

---

[20]   i.e. that the disciples were to see more of Jesus in [Mark] Chapter 8, and this serves as a contrast, given the special turning point in Chapter 8 (Fieldnotes, A3).

than one aspect of God that comes out, through one particular passage ... and when you have a number of people look at it, then you see that reflected.

TheresinaF thought such reader indeterminacy beneficial, so:

> **TheresinaF:** ... people have different ways of looking at different verses from the Bible, and you still get different interpretation, and sometimes you just think, "Wow, I never thought of it in that way" ... and it's just great to hear that from somebody, after reading it yourself, to get what the other people are getting from the same verses ...

> **Andrew:** If you're getting these different interpretations, how do you judge between?

> **TheresinaF:** I don't really judge, I just think, "Wow, is that what he thinks?"

This strong indeterminacy may not have been shared to the same extent by all interviewees, but it does seem likely that the value placed on generating 'different interpretations' within small groups would reduce concern for judging between them (so also NinaF above). MattF amplified this point when he spoke very positively of a 'big old nice discussion' in a large mixed group of young people[21] which 'wasn't meant to be aggressive or attacking' on the theme of men and women and God in the Bible. The Bible study was 'just set up with the intention of not coming to any kind of ... conclusive point'. He recognised that some churches did not allow women to be in leadership, and even though 'I'm not entirely sure I agree with that' he did 'respect the fact that they are drawing from biblical sources to enforce that' and concluded that he was 'unresolved'. For MattF, indeterminacy was seen as something to be encouraged and celebrated – a spiritual good. Although the resolution of texts was not ruled out, nevertheless there was an almost sacramental value ascribed to the exchange of differing text interpretations. It would seem that this celebration of reader indeterminacy in Fellowship small groups, in combination with their other epistemological characteristics, suggests that a functional textual indeterminacy was also implicitly operative. Having said this, the epistemological characteristics described here were less marked in church Bible studies, since the pastor directed them towards a greater resolution of meaning.

Hermeneutical indeterminacy was understood to result partially from God speaking to individuals in relevant ways through Scripture, and therefore multiple interpretations were produced to account for the multiple individual horizons within a small group. As discussed in Chapter 4, it may be that the

---

21   Outside of Fellowship, but within the Ekklesia network.

practice of Words also fostered indeterminacy in small group settings, due to members having learned to expect that God will speak to them (including through the Bible) in ways relevant to their own lives. However, hermeneutical indeterminacy was also understood to cultivate a mutual hermeneutics, whereby group members learnt from and sometimes were challenged by each other's understandings of Scripture. In addition, the freedom to ask critical questions of the text appeared to encourage genuine attention to the text horizon.

The strong theme of hermeneutical indeterminacy in Fellowship small groups was echoed in personal settings,[22] through interviewees having some degree of *comfort with unresolved Bible difficulties* (see Appendix F). For example, MattF spoke of the 'two creation stories' in Genesis, noting 'there's so many sort of theories and response to what happened' and so 'a part of me doesn't really want to know for certain'. Similarly MichelleF and PenelopeF were not unduly concerned with resolving their interpretation of Gen 1–3 more fully, describing the resolution of the issue as 'a red herring' (MichelleF) and 'not that important' (PenelopeF).[23] Others were slightly less comfortable with unresolved texts, so AmyF struggled with passages that might imply a doctrine of predestination, and acknowledged that 'we're not meant to understand everything', adding 'there's things that are bigger than us and my relationship with God is more important than my understanding of one particular issue'. However, she added that when the interpretation 'hits home … I tend to get more like "No, I want an answer to this"'. NadineF wondered about texts that might be related to healing, concluding 'I just tell myself, you have to trust and you can't see the full picture'. For both of these women, hermeneutics was perceived as a task carried out in the primary context of a relationship with God, which for them put resolving textual meaning in perspective.[24]

There was also a minority tendency towards greater resolution of textual meaning, once again indicative of Fellowship's heterogeneous nature. This has already been noted of DerekF-mediated small groups, but there were other minority tendencies as well. ReneeF was particularly exercised about hermeneutical indeterminacy, through an encounter at University with a friend who 'thought all Christians should be teetotal, and he argued Scripture to persuade me'. Her gut feeling was that 'alcohol's OK', which was a puzzle for her, since 'how can we be two Christians and reading the same Bible and coming up with different arguments?' In response, ReneeF explicitly identified the process of exegesis as putting 'limits on what [the text] could have meant', and she mediated this and related points in her Housegroup C (see Chapter 7).

---

[22] Interviewee comments on indeterminacy tended to focus on small groups.

[23] Interviewees tended to dissociate themselves from 'literal' readings of Genesis, which BruceF implied were 'fundamentalist'.

[24] A point also made regarding the role of the Spirit at Fellowship in Chapter 5.

A few congregants also appeared to take a view related to the perspicuity of Scripture. For example, WilliamF spoke to me after a Sunday service regarding a four-fold approach to interpreting the Bible, with one aspect being to 'take the Bible as it was' (SunAM11f). More explicitly, GordonF employed a hermeneutical Occam's razor in talking about 'a straightforward interpretation of the text', which he explained as 'I have a bias towards a feeling that if you can understand the Bible in a straightforward way, that ought to be the right way'. He added later that 'some parts of the Bible ... are so clear that they don't really need interpretation, or, at least, clear for most of the time', acknowledging that for 'other parts ... changes in time and culture' means there is 'more need for interpretation'.

Holder Epistemology

Closely associated with the Bible-centredness identified in Chapter 4, Holder appeared to operate with an implicit foundationalist epistemology. This was observed through a network of features that were coherent with a foundationalism of the Bible. In apparently explicit language, HarryH prayed of the Bible during a service, ' ... Lord God, we thank you that it is the solid truth, the rock on which we can base our lives ... ' (SunAM8h).[25] This made more explicit what was implicit in much of Holder's public discourse – that Christian faith was understood through making the Bible foundational for Christian faith.[26] As OwenH asked in a sermon 'if you can't really trust the Bible, what else can you put your trust in? What is there that's more reliable than Jesus?' (S12h). Since Holder's noetic structure appeared to be founded on basic beliefs about and derived from the Bible, it was not surprising that Holder speakers expressed a good deal of certainty about what 'the Bible says', in contrast to a 'world that's filled with uncertainty' (OwenH, S12h). Such certainty meant that questioning the text in public was very rare and even then muted when it occurred. When preaching on Ezra 2, OwenH anticipated that the congregation might find it unpromising material, but his response was to declare 'I'm a good evangelical, I believe that all Scripture is profitable' (S10h). Coherent with this certainty was the tendency of most Holder preachers to speak authoritatively and sometimes with raised voices.

A key basic belief for this foundationalism was Holder's default assumption of historicity, made explicit in S8h regarding the virgin birth, and in S10h regarding the detailed accounts in Ezra 2. Of the latter, OwenH commented:

---

[25]   Notably such characteristics might well be applied to Christ.
[26]   This resonates well with the ordering of Affinity's doctrinal basis (see Chapter 4).

Historians would have been salivating over such an account. To us it looks boring –
but such an accurate, specific list of people, also numbers, jobs, actions – what we
need to remember is that these are real people, real events and real history ... these
are real names that are going to last through all eternity.

Similarly, in Theo's much vaunted sermon on the parable of Abraham and Lazarus
(Lk 16:20–31), the 'chilling realities' of heaven and hell were addressed in a
surprisingly historically realist fashion (S9h).[27] As will be seen, this assumption
of historicity was yet more explicit in small group and personal settings.

The expression of a direct realism, which seemed to diminish the
hermeneutical task, further cohered with Holder's implicit foundationalism.
Indeed, KarlH described Holder's approach to the Bible as 'positivist', although
he was a fringe and sometimes critical congregant. Such direct realism was
evident in S1h when OwenH was fusing Rev 2:14–15 with the congregational
horizon. He stated 'we don't want our own teaching to come across, we only
want to teach what Jesus Christ wants the children and the young people to
know and to learn'. Similarly prayers said before the sermon Bible reading or the
sermon nearly always expressed the desire for God to speak through the preacher,
and that the human contribution would be small, for example DougH prayed
for JustinH before he preached as follows: 'we pray that as [JustinH] speaks to
us now, we pray that he would speak only your words ... reveal to us the truth
that you have prepared for us today' (SunAM3h). Here and in other prayers, the
sermon was understood as revelatory. That Scripture may be apprehended in this
direct form was heightened by regular use of the phrase 'the Bible says' and other
Bible personifications[28] along with a strong emphasis on how the Bible 'speaks
the truth *very clearly*' (OwenH, S12h). Associated with this direct realism was
a diminishing of hermeneutical indeterminacy, which seemed to be implied
when OwenH satirised the possible situation for the leaders of the church at
Pergamum in Rev 2 as: 'We're not going to agree on everything, but, well, we'll
just have a few different interpretations' (S1h).

There were a number of remarks in sermons, however, that acknowledged a
very limited hermeneutical indeterminacy of even the textual variety. OwenH
noted wryly of Rev 2:17b that 'there are ten different translations of what
this means, all the commentators in the six books I read, they all completely
disagree' (S1h). This comment could be understood as relativising the value
of commentaries, although its tone was somewhat ambiguous. The Holder
homepage also made reference to the need for *explaining* God's Word, as has been
seen (in Chapter 4), which may imply some recognition of the hermeneutical

---

27   Given Theo's opening remarks 'I don't want to go in for medieval literalism here, this
is not meant to be history'.
28   Also 'The Bible teaches / describes / tells us / gives us'.

task, although it is also coherent with Holder's emphasis on congregational boundaries and authoritative teaching. The tension between this very limited public indeterminacy and the realist, foundationalist epistemology was not addressed or resolved in public discourse.

Small groups at Holder had the key epistemological function of being a safe testing ground for Holder's tradition. This was seen through the groups *encountering problems in resolving the meaning of texts* and also in *significant exposure to bounded indeterminacy*. In certain respects, Holder small groups were carriers of their public epistemology, although they were far less explicit. Bible-centredness was implicit in the practice of numerous small group Bible studies meeting frequently to study the Bible, especially as Bible study was their main focus and the majority of the congregation participated regularly.[29] More explicit aspects of Bible-centredness were also noticeable – so in a rather Bible-centred impulse, HarryH stressed the importance of 'good, solid, Bible-based teaching' and 'quiet devotional times' as one way of avoiding the 'low spiritual ebb' of 'God's people' in Mal 1 (X2h).

There were two main types of problem with the text in Holder small groups. Firstly, there were problems with understanding the meaning of a passage, such as Mal 3:1–5 in X4h:

> See, I will send my messenger, who will prepare the way before me. Then suddenly
> the Lord you are seeking will come to his temple; the messenger of the covenant,
> whom you desire, will come", says the LORD Almighty (v1, NIV).

The issue here was whether the passage referred to Christ's first or second coming or both.[30] Prompted by the hand-out sheet questions, references to 'my messenger' and 'the Lord' were initially identified as John the Baptist and Jesus respectively. However, SiobhanH struggled to see how this corresponded to a perceived language of judgement in v2–5, causing her to remark 'he didn't judge us on his first coming, did he?' The leader, JamesH, who acknowledged his dependence on a commentary by James Montgomery Boice, supposed that the passage 'can be looked at with the two senses'. This passage provoked problems for the group as they did not find it matched a messianic and/or an eschatological interpretation exactly, and therefore its meaning was not fully resolved for all members during the session.

The second type of problem was where the text appeared to be in tension with doctrine, experience or reason. In the Y2h study on Job 1:1–2:9, the leader, RodneyH, asked 'Who struggles with this?', probably following the Bible Study

---

[29]   77% of respondents attended housegroups (N=105), with 75% of attendees attending always or nearly always (N=80).

[30]   Possible historical referents for the passage were not discussed.

Guide (Nystrom, 2000: 16). Regarding doctrinal conflict, PaulH said he was surprised to find Satan in the throne room of God (cf. Job 1:6), and in interview, DennisH explained he had 'found that kind of funny' since 'God banished [Satan] from heaven'. No answer was found for this tension in the session. Tensions also arose between the text and group members' experience and reasoning. In response to a hand-out question arising from Mal 1:2–3 in X1h, SiobhanH found it hard to 'consider God's elective love', asking why God had chosen her and not her husband? After all, she had done lots of things wrong. In interview she explained that the doctrine of election had 'overwhelmed' her when she first encountered it at Holder and 'out of everything that knocked my faith'. The relative priority given to reason and especially experience in small group hermeneutical discourse was significant when compared to public settings.

The second key epistemological distinctive found in Holder small groups was exposure to multiple understandings of the same text, or hermeneutical indeterminacy – something that was quite rare in congregational settings. The multiple meanings of Mal 3:1–5 in X4h above was a good example of textual indeterminacy. A number of narrative studies in Housegroup Y also lent themselves to demonstrating indeterminacy towards the textual end of the spectrum. For example, there was a discussion as to whether Joseph was tempted by Potiphar's wife in Gen 39:1–23 (Y4h). The co-leader, PaulH, asked 'Where is, in the narrative, any suggestion that Joseph was tempted by [Potiphar's] wife?' He added: 'She was trying to tempt him, but was he tempted?' and concluded 'We don't know'. PaulH reiterated the indeterminacy of the text by adding 'I'm not sure, from the passage, that we can tell whether he's tempted or not'. Strikingly, hermeneutical indeterminacy was the predominant theme for interviewees when talking about housegroups, mostly of the reader type, as WendyH explained:

> I think it's a good forum to actually talk about how we understand things. Because I think it's quite interesting when we do study Scripture, how one of us can believe one – **not huge doctrinal thing**, but we could have understood one thing from a verse and somebody else could read something quite different. [My emphasis]

Significantly, distinguishing between text and reader indeterminacy was rare, with only DennisH noting any sort of difference. He agreed with reader indeterminacy, but specifically denied textual indeterminacy, saying 'there's no disagreement in what the Word is actually saying, just a different version of how they actually see it'. Some interviewees, like WendyH in the quote above, understood reader indeterminacy in housegroups to be bounded, which was coherent with the explicit distinction between salvation and secondary issues that emerged in personal settings below.

At first this degree of indeterminacy appears to be in rather stark contrast to that expressed in public settings. This was nuanced, however, by the number and nature of (almost always courteous and friendly) disagreements that took place within Holder small groups. Disagreements were sought for a pedagogic purpose in Housegroup Y, as one of its leaders, RodneyH, acknowledged that 'I wanted to push the barriers and I wanted to really challenge people to make sure they knew what their Scriptures were'. In this pedagogic spirit, RodneyH had suggested (in a session prior to the fieldwork) that the book of Jonah 'was just a story to illustrate Christ'. RodneyH recalled that in response the group 'rallied round' saying 'Oh don't be ridiculous', causing them to 'go away and find verses' so the exercise was 'very beneficial'. The incident had become a traditional point of banter within the group by the time I joined. Notably, during interview, RodneyH wanted to 'say for the record' that 'Jonah is a historical fact'. This was a clear instance of the boundedness of any hermeneutical indeterminacy within small group discourse.

Other small groups observed did not court controversy in the same way as Housegroup Y, but still had plenty of less provoked disagreement regarding the text. Possibly the strongest example of disagreement came about in Housegroup X on Mal 3:6–12 when KarlH disputed the relevance of tithing in the passage for Christians today (X5h). He foresaw 'a whole series of problems ... with applying this principle to us' from Malachi, which was 'deeply unbiblical'.[31] What seemed to be underlying many of these disagreements was an implicit assumption that a correct understanding of the text may be achieved. The frequency and style of disagreements tended towards a more objectivist approach to biblical interpretation, compatible with the foundationalist epistemology witnessed in congregational settings, although this was significantly restrained in small groups by a limited but genuine indeterminacy.

Regarding personal horizons and epistemology, a marked *rationalist emphasis* for hermeneutics, a tendency towards *resolution of textual meaning*, a *limited hermeneutical indeterminacy* and a *'taking it as it is' perspicuity* were the four distinctive issues inferred from interviewees' accounts at Holder.

Firstly, personal Bible reading (PBR) was described by interviewees using educative language such as teaching, training, instructing, informing and learning, although the language of rebuke and challenge was also common.[32] Although never made explicit, such language pointed to a marked rationalist emphasis for PBR hermeneutics, which was similarly evident in the other

---

[31]   Strong language indeed within Holder discourse.

[32]   It would seem highly likely that some of this language reflected the mediation of 2 Timothy 3:16 – 'All Scripture is God-breathed and is useful for teaching, rebuking, correcting and training in righteousness, so that the man of God may be thoroughly equipped for every good work'. (NIV).

Holder settings. This cohered with Holder's concern for maintaining doctrinal boundaries and so the need for a correct understanding of Scripture, as well as the high premium placed on Bible knowledge – itself related to the congregation's Bible-centredness. It is likely that the tendency to treat the Bible propositionally, with the category of 'story' being eschewed, also contributed to this rationalist emphasis. Ameliorating this effect to a small extent was the *hermeneutica sacra* also spoken of by interviewees which emphasised the Spirit's role in the hermeneutical process (see Chapter 5).

The second epistemological issue was a drive towards resolution of textual meaning,[33] evident when interviewees were asked if there were any parts of the Bible or related doctrines that they (had) found difficult to understand. The pastor, OwenH, only slightly flippantly replied 'Yeah, where do you want to start?' The many passages cited by interviewees divided into two types of difficulty – those where it was difficult to find any relevance for today, and those which raised potential theological/moral/rational objections. For this latter group it was notable that creation was not raised as a difficult issue, with JoeH indicating that 'the majority of the church would be ... creationists'. As was seen in Chapter 4, LucyH tellingly captured the limited degree of tension and typical Holder resolution when wondering about whether the children 'ever had a chance' in The Flood and 'what will happen to them?' Her resolution was to say to God 'But you are sovereign' – which was often the conclusion to interviewees' Bible difficulties. Somewhat ironically, the commonest Bible difficulty was with aspects of Calvinistic doctrine, expressed in moving terms by some interviewees, so WendyH:

> It was soon after I became a Christian, and we had a visiting preacher come to [Holder] ... And he went into the theory of predestination. And this lady who I'd gone to, she brought me to [Holder] first, she was very kind to me and she explained to me exactly the Scriptures involved. And I went away and I thought about it and I prayed and I read it for myself, and I cried and I prayed and I cried, and I begged God that it wouldn't be true. And now I've just had to accept that, yeah, He knows – and I do believe that He knows just what he's doing ... I don't like it but I believe in it.

It seems likely that, given the prominence of Calvinistic teaching, particularly in Holder's past, it was not easy for congregants to avoid engaging with difficult aspects of Calvinistic doctrine. Both of these examples reflected a Holder attitude that wanted to move towards hermeneutical resolution, even if 'I don't like it' (WendyH) since 'in the end, I have to get over it' (IonaH). A strong example

---

[33] This is another aspect of hermeneutical indeterminacy, but it is treated separately here to emphasise the distinctive aspects of the same concept.

of this tendency was given by RodneyH, who would 'rather have a belief ... that can be contradicted, rather than leave something open and then not really know, be in the grey area'. Many other interviewees talked of passages that *had* been difficult for them, but now they had come to some sort of resolution. Underlying this tendency was an objectivist epistemology, where lack of resolution was only a temporary state, rather than an intrinsic property of the text.

The third epistemological issue was again of hermeneutical indeterminacy, which was nuanced further by many interviewees appealing to a distinction between salvation issues and secondary issues. Such a distinction is at least centuries old (Thiselton, 1992: 181), although no reference was made to its traditional nature. OwenH spoke of 'different interpretations amongst different Evangelicals' that were 'secondary' because they '[don't] have an impact on issues of faith and salvation'. So indeterminacy was bounded, in that it was permitted for secondary issues, but salvation issues were ring-fenced against hermeneutical indeterminacy, although whether this was textual or reader indeterminacy was not made clear (as was the case in small group settings). Interviewees were not all in agreement over the location of the fence, so PatriciaH and RodneyH thought creationism was a salvation issue, whereas JoeH and DorisH allowed that it was secondary. Indeed, for RodneyH, the language of foundationalism was applied to salvation issues such as creationism, so Genesis 'is the foundation Scripture' which 'Satan ... aims to undermine' and he recalled approvingly a picture where 'Satan's got a cannon aimed at the foundations of Scripture'.[34] Uncontested secondary issues were particular millennialist schemes, cessationism and 'women wearing hats in church', although the size of the salvation issues fence appeared to be quite large in practice, as previous chapters would suggest.

The fourth epistemological issue was raised through a number of interviewees talking of their Bible reading in terms of 'taking it as it is'. For DorisH, this was partly due to her self-perception that 'I'm not really a very deep thinker', so 'I just tend to take the Word for what it says, and that's good enough for me'. She continued: 'If someone says something to me, and it's in the Word, then I'll accept that'. Knowing if 'it's in the Word' appears to be understood here as a straightforward matter. 'Taking it as it is' was not only due to perceived intellectual limitations, but was also understood to be a consequence of the nature of Scripture itself. So with regard to the creation accounts, DorisH thought that 'six days is six days' because 'I don't think God wants to confuse and complicate things for us'.[35] More generally, IonaH thought the Bible 'very clear', but 'people's interpretations aren't very clear'. The 'taking it as it is' attitude agreed with a particular understanding of the Reformation doctrine of

---

[34]   This turned out to be on the Answers in Genesis website (2015).

[35]   Perspicuity or 'taking it as it is', then, is closely linked to the default historicity of the text, and as such resonates with Holder's public horizons on this point.

the perspicuity of Scripture, which may minimise the need for hermeneutical work. In tension with this particular understanding of the perspicuity doctrine, however, were the many comments regarding difficulties with specific biblical passages or books, as has been discussed above.

'Knowing' the Bible

Fellowship and Holder's implicit epistemologies are brought into yet sharper relief when contrasted. Although there were some variations within the congregations, particularly in small group and personal settings, nevertheless the stand-out commonalities fitted well-known epistemological positions. Holder was more foundationalist and objectivist, whereas Fellowship was much less foundationalist, and understood the text through a more subjective form of realism. In this regard, then, Holder exhibited certain marks of modernity, compared to Fellowship's many marks of the late-modern critique of modernity evidenced in their epistemological accommodation.[36] These interrelated marks at Holder were seen in the degree of their Bible-centredness (especially its status), certainty about what 'the Bible says', resulting authoritative statements about its meaning, a rationalistic/educative register, a tendency to move to resolution of textual meaning, minimal critique of the Bible, and limited indeterminacy. By contrast, Fellowship was less concerned with the Bible's status, since its authority was relativised to an extent by charismatic practices which were understood to be other ways in which God speaks. Fellowship also was marked by more perspectival/experiential language about the Bible, low authority discourse, comfort with unresolved texts, more open critique of the Bible, and more extensive indeterminacy.[37] It has been seen that these commonalities permeated each congregation and were a key factor in shaping their hermeneutical practices. As a category, epistemology captured the most significant difference between the two congregations. They were using two different epistemological languages.

---

[36] This throws up the less expected conclusion that Holder, embedded epistemologically within modernity, favoured the corporate (to guard against error), whereas the late-modern (postmodern) Fellowship favoured the individual, despite the individual and the corporate normally being associated vice versa.

[37] Bielo sees the 'theological lineage' of the Emerging church movement in America as 'grounded in an epistemological critique' of modernity (2011: 10). This has some commonality with Fellowship's implicit epistemology. While there was some interest in emerging church ideas at Fellowship (I attended two 'conversations' during the fieldwork), the church itself did not designate as emerging, nor did it connect to the British emerging trends in significant ways. This suggests that Fellowship type epistemologies are found in evangelicalism, at least, outside as well as inside emerging networks.

At Fellowship, their epistemology meant they were very open to hermeneutical innovation, and could consider a number of interpretative options. Their epistemology contributed to a greater emphasis on the individual as opposed to the congregation. Far greater engagement with culture was possible, since their epistemology did not require them to work deductively from Scripture. Epistemic caution did mean that the Bible sometimes spoke with an uncertain voice, and there was difficulty at times with generating enthusiasm for Bible study, thus the Bible passion. To some extent, the epistemology evident in relation to the Bible allowed for a congregational tradition that was dynamic yet also unstable.

At Holder, their epistemology heavily restricted the hermeneutical options available due to inerrancy and historicity being basic beliefs. Indeterminacy is corrosive for a foundationalist belief structure, since it weakens the warrant for one's beliefs, and thus destabilises the whole noetic structure.[38] Warrant for their beliefs was largely asymmetric; hence a deductive and one-way hermeneutics predominated. Strict boundaries were evident between church and world and other churches, which can be traced partially to their epistemic preferences. Well defined ecclesial boundaries are important for a foundationalist epistemology, in order to prevent alternative interpretations of Scripture from 'infecting' the congregation.[39] There were also pastoral implications for Holder's epistemology of certainty, with congregants experiencing great anguish about resolving matters of Calvinistic doctrine in particular. Objectivist and realist positions also meant that Bible study was taken quite seriously, as there was little room for negotiation with the conclusions.

This epistemological split between Fellowship and Holder has significance for wider evangelicalism and beyond. With hermeneutical practices shaped by very different epistemological horizons, it is not surprising that churches from either side of the split have difficulty in understanding 'how the Bible works' across the divide. This point has been recognised by a number of scholars. In Warner's model of English evangelicalism examined in Chapter 4, he considers Holder and Fellowship type churches as operating with mutually exclusive epistemologies – one of enlightenment, common sense rationalism and the other tending to a postmodern, critical realist framework (2007: 232). The tale of two churches does not support a judgement of 'mutually exclusive', but nevertheless indicates that the lingua franca is not extensive. Paul Hiebert develops the implications of the epistemological divide through considering how the different epistemologies require different responses to disagreement. In a somewhat one-sided analysis, he argues that critical realists 'can accept theological disagreements without calling the Christian commitment of others into question', since they

[38] So the 'all or nothing' view of Scripture expressed in Chapter 4.
[39] See the use of this language at Holder in Chapter 4.

recognise that 'one or both parties may have misunderstood the biblical texts'. Foundationalists, on the other hand, are required by their epistemology to take a 'confrontational' stance, since different interpretations of Scripture threaten the stability of the noetic structure. Despite the overstatement involved, Hiebert identifies an important point when he concludes 'the fact is that many disagreements in theology have less to do with the contents of theology than with its epistemic nature' (1999: 103). For congregational hermeneutics, then, a way of crossing the epistemological 'language barrier' is needed, both within and without congregations. Possibilities are offered in this and subsequent chapters.

Such an analysis and evaluation of implicit epistemologies means the 'F' word can be avoided no longer.[40] Were either of the two congregations 'fundamentalist' and should such a term even be used? Epistemology is often identified as critical when scholars use the fundamentalist label, since biblical foundationalism is frequently associated with fundamentalism (e.g. Harris, 2006). Specific elements of foundationalism are also said to be fundamentalist, so Holder's 'all or nothing' view of inerrancy is critiqued as such by the biblical scholar James Dunn. In an Anglican evangelical journal, he argues that this treats truth as a 'seamless robe' such that 'to doubt any part of it is to doubt the whole'. The quest for such certainty, according to Dunn, is a particular feature of fundamentalism. Dunn also claims that the ring-fence expansionism designed to protect 'salvation issues' at Holder is also a feature of fundamentalism (2002: 109, 115f). Gordon Fee argues that a rationalistic approach to the Bible is symptomatic of a fundamentalist use of texts (1990: 38f). Many scholars have identified the focus on corporate hermeneutics and boundaries seen at Holder as an ironic feature of fundamentalism. In Kevin Vanhoozer's words: 'Fundamentalism thus preaches the authority of the text but practices the authority of the interpretive community'. The irony is further reinforced, argues Vanhoozer, since fundamentalists therefore share hermeneutical ground with the likes of Stanley Fish (see Chapter 3) in 'privileging their interpretive community' (1998: 425).[41] It is therefore possible to match Holder to a number of fundamentalist 'identifiers', but such matches would be much harder to establish for Fellowship. Consequently, it is not possible to maintain that fundamentalism and evangelicalism are identical or even have substantial

---

[40]   The following discussion draws on Rogers (2013b), which formed part of a larger AHRC funded network on Evangelicalism and Fundamentalism in Britain from 2008 to 2009 (Bebbington, 2009).

[41]   On this point, see also Kathleen Boone (1989: 72) and Mark Noll (2004: 205).

overlap within the British context (and possibly beyond),[42] particularly given the epistemological split between the two.[43]

Should we be using the 'F' word of such churches anyway? To what does it refer? Briggs quips that a fundamentalist is anyone more conservative in their interpretations than me (2005: 92). Harriet Harris distinguishes between the historical movement originating in early twentieth century America and 'a certain way of thinking' (and behaving) (1998: 1). These are certainly overlapping senses, but it is clear that the characteristics and critique considered above tend towards the latter.[44] Indeed, 'fundamentalist' as a term appears to be a gathering point for a set of largely epistemological critiques (and so also hermeneutical critiques), at times somewhat disconnected from its original historical trajectory. Fundamentalist was not an insider term – no-one in either church described themselves as such, and some would argue that self-designation is the prime criterion (Chapman et al., 2009; cf. Malley, 2004: 20). Briggs is not far from the mark regarding the 'F' word's common usage in popular and often academic circles – as a label of dismissal and exclusion. There seems little benefit in perpetuating the use of the 'F' word when its meaning has become so toxic throughout church and society.[45]

Epistemological problems have been identified in both Fellowship and Holder, captured in the terms 'caution' and 'certainty' respectively, demonstrating that such critique should not be solely confined to 'fundamentalism'. Uncritical embrace of a worldview is problematic, whether that worldview is pre-modern, modern or late modern/postmodern. In addition, the nuances of congregational practice, evident in epistemological tensions in both churches,[46] highlight the need to use macro categories with care, since the lived epistemology may include

---

[42]   This has been Harriet Harris's position, in that she expresses suspicion of many evangelical claims to not be fundamentalist, especially claims that hermeneutics (in her normative use of the term) may be able to 'rescind' fundamentalism. Harris does uncover weaknesses in some evangelical scholars' pragmatic and partial adoption of (normative) hermeneutics. However, she does not address congregational or ordinary hermeneutics and a case such as Fellowship and others like it substantially weakens claims that evangelicals are unable to accept a subjective dimension to biblical engagement (1998: 311–12; see also 2001a; 2001b; 2002; 2006; 2013). Her fundamental critique does not appear to have been sufficiently modified alongside the dramatic changes in evangelicalism over recent decades.

[43]   This was also the broader conclusion of the AHRC Evangelicalism and Fundamentalism in Britain project (Bebbington and Jones, 2013; Goodhew, 2013).

[44]   As I have argued previously, the historical trajectory of fundamentalism is particularly frail within England anyway (2013b: 501).

[45]   David Goodhew, based on his case study of churches in York, points to the poor fit of the fundamentalist label and argues instead for 'conservative' (2013).

[46]   Drawing on Warner, I have argued previously that 'fundamentalising tendencies' is preferable to the rather static 'fundamentalism' (Rogers, 2013b; Warner, 2013).

many possibilities for transformation. This is one reason why ethnography is so useful for looking at the church, as it details the rough edges and fractures within the macro categories, which may otherwise appear rather static and monolithic.

With this in mind, what criteria can be offered for epistemology? Just as the Bible is not a textbook for hermeneutics, neither is it a textbook for epistemology. Murray Rae observes that 'we do not often discover an explicit epistemology in the biblical writings' (2007: 163). As has been seen for congregational hermeneutics, however, 'an epistemology need not be explicit to be operative in any given case' (Schindler, 2007: 183). In an important analysis for congregational hermeneutics which is worth quoting at length, Rae expands his account of 'biblical epistemology' as follows:

> The consistency of the biblical testimony to the primacy of revelation should come as no surprise, and yet the epistemic practices that the primacy of revelation requires are easily forgotten, especially among those of us who seek theological knowledge under the auspices of the modern academy. We need to be constantly reminded, therefore, that theological knowing is inseparable from the life of obedience and faith. It is fostered through worship and prayer – those practices by which we submit ourselves to the Word and Spirit of God – and it is borne of humility before the Word (2007: 163).

In identifying these practices of worship and prayer (and hermeneutical practices are implied), the relational nature of such knowledge is also emphasised (Rae, 2007: 166f; Schindler, 2007: 183). As I have argued of methodology in Chapter 2, a relational epistemology does not leave the knower unchanged (cf. Rae, 2007: 179) and Vanhoozer also observes that 'epistemology is an affair of the heart' (2002: 352–3). This then links to the argument running throughout this book that virtue language is particularly appropriate for speaking normatively about congregational hermeneutics, including the case of epistemology. The theological ethnographic look at Fellowship and Holder would appear to support this claim, in that epistemology is embedded in hermeneutical practices that form congregants and congregations.

How might the tale of two churches inform the forming of virtue in relation to epistemology? The epistemological characteristics of Fellowship and Holder might be construed as problematic, given the weaknesses already identified with caution and certainty. One could optimistically read certainty and caution as being missional strategies of epistemological inculturation within modern and postmodern worldviews respectively. However, the intensely implicit nature of such epistemology suggests it was less an intentional move, but rather an overwhelming process of osmosis from world(s) to church. Furthermore, the church is called to be appropriately counter-cultural and this includes epistemology. Certainty and caution may look virtuous within their respective stories of modernity and postmodernity, but take on a somewhat different appearance when placed within the Christian Story. In this Story, the epistemological virtues of humility and confidence are much more at home. Humility and confidence also need to be in balance, or perhaps tension, with one another. In such a tension lies the hope of *rapprochement* between churches on either side of the epistemological gap. The contours, narratives, and justifications for these hermeneutical virtues of humility and confidence will be developed further in Chapter 8.

Chapter 7
Mediation

Mediation is about standing in-between, of being an intermediary. This is certainly its biblical sense.[1] When it comes to the Bible in churches, there are many intermediaries. It is therefore not enough to know the shape of hermeneutical practices. One also needs to know why they are the shape they are. Mediation and mediators, then, are a critical dimension of understanding congregational hermeneutics. Ward recognises the significance of mediation in the Christian community more generally:

> ... mediation is clearly evident in the way that churches have adopted the communication and information technology associated with popular culture. Christian websites, radio stations, festivals and publishing exist as intermediaries communicating across distances. Mediation, however, is also found in more traditional forms of communication in the Church such as preaching, the construction of liturgies, the parish magazine and theological publishing ...

Such mediators are 'active agents' who shape 'ecclesial expression' through circulating and moving theology (2008: 108). To varying degrees, this was also found to be the case for hermeneutical practices.

In this study, mediation refers to the process of transmitting hermeneutical practices through a variety of mediators (cf. Negus, 1996: 66). The key mediators considered are listed here, according to whether they are internal or external to the congregation:

Internal: Sermons, Bible Display, Liturgical Use (including Prayer, Rites of Passage, Bible Readings and Words), Congregants, Housegroups, Church Bible Studies.

External: Visiting preachers, Friends and Family outside the congregation, Songs, General Christian books, Bible-related books (including Study Bibles), Bible Study Guides (BSG), Personal Bible Reading (PBR) Aids, Other churches, Parachurch agencies, Christian events, Bible-related courses.[2]

---

[1] E.g. Moses and the law in Gal 3; Christ in 1 Tim 2:5; Heb 8, 9, 12.

[2] Software, Internet, Recordings, Radio, and TV did not feature highly in the ethnographic accounts. Mediators from outside the Christian church were rarely identified by congregants in the context of hermeneutical mediation.

Those mediators which are not self-explanatory will be defined more fully as they occur, but a few definitions are necessary here. All mediators in print form are referred to collectively as 'print mediators', with Bible-related books including academic books on hermeneutics, books of the How-To-Read-The-Bible variety, Commentaries, Bible reference books (Concordances, Dictionaries etc.) and Study Bibles. Although BSGs and PBR aids are Bible-related, they are sometimes treated separately as their fieldwork use dictated. General Christian books are then those books that are not Bible-related in the sense given here, nor are they BSGs or PBR aids.

Distinctions are made regarding the form of internal mediation, so 'trickle-down' mediation takes the metaphor at face value, indicating slow and/or low authority internal mediation, in contrast to 'stream-down'. A similar comparison is made between 'hierarchical' and 'horizontal' forms of internal mediation, where the latter refers to mediation apart from formal congregational means. From engaging with the fieldwork congregations, four heuristic dimensions can be postulated regarding the effectiveness of a hermeneutical mediator, namely their *numerical reach, frequency, level of explicitness* and *intensity*. That is, in order, the number of congregants accessing a mediator (e.g. songs were sung by all congregants); how frequently a mediator is accessed (e.g. PBR aids might be accessed every day); how explicit or implicit a mediator is in hermeneutical terms (e.g. Bible-related courses could be very explicit, but General Christian books might be quite implicit in their hermeneutics); and the degree of mediator intensity (e.g. Christian events can be quite intense). Reference is made to these dimensions throughout the chapter regarding mediator effectiveness. 'Resistance' to mediators is also examined, ranging from critical appropriation to outright rejection. The whole configuration of hermeneutical mediators in a congregation is described along a spectrum of homogeneity to heterogeneity, capturing the degree of difference across mediators.

Mediation in this chapter develops the exploration of tradition in Chapter 4, through looking particularly at the process of mediating tradition. Mediation in a congregation also has much to do with how congregants learn their faith. The nature and extent of hermeneutical apprenticeship (introduced in Chapter 1) is developed here and continued in Chapter 9. In order to ascertain what hermeneutical mediation was taking place in Holder and Fellowship, a combination of participation observation, interview and questionnaire was utilised. Regarding the questionnaire, in addition to straightforward questions about mediator engagement, there was an attitude question that assessed the degree of influence of a list of mediator items upon a congregant's understanding of the Bible. Such a question addresses the combined perceived influence of the four mediatory dimensions proposed above. In allowing for the approximate nature of this question, I have opted to tell a descriptive story regarding the results, in terms of top, middle and bottom influence rankings for both respondents and the sample.[3] Somewhat typically for the two churches, the mean value for each influence item was higher at Holder for every item except one.

The tale of hermeneutical mediation in the two churches is told through assessing mediation in public, small group and personal settings. Of all the mediators listed above, those related to these three settings have been chosen as they were the critical *congregational* means of mediation.[4] Researching mediation reveals that there is a very large range of mediators influencing any one congregation, and it would be impractical to include detailed analysis of them all. Nevertheless, in the last section of the chapter, there is a broader comparison of Holder and Fellowship, including the whole range of hermeneutical mediators encountered as significant. The chapter finishes by drawing out the significance of hermeneutical mediation for a virtuous reading of Scripture.

Public Mediation

Sermons and songs are the focus of public mediation in this study, since they were the key Bible uses in public settings for both churches. Words at Fellowship did not always make use of Scripture, and although it was difficult to determine the mediatory significance of liturgical uses of Scripture such as Bible display and Bible readings, it appeared to be slight. This may have been due to their hermeneutical minimalism and embeddedness within congregational horizons. There were also some key instances of intentional mediation in public settings, which will be addressed at the end of this section, as they are revealing for congregational perceptions of mediation.

Sermon Mediation

At Holder, although sermons were never explicit in their hermeneutics, they provided weekly examples of hermeneutics for the whole congregation through some form of engagement with the biblical text. Cohering with Holder's

---

[3]   The question used a 7 point scale adapted from Cartledge (2003: 43) to indicate little to high influence of 19 or 18 hermeneutical mediator items at Holder and Fellowship respectively. Means were then calculated and items ranked accordingly, with the items then grouped into top, middle, and bottom influence rankings (see Appendix E). Two sets of rankings are used for each church – respondent and sample. Respondent ranks items according to those who indicated a preference for an item, whereas sample ranks items according to the whole sample, including those that missed out items.

[4]   The tale of mediation is structured differently in each of the three settings, since hermeneutical mediation had distinctive characteristics in each setting.

Bible-centredness, sermons were ranked first by a large margin according to the questionnaire influence items.[5] Interviewees were positive about sermon mediation, so AnnaH said of sermons 'that's where I have to start' since 'God uses ... a preacher ... to speak to us', and wondered if there were no sermon then 'why do we go to church?' Others understood listening to sermons as a matter of duty, drawing on Heb 10:25 to again identify the essential element of 'meeting together' as preaching. OwenH was praised as 'an excellent preacher' (HarryH) and he was named as the most influential person in aiding Bible understanding in the questionnaire.[6] Indeed, SiobhanH drew a parallel with the inspiration of Scripture as being 'the same way as with the help of God that [Owen] speaks'. A few interviewees spoke of the limitations of sermons, such as the assistant pastor, JoeH, who thought that 'in theological terms' learning about the Bible 'comes more from your own study or even housegroup'. Sermons were more for 'impact' in terms of conduct – 'what I should do ... how I should live'. Despite limited resistance, preaching appeared to be an effective form of internal hermeneutical mediation for Holder, given their relative homogeneity of speakers and centralised monthly training sessions (i.e. SatAM).[7] Indeed, one might characterise their internal mediation as hierarchical and 'stream-down' in nature, although this seemed to be more effective for horizonal starting points and goals than for the less explicit fusion processes.

Fellowship sermons provided some explicit hermeneutics, as has been seen, as well as weekly examples of diverse hermeneutical practices through quite varied degrees of exposure to Scripture.[8] The influence of sermons on Bible understanding was highly ranked in the questionnaire, but notably second to 'My Christian friends'.[9] This slight diminishing of the sermon's importance coheres well with the symbolism of preachers standing on the same level as the congregation, as well as the sermon being the second liturgical climax of the service. Interviewees were also ambivalent about preaching as a hermeneutical mediator. The pastor, DerekF, stated his gifting was as a pastor, rather than primarily that of a teacher/preacher – an assessment that was confirmed by

---

[5]   For both respondent and sample means.

[6]   28%, N=105.

[7]   The monthly training sessions (SatAM) were led by OwenH and included 'preaching development' for speakers (OwenH, JustinH, RodneyH). SatAM was also for small group leaders, see n26.

[8]   Fellowship sermons incorporated a significant external mediator during the fieldwork, namely the 'official follow-up' book to the Alpha course, *Challenging Lifestyle* (Gumbel, 1996). Structured around the Sermon on the Mount, it was used as the basis for the sermon series during the fieldwork, and was made available to speakers. This was therefore a significant external mediator, from within the same broad charismatic evangelical tradition as Fellowship.

[9]   For both respondent and sample means.

questionnaire and interview responses.[10] RossF acknowledged that some of the time during sermons 'like most people, I switch off' and did not always 'necessarily agree with everything that is said', nevertheless 'especially for someone like me who doesn't read the Bible' sermons were significant because 'it's the only, or one of the few places, that I can actually get any understanding of the Bible'. MattF and others struggled with the non-interactive dynamic of sermons, since a preacher 'might put something forward' that 'I haven't agreed with', then 'they've moved on' yet 'I've still been stuck … I can't say anything to it'.[11] BruceF had 'a mixed view about the role of sermons in church life', because positively, 'it's very important to … struggle with God's Word … spend time in God's Word … hearing from God' and 'the sermon can be a very good vehicle' for those things. Negatively, however, the sermon can be 'a much abused vehicle' and its 'whole role' in 'communal life' needs 'revisiting' so they can take a 'more creative approach' to 'how we … expose ourselves to God's Word'. GordonF made an explicit critique of Fellowship sermons, saying 'for my taste, there's not enough clear biblical teaching and use of the Bible in the services' which sometimes needed to be 'more authoritative and less apologetic'. As these extracts indicate, many Fellowship interviewees thought preaching *ought* to be 'biblical'. For SteveF, a sermon 'has to be backed up with Scripture'. This was qualified by a desire for sermons to be more than just repeating the Bible. AmyF was critical of sermons that were 'just completely what's already there in the Bible, nothing inspired, nothing revealed, it doesn't seem like God's really there, they're not really anointed'. Sermons needed to perform the spirit-inspired hermeneutical task of bringing 'something new' (NinaF) and 'a revelation' (AmyF) from the Bible that is God's Word for now.

Sermons at Fellowship mediated both implicit and explicit hermeneutics, but appeared to have a reduced mediatory function, particularly meeting with significant resistance from interviewees. Mediatory limitations may have been due to their liturgical status, low authority style/low intensity, relativised status of Scripture and wide range of preachers.[12] Regarding the latter, such a range of mediators brings a variety of hermeneutical practices to the congregation, with the potential to challenge existing understandings of texts, but too much diversity may disrupt the continuity of effective mediation.

---

[10] So just 7% of respondents cited DerekF as an influential person on Bible understanding, below Scholars (8%), Famous church leaders (20%) and Charles from Ekklesia (25%), N=75.

[11] MattF's preference was amplified in Chapter 6.

[12] So ReneeF, 'we have such a huge range of speakers at [Fellowship]'.

Song Mediation

Songs were largely external hermeneutical mediators for Holder public settings, although a number of them were composed by songwriters from within Holder's own evangelical tribe. Song mediation is almost always implicit, much more so than sermons, since the biblical provenance of song lyrics is not always obvious. Nevertheless, songs can act as hermeneutical examples that may become part of the congregation's hermeneutical milieu.

There were mixed responses from Holder interviewees when asked specifically about the influence of songs on their understanding of the Bible. SiobhanH supposed song words 'bring into context what you read in the Bible' which makes them 'hit home'. A number of interviewees commented on the power of songs to 'embed Scripture in your mind' (PatriciaH) due to the memorability of the accompanying tunes. WendyH found this embedding 'kind of lovely' since 'you know what you're singing is in line with God's Word', and 'not just nice words strung together'. Interviewees also spoke of certain songs exciting strong feelings during services, as songs could 'express, sometimes, what you can't express ... express what you're feeling' (DotH). Songs were said to have Holder's imprimatur on them, since RodneyH spoke of the 'elder's responsibility' to 'check ... what we're singing is doctrinally correct'. Asking if a song was 'scripturally correct' would particularly apply to new songs and children's songs.

There was also a critique of songs voiced by Holder interviewees, so the danger of familiar songs for PatriciaH was that 'sometimes people sing unintelligently' and so she tried to 'process them so that I am singing intelligently'. The preference for the objective over the subjective at Holder was in tension with a perceived turn to the subjective in songs by a few interviewees, so BridgetH noted:

> Someone once said something to me about some of the modern hymns are very much, "I, I, I", rather than, "God, God, God", that kind of emphasis, and how that, that can put it on, it's all about us, when it's not, it's about God.

Songs mediated Holder's Bible-centredness and corporate tendency in hermeneutics, as well as exposure to Scripture itself (as seen in previous chapters). Songs also mediated a Christocentric theology that made infrequent specific reference to the Father or Spirit, much as in wider Holder discourse. However, songs mediated dissimilar hermeneutical features as well, such as the reconstructive use of Scripture, which was more pronounced than in Holder's own hermeneutical practice.[13] Further dissimilarity was found in songs that

---

[13]   E.g. *O Lord Our God How Majestic Is Your Name* (MP507) combined at least 7 passages from the OT and NT, namely Psa 8:1, (possibly 9:7), 72:19, 93:1; Col 1:17; Heb 11:3; Rev 5:13.

mediated a Christological hermeneutics uncommon elsewhere in Holder public settings[14] and through conflicting theologies. The latter included Christus Victor references to the atonement, social justice emphases, non-Calvinistic views of God's agency, spiritual warfare and healing ministry. A number of these features, both similarities and dissimilarities with the Holder public horizon, suggest the greater influence of charismatic spirituality on the songs.

As at Holder, songs were implicit and largely external hermeneutical mediators in Fellowship public settings, although many of them originated from within the same broad charismatic tradition. Songs were appreciated by most interviewees, for instance, RossF described them as 'kind of joyful, uplifting', adding:

> Sometimes, reading the words of the songs, it's easier to read that, than read the Bible ... some of the images that it conjures up and so on. I think it's a really important part of going [to church], I really like it.

Interviewees spoke approvingly of songs with perceived biblical content, such as SteveF who commented 'I like stuff that's lifted completely from Scripture'. Song music was also important for some interviewees, so GrahamF explained that 'as soon as there's good music going on' then 'it's a hotline between me and up there', since a worship song can be 'a direct line for God to speak to me'. Songs were perceived as a vehicle for this distinctive hermeneutical goal of Fellowship by the worship leader BruceF, since they were:

> ... more than just a way to deal with the word of God, the written word, it's a way of dealing with the revealed word of God, and hearing from God in that broad sense of releasing prophecy, words of knowledge, the gifts. It's a context in which spiritual activity can take place, a vehicle, if you like, for it.

According to this extract and other evidence already provided, songs in worship appeared to function as the primary sacramental act in Fellowship (Ward, 2005: 199; cf. Stackhouse, 2007: 152f). Despite Fellowship songs being this significant, and the time spent singing them, interviewees had numerous criticisms to make, with some striking resemblance to Holder critique. They disliked songs that 'sound simple ... like a nursery rhyme' (SarahF) or were 'a bit too buddy-buddy' (SteveF), as well as songs that focussed on feelings. On this latter point, TomF preferred songs 'which sort of state things about the character of God, and ... less about my

---

[14] E.g. *Who Paints the Skies Into Glorious Day?* (SF1118) asks a series of qᵘ· alluding to (possibly) Isa 61:10; Ezek 36, 37; Dan 7:10; Mi 4 all with the answᵛ· Jesus'. Extract taken from 'Who Paints the Skies Into Glorious Day?' by Sᵗ Copyright © 1995 Thankyou Music*.

feelings'. Some interviewees made critiques of specific songs, so SarahF did not feel like singing the line 'You give and take away' (from Job 1:21) in *Blessed Be Your Name* (SF1193), because that was not her understanding of God's character.[15] There was also some explicit hermeneutical critique of song fusion processes, so TomF commented of *These Are The Days Of Elijah* (SF1047) 'it's like you're ... jumping from thousands of years ... from then to now ... there's this ... odd time-shift', and similarly ReneeF spoke of 'applying quite literally OT stories to modern day'. Of *Lord Let Your Glory Fall* (SF1430), ReneeF thought that without knowing the biblical context of the song (2 Chron 5–7), she was not sure 'what people get out of singing this'.

As has been seen in previous chapters, Fellowship songs mediated a focus on the individual, Christocentrism, this-is-that hermeneutics and text-linking. These features were largely consonant with other aspects of Fellowship's public horizon, including most of their theological emphases. Such mediated features support the claim that there is a charismatic centre of gravity for the spirituality of contemporary worship songs. There were *some* differences between Fellowship's public horizon and songs, such as songs' epistemic confidence, high incorporation of Scripture and more balanced use of the OT/NT[16] compared to other public uses. Furthermore, songs brought limited dissonance to the public horizon through Calvinistic[17] and penal substitution[18] references. As at Holder, reconstructive use of Scripture could generate new meanings for the biblical text, or make Scripture more understandable to worshippers – thus reshaping or enlarging their horizons. Despite these differences, Fellowship songs in their liturgical context were largely representative of their wider public horizon in terms of hermeneutical starting points, processes and goals. By this measure, songs may be effective hermeneutical mediators, but explicit resistance to song hermeneutics implied an attenuation of their mediatory function.

Intentional Mediation

Intentional mediation for Holder and Fellowship was at the broader level of congregational tradition, although, as has been seen, this provides an important context for hermeneutical mediation. The instances below were the most explicit references to mediation in the whole fieldwork period.

---

[15]   Extract taken from 'Blessed Be Your Name' by Matt and Beth Redman, Copyright © 2002 Thankyou Music*.

[16]   See n70.

[17]   E.g. *Blessed Be Your Name* (SF1193).

[18]   E.g. *In Christ Alone* (SF1346).

At Holder, a concern for passing on 'the truth from your Word' was made explicit at the Anniversary service, when DougH was asked to pray for the children and youth of the church:

> ... we thank you heavenly Father for the faithfulness of those Sunday School teachers and youth leaders who have faithfully taught the Gospel and preached the Gospel to these young children. There are many of us here this afternoon who can bear witness to the way in which we have grown through their teaching and have come to know you through the Bible ministry amongst the young people here at [Holder]. Heavenly Father, we thank you for preserving that ministry over these years, and ... we pray ... that you would equip and continue to equip our youth leaders to be able to hold to the truth of your Word, in a world which has so much to say, so many counter-gospels to teach ... we pray that you would help us only ever speak the truth from your Word and we pray that your Word would reach into the hearts of these young ones ... We pray ... that we would continue to see those young ones coming to a knowledge of your Son, the Lord Jesus Christ, coming to salvation and in turn taking their place in teaching others and in telling others about you.

That the theme of mediating the Word was chosen in this showcase service context underlines once again the importance of the Bible for Holder's self-understanding. In particular, the prayer expresses the desire for the mediation of the Word to be effective, where the emphasis is on holding to the truth already known.

At Fellowship, the importance of mediating 'truths ... passed down to us', was highlighted at their Church Consultation. In the context of discussing youth work, DerekF gave his own loose rendition of Psa 78:

> We will not hide the word of God from our children, we will tell the next generation the fantastic things that God has done, his power and wonders, God gave his word and commanded our forefathers to teach their children so that the next generation would know them, even the children yet to be born, and they in turn would tell their children, then they would put their trust in God.
>
> This whole generational business, we are inheriting the truths that God passed down to us. We have the responsibility to communicate it to our youth and children, and they will run with it, in the great story and plan and destiny of God, and we're caught up in the story, and his purposes ...

At the same meeting, a member of the leadership team (MelissaF) made a strong statement regarding the mediation of the Bible in the context of reporting on the children's work:

> ... the main thing though is we wanna get the Bible into the kids at an early age, and teach them the full range of Bible stories, so that they grow in their faith right from the beginning ...

> ... there are things we want to make sure the children know over the six years that they're in our Sunday school classes, we don't want them to kind of go out not knowing that Jesus can turn water into wine, or not knowing that you build your house on a solid foundation when the storms come, it'll stand, so that's important to us ...

These two extracts expressed the aspiration of Fellowship to mediate the 'word of God' to the next generation, understood, like Holder, to be inherited truths. Given the differences noted between the two churches, it is striking how their explicit views on mediating tradition and Scripture are so very similar, excepting the hint of theodrama in the first Fellowship quote. Such similarity of espoused mediation suggests that, despite their significant differences, the common evangelical roots of the two churches should not be overlooked.

Small Group Mediation

Fellowship small groups had a variety of Bible uses, reasons for meeting, and diverse fusion processes, all of which indicated the 'trickle-down' nature of Fellowship's internal mediation. There were few formal internal mechanisms for shaping small groups, with no member of the leadership team specifically assigned to such a portfolio[19] – hence housegroups were able to operate autonomously, as has already been noted. For church Bible studies, however, DerekF functioned as their key hermeneutical mediator through generating a more sustained interaction with the text than in any other Fellowship Bible setting observed. Furthermore, and in contrast to housegroups, these studies had a greater movement towards resolving the meaning of the text under consideration. It was interesting to see DerekF's approach amplified enthusiastically by the two youth leaders in the ThursAM group, which had been set up with the 'main aim' of training youth workers in Bible study (DerekF, interview). This group had a similar hermeneutical style to TuesAM, but with more time given to exegetical discourse, including verse by verse analysis and (sometimes frequent) commentary use.[20] The youth leaders 'drew on' Derek's

---

[19] 'Teaching Programme' and 'Pastoral Care' were the closest (*Leadership Portfolios* document). A member of the leadership team, JackF, said that responsibility for housegroups 'was shared out' (Phone, 4/5/05).

[20] Matthew Henry and the Tyndale series.

'style' and 'the teaching ways he gave us' when they subsequently led Bible studies with Fellowship's large youth group (SteveF, interview). TuesAM may also have had a mediatory role amongst other small groups, since it included members and leaders from various housegroups.

Housegroup leaders tended to be less directive than Derek, although FrancisF had a significant mediatory role as leader within Housegroup B.[21] FrancisF assisted individuals in the preparation of their own (often ambitious) study sessions, contributed many grammatical and historical observations regarding the Scriptures under discussion, and also mediated doctrines that were distinctive for the Ekklesia tradition (e.g. conditional immortality and open theism). FrancisF was much respected for his knowledge of the Scriptures, with MichelleF of the group describing him affectionately as a 'Bible Boffin',[22] adding in interview 'I do trust [him] – I think he's a wise man'. Being the final authority on exegetical matters had the effect of constraining some text horizon discussion, but this did not appear to be a problem for the group, nor did it seem to close down freer group discourse that moved away from the text towards the group horizon.[23] FrancisF preferred to describe his theological stance as 'centrist' rather than 'evangelical', recognising that he was more liberal than the 'vast majority' of the congregation. Given that he had held significant responsibilities within Ekklesia/Fellowship, this was another indicator of the congregation's fuzzy boundaries.

In addition to DerekF and FrancisF, a number of interviewees said they would turn to their housegroup leaders for help with issues of Bible understanding, with some describing them as 'mentors' (e.g. TheresinaF, MattF, TomF). The mediation of the whole group was significant for ReneeF who would talk to 'not one individual' but consult 'their collective wisdom'. SarahF spoke for many when she was asked about the most helpful ways of learning about the Bible in church:

> Interaction, talking with others, where you discuss something ... with people who are knowledgeable ... I think that's a good learning place because you're using your intellect, you're using your own mind, because if you're just listening, it's all coming towards you.

Other interviewees also included SarahF's caveat that the group should contain someone who 'really knows the Bible' (TheresinaF) or is made up of those who are 'soaked in the Bible' (ReneeF). All these positive perceptions of

---

[21] In this paragraph I am following an earlier article (Rogers, 2007: 89–90).

[22] MichelleF in conversation (SunAM5f).

[23] Gerald West's work on scholars 'reading with' ordinary readers develops these issues – see the summary of his work in Chapter 1.

small group mediation resonated with their top third ranking for influence on Bible understanding[24] and with the high levels of housegroup membership at Fellowship.[25]

Bearing in mind Holder's Bible-centredness and other congregational emphases, shaping the internal mediatory function of Holder small groups was a high priority. In addition to having an elder (JustinH) who organised the groups centrally, including allocation of persons and study materials, there was the SatAM training session for all housegroup leaders.[26] This was thought 'important' since small group leaders have 'far more spiritual authority' than some other elected church leaders. Indeed, in keeping with Holder's identity, small group leaders were encouraged to actually *lead* sessions, exercising a degree of hermeneutical authority within their groups. The account in Chapter 5 indicates that this was a significant mediatory function, given the frequency of leader's contributions in group discussions. Furthermore there were two other elders 'who go to different housegroups each Tuesday night ... by way of encouragement' but also for 'the crude term – quality control' (OwenH, interview). A mentoring system was also in place where a more experienced leader would co-lead with a newer leader, which might take the form of 'just engaging over the passage' before the session and deciding 'what the main elements might be that are going to be brought through'.[27] Somewhat unusually, there was also a system of completely redistributing housegroups every three years or so to prevent 'cliques within the church' from forming[28] – a practice with the potential to destabilise group horizons.[29]

Holder small groups were ranked in the top third for their influence on Bible understanding in the questionnaire.[30] The degree of participation and regular attendance further supports this positive perception.[31] In addition to the specific hermeneutical benefits of small groups discussed in Chapter 5, DennisH spoke of housegroups as a setting where 'you get to discuss what the real meaning of what [the biblical books/authors] are saying'. In church 'you probably just hear

---

[24]   Both respondent and sample means, for Housegroups and Church Bible Studies.

[25]   85%, N=75, although 67% of attendees met twice a month or less, and 39% attended 'about half the time' or less (N=64).

[26]   OwenH said 'we will actually go through passages, books of the Bible' – the session was for 'preaching and teaching development' (interview).

[27]   This arrangement was in place in Housegroup X.

[28]   E.g. JustinH, interview; RubyH, conversation, 18/12/05.

[29]   This practice dated from their inception in the 1980s (Anniversary Service exhibition field notes).

[30]   Both respondent and sample means, for Housegroups and Other Bible studies, with Housegroups ranked slightly higher, see Appendix E.

[31]   77% of respondents attended housegroups (N=105), with 75% of attendees attending always or nearly always (N=80).

it, but it's probably just something that's just straight off of your head' but in housegroups 'you get to discuss ... the reason for this and the reason for that'. A conspicuous benefit of small groups according to a number of interviewees was the space they gave to ordinary female readers to engage in hermeneutics. So LucyH said 'if somebody asked you something in church, you would curl up and die, some of us would' but in a small group 'you don't feel so threatened, and you can share ... and ... say what this means to you'. AnnaH similarly recognised the different mode of congregational services on Sundays, saying 'you can't ask many questions, really, you can't share your opinion, your ideas'. Being able to ask or listen to questions in housegroup meant 'you learn more in housegroup' than services or in PBR.

External Mediators

Small groups at Fellowship accessed a notably diverse range of external mediators, particularly Derek's theological college which was a substantial influence on his view of Scripture[32] and practice of hermeneutics. The college was therefore an indirect mediator to all church Bible studies. Another external organisation, Christian Aid, acted as mediator in B4 through a session on Trade Justice led by a visiting speaker – again indicative of Fellowship's broad range of theological influences.[33]

Print mediators from across the evangelical theological spectrum were also observed in Fellowship small groups, some mediating an explicit hermeneutical agenda. So the BSG on Mark's Gospel used in Housegroup A was from a 'reformed, evangelical publishing house' (Bolt and Payne, 1997; cf. Matthias Media, 2008),[34] and headlined its narrative theological approach in the first study[35] as follows:

> ... many of *us* are not used to reading Mark's Gospel (or any of the Gospels for that matter) as one continuous story. Instead, we are more used to regarding the Gospels as a collection of lots of different stories that don't have much to do with each other ... many of *us* have grown up with these Gospel stories without pausing to think that there might be a connection between all these different incidents, that the Gospel author might be trying to tell a big story of which all the different episodes are only a part (p. 10). [*My italics*]

---

[32] So 'I've got my position on reliability [of Scripture] ... from [Ian's] lectures at [college]'.

[33] Notably the speaker commented that Trade Justice had been a liberal church issue, but that evangelicals were catching up (Fieldnotes, B4).

[34] Page numbers only will be given from here on.

[35] This took place in Housegroup A before the fieldwork period.

Here the BSG critiques a presumed ordinary hermeneutical characteristic of non-narrative reading. This is thought to be widespread enough for it to mean something to the 'us' of a largely evangelical publishing constituency in Australia, the UK, South Africa and the USA (Matthias Media, 2014).

Apart from Housegroup A, print mediators were not particularly conspicuous in Fellowship small groups, neither were they accorded high authority, but they were nevertheless able to provide hermeneutical reinforcement. As has been noted, substantial use was made of commentaries in ThursAM[36] and to a lesser extent in ThursPM. In TuesAM1, reference was made to Andrew Perriman's explicitly hermeneutical book *Speaking of Women: Interpreting Paul* (1998) regarding the cultural context in which Ephesians was written. Popular Christian (auto)biographies were also cited, such as the (then) bestseller *The Heavenly Man* (Brother Yun and Hattaway, 2002), in relation to a TuesAM5 discussion of Paul's situation and mindset in Php 1:12–30. Regarding v21 'to live is Christ, to die is gain', SteveF said:

> Yeah, I think, I'm just coming to the end of the *Heavenly Man* book ... and he's very much like that, isn't he? And ... near the end ... when he's out of China, and he's saying to other churches and people are saying, "Oh, how can we pray for you? We're praying that persecution will stop in China". He said, "No, don't pray for that ... persecution's the best thing, 'cause it stops us from ... falling asleep, and when we're persecuted, we get into God deeper". And so I don't think that we can experience sometimes what it is to live as Christ, but only sometimes, and I think the – the true thing is when you're through persecution, actually.

Such popular (auto)biographies put stories into circulation which provided ideal yet concrete examples on which group members could hang their understanding of the biblical text.

The remaining observed external mediator at Fellowship was this research, which stimulated varying degrees of explicit hermeneutical discussion.[37] The most pronounced and explicit example was in Housegroup C after the fieldwork period, where ReneeF led a session entitled 'The Exegesis and Hermeneutics of the Epistles, Or, How do we know which bits of the New Testament Letters apply to us today?'[38] This study was based on the popularisation of hermeneutics in Fee's book *How To Read The Bible For All It's Worth* (Fee and Stuart, 2003), and arose partly out of conversations with ReneeF. This and other examples suggested a certain openness to academic hermeneutics within Fellowship.

---

[36]   See n20.

[37]   The questionnaire also stimulated a discussion in Housegroup C regarding the meaning of 'evangelical'.

[38]   Email, 22/1/06.

Given the 'control' mechanisms at Holder, the pastor and housegroup organiser had a significant role in effecting internal hermeneutical mediation through leadership training and writing in-house study material/selecting BSGs. Small group leaders also had a platform to mediate their choice of academic mediators, particularly through commentaries, some of which had been recommended in SatAM.[39] The leaders observed mostly directed the session discussions and often acted as 'boundary patrol' for the Holder tradition. Significant mediation was also witnessed through group references to 'branded' study Bibles (e.g. MacArthur, 2004),[40] indicating their powerful potential to mediate hermeneutics and a doctrinal tradition, by the very nature of their format. The study Bibles and commentaries used were from a very similar theological tradition to Holder, with the most popular all being American. So frequent were references to these sources in small groups that they functioned almost as extra members of the groups. The BSG in Housegroup Y drew on a slightly more diverse range of sources including the Church Fathers and a broader range of evangelical scholars,[41] but these were only included in the leaders' notes and not obviously used (Nystrom, 2000). Indeed, the BSG was so integrated into Y discourse that participants could easily be unaware of its use in general.[42]

The power of the bestseller was also evident in Y4 through an apt contribution from WendyH regarding temptation, which was taken from Rick Warren's *The Purpose-Driven Life* (2003). Its difference as a mediator, if only slight, was suggested by MossH in Y1 who said the book had changed his life, but he thought it unlikely it would be studied at Holder. Occasionally, more heterogeneous mediators were introduced, so in WedAM the leader (LindaH, the pastor's wife) referred to a book on singleness in relation to Dorcas in Acts 9. She reported its argument that single women did not feel respected in their churches, with which the group disagreed. It was an unusual mediator for Holder given its contrasting theological stance on the role of women, although LindaH thought it useful to see this perspective (Aune, 2002).

The diffusion of new hermeneutical ideas was evident in MossH's interjection in Y1 when he spoke of Roman soldiers only being able to pressgang civilians to carry their packs for one mile. The idea was to go the extra mile to 'embarrass them' since 'even psychopaths know you are doing good to them' since 'grace breaks people down'. He had heard this interpretation of Matt 5:41 through a friend at an emerging church meeting (Asylum, nd), who he knew had learnt

---

[39]   So James Montgomery Boice had been recommended for all leaders (RodneyH, interview).

[40]   RodneyH reported being told at the FIEC conference of John MacArthur 'Well, you know he's got a Bible out'.

[41]   Chrysostom, Augustine, other IVP commentaries (such as the Tyndale Old Testament Commentary series) and drawing on some British scholars.

[42]   Only the leaders had a copy.

it at a part-time theological course run by Workshop (interview) – a quite distant relation to Holder in terms of theological tradition (Workshop, nd). The original source in this diffusion chain is likely to be the biblical scholar Walter Wink (2003). The manner of his interjection, its novelty, and the fringe status of MossH may all have contributed to it being politely ignored.

Resistance to Mediation

Outright *resistance* to BSG mediation at Fellowship was noticeable in Housegroup A, partly due to their adaptive use of the materials, but also due to the BSG's unfamiliar emphasis on exploring the theological framework of Markan passages (Bolt and Payne, 1997: 42). For instance, in A3 on Mk 6:45–56 (Jesus walking on water), the BSG required the group to look up six sets of allusive references in the OT 'that add meaning to the event'.[43] However, the allusions in Mark to the OT passages were not clear to the group, or to the leader, and the BSG provided no answers (as part of its study philosophy). Consequently, session leaders were sometimes critical of the BSG, such as PenelopeF, perhaps pointing to the inertia that groups may face when adopting new hermeneutical strategies.

Some interesting resistance to DerekF's own hermeneutical programme was observed in ThursPM2 on Jas 1:1–11. After a lengthy discussion regarding the intended audience of James' letter[44] and other grammatico-historical issues, TomF then reflected on the childlikeness of Paul and Silas singing in prison (cf. Acts 16:25) and Jesus' saying that 'we have to become like children to enter the kingdom of God' (cf. Mk 10:14–15) as follows:

> It's child-like in the right kind of way. And I wonder if … in our search to – like …
> we're doing tonight really – to … really … get hold of what the Bible's saying, if
> we're losing the point of – again, I'm probably completely wrong here – but … if
> we're losing that child-like, just chasing after God, and that … sense of … let's, just
> kind of go with what … just kind of praising and enjoying being with God,
> enjoying the presence of God. And if we kind of … possibly throughout church
> history, if we traded that for a more academic approach to Christianity, which is
> not quite the same.

Whilst TomF appreciated ThursPM as a forum for questioning of the text, his caution towards Derek's grammatico-historical approach was a sign of

---

[43]   This was not 'proof-texting' since Mark is 'deliberately using language … which should spark off Old Testament images in your mind' (p. 42). Once again, the BSG distanced itself from a perceived ordinary hermeneutical practice.

[44]   Someone asked 'Why is it important to know?'

its relativised value for Fellowship – a point that also resonates with Stibbe's characterisation of charismatic hermeneutics discussed in Chapter 3.

Criticisms of Holder housegroups were remarkably few, but the elder, JustinH, told me in critical tone of those who resisted the pedagogical style praised by many above:

> There are some people in the church that do not like housegroups, full stop, because they do not like the style. They just don't like the idea of not being taught, of actually having to sit and to be questioned and to think and to respond.

For those in small groups, resistance to mediation was most commonly low-key, of the sort expected in small groups – disagreement with each other. Notably those with some academic background were often those with the confidence to challenge the view of the leaders and other group members (e.g. KarlH in X, PatriciaH in Y and WedAM). The reception of the external mediators described varied according to their use. Extracts from study Bibles and commentaries were often read out in relation to a point, but small groups often failed to engage with what had been read beyond polite nods and 'Hmmms'. This appeared to be due to the formal and authoritative register of such extracts not being in keeping with their small group discussion dynamics. Where external mediators had greater integration into a person's speech and flow of discussion, the group engagement was more substantial.

The greatest resistance to external mediators was observed in Housegroup X, although this may have been due partly to their authoritative appropriation by the leader (JamesH). X4 saw a near rebellion in resisting Boice's commentary on Mal 3:1–5. JamesH said he was 'coming back to James Montgomery Boice for the last time' raising the point that 'between this prophecy and Jesus actually coming there was a period of about four hundred years', so 'we've had ... five times that long since the coming of Jesus'. Boice asks 'Why hasn't God said anything more between Jesus coming and now?', and concludes that 'He does not speak' since 'God's said everything' (meaning the Bible). But Boice continues to wonder about this silence, noting 'how even strong believers would have liked a ... pointed directing word in crisis'.[45] Once the group had grasped what was being said, the following lengthy exchange took place:[46]

[laughter]

anon: We're all dumbfounded here.

---

[45] Boice is in fact quoting approvingly from a book (reference unknown).

[46] 'anon' does not indicate a single individual.

anon: We're hearing all the time.

    ...

JamesH: I'm stimulating discussion ...

anon: It sounds a bit like that guy –

anon: We can't get over it, we're dumbfounded.

anon: Who's that one that doesn't believe in the resurrection – the Durham ... ?

Andrew: The Bishop of Durham, David Jenkins.[47]

anon: It sounds a bit like him –

    ...

JamesH: No, no, I think he's saying ... if we are very, very honest, would we not even say ... we would sometimes like to hear?

anon: Well, we do.

JamesH: ... in a loud, booming voice, or speak in terms of revelation?

anon: But you get that from here [the Bible], the revelation –

JamesH: Well ... that's the answer, yes.

anon: You're talking about physical hearing or –

JamesH: Yeah ...

anon: I mean, I've often said, I'd like Jesus to come down in person and put his arms round me, but I realise that he's putting his arms round me all the time, because as – the Spirit's in us and, so, he's in us, and he's doing that. So, you know, it's the same with revelation and things here [the Bible], we've got all we need there, there isn't silence.

---

[47]   A previous Bishop of Durham in the 1980s and notorious figure within evangelicalism at the time, making this quite an insult.

[laughter]

JamesH: No.

anon: I think it's most peculiar.

...

JamesH: And James Montgomery Boice is saying, "Yes, God has said everything that needs to be said".

anon: Oh.

JamesH: And if He said anything more –

SiobhanH: But He does ongoingly speak.

JamesH: Yeah, as Andrew drew out, there is, I think, we're talking about the kind of revelation that we find in Malachi and in the words of Jesus, rather than the day-to-day communication we can all have, as Christians, with God.

SiobhanH: And in His words. I mean, even my [husband], who's a non-Christian, would say, when he's up on a mountain or he feeds [my son], he'll say that there is something.

JamesH: Yeah, yeah, so that's encouraging, then, that we all do hear God.

SiobhanH: Yeah.

anon: You have to, or we couldn't live. This is how we live.

anon: He doesn't have to speak just through the Bible, He can speak through a friend.

...

anon: I'm interested in the silent bit.

TommyH: Well, what does he think – does he say anything about ... tongues and prophecies there?

...

JamesH: I think we're running a bit late to –

[all speaking, laughter]

Andrew: [TommyH] has got a question.[48]

TommyH: There's a lot of churches who do tongues and prophesy. [Holder] doesn't. So, are we – is [Holder] – are we missing out on that, the Spirit speaking to each of us, as a group, as each other? Are we missing out on that?

JamesH: But it still wouldn't be final revelation in the same way as –

TommyH: Well, it could be … it depends what the Spirit says … and … like Matthew Henry, he believes that it stopped with the Disciples. But, I've known –

SiobhanH: I've never been to any other church, have I?

anon: No, well, this is the thing.

This exchange is fascinating in bringing out the reactions of ordinary readers to strong statements of doctrinally orthodox distinctions (for Holder) arising out of a hermeneutical move from Mal 3. The group do not accept that God is silent, nor that there is any meaningful distinction between God speaking through the Bible and 'ongoingly' – points made on the basis of their Christian experience. Such is the resistance to Boice that TommyH eventually questions the implied cessationism in Boice's commentary, goes on to challenge Holder's tradition of functional cessationism, and SiobhanH then wonders if only knowing the Holder tradition is enough. Here the mediated fusion of text and doctrinal horizons is contested, leading to a re-examination of the group's horizon, and also revealing greater heterogeneity in the Holder tradition than public discourse would suggest.

Personal Bible Reading Mediation

Other vehicles for hermeneutical mediation were plentiful, but not necessarily related to specific congregational Bible settings. Space does not permit a full account of these many mediators, although they will be drawn on selectively

---

48   Participant observer troublemaking.

later in this and then subsequent chapters.[49] The focus here, however, will be on mediators relating to personal Bible reading (PBR), or 'Bible reading aids', since this was a key Bible use in both churches.

81 per cent of questionnaire respondents at Holder used a variety of aids,[50] with 18 per cent of the questionnaire sample using commentaries for PBR.[51] This high use of Bible reading aids was probably due in part to centralised ordering through a designated book person, CharlotteH, who also promoted them in public settings.[52] The enthusiasm for PBR at Holder was considered in Chapters 4 and 5, although there was some evidence that expectations of PBR were ideals that were aimed for but not always achieved. Sometimes it was 'more of a habit than an actual delight' (JustinH), or 'quite dry' and 'can become a superstitious ritual' (BridgetH). Only a few interviewees expressed some guilt about not reading regularly enough, so SiobhanH said 'I know I beat myself up about it, but I do feel that I should read it more'. Interviewees were also asked about parts of the Bible they found difficult to understand, and many referred to passages in which it was difficult to find any relevance for today (commonly OT books and even the OT itself).[53] SiobhanH said 'I never knowingly go to the OT' since 'the list of names is very off-putting to me' so instead 'I comfort read' which she thought was 'a bit naughty'. Most other interviewees, however, wanted to be more positive, so WendyH said of OT reading 'I don't think anything's ever wasted'.

In terms of hermeneutics, however, it may be inferred that most congregants perceived PBR as an effective mediator, since PBR aids were ranked in the top third of influence items.[54] Of *Explore*, produced by a publisher within the same Reformed evangelical tradition as Holder (The Good Book Company, 2007), JustinH commented 'they're not simplistic' and 'they challenge thinking' by giving 'a core of understanding to the passage but actually challenging further thinking beyond it'. Commentaries were also significant hermeneutical mediators for PBR, since they have 'something you can get your teeth into a bit', whilst not being 'big heavy scholarly things' (HarryH). RodneyH found Wiersbe's commentaries 'brilliant' because 'they're very accessible', and he would incorporate them into his PBR. Study Bibles were owned by 49 per cent of

---

[49] Three main categories of hermeneutical mediators emerged, namely the wider church (including Christian events), print, and bible-related courses.

[50] N=97. The Bible Society survey discussed in Chapter 1 had 43% of non-leaders and 46% of leaders using PBR aids (excluding commentaries) (Bible Society, 2008).

[51] N=105. This was a separate question.

[52] CharlotteH in conversation, 16/10/05; JoeH, LucyH, BridgetH in interview.

[53] See Appendix F for the list of Bible problems.

[54] Both respondents and sample.

respondents,[55] and since the commentary is placed alongside the biblical text, it seems likely that they too were influential hermeneutical mediators for PBR.[56]

The Bible passion of Fellowship translated into some enthusiasm for PBR, as at Holder, although not to the same degree. Expectations were similarly qualified by the admission that God did not always speak directly to the individual through PBR, but there were always other benefits mentioned such as a sense of peace, or greater engagement with the text. More widely there was an underlying sense that one 'ought' to be reading the Bible more regularly, although feeling guilty about failing to do so was often attributed to earlier stages of interviewees' Christian lives.

PBR aids were used by 43 per cent of questionnaire respondents,[57] and were ranked in the middle third for influence on Bible understanding.[58] 11 per cent of the sample used commentaries for their PBR,[59] and 46 per cent of respondents owned a Study Bible,[60] which may also have had some influence on PBR. The use of PBR aids by interviewees varied from a current loyalty to just one type such as *Every Day With Jesus* (EDWJ) to a more promiscuous mixing of various types of aids combined with the self-selection of biblical chapters. SarahF spoke positively of EDWJ because 'nearly always something in [the EDWJ] readings strike me as "Hey, that's a pull up"'. She added that EDWJ 'speaks very personally to me', although 'the Scriptures do, of course' but the 'personal way [EDWJ] is written' enabled her to 'link it' to actions in her life. In her past use of PBR aids, PenelopeF had encountered some hermeneutical difference:

> **PenelopeF:** I went through a phase of using some really good Bible study notes ... Is it William Barclay? Which was quite interesting ... because ... I'm not sure if he believed in many of the miracles actually ... I think that ... the sort of theology that he did, and history, that I found quite interesting, some of the insight that he gave.

> **Andrew:** And he has ... a different theological approach to perhaps your own standpoint, was that a problem for you?

> **PenelopeF:** No, I don't think it was, because ... I think I was ... using it more from the ... background knowledge he would give about Jewish customs ... what things would have meant in religion then, that sort of thing.

---

55   N=100.

56   So DennisH said of his 'Spirit-Filled Bible' when reading 'sometimes "I wonder what that means", so, I turn the page and I say, "Oh, that's what it means"'.

57   N=73.

58   Both respondent and sample means.

59   N=75.

60   N=72.

This 'interesting' mediation regarding the cultural context of the Gospels was a telling instance of the acceptability of diverse mediators within Fellowship.

Hermeneutical problems with PBR aids were also identified by interviewees, so SteveF found *The Word for Today* 'good' and encouraged the young people to use the 'youth' version, but added:

> The danger is ... that sometimes you can just get into the whole thing of just reading the application and that can become your Bible, and I think it can be dangerous in that way ... I do believe strongly that God does speak through it, but he also speaks through the Bible – I've heard many people say, "Oh, I did *The Word for Today* and it was ace, it just spoke to me", but they're talking about that little application part, not the Bible passage.

The potential hermeneutical 'danger' perceived by SteveF here is that the 'application' or contemporary horizon can almost engulf the horizon of the biblical text. A veiled critique of PBR aids was made by a number of interviewees, who talked of their use when they were younger or new Christians. Those who did not use PBR aids were often critical, with TomF the most damning:

> I think passages which I think would probably strike me in one way ... quite often ... I ... read what somebody else has written and just think that's really quite cheesy.
>
> ...
>
> ... well, to be honest, I've not read one for sort of ten years or more, but ... I think the Bible itself has some very strong things to say, and then I think these Bible reading notes, quite often, something quite twee ... comes out of it.

TomF here demonstrates the relative freedom in Fellowship to be quite critical of their hermeneutical mediators, as he effectively implies in this excerpt that PBR aids can emasculate the Scriptures. This quote also points to the role of internal hermeneutical critics within congregations, and how they might themselves function as significant mediators.

Comparing Mediatory Dynamics

Hermeneutical mediation, both internally and externally, differed significantly between the two congregations. *Internal mediation* at Fellowship was very much 'trickle-down' in nature, since the diverse preaching was low authority in nature, the housegroups were largely autonomous, and there was no centralised system for print mediators. By contrast, Holder's mediation was more 'stream-down', with a narrower range of preachers,[61] a much greater emphasis on the importance of preaching, a membership process which included doctrinal commitments, as well as centralised mediatory systems for housegroups, PBR and Christian books. The dynamics of these contrasting mediatory systems largely cohered with their broader congregational values, emphasising informality and low authority at Fellowship, compared with a concern for guarding congregational identity and boundaries at Holder. These contrasting dynamics also contributed to how substantive a hermeneutical apprenticeship was to be found in each congregation. Unsurprisingly, given their 'stream-down' mediation and greater exposure to Scripture, Holder was able to inculcate its own hermeneutical practices amongst its members more optimally than Fellowship.

With regard to *external mediation*, Fellowship was a more permeable congregation than Holder,[62] with horizontal mediation being more significant. That is, Fellowship congregants accessed external mediators more readily and in less dependence on their formal internal mediators than at Holder. Factors of congregational make-up also fitted this pattern, so Fellowship congregants had a more diverse range of prior Christian traditions,[63] a much shorter tradition,[64] and fewer family interrelations. The degree of congregational permeability towards external mediators (and their hermeneutical innovations) was in continuity with Bebbington's historical account of cultural diffusion within evangelicalism, whereby permeability is related to certain factors of congregational make-up, namely education, class, and age (2008).[65] Such permeability was evident through Fellowship congregants visiting other churches far more often,[66] and although a greater proportion of Holder congregants attended Christian events,[67] these were

---

[61]   OwenH gave the sermon at 60% of Sunday services during the fieldwork (N=10), whereas DerekF delivered just 33% of Sunday morning sermons (N=12). Furthermore, four Fellowship Sunday morning sermons were by visitors, compared to one at Holder Sunday services, see Appendix A.

[62]   See also Ammerman for this terminology (1998: 81).

[63]   26% of Holder respondents had no church affiliation prior to Holder (N=104), compared to 4% at Fellowship (N=74).

[64]   Over one hundred years at Holder and just over thirty years (by the most generous congregational trajectory) for Fellowship. Also congregational longevity, so 56% of Holder respondents had been at the church over 10 years, compared to 44% at Fellowship (N=105/75).

[65]   Educational level was higher at Fellowship, and Fellowship had far fewer older people (12% ≥ 60 years old at Fellowship, N=75; 30% ≥ 60 years old at Holder, N=105).

[66]   49% at Fellowship (N=63) and 19% at Holder (N=99), although Holder had a Sunday evening service which meant there was less opportunity for congregants to visit other churches.

[67]   49% at Holder (N=98), and 35% at Fellowship (N=68).

largely within Holder's own evangelical tribe compared to Fellowship's slightly more diverse attendance patterns. There was little overlap for Christian events between the two congregations, as was also the case for Christian periodicals and books that were thought helpful in aiding understanding of the Bible. However, a number of (mostly minimally explicit) bestselling Christian authors were being read by interviewees in both churches,[68] which may point to the mediatory power of the Christian book industry and bookshops to reach across evangelical boundaries. To the extent that the congregations drew on tribal and theologically homogenous mediators – more pronounced at Holder – there is then some evidence for David Clines's contention that hermeneutics is dictated by the demands of the market (1997). Songs, however, were exceptional in having the greatest mediator overlap between the two churches, with approximately 20 per cent being common to both congregations during the fieldwork.[69] This commonality points to the influence of the charismatic movement on contemporary worship songs across the evangelical tribes (cf. Stackhouse, 2004: 44–5; Tomlinson, 1995: 15f; Warner, 2007: 70f; Ward, 2005). It was not surprising, then, to find greater theological dissonance in Holder's songs than in Fellowship. In addition songs mediated a high incorporation of Scripture and balanced use of the OT/NT to Fellowship.[70]

Notably for hermeneutics, Holder's key mediating biblical scholars (normally through print) were largely missing from Fellowship (and vice versa), although Fellowship did not have key scholars in the same way, with the possible exception of Charles. Print mediation was more hierarchical at Holder than at Fellowship, this being boosted through their focussed Christian event attendance. Holder's relational forms of mediating print were partially driven by a concern for whether the print mediator was within congregational doctrinal boundaries, rather than the more social mediatory dynamic of Fellowship. Holder congregants read more Christian books in general,[71] and a slightly greater proportion of Holder

---

[68] E.g. John Eldridge, Bill Hybels, John Ortberg, Rick Warren, Philip Yancey, Brother Yun.

[69] Holder 20% / Fellowship 21% (N=65/62).

[70] Bible use was usually higher at Holder, but Scripture incorporation was higher in Fellowship songs (Holder 68%; Fellowship 77%; N=65/62), and OT/NT use was much more balanced than in all other Fellowship Bible uses (all other settings: >80% NT, <20% OT; songs: 59% NT, 43% OT). Holder's OT/NT balance was not distinctly different to its other settings (all other settings: 50% NT, 50% OT; songs: 62% NT, 42% OT).

[71] At Holder 78% had read one or more Christian books in the last three months (N=102); at Fellowship, 59% (N=75).

congregants used commentaries,[72] but they owned less of them,[73] as well as fewer other Bible-related books (with the exception of Study Bibles), particularly those of maximal hermeneutical explicitness. Small group use of print mediators partially matched this arrangement, with Holder housegroups making frequent reference to commentaries and Bible-related books at a low to medium level of explicitness, whereas Fellowship housegroups made more occasional use of some maximally explicit hermeneutical mediators.[74] Services and sermons saw almost no references to biblical scholars in both churches, perhaps due to the perception that this was inappropriate for public settings, although again Fellowship had one sermon (S1f) that explicitly drew on insights from biblical scholars.

Proportions of congregants who had or had not taken Bible-related courses were similar for the levels up to and including the Higher Education level of Certificate/Diploma.[75] Those with a degree or higher were absent in the Holder sample, but 4 per cent at Fellowship.[76] The qualitative accounts would suggest that the church-based courses at Fellowship, of which there was a greater variety, were more hermeneutically explicit on average. Furthermore, Fellowship interviewees appeared to have been exposed to a greater variety of hermeneutical approaches on Bible-related courses. Strikingly, 'Training/Theology' courses at Fellowship were perceived to be much more influential on Bible understanding than at Holder, although it was still only ranked in the middle third.[77] Notably, the pastor of Fellowship, DerekF, was able to mediate maximally explicit hermeneutics from his theological college into small groups and to other settings through links he had established.

Resistance to mediation was a function of congregational identity. Although criticism of internal hermeneutical mediators was limited at both churches, Fellowship congregants appeared to be freer in their resistance to hermeneutical aspects of Bible settings. This cohered with the lower authority structures at Fellowship, and also Fellowship's much shorter tradition that was still in the initial stages of formation. Holder congregants were much less critical of their internal

---

[72] All types of commentary use were proportionately slightly higher at Holder. Furthermore 21% of the Holder sample could name a helpful commentary series, whereas only 11% could do so at Fellowship (N=105/75).

[73] 5% of Holder congregants owned seven or more commentaries (N=98), compared to 15% who owned eight or more at Fellowship (N=73).

[74] This pattern of difference for print mediators was less marked for PBR aids, in that Holder PBR aids appeared to be at the same level of hermeneutical explicitness as at Fellowship.

[75] These correspond to the first and second year of a British undergraduate degree respectively.

[76] N=99/69.

[77] Holder/Fellowship (N=55/45). This was the *only* influence item in which the absolute mean respondent value for Fellowship was higher than at Holder.

mediators, which may reflect the greater doctrinal commonality at Holder, their higher authority structures, and the greater 'reverence' they accorded to Bible settings. Regarding external mediators, resistance to other churches and Christian events as mediators was more marked at Fellowship, probably because they were more diverse in their patterns of attendance, but possibly also due to their low authority 'habit'. Through Holder congregants visiting fewer other churches and less diverse Christian events, there was an implicit rejection of evangelical mediators from outside their tribe. However, resistance was lower than at Fellowship due to lack of contact with these mediators from the wider tradition. The same pattern was seen with print mediators, although somewhat amplified, where Holder congregants resisted print mediators less, due to the enthusiastic and hierarchical mediation of select scholars, as well as there being less individual (horizontal) access to print mediators. Resistance to PBR aids was particularly marked at Fellowship in comparison to Holder, both in terms of much lower usage at Fellowship, and also many critical comments from Fellowship interviewees, which again were less pronounced at Holder. Small groups in the two churches were special cases for resistance of both internal and external mediators. Disagreements in Holder housegroups were generally taken more seriously and were often related to doctrinal or hermeneutical issues. Fellowship disagreements did not have the same drive towards resolution, and tended to be more pragmatic in nature. This difference between small groups in the two churches further cohered with their respective epistemologies. Bible-related courses that were church-based were largely well-received in both congregations, with guaranteed theological homogeneity and highly relational mediation likely to be factors. Fellowship were more cautious about Bible-related courses in general, and had more 'scare stories' about external courses than Holder,[78] but Holder participants appeared to have experienced a greater challenge to their hermeneutical framework through external courses.

Mediating Hermeneutics

What emerges from this analysis of hermeneutical mediation? This chapter has demonstrated that mediation, both internal and external, cannot be ignored when seeking to engage with congregational hermeneutics. Hermeneutical practices are shaped by how they are learned (cf. Astley, 2002: 4f). It should also be evident, then, that hermeneutical mediation includes the multiple ways that congregants learn about the Bible, whether intentional or not. Hermeneutical

---

[78] So SteveF had friends that had studied Theology looking at it 'in this kind of cynical, critical way' where he had 'seen people lose their passion for Jesus with Theology, which is a shame'.

mediation therefore provides significant insight into the processes of formation and transformation within congregations. Resistance to such mediation may also be critical for transformation, as has been seen, although in less predictable ways.

Following the distinction made between affirmative and disruptive reading introduced in earlier chapters, there were certain associations attached to Holder and Fellowship's mediatory dynamics. Affirmation of horizons through scriptural encounter was associated with stronger mediatory dynamics and more homogenous hermeneutical mediators. Disruption of horizons was associated with weaker mediatory dynamics and a congregational permeability that allowed for more heterogeneous mediators. There were varying degrees of intentionality regarding mediation in general, but little explicit mediation of hermeneutical practices at both churches.

These points raise questions of normativity for hermeneutical mediators. What is theologically desirable for such mediation? From the tale told in this chapter, and building on arguments made earlier, there needs to be a balance or even tension between affirmative and disruptive readings. This applies to individual horizons, as well as the less tangible but nevertheless significant congregational horizons. Mediators have a critical role to play in terms of achieving this balance. For Holder and Fellowship, mediatory dynamics and location on the homogeneity/heterogeneity spectrum were significant for transformation. There were strengths to both configurations, but weaknesses were also evident. Too much homogeneity combined with strong mediatory dynamics suggests an overly affirmative approach to biblical engagement. Too much heterogeneity combined with weak mediatory dynamics suggests an overly disruptive approach to biblical engagement. One has the danger of fossilising tradition, so that congregations cannot hear new things from Scripture, the other destabilises tradition and relativises the value of Scripture. The importance of affirming tradition was underlined in Chapter 4. For both Holder and Fellowship, however, the encounter with difference through heterogeneous hermeneutical mediators was often a fruitful and even profound experience. The tension between affirmation and disruption might be described in virtue language as the tension between *faithfulness* and *openness*. As has been seen, the terms 'faithful' and 'radical' were prevalent at Holder and Fellowship respectively. Some of the examples considered here also provided instances of the related virtue of *courage*, which is sometimes needed for virtuous resistance to mediation and tradition. Out of this chapter, then, faithfulness and openness in tension, alongside courage, are held up as virtues for hermeneutics, especially the importance of openness to heterogeneous mediators (further developed in Chapter 8).

A notable example of structured openness in the churches was the significance of boundary crossing mediators. That is, there were some mediators that were able to cross the boundaries of theological and congregational tradition, mainly certain songwriters and bestselling Christian books/authors. Openness to such mediators appeared to be due to their high profile and trusted 'brand' status; hence their slightly dissonant theologies (and thus hermeneutics) were gifted to the congregations with no apparent resistance. Admittedly, these mediators were mostly quite implicit hermeneutically, but boundary crossers still provided a safe route for exposing congregations to limited hermeneutical diversity. Writing of songs, but with relevance for other mediators also, Thomas Troeger notes that theological reconstruction is a key function of songs. They help to 'save the church from bibliolatry' by generating new and multiple meanings via a midrashic hermeneutics and concern. Such hymnody will 'reveal the [theological diversity] that their dogmatics have tried to discourage' (1998: 15). This concrete instance helps to give some content and shape to what hermeneutical openness might look like.

Chapter 8

Virtue

Virtue is the hinge for this account of congregational hermeneutics. Introduced in Chapter 2, hermeneutical virtues are those characteristics needed for a Christian reading of Scripture. Through the tale of two churches, the shape of seven hermeneutical virtues has begun to emerge. The purpose of this chapter is to substantially thicken the account of hermeneutical virtue told thus far.

Before launching into the theological ethnographic case for hermeneutical virtue, a selective sketch of the virtue ethics story will provide some valuable context and categories. The English 'virtue' derives from the Latin *virtus* which is a translation of the Greek, *aretē*, which is usually translated as 'excellence'. Virtue ethics has an ancient pedigree, stretching back to the Greek philosophers Plato and Aristotle. Aristotle understood human beings to have a goal or *telos*, namely *eudaimonia*, which may be best captured by the English phrase 'human flourishing'. Virtues are therefore the excellences of character required to achieve such human flourishing. Virtues are also acquired excellences, in that 'nature gives us the capacity to receive them, and this capacity is brought to maturity by habit' (*NE*, 2.1.3). Aristotle expands on this point:

> The virtues on the other hand we acquire by first having actually practised them, just as we do the arts. We learn an art or craft by doing the things that we shall have to do when we have learnt it: for instance, men become builders by building houses, harpers by playing on the harp. Similarly we become just by doing just acts, temperate by doing temperate acts, brave by doing brave acts (*NE*, 2.1.4).

Four primary virtues emerged out of this Greek philosophical tradition, namely prudence (*phronēsis* or practical wisdom), justice, courage and temperance. It was argued that human flourishing hinges upon these four virtues, so they became known as the cardinal virtues (from the Latin *cardo*, meaning 'hinge'). For Aristotle, practical wisdom unites all the virtues in the sense that it is necessary for the exercise of any virtue (*NE*, 6.13.5–6). The virtuous person is able to avoid the vices of excess or deficiency through the exercise of practical wisdom in a given situation (*NE*, 2.6.15–16).[1] Of particular and controversial interest for hermeneutical virtue, Aristotle makes a distinction between moral

---

[1] This view is often referred to as the 'doctrine of the mean'.

and intellectual virtue, the former acquired through habit, the latter through teaching (*NE*, 2.1.1).

Christian theology has drawn on this classical inheritance of virtue ethics, but has sought to baptise the tradition over the centuries. At first glance, Scripture itself does not appear to be overly concerned with virtue ethics. The standard Greek word for virtue, *aretē*, is very rare in the NT (Wright, 2010: 53–4, 155). John Barton has commented that one will struggle to find an explicit virtue ethics in the Old Testament (1999). Second and subsequent readings of Scripture would suggest that an implicit virtue ethic is much easier to find. Implicit here does not mean hidden, but rather virtue construed in a different form. Barton tentatively argues that the extensive narrative and narratively shaped material in Scripture present 'unvarnished and complex characters for the contemplation of the reader', which may contribute to 'a kind of profile of the good life' through 'helping to shape and train' our minds (1999: 19, 21). With a greater degree of confidence, Ellen Davis argues that the Israelite wisdom literature, especially Proverbs, might function as 'an exegetical base for renewing a biblically informed virtue tradition'. Amongst many passages, she cites the woman of Proverbs 31 as an '"A to Z" demonstration of what the virtues look like in embodied action' (2002: 186, 195). Within the New Testament, Tom Wright makes a bold case for a distinctively Christian 'rebirth' of the classical virtue tradition (2010).[2] Of the Pauline writings, he plausibly argues that Paul teaches a virtue ethic, which includes notions of moral progress and the hard work that this entails, held within the framework of God's grace to us (2010: 54; 2013: 1374). Drawing on a wide range of biblical passages and themes,[3] Wright particularly identifies Col 3 as a 'primer in Christian virtue' (2010: 126). It is not hard to see why:

> As God's chosen ones, holy and beloved, clothe yourselves with compassion, kindness, humility, meekness, and patience. Bear with one another and, if anyone has a complaint against another, forgive each other; just as the Lord has forgiven you, so you also must forgive. Above all, clothe yourselves with love, which binds everything together in perfect harmony (Col 3:12–14, NRSV).

---

[2]   Wright is not alone in making this case. Within a pessimistic account of explicit biblical virtue ethics, Barton still asserts that 'the Pauline epistles abound in the language of virtues and vices' (1999: 14). Wayne Meeks sees the purpose of Philippians as 'the shaping of Christian *phronēsis*, a practical moral reasoning that is conformed to [Christ's] death in hope of his resurrection' (1991: 333; see also Rooms, 2012).

[3]   Key passages are Rom 5, 12; 1 Cor 13; Gal 5; Eph 4:1–16; Col 3; Jas 1:2–4; 2 Pe 1:5–8; Php; 1 Thess 4:1–8, 5:1–11. The fruit of the Spirit are understood as another way of talking about virtue (2010: 177f; cf. Davis, 2002: 184). Martin Luther, in his commentary on Galatians, describes the fruit of the Spirit as a better name for virtue (1949).

Christian virtue is distinctive, firstly, because there are virtues in the New Testament that would not have been recognised as such in the ancient world, in particular patience, humility, chastity and love (Wright, 2013: 1116). Faith, hope and love, especially love, are singled out for special emphasis (so 1 Cor 13; Col 1:4–5; 1 Thess 1:3, 5:8). More distinctive still is the different Story in which Christian virtue is set, thus giving them a radically different shape and *telos*. As discussed in Chapter 2, Christian virtue is understood within the formation and transformation of Christians in community, where that transformation is directed towards God's new creation.[4]

An early Christian development of virtue is found in Augustine, who understood virtue 'to be nothing else than perfect love of God' (*Mor. Ecc.*, 15.25). The cardinal (and all other) virtues are directed toward the love of God, and find expression in the love of neighbour. Consequently, the virtues of non-Christians are 'rather vices than virtues so long as there is no reference to God in the matter' (*Civ. Dei*, 19.25).[5] Beyond the Patristic period, Aquinas stands out as the medieval systematiser who integrates Christian and Aristotelian thought on virtue and much else besides.[6] Drawing on Augustine and the work of others from the scholastic period, Aquinas made the case for three theological virtues in addition to the cardinal virtues, namely faith, hope and love. For the three theological virtues, their 'object is God, inasmuch as they direct us aright to God' and 'they are infused in us by God alone' rather than acquired as other virtues.[7] Infused virtues are only made known to us through 'Divine revelation, contained in Holy Writ' (*ST* I–II 62.1). Such theological virtues are 'superhuman', for 'they are virtues of man as sharing in the grace of God' (*ST* I–II 58.3).

The decline of virtue ethics within the Christian tradition and beyond, from the Reformation until the twentieth century, has been well documented, as well as overstated at times (Frede, 2013). Martin Luther was famously no fan of Aristotle, describing the *Nicomachean Ethics* as 'the worst enemy of grace' and 'directly contrary to God's will and the Christian virtues',[8] although his objection was to virtue acquired apart from God's grace, rather than virtue

---

[4]   Wright contrasts the Pauline eschatologically driven communal virtue ethic (e.g. Rom 12:2; Eph 4: 23–4; Col 3:10) with the heroic this-life focus of virtue in classical accounts (2010: 149).

[5]   Thus the 'splendid vices' of the pagans, a phrase which cannot be ascribed directly to Augustine (Wetzel, 2004: 271).

[6]   So Aquinas maintains Aristotle's distinction between moral and intellectual virtues (Copleston, 1955: 215).

[7]   So Aquinas diverges from Aristotle over the ends to which virtue is directed (Copleston, 1955: 216–17). He also diverges from Augustine on pagan virtue – these are not vices, but genuine virtues in a limited sense (Porter, 2006: 102–3).

[8]   *Disputation* 41, 2012 and *Twenty-Seven Articles* 25 in *To The Christian Nobility*, 1883.

per se.[9] Space does not permit examination of the complex post-Reformation history of virtue, except to note its renaissance in the mid-twentieth century[10] and its subsequent development in the work of the philosopher, Alasdair MacIntyre, and theologian, Stanley Hauerwas. MacIntyre argues for a recovery of Aristotelian virtue ethics, since 'the Enlightenment Project' failed due to its loss of *telos* as a meaningful category. Weaving together the concepts of narrative, tradition and practices, MacIntyre makes the case for virtue as narratively construed within a particular tradition. He argued that 'I can only answer the question "What am I to do?" if I can answer the prior question "Of what story or stories do I find myself a part?"' (1985: 216). With such talk of stories and echoes of eschatology, it is not surprising that MacIntyre has been influential within some theological circles, with Hauerwas perhaps the most well-known. In his memoir, Hauerwas summarises the 'primary task' of his work as 'to demonstrate the link between the truth of what we say we believe and the shape of the lives we have' (2010a: 69). This is exemplified in the introduction to *A Community of Character*, where the church is described as 'a distinct society with an integrity peculiar to itself'. Hauerwas continues '[Christians] most important social task is nothing less than to be a community capable of hearing the story of God we find in the scripture and living in a manner that is faithful to that story' (1981: 1). Character formed in community is the signature theme of Hauerwas's work.[11] 'Hopeful' virtues are to be developed, distinct from non-Christian traditions, since we are an eschatological community (Hauerwas and Pinches, 1997; 2010).

While virtue is an important theme for this book, space does not permit a detailed examination of the debates around virtue ethics. The intention rather is to build on existing virtue theorists as far as they are relevant for the concerns of congregational hermeneutics. This selective sketch of virtue above does, however, call for some positioning on my part. I contend that a reasonable biblical and theological case can be made for the ongoing significance of Christian virtues today, and that such virtues do not need to undermine justification by faith or devalue the grace of God. As Hauerwas and Pinches note of Romans 5, virtue and justification talk sit very close together. Are virtues infused or acquired through habituation? Virtue is a gift from God that also leads to growth in grace. Simply put, both (Wright,

---

[9]   Such a pretence of virtue was hypocrisy according to Luther. Jennifer Herdt's chapter entitled 'Saved Hypocrites' navigates the complexities of this point (2008: 173f). I am grateful to my colleague, Dr Neil MacDonald, for clarifying this point.

[10]   Many commentators point to Elizabeth Anscombe's 1950s article as a key turning point for virtue ethics in the wider academic world (1958).

[11]   In one of his earliest books, Hauerwas identifies the 'task of contemporary theological ethics' as 'to state the language of faith in terms of the Christian responsibility to be formed in the likeness of Christ' (1974: 29).

2010: 170; Hauerwas and Pinches, 1997: 114, 128). I also contend that the traditional distinction between moral and intellectual virtue does not stand up well to explorations of hermeneutical virtue – a point developed at greater length at the end of the chapter. While affirming MacIntyre's emphasis on the importance of narrative for understanding virtue, I would concur with many critiques that his account of virtue is still too Aristotelian in emphasis.[12] Similarly, while benefitting greatly from Hauerwas's account of virtue, there are a number of points of divergence, especially in terms of needing to describe the practices of actual churches, and to do so within a more realist framework (cf. Scharen and Vigen, 2011: 50–53; Vanhoozer, 1998: 379).

A Tale of Hermeneutical Virtues

It is time to move from virtue ethics in general to hermeneutical virtue in particular. Hermeneutical virtue was introduced in Chapter 2 using Vanhoozer's definition as 'a disposition of the mind and heart that arises from the motivation for understanding, for cognitive contact with the text' (1998: 376). It was noted that virtue hermeneutics has a long history, although nearly all the explicit treatments have emerged in recent decades. Augustine offers the only (nearly) explicit ancient approach, when he argues that our interpretations of Scripture should always aim to 'build up this twofold love of God and our neighbour' (*Doc. Chr.* 1.36).

Table 8.1 (below) shows that love and humility are the hermeneutical virtues of choice, yet there is also a wide variety of other hermeneutical virtues that have been proposed by theologians over the last three decades. There is also a parallel tradition of 'intellectual virtue' within philosophy, from which theologians may benefit.[13] For example, Linda Trinkhaus Zagzebski proposes carefulness, perseverance, humility, vigour, flexibility, courage, thoroughness, open-mindedness, fair-mindedness, insightfulness and integrity as intellectual virtues (1996: 155).[14] W. Jay Wood contends that for Christians 'forging virtuous habits of moral and intellectual character is part of what is required of us to grow to the full stature of all that God intends for humans to be' (1998: 19).

---

[12] 'If the language and logic of virtue tips in any direction, it is away from Christianity and toward the Greek context in which it originated. For Christians, it can be used with great reward, but it must be purified as used or else bear bad fruit' (Hauerwas and Pinches, 1997: 57). This dimension of Christian virtue is one area where Hauerwas diverges from MacIntyre (2010: 86).

[13] As have Vanhoozer (1998: 443n49) and Briggs (2010: 24f).

[14] See also W. Jay Wood (1998) and Michael DePaul and Linda Zagzebski (2003).

Table 8.1 Summary of Proposed Hermeneutical/Interpretative Virtues

Name	Implicit or Explicit	Work(s)	Hermeneutical / interpretative Virtue(s) identified
Augustine 397	Implicit	*De Doctrina Christiana*	Charity / love
Stephen Fowl and L. Gregory Jones 1991	Explicit	Reading in Communion	Practical wisdom, 'critical virtues of professional biblical scholarship'
N. T. Wright 1992	Implicit	The New Testament and the People of God	Love
Eugene Rogers 1996	Implicit / Explicit	How the Virtues of the Interpreter Presuppose and Perfect Hermeneutics	Prudence
Stephen Fowl 1998	Explicit	Engaging Scripture	Charity, (vigilance)
Kevin Vanhoozer 1998 / 2006	Explicit	Is There a Meaning in this Text? / 'Imprisoned or Free?'	Faith, hope, love, honesty, openness, attention, obedience, (humility, conviction)
Alan Jacobs 2001	Implicit	A Theology of Reading	Love
L. Gregory Jones 2002 / The Scripture Project 2003	Explicit	'Formed and Transformed by Scripture' / The Art of Reading Scripture	Receptivity, humility, truthfulness, courage, charity, (humour), imagination
Daniel Treier 2006	Explicit	Virtue and the Voice of God	*Phronēsis* (prudence)
Angus Paddison 2009	Explicit	Scripture: A Very Theological Proposal	Patience
Richard Briggs 2010	Explicit	The Virtuous Reader	Humility, wisdom, trust, charity, receptivity
Richard Wyld 2014	Explicit	The Hermeneutics of Hope (PhD, Durham)	Hope
Uche Anizor 2014	Explicit	Kings and Priests: Scripture's Theological Account of its Readers	Fear, humility, delight
Jacob L. Goodson 2015	Explicit	Narrative Theology and the Hermeneutical Virtues	Humility, patience, prudence
Andrew Rogers 2013, 2015	Explicit	'Towards Virtuous Apprenticeship' / Congregational Hermeneutics	Honesty, faithfulness, openness, courage, humility, confidence, community

Note: I have limited the table to those who, either implicitly or explicitly, have a significant constructive focus on how virtues may inform biblical hermeneutics. With this proviso in mind, I have attempted to identify all works in English addressing virtue hermeneutics up until 2015.

The seven hermeneutical virtues emerging from the tale of two churches, introduced in Chapter 2, are honesty, faithfulness, openness, courage, humility, confidence and community. Each of these hermeneutical virtues will now be considered in turn,[15] working towards answering 'Why these virtues?', 'Who should have these virtues?', and 'How are these virtues developed?' alongside related critical questions. The key contention is that growth in Christian character is significant for how well we read Scripture, and therefore virtue language provides us with a theologically natural hermeneutical vocabulary.

Honesty

There were indicative signs of hermeneutical honesty in both Holder and Fellowship, as has been seen in Chapter 4 particularly. At Holder, in Housegroup X, a pointed handout question asked in relation to Mal 1:6–14: 'Is there such a thing as empty and useless religious practices within the Christian Church?' KateH replied emphatically 'Yes', and her husband, KarlH, then commented: 'Scripture getting in the way, to the extent that a church has a great focus on Scripture, but other relationships are not right in the church'. ThelmaH, as we have heard, interjected that 'Reformedness' was a better example of 'getting in the way' (X2). Interestingly, JustinH in interview also understood Holder in its earlier days to hold that 'Calvinism was the doctrine, rather than what Christian truth is'. RodneyH, from a leadership point of view, spoke of 'always reviewing what we do, biblically, and making changes where we feel we need to, to get back to what Scripture would intend'. Examples were plural (male) leadership and discontinuing female housegroup leaders. At Fellowship, the pastor, DerekF, understood their functional Christocentrism to have displaced a Trinitarian concept of God to a degree, and noted a 'swing back' towards being 'more explicitly Trinitarian'. Such an awareness had been prompted by an outsider visiting Fellowship. TomF spoke movingly of changing from a 'me-centred' Bible reading perspective that 'weakened the message of the Bible very significantly', to one that perceived Scripture to have a broader scope. At the same time, as has been seen, there remained substantial areas of their congregational horizons (and so traditions) that were not uncovered when engaging with Scripture.

Honesty is both a very hermeneutical and theological virtue.[16] As discussed in Chapter 3, Gadamer asks 'how we can break the spell of our own fore-meanings',

---

[15] Drawing on all of Chapters 4–7, as explained in Chapter 1.

[16] As can be seen in Table 8.1, apart from my publications, only Vanhoozer identifies honesty as an interpretive virtue. However, 'truthfulness' is certainly very close to honesty, and this is identified by both Jones and the Scripture Project. Explicit biblical reference to honesty and its corresponding vice, dishonesty, are largely found in the Old Testament in the context of economic justice (e.g. Lev 19:36; Deut 25:15–16; Jer 22:17; Ezek 22; Prov 16:11) and to a lesser degree as a general character description (e.g. Gen 42; 1 Sam 29:6; but also Lk

and so argues that the interpreter should be 'situating the other meaning [of the text] in relation to the whole of our own meanings or ourselves in relation to it' (2004: 270–71). To know where we stand in relation to the text, we must know the truth of our own horizons. As Vanhoozer says of interpretive honesty, it means 'acknowledging one's prior commitments and preunderstandings' (1998: 377). Admittedly, God speaking through Scripture may bring that knowledge into being, particularly in conversion, but that is no reason for dismissing the need to grow in hermeneutical honesty throughout our Christian lives. Honesty prompts the self-examination or even self-criticism of congregational horizons, as the signs from Holder and Fellowship indicate above. Indeed, the congregants were seeking to reflect truthfully upon themselves and their church. Such horizonal honesty is a fundamental part of theological reflection, which underlines the importance of rooting aspects of practical theology education within the church. When hermeneutical honesty is not valued, it is all too easy to collapse the distinction between congregational horizons and the Scriptures (as per the analysis in Chapter 4). Positively, honesty can engender a celebration of congregational tradition formed by Scripture over many years, as also argued in Chapter 4. Negatively, honesty compels Christian communities to acknowledge the potential impact of sin upon their understanding of Scripture.[17] There are interests and ideologies in our traditions that may need unmasking, and honesty is required. Fowl majors on this point when he almost adds 'vigilance' to charity as an interpretative virtue, developed through an exegesis of Lk 11:34–5, as follows (Fowl's translation):

> Your eye is the lamp of your body; when your eye is single then your body is full of light; but when it is not sound, then your whole body is full of darkness. Therefore, be vigilant lest the light in you (prove to) be darkness.

Fowl argues that the expression translated as 'when your eye is single' conveys the idea of 'focussing one's attention on God alone' (1998: 75f). Fowl concludes that this passage is crucial for:

> ... understanding how a body of believers is to read and perform Scripture in ways that do not simply underwrite and replicate sinful actions ... this passage calls followers to a life of vigilant self-reflection, ever seeking to keep their "eye" single-mindedly focused on Jesus (1998: 77–8).

16:1–13). The prevalence of honesty as a biblical theme is greatly increased if 'truthfulness' and its variants are included.

[17]   Sometimes referred to as the 'noetic effects of sin'.

Christian communities therefore need to be vigilant communities, especially in relation to Scripture, who ask themselves whether what was thought to be light might in fact be darkness. Vigilance, as a sister characteristic to honesty, requires the practices of confession, forgiveness, and reconciliation to be in place in any Christian community (so Fowl, 1998: 62f), if honesty is to have its effect. Hermeneutical practices, as seen through the prism of honesty, are therefore inextricably linked to other Christian practices.

If it is possible to have a starting point in the virtuous circle, then after community, honesty may well be the next best hermeneutical candidate. Honesty enables many of the other hermeneutical virtues. We need to be honest about ourselves in relation to God and others, in order to excel at reading with faithfulness, openness, humility, confidence and courage. Especially for churches with a high view of Scripture, hermeneutical honesty should be one of our highest priorities, so that we can celebrate *and* be vigilant about our traditions.

Faithfulness

Of the seven virtues explored in this chapter, 'faithfulness' is the one that occurs most frequently in Scripture.[18] Indeed, 'faithfulness' is the only one to be listed as a fruit of the Spirit (Gal 5:22). Faithfulness was one of two explicit hermeneutical virtues at Holder and Fellowship. As has been seen, the term 'faithfulness' was especially prevalent in Holder discourse, and was used of both divine and human faithfulness. It was significant that at the showcase Anniversary service, there were two public prayers that used 'faithful' language. JoeH thanked God 'for those people who have faithfully preached your word and taught it' (so Chapter 4) and DougH similarly prayed later in the service for 'those Sunday School teachers and youth leaders who have faithfully taught the Gospel and preached the Gospel' (so Chapter 7). 'Faithful preaching' was the particular focus of faithfulness language, and this was notable in congregant interviews as well as public discourse. With a more specifically hermeneutical focus, OwenH, the pastor, thought it important to be 'faithful to the original text' which he understood to mean paying attention to its historical context (so Chapter 5). There were many more examples of implicit faithfulness at Holder, as was seen with JustinH in Chapter 5, where the priority in biblical interpretation was to discover 'what was the real essence of the communication at the time'. JustinH wanted to maintain 'a measure of consistency' so Scripture does not become a series of 'one line catchphrases' taken out of context. In DougH's prayer above, he also prayed that God would 'equip our youth leaders to be able to hold to the truth of your Word ... help us only ever speak the truth from your Word' (so Chapter 7).

---

[18] Including variants.

Faithfulness was made explicit as a hermeneutical virtue by DerekF, the pastor of Fellowship, but it was rarely mentioned in other settings. In Chapter 4, it was seen how DerekF drew on Tom Wright when he spoke of being 'faithful' to Scripture, while recognising 'God needs to interpret it to you, in our own day and age and culture'. Ian, a visiting speaker, was even more explicit in detailing Tom Wright's five act play analogy in a highly compressed summary at the end of his sermon (S1f). He explained that the fifth act has to be 'faithful to the old but also new ... You and I are the fifth act'. It was not surprising to hear DerekF acknowledge that he and Ian were kindred spirits. There were many examples of implicit faithfulness at Fellowship focussed around extended engagement with the text horizon. From Chapter 7, 'The Exegesis and Hermeneutics of the Epistles' was one example from Housegroup C, mediated by ReneeF. As seen in Chapter 5, hermeneutical faithfulness was in view when GordonF identified 'What does it say?' as a key hermeneutical question for Scripture, observing 'we don't actually read what's there' or 'we read the first half of a sentence and forget the second bit'.

Three interrelated senses of faithfulness emerge from the Holder and Fellowship story. The *first* sense is found in both churches, that of paying attention to the text of Scripture itself. As discussed in Chapter 2, Wright argues for a form of relational knowledge, where 'the "knower" must be open to the possibility of the "known" being other than had been expected or even desired'. Wright goes on to describe this as a 'form of love', to which faithfulness language seems very well suited (1992: 45). The *second* sense, which was particularly strong at Holder, was that of reliable[19] performance of practices such as preaching and teaching the Bible. Underlying this sense was an expectation that such practices would affirm the truth of Scripture, as understood within the congregation. Structured forms of faithfulness, through practices and mediatory configurations that contribute to affirming congregational tradition through Scripture, also belong to this second sense. The *third* sense, evident mainly at Fellowship, was faithfulness as appropriate contextualisation, mediated by N. T. Wright's theodramatic understanding of Scripture. This sense in particular operates in tension with openness.

Faithfulness is a hermeneutical virtue that has some close relatives. Clustering around the first sense of faithfulness above, Vanhoozer's 'attention' and 'obedience' and Fowl and Jones's 'critical virtues of professional biblical scholarship' have varying degrees of overlap. Vanhoozer describes the attentive reader as 'focused on the text', 'observant', 'attending to the details' and 'having insight into the nature of the whole'. The obedient interpreter 'follows the directions of the text rather than one's own desires'. Obedient readers 'indwell the

---

19   Leon Morris gives 'complete reliability' as the sense of faithfulness in Gal 5:22 (1993: 288).

text' by 'adopting a reading genre that corresponds to the genre of the text' (1998: 377). Certainly such descriptions of ideal faithful readers would encompass the hermeneutical dispositions of real readers at Holder and Fellowship, with the proviso that real readers are lifelong learners of hermeneutical virtue. Fowl and Jones's critical virtues are by definition more specialised, for example, enabling the analysis of 'textual traditions in order to discern the final form of the text' and enabling 'linguistic skills for discerning how best to translate particular texts' (1991: 39). Such instances of critical virtues were not evident in either Holder or Fellowship, although critical virtues need not be exhausted by specific hermeneutical skills. Faithfulness, particularly in its first sense, is the most textual of the seven hermeneutical virtues considered here. If there are 'critical virtues', then faithfulness is one of them.[20]

Inter-connected signs of hermeneutical faithfulness have been seen in this and the preceding chapters, indicating a number of potential challenges for wider congregational engagement with Scripture. Regarding the first sense, there is a need for attending to the text horizon, which may lead to affirming readings, but also disruptive readings that make the biblical text strange. That faithfulness may be disruptive suggests that faithfulness and openness come very close to each other at certain points. Such faithfulness needs spaces where the reading process can be slowed down (cf. Melchert, 1998: 273f), so that congregants have the time to attend to the text – perhaps pointing to the importance of providing opportunities for smaller group Bible studies. Extending the first sense, it is important for a hermeneutical tradition to be established within congregations, so that attention to the text is not swept away by traditioned readings that affirm the status quo in a way that is not transformative. Faithfulness in terms of a hermeneutical tradition elides into the second sense of faithfulness, that of more structured practices and mediatory configurations that foster hermeneutical faithfulness. Ruled reading is another of those hermeneutical practices that is motivated by faithfulness, as is having a degree of hermeneutical stability through sufficiently homogenous mediators. The third sense of faithfulness, albeit muted, motivates the church to know its bigger story, to enable faithful contextualisation.

Openness

Signs of virtue that might come under the canopy of openness were noticeable in both Fellowship and Holder, albeit with different emphases. For Fellowship, openness was close to an explicit virtue, given their emphasis on being 'radical', which interviewees variously took to mean new, different, change, challenging

---

[20]   Brueggemann writes of 'faithful interpretation' (without dwelling on the virtue aspect), where he overlaps with all of these senses (2009: 20–29).

and counter-cultural. Openness was a strong theme for Fellowship in Chapter 6. NinaF liked it when Bible study was 'opened up for everyone to say what they think'. FrancisF, leader of Housegroup B, liked an 'open style of discussion' with a 'fairly open agenda'. GordonF saw such freedom in Bible study groups as significant for building community. According to GrahamF, such open settings allowed 'more than one aspect of God' to emerge from Scripture. As seen in Chapter 7, Fellowship operated with a heterogeneous configuration of hermeneutical mediators, which was associated with disruptive readings of Scripture. Disruption of horizons was evident when AmyF spoke of moving to Fellowship from a church culture where 'all the Christians were of the same opinion' that 'women shouldn't be in leadership'.[21] AmyF explained 'I hadn't really opened myself up to another opinion' and then she came to Fellowship where suddenly 'all the Christians I knew thought women should be in leadership'. It provoked 'reading and thinking' and 'some conclusions but not all', eventually leading to changed practice as she took on leadership roles within the church. MichelleF captured well Fellowship's openness DNA when speaking of events held in the early days of Ekklesia:

> ... we'd have speakers invited to big meetings who I know they didn't agree with their theology. And I used to sit there and think, "Oh, we don't believe that, oh, I don't believe that", but, actually, it helped you understand what your background was, what you – it helped you understand what you really believed.

MichelleF here makes a case for openness to theological difference bringing about fuller awareness of one's own horizons.

As considered in Chapter 7, there was less structured openness in Holder's mediatory configuration than at Fellowship. Holder also had a tendency to greater resolution of textual meaning, with some congregants preferring 'a belief ... that can be contradicted, rather than leave something open' and 'not really know' (RodneyH in Chapter 6). Within this tighter mediatory configuration, however, were some striking examples of openness. As was seen in Chapter 5, HarryH prayed at the beginning of Housegroup X 'Lord God, I really do pray that you will open up new truths to us' (X3). Talk of the Spirit led DennisH to comment 'the Bible will only speak to people who are open, who the Holy Spirit has actually opened their eyes'. Ecumenical thinking and practice was evident when PatriciaH spoke of her role as a spiritual director for a Christian retreat organisation. She commented 'it is very ecumenical, which is why I don't say a lot about it in [Holder], because they try and steer away from things ecumenical'. DennisH commented more broadly:

---

[21]   Where no chapter reference is given, the examples are additional to those found in preceding chapters.

I think it's good to mix with other Christians from other churches ... For
me, personally, I reckon all churches, rather than bickering and "Our doctrine's
better than yours, blah, blah, blah", I think they should all come together, because,
I believe that if they come together in one, I think they'll be so much stronger. But
there's too much of this, "Well, I'm pentecostal, so, I preach a better sermon than
you, we have better worship than you", or, "We're evangelical", whatever.

JoeH, the associate pastor, found the encounter with lecturers at Bible college
'quite liberating' in finding that 'you can still be thoroughly scriptural, biblical,
and yet actually come to different conclusions'. Greater heterogeneity was
desired by HarryH, who thought that 'as good Reformed evangelicals':

... we can often be overly narrow-minded in what we read, and actually end up
missing out on some very good books. Perhaps an extreme example, one of the
best books I've ever read is *The Return of the Prodigal Son*, by Henri Nouwen.[22]
But that is not something that a Reformed Evangelical would immediately make
for to read. But someone who I trusted recommended it to me, I read it, and it
is, indeed, a great book. And I think that the problem is, often, we are so narrow-
minded and focused that we do miss out on very edifying and encouraging books
that are outside our sphere of reference.

These extracts from previous chapters and additional examples point to a tension
inherent within Holder between its strong congregational boundaries and a not
insignificant openness towards 'new truths'.

Openness, as it emerges from Fellowship and Holder, is about being open to
different interpretations of Scripture, different Christians and their traditions,
and different mediators. It is ultimately about being open to God. 'Being open'
here indicates a willingness to listen to and consider that which is different and
new and potentially disruptive. This is not to suggest that signs of openness
are necessarily transformative theologically, but rather that such possibilities
should be considered. Vanhoozer also identifies openness as a hermeneutical
virtue, contrasting it with the vice of 'closed-mindedness'. The characteristics
of openness he elucidates overlap with those given here, commenting that
'readers display interpretative openness when they welcome the text as other,
with courtesy and respect', adding that 'openness implies a willingness to change'
(1998: 377).[23] As noted previously, when talking of openness to the text, there is

---

[22]   The late Henri Nouwen was a Dutch Roman Catholic priest (1992).
[23]   Tom Greggs calls for a programmatic 'opening' of evangelicalism in his edited
volume *New Perspectives for Evangelical Theology: Engaging with God, Scripture and the
World*. With academic evangelical theology in view, Greggs argues that evangelical theology
should be orientated in an eschatological direction, *ecclesia semper reformanda*, that is 'an ever

virtuous resonance with faithful hermeneutical dispositions as well. Receptivity, identified as a hermeneutical virtue by a number of scholars (see Table 8.1), also has overlap with openness. Briggs argues from Isaiah 6 that receptivity is a hermeneutical virtue for the implied reader of the Bible. He urges the 'reader of scriptural texts' to attend to the *Sache* of the text before them. This German term indicates 'the reality, the subject matter, the "what it is about" of the text'. For Briggs, *Sache* is shorthand for 'what is really there'. Receptivity, then, draws on the Isa 6 picture of being summoned by God, which for hermeneutical virtue means 'conceiving oneself as being summoned by the text', by what is really there, 'willing to have one's perspectives transcended and taken up into mysterious divine purposes' (2010: 188–92). Scripture itself does not use words directly equivalent to 'openness', but as was argued earlier in the chapter, and here by Briggs, there are implicit narratives and characterisations of hermeneutical virtue, with openness being such an example.[24]

The hermeneutical virtue of openness leads us to examine our hermeneutical traditions within congregations, so that they may foster virtuous openness to the text and to others and their mediators. Such openness is an important partner of faithfulness in order for Christian communities to improvise the Christian Story today. Openness to the other is a disposition that Gadamer once called the 'soul of hermeneutics' – 'the possibility that the other person may be right' (Grondin, 1994: 124).[25]

Courage

Critique of congregational tradition and hermeneutical practices may create a breeding ground for hermeneutical courage, albeit much else besides. Resistance to such tradition and practices may enable embryonic forms of courage to develop. As has been seen, predominantly in Chapter 7, there were plenty of examples of critique and resistance in both Holder and Fellowship. The dynamics of critique and resistance have been described as a function of congregational identity, with Fellowship broadly having more freedom to do so than Holder, although there were some variations. Relative to the other seven virtues, hermeneutical courage is not that easy to spot. Interviewees critiquing tradition and practices may or may not be particularly courageous, yet the more promising small group/public settings also need reading carefully for persuasive signs of courage.[26]

---

unfolding and progressive engagement in the present as we move into the future with the tradition of the church' (2010: 2–3).

[24]   In Bible Society's *h+* course, discussed in Chapter 9, the story of Peter's vision in Acts 10–11 is offered as an implicit example of openness.

[25]   Quoted from the Heidelberg colloquium on 9th July, 1989.

[26]   Courage within the wider world, which is likely to be a significant arena for hermeneutical courage, was outside the scope of this study.

In Chapter 7, the discussion in Housegroup X in response to the mediation of a commentary on Mal 3:1–5 saw something like group courage in resisting a hermeneutical authority on the basis of their Christian experience. The group setting appeared to embolden participants to contribute to the rebellion, notably opening up other controversial doctrinal issues for Holder tradition. More explicit courage was apparent in Chapter 6 when RodneyH decided to question the genre of Jonah in Housegroup Y for what he says were pedagogical reasons. DotH had been impressed with her late husband's distance learning course through 'the London Bible College',[27] and spoke of his reasons for studying:

> **DotH:** ... he was a person that had to find everything out for himself, he didn't used to take your word for it, so he had to ... satisfy himself.
>
> ...
>
> I think he just wanted to learn more ... about the Bible and everything ... But ... when he was doing the Bible course ... he used to go to the housegroup of a Thursday afternoon and teach them what he'd learned, so they got it as well ... so what he learned from there, he used to go and give it to them.
>
> **Andrew:** Did he talk to you about what he was learning?
>
> **DotH:** Oh yeah ... And I couldn't understand some of the questions, really, what he had to answer. I thought that they made you disbelieve the Bible. But then that's what you would get with people asking you them sort of questions. I find that hard ... but he really enjoyed learning and doing it.

It seems likely that courage was needed to deal with questions that 'made you disbelieve the Bible'. JustinH spoke of a similar situation where he had resisted aspects of hermeneutical mediation through his theological studies over thirty years previously, where 'the Theology department wasn't Evangelical':

> **JustinH:** I found some of it very threatening, very challenging, because of having been brought up in [Holder] for my whole life prior to that, it was like, this is something new, this is something different, and this is potentially going to threaten my faith, because of looking at things from a different perspective and being challenged in that respect. So, yes, having said that ... I had a sort of a mindset that I am not going to allow this to throw me, so, whatever I take from all of these studies, there still is an essence of a need for faith in God, and that the Scripture is genuine and it is God's Word. So, there were certain aspects of the

---

27   Since renamed *London School of Theology*.

course that were obviously challenging that, that [the Bible] was just a concoction of ideas that were brought together from all over the place and thrown together, and this is the way the Scripture happened.

Andrew: Was there anyone you were able to talk to about some of the issues raised?

...

JustinH: ... There were people, families within the church, that I did share some things with and discuss things through with. But, because they were from an Evangelical background ... and because it was seen to be ... almost heretical to ask certain questions, I didn't pursue that with them.

Andrew: You talked about it being heretical to ask, is that something you still see as the case in Evangelical tradition or in some parts of the tradition?

JustinH: Some people would consider certain things wrong to ask, yeah. But I wouldn't personally have that. You know, I think God's Word is strong enough to stand up for itself, it doesn't need me to defend it in that way. But, I think, for some people whose, perhaps, faith is somewhat at risk, as it were, it would be too overwhelming for them to be asked or to consider certain issues.

This certainly seems to describe a situation where hermeneutical courage was needed. For both prior examples, however, it is unclear whether courage was needed to resist mediation or to accept it, or a mixture of both.

Courage was less obvious within Fellowship, perhaps because there was less to kick against, with critique, resistance and change being more ingrained within their congregational tradition. There was a sustained critique of song words in both churches by interviewees, as has been seen in Chapter 7, but this was taken a little further in Fellowship with SarahF refusing to sing one song, as it conflicted with her understanding of God's nature. As discussed in Chapter 4, courage contributed to BruceF's significant Word on a Sunday morning where he spoke about Fellowship's difficult recent history and the 'new words' God had for their self-understanding (SunAM9f), although this was hermeneutical in terms of interpreting Words rather than the Bible. In Chapter 7, some hesitant courage was demonstrated at ThursPM when TomF effectively questioned the pastor's grammatico-historical approach to Scripture, through contrasting a 'child-like ... chasing after God' with 'a more academic approach to Christianity' (ThursPM2). Also in Chapter 7, the Bible Study Guide from Housegroup A provided an explicit yet gentle hermeneutical critique of an assumed congregational hermeneutics that required some courage on the part of its publishers (Matthias Media, 2014).

Hermeneutical practices sometimes need to be courageous. As Ron Beadle and Geoff Moore have argued more generally of organisations, 'practices could not resist the institutions without the virtues to shape them' (2006: 333). A more focussed example of hermeneutical courage in both Holder and Fellowship came from certain congregants who had the ability to look at biblical texts and their uses within the church in different ways. Some of these congregants had undertaken formal theological training, but it was striking how a number of ordinary congregants fulfilled this role as well. ReneeF, TomF and RodneyH all had this function to varying degrees. We have seen how all three of them, especially ReneeF, felt free to test the limits of their congregational tradition, sometimes critiquing hermeneutical practices, sometimes catalysing hermeneutical discussion with others. Such a role matches well with that of an 'organic theologian' – a concept proposed by McGrath, and derived from Antonio Gramsci's concept of the 'organic intellectual' (1971). An organic theologian is defined by *how* they use their scholarship or understanding of their Christian tradition or their critical faculties, as McGrath explains:

> An organic theologian is an activist, a popularizer – someone who sees her task as supportive and systematic within the community of faith, and as evangelistic and apologetic outside that community.
>
> ...
>
> The organic theologian will see herself as working within the great historical Christian tradition, which she gladly makes her own. Even when she feels she must critique the contemporary expressions or applications of that tradition, she will do so from a deep sense of commitment to the community of faith and its distinctive ideas and values. She will not see her task as imposing alien ideas upon her community ... Her responsibility within the community is to explore and apply its tradition; outside the community, her task is to commend and defend its ideas and communicate them as effectively as possible.
>
> ...
>
> The organic theologian does not simply arise within the community of faith; she is accountable to them, in that she speaks for that community (2002a: 151–2, 154).[28]

This description of organic theologians largely resonates with the individuals witnessed in Holder and Fellowship, given the emphasis in this quote on

---

[28] I have largely replaced male pronouns with female ones in this quote.

activism, popularising, critiquing, systematising, working within congregational tradition, and being committed and accountable to the congregation. All of these characteristics were identified in the tale of two churches. Examples given of organic theologians are often rather high profile, such as Karl Barth, and John Stott has been proposed as an organic theologian for evangelicalism (McGrath, 2000a: 156; 2002a: 154). Hitherto, the lack of academic attention to ordinary theology may well explain the tendency to cite high profile examples of academic mediators. The examples from Holder and Fellowship were home-grown Christians, growing in hermeneutical virtue, especially courage, and so liked to test their tradition by asking 'Why?' That they were free to do so, despite quite contrasting congregational identities, appeared to be due to their evident commitment and accountability to their congregations. Although this was also true of the pastors, OwenH and DerekF, their position of authority made it more difficult to fulfil this organic theologian role. Furthermore, KarlH, who was the most critical of hermeneutical practices and tradition at Holder, was not owned by the congregation in the same way as RodneyH. This is likely to be due to his position within evangelicalism being too distant from Holder's theological centre of gravity.

Courage is a common biblical theme, both explicitly and implicitly.[29] It has prompted much Christian reflection on how it differs from alternative narratives of virtue, as Rebecca DeYoung has noted. Drawing on Aquinas and Augustine, she argues convincingly that courage is not about exercising our own power, but involves 'setting *human* power aside in favour of reliance on divine power and grace' (2012: 163). Courage must be grounded in sacrificial love, not self-assertive heroics – so Augustine defines courage as 'love readily bearing all things for the sake of the loved object' (*Mor. Ecc.* 15.25).[30] Courage is therefore the prophetic hermeneutical virtue that enables critique of and resistance to the hermeneutical powers that be, whether in the church or world, ultimately for the love of Christ and his church. It disrupts affirmative readings of Scripture that are not genuinely transformative. To allow hermeneutical courage to grow, the church needs to make more space for organic theologians who can see Scripture differently and help others to do the same.[31]

---

[29] Explicit uses of the concept are well known in Joshua 1, and courage describes Israel, and its leaders in battle in Judg 20; 2 Sam 10; 1 Chron 19. Asa in 2 Chron 15 is described as responding to prophecy by taking courage and putting away idols. Jesus exhorts his disciples to 'take courage' or 'take heart' in the face of persecution in Jn 16:33. The Lord appears to Paul in Jerusalem in Acts 23:11, when his life was in danger, to encourage him to continue bearing witness.

[30] This is in the context of defining the cardinal virtues, of which courage is the only one identified here.

[31] Charles Melchert argues that courage (as well as humility) is pedagogically important, since 'it requires courage to follow where the truth leads – out beyond what is

Humility and Confidence

Humility and confidence are the most closely paired of the hermeneutical virtues identified. Humility and confidence are distinct, in that, unlike the other virtues presented here, they emerge from what I have argued are potential hermeneutical problems within the tale of two churches. That is to say, caution and certainty were lacking in confidence and humility respectively, and so pointed to these virtues. Humility and confidence are virtues that need each other. Without the pull of humility, confidence can slip into excessive certainty; without the pull of confidence, humility can slip into excessive caution. These hermeneutical virtues are epistemological in focus, since epistemology is so significant for hermeneutical practice, as argued in Chapter 6.

Examples of caution and certainty in the two churches are laid out in Chapter 6 in some detail, so I will not repeat them unnecessarily here. There were few specific signs of hermeneutical humility and confidence in the congregations, although worship songs and Words at Fellowship struck a confident note in some contrast to the prevailing epistemological tone. Some of the small groups at Fellowship, especially the church-based Bible studies, were less cautious about resolving the meaning of a passage. At Holder, those with some academic background displayed confidence (and also courage) in challenging the views of others in small groups. Of humility, it was very much a hopeful hermeneutical virtue for Fellowship and Holder, given the paucity of clear examples in the tale of two churches.

The contours, narratives, and justifications for hermeneutical humility and confidence only begin in the ethnographic accounts. The narrative is largely one of absence and the contours are construed from virtuous negatives. Therefore humility and confidence in particular need shaping by the Christian Story. After love/charity, humility features most often in accounts of hermeneutical virtue (so Table 8.1), and is a strong theme in Scripture and the Christian tradition. As discussed earlier, humility was a distinctly Christian virtue in ancient times, largely unrecognised by the world of antiquity. For example, humility is conspicuous by its near absence from the works of Aristotle and Plato, and Aristotle even appears to view humility as a vice (MacIntyre, 1985: 182; Pinsent, 2012: 243). By contrast, of the seven hermeneutical virtues identified in this study, humility is second only to faithfulness in terms of its frequency in Scripture. Key passages include the humility of Moses in Num 12:3; the injunction 'to walk humbly with your God' in Mi 6:8; the humbled/exalted sayings in the Gospels (Matt 23:12; Lk 14:11, 18:14) and the passage on humility in Php 2. Briggs has an extended treatment of humility as an 'interpretive' virtue, focussing on Num

---

accepted as normal and conventional – as Job, Qohelet, the prophets, Jesus, and many others have demonstrated' (1998: 240).

12:3 as follows: 'Now the man Moses was very humble, more so than anyone else on the face of the earth' (NRSV). He argues persuasively that what sets Moses apart from 'anyone else' in this passage is 'his unique status as a recipient of God's spoken word "face to face"' (2010: 60). Therefore humility in this passage is 'dependence upon God, and in particular, it is dependence upon God for any speaking of a divinely authorized word'. Such humility does not necessarily entail meekness, given Moses' bold cry to God on Miriam's behalf. Of this development in Num 12:13, Briggs comments 'it is a vigorous action engaging with God in the confidence of one who knows God face-to-face'(2010: 61). Although humility may often be in healthy tension with confidence, at times, it would seem the two enfold one another. In developing this example of Moses, Briggs argues that humility is implied for subsequent readers of Numbers, where 'dependence upon God' is 'the requirement of speaking for God'. In summary, 'humility, as it pertains to Moses in Num 12, is the root of faithful handling of the word of God' (2010: 63).[32] Humility as found in the New Testament shares in this theme of recognising one's dependence upon God, although there are variations in emphasis. The passage in Php 2:1–5 is worth further consideration:

> If then there is any encouragement in Christ, any consolation from love, any sharing in the Spirit, any compassion and sympathy, make my joy complete: be of the same mind, having the same love, being in full accord and of one mind. Do nothing from selfish ambition or conceit, but in humility regard others as better than yourselves. Let each of you look not to your own interests, but to the interests of others. Let the same mind be in you that was in Christ Jesus ... (NRSV)

The 'hymn' that follows immediately after this passage provides the exemplar of Christ's humility. The counter-cultural force of these verses has already been noted. In his commentary, Fowl points out that political concord at the time was assumed to depend on people knowing their place in society. These verses challenge that understanding with a concord found 'in Christ' that depends on the humility of all, where all others are regarded as of superior status, the upshot being looking first to the interests of others (2005: 84–5). The emphasis here is more social than in the Moses example, yet this humility too is rooted in our dependence on God for our 'in Christ' status. Such dependence makes looking to the interests of others possible.

How might such humility translate into a hermeneutical virtue? While the Moses example can be understood in a hermeneutical key more directly, I would contend that it is not difficult to see this social dimension of humility as also being relevant hermeneutically. In recognising our status before God, we acknowledge the limits of our understanding, and that we are sinners. As

---

[32] Briggs cites Deut 8:2–3 in support of this claim.

Fowl puts it 'being able to identify oneself as a sinner injects a crucial element of provisionality into one's interpretive practice' (1998: 82; cf. Jones, 2003: 158). Such humility therefore means we need to take the voices of others seriously, including their interpretations of Scripture, whether we are biblical novices, virtuosos or somewhere in-between.[33] Of course, humility is not the only virtue that governs handling of the Bible, and it must be developed alongside others. Confidence we will come to in a moment, but *honesty* about who we are, *openness* to others, and working at living in *community* together around the Scriptures are strongly related.

The passage in Philippians goes on to speak of Christ's humility as self-emptying or *kenōsis*. A number of thinkers have drawn upon this example of *kenōsis* as a hermeneutical theme. Alan Jacobs, in his *Theology of Reading*, makes the convincing case that to read charitably requires the practice of *kenōsis* (2007: 15). Genuine love of others requires 'an emptying out of one's self and a consequent refilling of the emptied consciousness with attention to the Other' (2001: 104). This is true for a theology of reading also, as 'one must take the chance of humbling oneself before what one reads, becoming its servant' (2007: 15). This language of *kenōsis* and humility resonates well with Gadamer's 'fusion of horizons' discussed in Chapter 3. The hermeneutically trained person (virtuous reader?) must be open to the text 'in all its otherness and thus assert its own truth against one's own fore-meanings' (Gadamer, 2004: 271–2). Hermeneutical humility is therefore also needed for the right disposition towards the Scriptures, in setting our status below the text, in order that we might respond to its address (cf. Slagter, 2007: 103–4; Vanhoozer, 1998: 464; 2006: 92–3). Humility is therefore also significant in the exercise of hermeneutical faithfulness as described above.

Confidence as a hermeneutical virtue is not identified by any other scholar in Table 8.1, although Vanhoozer argues for a balance between humility and *conviction* (1998: 463f).[34] As has been seen, confidence may be wrapped up in a humility that knows our dependence upon God. Eschatology, as Vanhoozer argues, provides a theological driver for confidence and humility. The kingdom of God is now and not yet, and so also is our knowledge. Now we know 'only in part' (1 Cor 13:12), but this is not nothing. Neither is it everything. A 'realised' epistemology means there are grounds for confidence in the Gospel; a 'futurist' epistemology means we also need humility (1998: 465).

---

[33] Briggs sounds a note of caution regarding postmodern thinking that 'appeals to a vague notion of humility as a bulwark against making any sort of definite claims about knowledge' (2010: 68). While this point is taken, humility as a hermeneutical virtue still has epistemological as well as ontological significance.

[34] Vanhoozer takes Martin Luther's 'Here I stand' as summing up these hermeneutical virtues. 'Here' is perspectival, thus humility; but 'I stand' manifests conviction about his interpretation of Scripture (1998: 466–7).

Confidence and its relatives occur frequently in Scripture, especially in the context of exhortation.[35] This is the confidence that is gained through the fear of the LORD/faith in Christ and being 'in him'. What is the connection between this confidence and confidence in our handling of the Scriptures? The answer has to be that it is one and the same confidence. Confidence develops alongside the other hermeneutical virtues such as faithfulness and humility, to enable 'rightly explaining the word of truth' (2 Tim 2:15). Such virtues are associated with certain hermeneutical skills and techniques, as discussed previously, but competence in such skills and techniques cannot be our primary grounds for confidence.[36] As Lesslie Newbigin argues in *Proper Confidence*, 'the locus of confidence is not in the competence of our own knowing, but in the faithfulness and reliability of the one who is known'. Commenting on Jn 14:6, where Thomas asks Jesus 'How can we know the way?', Newbigin stresses the committed and relational nature of knowing implied in Jesus' response and in passages like 2 Tim 1:12 (1995: 66–7).[37] 'Certainty' is better expressed as 'confidence' for a now and not yet epistemology.

This tale of two churches has provided insight into the shadow side of confidence and humility. To develop an epistemological lingua franca between churches, as discussed in Chapter 6, must at least mean cultivating the hermeneutical virtues of confidence *and* humility. Such virtues would foster sensitivity regarding labels such as the 'F' word, and would welcome the varied epistemological dialects of boundary crossing mediators discussed in Chapter 7. Where multiple epistemological languages exist within a single congregation, organic theologians may act as translators. Confidence and humility are combined in ruled reading, as discussed in Chapter 4. Confidence is needed to agree on a 'mere' Christian Story, but humility is needed to ensure that such ruled reading does not become bloated. Confidence in particular is needed in many churches where congregants have become wary of biblical engagement, due to a perceived difficulty in understanding Scripture.[38] Making hermeneutical traditions explicit, as discussed in Chapter 5, can lead to increased hermeneutical confidence if congregants can actually name the 'how' of Bible reading. Courses such as *h*+, addressed in Chapter 9, are deliberately designed

---

[35]   E.g. Prov 3:26, 14:26; 2 Cor 3:4; Eph 3:12; Heb 10:19, 11:1; 1 Jn 2:28. Commenting on Heb 11:1, William Abraham notes that 'at least one biblical writer is adept at deploying a host of epistemic measures and strategies to persuade believers and sustain them in their convictions' (2003: 74).

[36]   This is the epistemological/hermeneutical instance of the relationship between faith and works.

[37]   Abraham makes a similar point about Hebrews, where the capacities of human agents 'to see the truth about God are linked in profound ways to trust, obedience, the quest for virtue, and the like' (2003: 72). See also the discussion in Chapter 6.

[38]   See survey discussion in Chapter 1 and Bible difficulties in Appendix F.

to build the hermeneutical confidence of congregations, as are other forms of hermeneutical apprenticeship.

Community

Community is this book's title virtue in that it most closely relates to the 'congregational' focus of congregational hermeneutics. The significance of community for congregational hermeneutics, including hermeneutical apprenticeship, is the theme of Chapter 9. Therefore, unlike the other hermeneutical virtues identified in this chapter, this is where community is explored at length.

Why Virtue Hermeneutics Works

A theological ethnographic methodology was proposed in Chapter 2, where a research 'conversation' can lead to 'new or revised models, language, categories, and connections'. Hermeneutical virtue is a case of the latter in this study. It is hoped that the examples of hermeneutical virtue which have emerged will enrich its existing, albeit fledgling, theological discourse and currency. The seven virtues here identified became apparent from a reading of the ethnographic accounts, with faithfulness and openness being close to emic virtues. Such a reading was, of course, not neutral, but deliberately theological in its gaze. That the hermeneutical virtues are not necessarily explicit for congregants does not invalidate their identification, since I have already noted that virtue is often implicit in narratives, not least in Scripture.

Certain traditional points of virtue theory were not persuasive viewed through an ethnographic lens. It was not self-evident that hermeneutical virtues were straightforwardly the mean between excess and deficiency. It is difficult to see how honesty or community, for example, could be an excess. The pairings of humility/confidence and faithfulness/openness, however, have some resonance, albeit differently construed in terms of a balance of virtues. More significantly for hermeneutical virtues, the distinction between moral and intellectual virtue needs to be challenged. Following the work of Zagzebski, I am not convinced that there is a meaningful difference between moral and intellectual virtue. Zagzebski observes that this distinction is 'a commonplace of Western philosophy', although she notes the illustrious exceptions (1996: 137–40).[39] Zagzebski questions the Aristotelian position that the two kinds of virtue govern different parts of the soul (the rational and the non-rational), hence thinking and feeling are characterised as very different types of activity. She argues that

---

[39] Plato and Spinoza.

there are many states that are 'blends of thought and feeling' (1996: 140f, 148). Although these blends might vary in their proportions (if such things can be measured), it is not obvious that faithfulness or courage, for example, are only moral or only intellectual.[40] As to distinguishing virtues by their mode of acquisition (through teaching or imitation), Zagzebski compellingly maintains that this is actually about skills and virtues (1996: 150), a distinction to which I will return in a moment. Her conclusion is that 'an intellectual virtue does not differ from certain moral virtues any more than one moral virtue differs from another' and therefore intellectual virtues are 'best viewed as forms of moral virtue' (1996: 139). In my view, her conclusions apply equally to hermeneutical virtues, since they too engage the mind and heart, thought and feeling. Challenging the distinction between moral and intellectual virtue matters since it is then far harder to justify a subset of hermeneutical virtues that are for a few only. The tenor of Scripture is that Christians are to grow in all the virtues (e.g. Gal 5:22–3). That the virtues are closely interrelated has been evident in the accounts given in this chapter. Such a position is aligned with the view that love is the virtue at the root of all others, which is surely correct.

A tendency towards creating a subset of virtuous interpreters is apparent in Fowl and Jones, where they have written of 'the critical virtues of professional biblical scholarship' (1991: 43f). While agreeing with their argument that the church needs to 'nurture and develop people' who are skilled in interpretation and hermeneutics (see Chapter 9), I am not convinced that this is a matter of virtue. Briggs also tilts in Fowl and Jones's direction when he maintains that:

> ... a concern with the moral formation of the reader must go hand in hand with the deployment of as wide a range as possible of interpretive insights from the various critical methodologies of biblical studies. To be a wise reader is more than attaining to a mastery of critical tools, but it is not less than that (2010: 195).

Although I am sure that neither Fowl, Jones nor Briggs intends for hermeneutics to be an enterprise reserved for an elite, such arguments can lead in that direction. The distinction between virtue and skills may be of use here. A hermeneutical virtue may be associated with a set of hermeneutical skills, and motivates the wise exercise of those skills, but the virtue is not exhausted by those skills. Zagzebski constructs a solid case for this distinction, contending that 'skills serve virtues by allowing a person who is virtuously motivated to be effective in action' (1996: 113). She lists many intellectual virtues and skills, for example, honesty involves 'skills of communication – not misleading others' (1996: 115). A hermeneutical

[40] Zagzebski provides examples of the connections between moral and intellectual virtues, such as honesty, patience, perseverance, courage, humility, and discretion (1996: 158f).

virtue such as faithfulness may involve the skills of paying close attention to the text and being attentive to historical context, as was seen in the accounts above. Although 'we would normally expect a person with a virtue to develop the associated skills', nevertheless, it is possible to have the virtue without the corresponding skills (1996: 116).[41] Consequently, there does not need to be a subset of critical hermeneutical virtues, but rather critical hermeneutical skills and techniques that may or may not be associated with any Christian's growth in hermeneutical virtue. Therefore, I am arguing that all the hermeneutical virtues are for all Christians to cultivate.

This leads to questions regarding what hermeneutical virtues there are and why identify the particular seven in this study. Bearing in mind Table 8.1, there is clearly no agreed list of hermeneutical virtues, just as there is no consistent list of general virtues in Scripture. I expect a good case can be made for the value of all the hermeneutical virtues given in Table 8.1, so do not see the need for a list of agreed hermeneutical virtues. That said, we would do well to note the points of convergence in Table 8.1, such as love and humility. The seven hermeneutical virtues identified in this book arose from theological ethnographic interactions within the two churches, where it is hoped that these virtues, and the language of hermeneutical virtue itself, will be of value to many other churches beyond this study. Virtues could have been identified at higher or lower levels of abstraction for congregational hermeneutics, but for the purposes of showing and communicating hermeneutical virtue *in situ*, I opted for more concrete abstract nouns. Love and *phronēsis* are important hermeneutical virtues, but sit behind the more frontline hermeneutical virtues named here and in Table 8.1. That hermeneutical practices may need the exercise of multiple hermeneutical virtues at the same time has been very evident in the accounts above. It has also been seen that hermeneutical virtues work together, sometimes in tension, sometimes reinforcing each other. This is not surprising since hermeneutical practices may need multi-faceted dispositions to drive them to virtuous ends. This point is also further support for there being no subset of reserved hermeneutical virtues.

Another question raised of hermeneutical virtue is that it is too subjective. The rejoinder is to ask, 'Compared to what?' The hyperactivity of hermeneutics in the academy is no bastion of objectivity when it comes to the Bible (cf. Vanhoozer, 1992). Similarly, the church has not been entirely successful in agreeing what constitutes appropriate hermeneutical practice. A virtue account does not discount the importance of hermeneutical skills and tools, but also includes the character of the interpreter and so the ends to which hermeneutical skills and tools are directed. Given the relativism of hermeneutics that already

---

41   Stephen Pardue's point that 'it will not do ... to argue that a person takes a genitive subjectively instead of objectively because of moral deficiency', could be due to a lack of skill rather than virtue (2010: 305).

obtains, virtue hermeneutics has much to offer. Hermeneutical virtue gains its meaning from the Christian Story but is inculturated in a particular congregational context. Yes, hermeneutical virtue has risks of subjectivity, yet it explicitly looks to the genuinely transformative work of the Spirit through Scripture in a congregation, for whom there is a common *telos* to the myriad congregational experiences of learning how to read Scripture. Virtue provides a common theological language for hermeneutics, even if congregations have many dialects.[42]

It is time to return to Vanhoozer's definition of hermeneutical virtue as 'a disposition of the mind and heart that arises from the motivation for understanding, for cognitive contact with the text' (1998: 376). What is very clear from the tale of two churches is that congregational hermeneutics are constituted by a complex set of practices and relations that extend far beyond the biblical text. Consequently, while I would emphasise (and italicise) 'disposition of the mind *and* heart', the phrase 'cognitive contact with the text' is too narrow for the purposes of congregational hermeneutics. Furthermore, defining generic hermeneutical virtue may be of limited value compared to engaging with their specific instances, as we have done in this and previous chapters. If a definition is to be sought, then nothing has been seen to stop hermeneutical virtue being linked simply to transformation as 'a disposition of the mind and heart that allows for transformative engagement with Scripture'.[43]

Having made a case for why hermeneutical virtue works, I conclude this chapter by drawing out its benefits. The link between hermeneutics and virtue means that hermeneutics becomes part of Christian discipleship.[44] [45] Learning how to read Scripture – hermeneutical apprenticeship – is for every Christian, not for an expert few. This may also go some way to lessening the divide between 'academic' and 'ordinary' approaches to reading Scripture. I am not arguing that every Christian needs to become a biblical scholar, but that every Christian should be growing in hermeneutical virtues. Indeed, hermeneutical virtues are by no means a monopoly of the academy, since the connection between critical scholarship and virtue is not direct. An 'expert' reader may not be more honest or courageous than an ordinary one. Furthermore, virtue provides the church with an accessible and common theological language for hermeneutics that has

---

[42]   Pardue observes that a virtue account reframes the relativism of hermeneutics in 'ways more amenable to the Christian tradition', but adds (somewhat underplaying his hand in my view) that the primary function of hermeneutical virtue is 'to enrich the vocabulary and practices that permeate exegetical practice and training'. Biblical interpretation animated by the virtue tradition has 'the potential to help exegetes and their teachers understand and orient their tasks rightly' (2010: 308).

[43]   This connection is established in Chapter 2.

[44]   I am expanding on my argument in Rogers (2013c: 124).

[45]   ' ... the ideal reader of Scripture must be a disciple' (Vanhoozer, 1998: 381).

currency across different Christian traditions. They may act as critical pivots or hinges that inform interpretative decisions, where understanding of complex hermeneutical details may be only partially grasped or indeed inaccessible. Such relatively subjective criteria therefore also furnish us with a dynamic language that can aid the learning process of hermeneutics, the focus of our next chapter.

Chapter 9
Community

Six hermeneutical virtues were considered in the previous chapter. In this final chapter, there is a special focus on the hermeneutical virtue of community, understood through listening to operant, espoused, normative and formal theological voices. This then drives an argument about the significance of community for hermeneutical apprenticeship, which concludes with concrete examples of what such apprenticeship might look like.

Unlike the six other virtues in this book, whose primary sense is virtuous, Christian 'community' typically *describes* a group of Christians, often a congregation or local church. Like the other hermeneutical virtues, however, community is often used positively in everyday English as 'the condition of sharing or having certain attitudes and interests in common' (Pearsall, 1998: 371). The Christian discourse around 'community' is already semi-virtuous, as will be seen below, hence co-opting it as a hermeneutical virtue seems fitting and worth any potential confusion caused by multiple senses. Indeed, the descriptive and virtuous senses in this chapter merge into each other, further underscoring the suitability of 'community' for shaping hermeneutical practices.

Community in the Congregations

I begin by considering signs of community as seen in the themes of tradition, practices, epistemology and mediation at Holder and Fellowship. This then leads into a broader normative and formal exploration of what community as a hermeneutical virtue might look like.

Tradition

Tradition is transmitted by a community. Patterns of discourses, actions, artefacts and mediators are transmitted by a network of relationships over time (Chapter 4). In short, tradition is the product of community over time. For congregational hermeneutics, then, community is about historical as well as contemporary hermeneutical practices. Just as it would be almost impossible to conceive of a congregation without its own tradition, so too it would be difficult to imagine a congregation where communal engagement with Scripture had not contributed to that tradition in some way (even if through the wider

Christian community beyond the local church).[1] In relation to tradition, then, congregational hermeneutics is interested in the extent of communal engagement with Scripture over time.

This interest is mostly addressed indirectly since theological ethnography by its very nature looks at contemporary horizons. Nevertheless, there were identifiable horizons at both Holder and Fellowship in terms of both hermeneutical starting points and goals that were the end point of what had clearly been generated communally. Of particular interest for the virtue of community was the horizonal goal regarding the address of Scripture, whether it tended to the corporate or individual. The emphasis at Holder was on the corporate; especially in terms of how reading Scripture together can be a constraint on interpretation, thus protecting the boundaries of congregational identity. Fellowship, on the other hand, tended to an emphasis on the individual, captured by GordonF's 'What does it say to me?'[2] Distinctive theological traditions and 'ruled reading' informed engagement with Scripture for the two churches (albeit much more so at Holder) and these again both point indirectly to the communal processes that generated those traditions and 'rules'.

Practices

There were a cluster of practices in the two churches that came under the insider heading of 'hearing God speak through Scripture'. Such practices would appear to structure the ways in which a congregation may read in community. There was a sense in which sermons and especially personal Bible reading encouraged a focus on the individual, whereas small groups operated as the most intense forum for community readings in the two congregations. However, community reading is more multi-layered than this, since these general practices interacted with congregational horizons and tradition. Although sermons and other public uses of Scripture are mostly carried out by just a few people, there can be a strong communal dynamic to the address and reception of, for example, a sermon. It has been seen how in Holder there was a corporate tendency in sermons and songs, whereas this was much less marked in Fellowship public settings, with notable examples of Bible uses being directed to the individual (e.g. personal mission statements arising out of Luke 4 in S8f). Small groups brought out the interaction between practices and tradition yet further. Fellowship groups permitted a

---

[1]   Matthew Engelke's study of the Friday Masowe apostolics of Zimbabwe known as 'the Christians who don't read the Bible' points to possible exceptions, although the rejection of Scripture is also likely to require some engagement with Scripture (2007).

[2]   One might argue that the operant horizonal conviction that Scripture primarily addresses the individual may have been formed through the community agreeing on this point. That is, the community agrees to read as individuals. However, such a position is likely to undermine continued community agreement about hermeneutics.

significant degree of freedom for participants to engage with Scripture on their own terms. With less concern for arriving at the 'right' understanding of the text, such groups had *both* an individual and corporate dynamic. For Holder, small groups provided a safe space for individuals to test their tradition, although this testing was bounded by a strong corporate dynamic.

At the more detailed level of hermeneutical practices, most fusion processes, as described in Chapter 5, were not particularly related to either an individual or community reading of Scripture. The exceptions were those fusion processes that flourished in certain small group contexts. Text-linking at Holder gained its energy from small group communities who knew the Bible well enough to make multiple connections within Scripture. Text horizon engagement was also more prominent in small groups at both churches, seen in closer readings of Scripture and grammatico-historical approaches, as described in Chapter 5. Such engagement favoured a group environment with extended time for learning together, where that learning was normally directed by a leader. Explicitly naming hermeneutical practices, such as Jesus hermeneutics at Fellowship, did enable congregants to share in this practice, even if only aspirationally. As has just been described, however, certain implicit practices also fostered communal reading of Scripture, so it would appear that the structure of the practice is significant, as well as whether it is explicit or not.

In conclusion, although certain hermeneutical practices do structure the degree of communal reading of Scripture, they may do so with quite complex dynamics. The tale of two churches indicates there are multiple possible dynamics, deriving from the potential tensions between tradition/practice and individual/corporate, as well as whether it is implicit/explicit.

Epistemology

The theme of epistemology related to community in ways already hinted at in the themes of tradition and practices above. In Chapter 6, the freedom for small group members to chat together about how they understood a passage was explicitly identified by GordonF as building a sense of community that 'teaching' was less likely to achieve.[3] [4] Many Fellowship congregants valued the group interactions of an 'open' Bible study where they could 'say what they think' (NinaF). For epistemology and hermeneutics, then, this freedom and openness was facilitated by a tendency to indeterminacy at Fellowship. That

---

[3]   The related view that small group Bible studies primarily build community rather than develop biblical engagement receives broad support from a number of scholars (e.g. Bielo, 2009b; Todd, 2013; Walton, 2011). This study challenges aspects of such a view.

[4]   While building community and reading communally are not identical, it is plausible to see them as complementary arcs of the same virtuous circle.

is, the concern was less about resolving the meaning of a text and more about allowing for an exchange of interpretations. A mutual hermeneutics may then be fostered by such an epistemological trait.

As has been seen, Holder operated with limited indeterminacy in all three settings, with (relatively) greater indeterminacy possible in small groups. As in Fellowship, group interactions facilitated by a degree of reader indeterminacy were valued. This was a clearly bounded indeterminacy, however, in that textual indeterminacy was explicitly ruled out by some interviewees, and the corporate tendency in Holder Bible settings often functioned to maintain boundaries for indeterminacy (e.g. the Jonah incident in Housegroup Y). In the discussion of fundamentalism, where a foundationalist epistemology was understood to be the key component, it was noted that the authority of the text can become closely identified with the authority of the interpretative community. Where there are very strong internal mediatory dynamics, that authority may be concentrated in relatively few congregants, reducing the potential for hermeneutical community.

The equation greater indeterminacy = greater community is, however, only a partial account of the relationship between epistemology and community. Other factors also pertain. To a degree, indeterminacy permits communal reading of Scripture to flourish, but when taken too far, Scripture becomes so relativised that there is not enough substance to sustain a hermeneutical community – as was seen in some Fellowship settings. By contrast, the drive towards textual resolution in Holder generated a seriousness about engaging in Bible study *with each other*. This was heightened by the relative indeterminacy of Holder small groups which were able to test their tradition a little in relation to Scripture, where such testing was also a communal activity.

Mediation

As has been argued, all hermeneutical practices are mediated; hence mediation provides an important complementary lens for seeking signs of community in hermeneutical practices. The nature and dynamics of mediation are particularly in view here.

It is apparent from Holder and Fellowship that hermeneutical mediators are linked into a wider configuration or network of mediators that extend beyond the congregation.[5] The mediatory dynamics varied, but whether bounded or permeable, there was a global mediatory network that shaped their practices

---

[5]   Ward develops the theme of 'network' for Liquid Church following Manuel Castells (2000), giving the examples of a parents and tots group and a worship song as networks (2002: chapter 4). Networks in Ward correspond to both mediators and their configuration in this study.

to varying degrees. In short, no hermeneutical community is an island[6] – the hermeneutical community is bigger than the congregation (cf. Thiselton, 1992: 65). Alongside this point is the recognition that some mediators are more communal than they at first appear. For example, the preacher may preach and prepare alone, but the sermon may still be shaped by mentors, commentaries, anticipated audience, websites, current news stories and many other mediators. What was also interesting was the degree to which mediators did not always resonate with congregational tradition, practices, and epistemology, and how this was apparently difficult to control (e.g. worship songs that conflicted with congregational doctrine or epistemology). This might be described as *unintentional* community.

Resistance to mediation was also revealing for community. There were some instances of congregants not wanting to read Scripture in more communal contexts. At Holder, resistance to housegroups from some was said to be due to their interactive nature that did not allow for a more passive style of learning. For Holder and especially Fellowship, there were some indications that 'Bible study is something you do on your own' (JoeH, NadineF). As well as resisting community itself, there were striking examples of resistance-as-community. This communal resistance was more marked at Holder than at Fellowship, although Housegroup A exhibited significant inertia when trying to follow a new hermeneutical strategy mediated by a Bible Study Guide. Housegroup X, however, gained significant momentum when rejecting a particular reading of Scripture mediated by an expert (in commentary form). It is worth noting that the instances of communal resistance were for both more *and* less conservative readings of Scripture.

Not unrelated to mediatory resistance, the specific example of organic theologians (identified in Chapter 8) are of particular interest for community as a hermeneutical virtue. Organic theologians tested the limits of congregational tradition, sometimes critiqued hermeneutical practices, and through doing so catalysed hermeneutical discussion with others. McGrath describes organic theologians as those who have a 'deep sense of commitment to the community of faith', as well as being accountable to them (2002a: 152, 154). ReneeF particularly encapsulated these characteristics, through her questioning of hermeneutical practices and organising of study sessions that tackled hermeneutics explicitly. This role was not possible for all congregants, as has been seen, nor was it necessarily limited to the most hermeneutically virtuous or skilled. I suspect organic theologians need to be those who are hermeneutically courageous (so Chapter 8); who are growing in other hermeneutical virtues; who are learning

---

[6] I am drawing on David M. Csinos here, after John Donne, and in the preaching example that follows (2010: 47f).

how to mediate relationally and so can catalyse hermeneutical community. Such figures it would seem are critical within congregations for hermeneutics.

To conclude this theme, I address the following key question for mediation. Do mediatory dynamics, such as trickle-down and stream-down, have any significance for community as a hermeneutical virtue? There is only limited evidence in the tale of two churches, hence this must be a tentative response. My reading of the churches is that, as for epistemology, there are factors in tension on this point. Drawing on the theme of epistemology above, a low authority, trickle-down dynamic may favour a more mutual hermeneutics for congregants. Such a dynamic, however, also exposes congregants to greater hermeneutical difference, meaning less shared horizons and practices locally, but more diffuse engagement with the wider Christian community. By contrast, a high authority, stream-down dynamic may reduce the mutuality of hermeneutical practices by congregants. Such a dynamic, however, exposes congregants to limited hermeneutical difference, meaning more shared horizons and practices locally, and limited focussed engagement with the wider Christian community. Within this dynamic tension, at the more contextual level, a number of instances have been cited where the perceived 'expert' mediator tended to reduce the communal nature of Bible engagement.

Towards Community

Community is not found in other lists of hermeneutical virtue,[7] but it was clearly indicated as a virtuous theme by the tale of two churches. From our analysis of the tale, hermeneutical community is the product of historical practices that shape and are shaped by congregational horizons. Such community does not have to be face-to-face, but can also be experienced at a distance, and the hermeneutical community extends beyond the congregation, sometimes in unintended ways. There was a significance to certain hermeneutical practices, indeterminacy, and mediatory dynamics for community, but these were in a complex tension with other factors. Resistance to mediators and organic theologians more straightforwardly favoured community engagement with Scripture.[8]

The tale of two churches would suggest that community as a hermeneutical virtue is multi-faceted. The virtue may potentially contribute to building relationships, protecting congregational boundaries, resisting mediation,

---

[7]　　Although Fowl and Jones come close in emphasising *Reading in Communion* (1991), and Wright argues that unity is a virtue more generally (2010: 187). There are many others who imply community is virtuous by using terms such as 'communal hermeneutics', 'community hermeneutics', and 'hermeneutical community'. I will return to these uses later in the chapter.

[8]　　Congregants rarely referred to the local community outside the church or the wider world as mediators of hermeneutics (key exception is TomF in Chapter 4).

affirming or disrupting tradition, and aid learning from others. It is important to state, however, that reading the Bible together (whether directly or indirectly) is not necessarily virtuous. There is a dark side to community when it is not aligned with a Christian *telos*. Community can be an excuse for a hermeneutical free for all or for authoritarian policing of congregational boundaries. It is possible that both of these modes, although claiming to be disruptive or affirming of congregational horizons respectively, can actually be lacking in genuine Spirit driven transformation. As with all of the hermeneutical virtues, they do not stand alone, and community is not all, even though important.

The discussion of the four themes above has deliberately sought signs of hermeneutical community without closely defining what such community *should be* in terms of 'formal' and 'normative' theological voices.[9] This is now our pressing question.

Further Christian Perspectives on Community

What does community look like as a hermeneutical virtue when directed towards God? Scripture is not short of clues. Directions can be found in the notions of *ekklēsia*, *koinōnia* and the communal metaphors for church in the New Testament (e.g. household, temple/building, and body of Christ). Paula Gooder argues that 'community' is to be preferred over 'congregation' and 'church' as a translation of *ekklēsia* in the New Testament (2008a: 11). If this is correct, it would make 'community' very common in English Bibles.[10] Although *ekklēsia*-as-community is surely an eschatological concept,[11] nevertheless more specific direction is needed regarding where this 'community' points. *Koinōnia*

---

[9]   Village analyses the influence of community (in a descriptive sense) on Anglican biblical interpretation by quantitative means, and concludes that any community effect is 'partial rather than absolute'. For biblical interpretation, 'people carry with them some influences of their previous experience of other traditions, and that their present congregation has partly, but not fully, shaped their interpretative practice'. This result broadly concurs with the qualitative analysis of mediatory dynamics here, albeit community is found to be more significant in this study. Village acknowledges that 'in other traditions there may be much tighter control of individual interpretations and the "community effect" could be much stronger relative to individual difference' (2007: 137–8).

[10]   Probably second only to faithfulness in terms of the seven hermeneutical virtues identified here, since there are 114 instances of *ekklēsia* in the NT (O'Brien, 1993a: 124). Gooder prefers 'community' since 'congregation' has lost its universal sense and 'church' is anachronistic in the context of the NT.

[11]   According to O'Brien, some have argued that *ekklēsia*, when it occurs on its own in the NT, is an abbreviation of the original *hē ekklēsia tou theou*, 'the church of God'. That is, an eschatological designation, see 1 Cor 1:2; 10:32; 11:22; 15:9; 2 Cor 1:1; Gal 1:13 (1993a: 126).

is translated by the English words fellowship, communion, and sharing, with the NT emphasis being on 'participating "in something"', as in the 'fellowship of his Son' (1 Cor 1:9), 'communion of the Holy Spirit' (2 Cor 13:13), and 'sharing in the Spirit' (Phil 2:1) (O'Brien, 1993b).[12] The *koinōnia* characteristic of Christian community, then, is that their shared common life is gained through its shared life in Christ, empowered by the Spirit. The metaphors of temple/building,[13] household, and body provide further clues to what hermeneutical community should be. Temple identifies Christian community as a place in which God dwells, and points to its intended unity (1 Cor 3:16–17; 2 Cor 6:16; 1 Pe 2:4–6). Furthermore, the temple is being built together in Christ – a reconciling work in progress – where organic growth is a characteristic of Christian community (Eph 2:20–22). Household describes Christian community using the language of family (e.g. father, firstborn, children, brothers), in particular underlining the importance and quality of relationships within that community (e.g. 1 Tim 3:1–7; 5:1–2, 5, 16).

The body of Christ is an important biblical image for understanding hermeneutical community (e.g. Rom 12:4–5; 1 Cor 12:12–27; Eph 4:11–16). 'Body of Christ' is not a random image in Paul's writing, but is an appropriate metaphor for the church. It draws on the concept of corporate personality, where the many are included in the one. As all human beings are 'in Adam' by birth, so the church is 'in Christ' by new birth (Rom 5:12–21; 1 Cor 15:22, 45) (Fung, 1993: 78). 'Body of Christ', then, is the reconciled new humanity of Eph 2:15–16,[14] or as Wright puts it, the 'New Human', thus the apt metaphor (2010: 184).[15] Paul has his most extended use of the body image in 1 Cor 12 as follows:

> For just as the body is one and has many members, and all the members of the body, though many, are one body, so it is with Christ. For in the one Spirit we were all baptized into one body – Jews or Greeks, slaves or free – and we were all made to drink of one Spirit.

> Indeed, the body does not consist of one member but of many. If the foot would say, "Because I am not a hand, I do not belong to the body", that would not make it any less a part of the body. And if the ear would say, "Because I am not an eye, I do not belong to the body", that would not make it any less a part of the body. If the whole body were an eye, where would the hearing be? If the whole body were hearing, where would the sense of smell be? But as it is, God arranged the

---

[12] I am following O'Brien in this paragraph.

[13] The metaphors of temple and building merge into each other in Paul's usage (Schnackenburg, 1991: 125).

[14] See also Eph 4:13 (Schnackenburg, 1991: 115).

[15] Indeed, such aptness may push metaphor to metonym.

members in the body, each one of them, as he chose. If all were a single member, where would the body be? As it is, there are many members, yet one body. The eye cannot say to the hand, "I have no need of you", nor again the head to the feet, "I have no need of you". On the contrary, the members of the body that seem to be weaker are indispensable, and those members of the body that we think less honourable we clothe with greater honour, and our less respectable members are treated with greater respect; whereas our more respectable members do not need this. But God has so arranged the body, giving the greater honour to the inferior member, that there may be no dissension within the body, but the members may have the same care for one another. If one member suffers, all suffer together with it; if one member is honoured, all rejoice together with it.

Now you are the body of Christ and individually members of it. (1 Cor 12:12–27, NRSV)

The strong emphasis here is on wide diversity within unity, alongside the mutual dependence that the body of Christ entails. This mutual dependence is no respecter of apparent importance either. Such mutuality is for the healthy functioning of the body, which implies an organic growth that is developed more explicitly elsewhere in the NT. For example, Eph 4:16 speaks of each part of the body 'working properly' in order to promote 'the body's growth in building itself up in love'. As for all the communal metaphors considered, this body only gains its shared life and growth from being in Christ, the head of the body (Eph 4:15; Col 2:19). Commentators have also noted of this (and the other body texts) that the body of Christ may refer to a local congregation (v27) or to the Christian church more widely (v12–13) (O'Brien, 1993a; Fung, 1993).

What does this indicate for community as a hermeneutical virtue? Firstly, community loses its oddity as a hermeneutical virtue when considered in a Christian framework, since it is a thoroughly eschatological category. Secondly, that community is a particular outworking of the root virtue, love. For hermeneutical virtue, community is the more concrete frontline instance of love (see Chapter 8). If love is the driver for the virtue of community, then the quality of relationships will also be significant for virtuous hermeneutical practice. Thirdly, assuming that what is true of community in general is true of community as a hermeneutical virtue, it is evident that *we need each other* to read Scripture virtuously, whether within a local congregation or the wider church. Community is about recognising that all members of the body have something to contribute to virtuous hermeneutical practices. Reading in Christian community encourages all the hermeneutical virtues to flourish. In community, we are more than the sum of our virtuous parts. Fourthly, Christian community means reconciliation with God and others, hence certain congregational/

denominational/tradition and other barriers may well need to be broken down for the growth of hermeneutical virtue.[16]

If we listen to wider normative and formal voices, there appears to be a growing theological consensus that hermeneutical practices should primarily be located in Christian communities – 'the Bible in its true place' (Anglican Communion, 2012: 1). Justifications are drawn from biblical, doctrinal, ecclesial, ecumenical, missiological and liberative sources. It is not controversial to observe that the address of Scripture is largely directed to communities rather than individuals (e.g. Smart, 1970: 23f), and its pervasive communal metaphors have already been examined above. The Scripture Project at the Center of Theological Inquiry in Princeton boldly states the importance of community in the sixth of its *Nine Theses on the Interpretation of Scripture*, as: 'Faithful interpretation of Scripture invites and presupposes participation in the community brought into being by God's redemptive action – the church' (Davis and Hays, 2003: 3–4).[17] Thesis seven also identifies the importance of the historical church community, who help us today to see what it means to interpret the Bible virtuously (2003: 4; cf. Parris, 2006).

Theodramatic language has been used throughout previous chapters, and this is also revealing for community. One cannot improvise and embody the Christian Story alone. Indeed, properly speaking, as Billings highlights:

> In ourselves, we are not the central actors in God's inbreaking kingdom; we are members of the body of Christ, who is central in the drama's action. Insofar as we act in this drama at all, it is only as those united to Jesus Christ and filled with the Holy Spirit (2010: 201).

Scripture is therefore not the church's tool; it is 'the tool of the triune God' and so 'mediates "God's communicative fellowship" by extending "Christ's active, communicative presence" by the Spirit's power' (Billings, 2010: 199).[18] Such mediation is to be experienced corporately.

This embodied sense of Scripture in the church is found in many denominational and ecumenical sources. Rowan Williams states in a key Anglican document: 'To be a biblical Church is surely to be a community that lives out this great story day by day and commends it to people everywhere as the most comprehensive truth possible about the nature of God and God's world' (Foreword in Anglican Communion, 2012: 2). Lesslie Newbigin spoke in similar

---

[16]   Of 2 Cor 3:18, which was a focus for discussion around transformation in Chapter 2, Larry Kreitzer argues that the purpose of such transformation is to 'stress the idea of reconciliation as foundational to any understanding of ministry' (1996: 68).

[17]   Although speaking of community in very positive theological tones, it is not included in their list of 'interpretive virtues', see Table 8.1 in Chapter 8.

[18]   Citing Webster (2006: 46, 36).

terms when he declared 'the only hermeneutic of the gospel ... is a congregation of men and women who believe it and live by it' (1989: 227). Notably, such thinking is spelt out in some detail in the World Council of Churches Faith and Order text, *A Treasure in Earthen Vessels*. Under the heading of 'The Church as an hermeneutical community', paragraph 49 says:

> The Church, whether embodied in a local congregation, episcopal diocese, or Christian World Communion, is called to interpret texts, symbols and practices so as to discern the Word of God as a word of life amid ever-changing times and places. This hermeneutical task undertaken by the Church, with the guidance of the Holy Spirit, is a condition for apostolic mission in and for the world. To speak of the Church as a hermeneutical community is also to say that this community is a proper locus for the interpretation and the proclamation of the Gospel (1998).[19]

The language of 'hermeneutical community' used here is prevalent across many church traditions and theological subdisciplines.[20] This language is also strongly implied in Fowl's work, where he has an intense emphasis on how communities must be vigilant in resisting sinful performances of Scripture (1998: chapter 3), as seen in Chapter 8. A similar theme is raised from a missiological perspective by David Bosch in calling for the church to be an 'international hermeneutical community' where 'Christians ... from different contexts challenge one another's cultural, social, and ideological biases' (1991: 187; cf. Hiebert, 1999: 113; Walls, 2002).[21] Liberation hermeneutics also makes much of hermeneutical community, albeit not necessarily with that precise terminology. In Latin America, as introduced in Chapter 1, Carlos Mesters has written of how Base Communities[22] interpret Scripture. Mesters represents this as a communal activity that leads to a 'democratisation of the Bible' with the aim of identifying with the poor and fighting for justice (1980: 44; 1990; also 1989). Also highlighted in Chapter 1, Gerald West in South Africa developed the concept of 'reading with' over a number of decades, giving it form through the practice of Contextual Bible Study. Dube and West explain 'reading with' as 'a reading process in which the respective subject positions of ordinary, untrained readers and critical, trained

---

[19]   Contributors came from many ecclesial traditions, so Anglican, Anabaptist/Pietist, Lutheran, Methodist, Old Catholic, Orthodox, Reformed and Roman Catholic. See Simone Sinn for an evaluation of this text (2002).

[20]   See Bosch (1991: 187); Catholic Church and Baptist World Alliance (2006–10: paras 48, 49, 50, 53, 57b); Conder and Rhodes (2009); Hays (1996: 304–6); Hiebert (1999: 101f, 113); Murray (2000: 157f, 182); Sinn (2008).

[21]   Although unlikely to be in agreement with the overall approach argued for here, 'cultural exegesis' in biblical studies similarly argues for a 'chorus of perspectives' from different cultural contexts (Smith-Christopher, 1995).

[22]   *Communidades Ecclesiasticas de Base.*

readers are vigilantly foregrounded and in which power relations are structurally acknowledged' (1996b: 7–8). 'Reading with' in Contextual Bible Study begins and ends with contextual questions that are 'community consciousness questions' that 'draw on the resources of the community', their 'lived experience and embodied theologies' (The Ujamaa Centre, 2014: 9).

Community and Congregation

The hermeneutical virtue of community clearly has ecumenical potential and theological support. As seen in the quote from *A Treasure in Earthen Vessels* above, such community may find expression in a range of ecclesial structures and commitments. For example, as the Baptist – Roman Catholic dialogue on *The Word of God in the Life of the Church* expressed the matter:

> Catholics believe that the Spirit has guided them to locate the communal interpretation of Scripture in the historically extended ecclesial community that is represented by its episcopal leadership ... Baptists also locate the communal interpretation of Scripture in the ecclesial community, but primarily in the form of the gathered local congregation (2006–10: §49).[23]

The tale of two churches draws on accounts of hermeneutical community expressed within local congregations, but this need not limit what emerges to those who subscribe to a congregationalist polity. Congregational hermeneutics in my usage is the theological ethnographic study of local churches, however configured, and their hermeneutical practices.[24] What emerges for community as a hermeneutical virtue, in the remainder of this chapter, is how such practices are learned within community and how they might be enriched. This is of concern for a wide range of Christian traditions.

Towards Hermeneutical Apprenticeship

Four theological voices have been heard speaking of community. The conversation has included signs of community, both espoused and operant, as well as formal and normative voices from a wide range of contexts. There is resonance and dissonance between the voices, both of which may function as

---

[23]   The Baptist position in this document is described as 'congregational hermeneutics' (akin to Stuart Murray in Chapter 1), which is a much more ecclesially specific use of the term than mine.

[24]   As noted in Chapter 1, the same generic sense as in the subdiscipline of 'congregational studies' (e.g. Guest et al., 2004; cf. Cameron et al., 2005).

drivers for change. The potential of community for change in terms of enriched hermeneutical practices is under consideration here.

Although the virtue of community has been seen to have specific shape and dynamics, it is easy for it to be treated as a 'worthy' virtue that primarily consists of warm and fuzzy feelings towards others in a local church. Counter to this tendency, I propose that community as a hermeneutical virtue should have a particular focus within churches. From listening to the four voices, both resonance and dissonance, I would like to develop the ways in which community is necessary for the development of all the other virtues. These voices indicate that honesty, faithfulness, openness, courage, humility and confidence, and their associated practices, are not primarily developed as an individual. Such virtues need community so that they may grow and flourish. Since growth in virtue is a learning process, community is inextricably linked to the learning of all hermeneutical virtues. Community, as a hermeneutical virtue, therefore, has a strong educational focus. It is argued in the rest of the chapter that hermeneutical apprenticeship is the most appropriate educational mode for congregational hermeneutics.

Exploring Apprenticeship

Apprenticeship has traditionally been understood as the process of a novice learning a trade or craft from a highly experienced practitioner. This learning is not just 'saying' but also 'doing' and is highly relational. The novice watches the expert practice their craft, tries to imitate what they do, receives correction and feedback, revises their practice, and so gradually learns the habits and language of the craft.[25] It is my contention that learning virtuous hermeneutical practices takes the form of an apprenticeship, albeit configured in particular ways appropriate for Christian communities. As discussed in Chapter 1, hermeneutics is a science and an art; it is not simply about learning hermeneutical rules, principles, guidelines or rules of thumb. Hermeneutics requires practice. Vanhoozer captures very well the apprenticeship-like nature of learning to read texts, as follows:

> Developing interpretive virtues is not a matter of following, say, "thirty-six steps to better exegesis". It is not a matter of following rules or procedures, but of acquiring skills and learning good practice. To this end, readers must be apprentices of texts and of their authors. Right reading – reading that both fosters and exemplifies virtue – is ultimately a matter of cultivating good judgement, of knowing what

---

[25] Hauerwas is fond of the analogy of brick-laying as a picture of what it means to be a disciplined Christian community. The key ingredients of apprenticeship here are taken from Hauerwas (2010b: 45f).

to do when. This is as much a spiritual as an intellectual and interpretive task ... The wise reader knows not only how to interpret, but more importantly, what interpretation is for (1998: 377–8).

We need to be apprentices of texts, as some of the virtues discussed in Chapter 8 have indicated, but to extend Vanhoozer's argument further, in Christian communities we must also be hermeneutical apprentices of each other. This many-to-many model is a development from the traditional one-to-one conception of apprenticeship, and might be described as a corporate or community apprenticeship. Jos de Kock argues for a similar approach in relation to catechesis in church communities, particularly for young people. Critically, learners and teachers *participate* together in shared practices, creating a relational learning environment that enables identification with mature believers across the generations, and, I suggest, across other differentiations within the body as well. Such an apprenticeship model is fitting since it 'corresponds with a plea for taking the community, rather than the individual to be more accurately understood as the center of knowledge formation in churches' (2012: 190–91).

At the heart of community apprenticeship is imitation in relationship. Signs of this were seen in Holder and Fellowship, where hermeneutical patterns implied some imitation of practices, whether they were named or not. For example, there was evidence that text-linking, grammatico-historical approaches, Jesus hermeneutics, and congregational horizons were imitated within the congregations. Imitation, however, does not need to mean slavish or passive copying. My dictionary allows for imitation to have the sense of following a model (Pearsall, 1998: 913). Apprentices will not come to much if all they can do is copy their mentors. They need to develop the disposition of 'knowing what to do when', that is, to contextualise the hermeneutical virtues and skills they have gained from their community mentors. Apprenticeship should not entail a passive and submissive transmission of practices, as in some accounts of religious socialisation, but rather an increasingly critical appropriation of mentor models (Vermeer, 2010).[26] Hermeneutical apprenticeship, particularly of the more intentional variety, should be less prone to passive learning, since it is largely process that is being modelled, with both affirmative *and* disruptive reading processes being embedded in hermeneutical virtue.

Apprenticeship has many resonances within Scripture. Some point to the rabbinic traditions of apprenticeship that seem recognisable in Jesus' teaching of his disciples (Csinos, 2010; Melchert, 1998). Furthermore, the imperative to

---

[26]   In the context of Religious Education in faith schools in the Netherlands, Paul Vermeer argues for a 'modern' socialisation that focusses on the 'acquisition of hermeneutic and critical reflective skills' (2010: 115).

'imitate' occurs a number of times in the New Testament[27] and refers variously to Paul, churches, other believers, Christ and God. Christians are apprentices of Christ, in that they are disciples being transformed into the likeness of Christ (see Chapter 2), but as the body of Christ, they are also apprentices of each other. A sense of this is gained from Paul's appeal in 1 Cor 11:1: 'Be imitators of me, as I am of Christ!' (NRSV). As argued above, however, this imitation does not mean copying Christ, Paul or anyone else in every respect. In Paul's use of 'imitate', he is asking Christians to 'incorporate certain specific aspects of his life into their own lives', not for everyone to become tentmakers, for example (Fowl, 1993: 430). Dustin Ellington makes a persuasive case for Paul's imitation imperative in 1 Cor 11:1 being an exhortation for the Corinthian believers 'to share in his relationship to the gospel, working with it for the salvation of others and allowing its pattern and power to shape their life together' (2011: 303).[28] With regard to Christ, our ultimate mentor, it is evident that the early church did not copy him in every way. As Conrad Gempf points out, they did not use parables nor walk on water (cited in Tomkins, 2011). Paul was not able to save people as Christ does; indeed, there are many aspects of Christ's life and ministry that were unique to him. The popular hermeneutics slogan 'What would Jesus do?' (WWJD) leans towards over-imitation, despite its good intentions.[29] Imitation (and so apprenticeship) should instead be about doing what Christ has taught us to do in our own contexts, and in this way being formed into his likeness.[30]

Apprenticeship and Communities of Practice

Community apprenticeship, working with a mutual many-to-many model of mentoring and being mentored, has helpful resonance with communities of practice thinking. Not surprisingly, this link to communities of practice has been picked up by those who are concerned about learning in the church (e.g. Csinos, 2010; Faith & Leadership, 2009; Floding and Swier, 2011). Jean Lave and Etienne Wenger originated the term back in 1991 for what they recognised was an age-old process of situated learning (1991: 98). Wenger defines communities of practice as 'groups of people who share a concern or passion for something they do and learn how to do it better as they interact regularly' (Wenger, nd).

---

[27] E.g. 1 Cor 4:16, 11:1; Eph 5:1; Php 3:17; 1 Thess 1:6, 2:14; 2 Thess 3:7, 9; Heb 6:12, 13:7; 3 Jn 1:11.

[28] 1 Cor 11:1 is seen as the culmination of the discussion from 1 Cor 8:1 onwards.

[29] The Occupy movement raised a large WWJD banner outside St. Paul's Cathedral in London during November 2011 as part of their protest (Tomkins, 2011; cf. Bennett, 2013: 111f).

[30] Mark Galli argues that *The Imitation of Christ* by Thomas à Kempis does not advise its readers to 'mimic Christ' but rather focusses on 'how God can form their character to become the people Christ wants them to be' (2002).

Such a concept would certainly appear to have utility for Christian communities seeking to develop virtuous hermeneutical practices. Its development from traditional notions of apprenticeship parallels the discussion above at so many points it is worth quoting Wenger at length:

> Anthropologist Jean Lave and I coined the term while studying apprenticeship as a learning model. People usually think of apprenticeship as a relationship between a student and a master, but studies of apprenticeship reveal a more complex set of social relationships through which learning takes place mostly with journeymen and more advanced apprentices. The term community of practice was coined to refer to the community that acts as a living curriculum for the apprentice. Once the concept was articulated, we started to see these communities everywhere, even when no formal apprenticeship system existed. And of course, learning in a community of practice is not limited to novices. The practice of a community is dynamic and involves learning on the part of everyone (Wenger, nd).

I have argued similarly that the virtue of community entails learning hermeneutical practices through multiple mediators and relationships. Like the communities of practice here described, Holder and Fellowship operated with largely informal modes of hermeneutical apprenticeship, although there were also some formal elements. The case being made in this study is that a more intentional hermeneutical apprenticeship/community of practice is needed in some, if not many, churches. This need not be more formal, but certainly should be more explicit. Furthermore, the point has been made that hermeneutical apprenticeship is for all Christians, not just for novices but for 'old-timers' as well, and all in-between. Growth in hermeneutical virtue, as for virtue in general, is a lifelong process.

A key feature in communities of practice thinking is the importance of 'legitimate peripheral participation' for genuine learning. This important concept concerns 'the process by which newcomers become part of a community of practice' where they 'move toward full participation in the sociocultural practices of a community' (Lave and Wenger, 1991: 29). David Csinos has argued in general how legitimate peripheral participation informs learning in churches, and so broadly following Csinos (2010), I identify its usefulness for community hermeneutical apprenticeship. Firstly, congregants must have genuine *participation* in the church's hermeneutical practices through being invited to do so. This raises questions of how broadly participation is defined, especially how active or passive, whether acting on an interpretation of Scripture by volunteering at a food bank, or saying the liturgy during a worship service, or contributing to a Bible study group. It also invokes questions of authority – who is permitted to engage in congregational hermeneutical practices and in what roles? This leads into *legitimacy*, where newcomers and novices are granted sufficient legitimacy to make a genuine contribution to the hermeneutical practices of the church. Legitimacy in the church should come from being members of the body of Christ who can grow in hermeneutical virtue. Recognising this given legitimacy means that 'their inevitable stumbling and violations become opportunities for learning rather than cause for dismissal, neglect or exclusion' (Wenger, 1998: 101). Such legitimate participation also needs to be *peripheral*, which is to say that novice practitioners should only have 'an approximation of full participation that gives exposure to actual practice' (Wenger, 1998: 100). In the ongoing practice of hermeneutics, congregants move from peripheral to full participation, and in so doing may transform *and* be transformed by their Christian community. Peripherality is not a negative term, but rather a positive in that it 'suggests an opening, a way of gaining access to sources for understanding through growing involvement' (Lave and Wenger, 1991: 37). These 'sources for understanding' I will address in more concrete terms later in the chapter.

A few more points emerge from communities of practice thinking. Csinos warns of how some key individuals in a church can be unwilling to share their authority, thus withholding legitimacy from key practices to many in the congregation. Alternatively, novices are sometimes given full participation too soon, and are 'robbed' of the journey from peripheral to full participation, that 'affirms their worth yet grounds them in the community's practice' (2010: 60). In my own experience of hermeneutical practices in churches, many congregants feel they have little of value to contribute, possibly due to the lack of conferred legitimacy. This can also be heightened by a less than virtuous use of 'expert' mediators.

Community of practice thinking reinforces and nuances much of the community hermeneutical apprenticeship discussion that has gone before, but inevitably it does not fit in every respect. Christian communities are eschatological, so in the case being made here, their hermeneutical practices are to be shaped by certain virtues, which may or may not be part of a community of practice account. In Gospel fashion, this may also upset any straightforward progression from newcomer to old-timer, since growth in virtue is not necessarily correlated to time. Consequently, the distinction between newcomers and old-timers may well be less sharp, where there are many shades of peripherality and 'old-timers' continue to learn. More problematically, the tale of two churches indicates that some churches may not recognise that there are any practices to be learnt! Before legitimate peripheral participation can be effected, greater explicitness and intentionality may be needed in congregational hermeneutics.

The Scope of Community Hermeneutical Apprenticeship

Wenger also notes that the characteristics of a community of practice may make them 'a challenge for traditional hierarchical organizations' (nd). This point leads us to revisit the broader question addressed previously, namely is community hermeneutical apprenticeship fitting for all church structures and ecclesiologies? Certainly the tale of two churches is rooted in congregationalist structures, but this need not limit its wider relevance. Hermeneutical apprenticeship may be configured through different Bible uses and settings appropriate to the church tradition, as long as there is room for legitimate participation in the practice of 'hearing God speak through Scripture'. The Apostolic Exhortation of Pope Francis is highly suggestive on this point (*Evangelii Gaudium*). I quote from the section entitled 'Centred on the word of God':

> 174. The sacred Scriptures are the very source of evangelization. Consequently, we need to be constantly trained in hearing the word. The church does not evangelize unless she constantly lets herself be evangelized. It is indispensable that the word of God "be ever more fully at the heart of every ecclesial activity" ...

> 175. The study of the sacred Scriptures must be a door opened to every believer. It is essential that the revealed word radically enrich our catechesis and all our efforts to pass on the faith. Evangelization demands familiarity with God's word, which calls for dioceses, parishes and Catholic associations to provide for a serious, ongoing study of the Bible, while encouraging its prayerful individual and communal reading ... (2013)[31]

The emphases here appear to have a strong resonance with communal hermeneutical apprenticeship, expressed in the language and structures of a particular Christian tradition. Other traditions will express this desire in different ways, such as the less specific 'Bible passion' of Fellowship, not so dissimilar from Rowan Williams's desire for the *Bible in the Life of the Church* project:

> This project looks towards a future in which we can not only read Scripture with clearer eyes but understand each other's reading with clearer eyes as well – with more love and patience and willingness to be taught and enriched by each other ...

> One of the things that I personally hope this project will help us develop in the Communion is a wider and fuller biblical literacy, in which the outlines of the one great story of creation and redemption will be clear (foreword in Anglican Communion, 2012: 1–2).

Having argued that the tale of two churches, alongside other voices, points to the need for a communal, intentional and virtuous hermeneutical apprenticeship

---

[31]   See also *Lectio Divina* in Pontifical Bible Commission (1993).

for many churches, it now seems appropriate to look at some practical examples of what such apprenticeship might (and might not) look like.

What Does Hermeneutical Apprenticeship Look Like?

Hermeneutical apprenticeship ought to be something ongoing in the life of a local church. Both internal and external ways of mediating virtuous hermeneutical practice are considered here, some suitable for particular traditions, others more generally applicable. This is approached through considering those Bible settings given in the tale of two churches, namely public, small group and personal.

For many Christians, especially historically, participation in liturgy has been their main exposure to the Bible. This is a very important form of Bible engagement in the church, particularly in terms of increasing familiarity with biblical themes and passages, so as to enter the 'strange new world of the Bible'. Having said this, in terms of virtuous hermeneutical apprenticeship, such 'minimalist hermeneutics' is often not enough. It is too passive to be the staple hermeneutical diet of congregants. A more explicit form of hermeneutical apprenticeship is the sermon, although this is still typically passive in terms of congregational participation. To counteract this passivity, some churches have experimented with interactive sermons that involve a degree of discussion and/or feedback.[32] I have occasionally been present in relatively traditional format churches where this has taken place, and noted its counter-cultural and logistical difficulties, but recognise its value in communicating that the Bible needs to be read in community. An alternative to this approach is to remove the 'real-time' aspect of this interaction, by discussing with other congregants prior to the sermon. When preaching in my home congregation, I often invite my homegroup to offer their insights on the passage in advance and have then incorporated them into the sermon. Much preaching advice stresses the importance of 'exegeting' the congregation alongside the Scriptures. In her book *Preaching as Local Theology and Folk Art* Leonora Tubbs Tisdale argues that the preacher is a local theologian, albeit one who recognises they are not the only 'resident theologian' in the local community of faith. She argues:

> Instead of viewing preaching as an act in which theologically educated pastors help uneducated lay people attain unto their level of knowledge and expertise, preaching as local theology calls us to view our task with greater humility – respecting and affirming the wealth of theological knowledge and wisdom already present within the congregation, and the many ways in which congregations shape and feed the theology which finds its voice in the pulpit (1997: 42).

---

[32] Cory Labanow documents such a practice in his study of Jacobsfield Vineyard, which he describes as 'congregational hermeneutics' in the prescriptive sense (2009: 49–50).

A sense of community hermeneutical apprenticeship is therefore evident with the minister who knows their congregation very well, as they speak not only 'to' the congregation, but also 'on behalf of'. Preachers may be pro-active in this respect through becoming 'amateur ethnographers – skilled in observing and thickly describing the subcultural signs and symbols of the congregations they serve' (1997: 60).

More generally, there is a question as to how explicit a form of apprenticeship the sermon should be. After completing a Master's degree on the subject of Biblical Hermeneutics I was keen to communicate all I was doing when preaching, by 'showing my working out'. This was not entirely successful, since hermeneutical moves do not always hold people's attention. On the other hand, as ReneeF (typically) asked me: 'If we never see it, how do we learn to do it for ourselves?' Apprenticeship does need some transparency from those in a mentoring role. My experience of preaching and this research has led me to integrate the two by selectively highlighting hermeneutical moves and difficult issues where it has been appropriate for the congregation and the message.

Small groups emerged from this study as the most intense forum for community hermeneutical apprenticeship, relative to the other settings considered. On balance, there was greater potential for the flourishing of hermeneutical virtues. It is also recognised that small groups serve multiple purposes for their members, besides that of hermeneutical apprenticeship (e.g. GordonF in Chapter 6). Roger Walton has provided a sobering critique of contemporary small groups in English churches, based on qualitative and quantitative fieldwork, confirming and extending the work of Robert Wuthnow in the USA (1994a; b). Walton concludes that such groups are based on the contemporary cultural form of the self-help group, and as such diverge from kingdom values in significant ways. In particular, groups can focus inwardly on developing 'personal qualities' and 'the care of the church community' at the expense of a more outward focus on 'discovering God in the life of the world' and being formed through 'active engagement in mission' (2011: 112; cf., 2014). As someone who leads and coordinates small groups, I am disheartened by these findings, but recognise much of what is presented.[33] However, from the perspective of hermeneutical apprenticeship, the tale of two churches indicates that small groups are a significant setting within congregations, somewhat counter to Walton's account. I do agree, nevertheless, that small groups need to be based upon broader kingdom values (or virtues), which will include a more intentional hermeneutical apprenticeship.

One externally mediated form for small groups identified in Chapter 1 and earlier in this chapter is 'Contextual Bible Study' (CBS). Developed by Gerald

---

[33]   I would want to maintain the importance of *both* an inward and outward focus for small groups, where 'inward' need not be pejorative.

West in South Africa, the approach has much in common with the liberation hermeneutics of Latin America, with origins in 'the interface between socially engaged biblical scholars, organic intellectuals, and ordinary Christian "readers" of the Bible' (The Ujamaa Centre, 2014: 4). As discussed earlier, CBS deals with community consciousness questions (context), as well as critical consciousness questions (text), where the latter are informed by the three dimensions of behind, within, and in front of the text (see Chapter 3). Studies follow a version of the pastoral cycle outlined in Chapter 2, known as See–Judge–Act, as follows:

> ... the Bible study process begins with analysis of the local context (See), and then re-reads the Bible to allow the biblical text to speak to the context (Judge), and then moves to action as we respond to what God is saying (Act). Social analysis enables us to understand our reality; re-reading the Bible enables us to judge whether our reality is as God intends it to be; and our plan of action enables us to work with God to change our reality (The Ujamaa Centre, 2014: 4).

In summary, CBS is about 'reading and studying the Bible in the church and community so that we can hear God speaking to us in our context' (West, 1993: 7). The approach has been picked up and adapted in various other parts of the world, particularly by Louise Lawrence in the West Country of England (2009) and John Riches in Scotland (Riches, 2010; cf. The Contextual Bible Study Development Group, 2005). The CBS approach has much to offer for hermeneutical apprenticeship in churches, particularly its strong participatory emphasis driven by members' experience and context alongside the expectation of action arising out of Bible engagement. Questions remain for some regarding its very strong focus on experience and context, as well as its transferability from situations of marginalisation to those of relative advantage, although I do not think these issues are insurmountable.

Regarding personal Bible reading, I consider this an important part of hermeneutical apprenticeship, where mentors are mediated by Bible reading aids in a variety of media (Chapter 7). The attitude of condescension or even dismissal applied to 'devotional reading' or *lectio divina* common in some circles (especially academic), is inappropriate since many will testify that the Spirit works to transform through Scripture in this setting as in others. Such testimony was heard in the tale of two churches. Congregations can certainly generate mediatory configurations that allow for the dissemination of helpful Bible reading aids that might contribute to virtuous hermeneutical apprenticeship. The dangers of personal Bible reading, however, especially of an inward individualism, are captured in the memorable words of James Smart, writing of the 'private practices of Christians' in relation to the Bible in 1970, albeit with a touch of overstatement:

> But the Bible was not written to be used in that way and certainly not be read in snippets of five or six verses each. No part of it (with the exception perhaps of a few psalms) in its origin was intended for private consumption. It is distinctively a public book ... The Bible is marching orders for an army, not bedtime reading to help one sleep more soundly. The Bible is a book to be studied by the Christian community. Make it primarily devotional literature for private use and no longer is it given the attention it requires but, more seriously still, it is subjected to an intensely individualistic interpretation and thereby silenced at the most incisive points of its message (1970: 23–4).

While wanting to argue that there are still appropriate ways to read the Bible individually – a both/and rather than either/or – nevertheless, Smart's critique has some force that needs to be taken seriously for community hermeneutical apprenticeship.

A number of non-specific setting apprenticeship strategies have been mentioned throughout the previous chapters, such as being more explicit about hermeneutics in ruled readings and making space for organic theologians in a congregation. It is recognised there are many settings that are outside the scope of this study. One that is strongly linked to congregational hermeneutics is the teaching of biblical hermeneutics in theological colleges and, in some countries, universities. The fragmentation of theology in academia has been lamented for many years now, and the knock-on effect of this is evident in churches' struggle to address hermeneutical apprenticeship within congregations. Interdisciplinary modules and courses are needed that bridge some or all of biblical studies/ hermeneutics, practical theology and education. Ministers need to develop hermeneutical skills and virtues for themselves, but also need to acquire the habit of critical reflection on their hermeneutical practices and those of their congregants, as well as knowing how to inculcate these skills and virtues within their communities. Such hermeneutical education is not just for ministers, however, but is also an investment of time and money for lay people/organic theologians that will bear fruit in congregations.[34]

One such course designed for churches and Christian organisations is the Bible Society's *h+ (Making Good Sense of the Bible)*, which drew directly on this research and for which I was the lead author (Bible Society, 2011a; b).[35] The aim

---

[34] As part of the 2011 400th anniversary of the King James Bible celebrations, I ran a module at the University of Roehampton entitled *Congregational Hermeneutics* which combined biblical hermeneutics with reflection on students' hermeneutical practices (sermons, small groups, personal bible reading), along with hermeneutical apprenticeship strategies. In 2015–16, the module is being relaunched as *Biblical Hermeneutics* and team-taught between a biblical scholar and me, a practical theologian.

[35] With significant input from my colleague, Mike Simmonds, and members of the Bible Society project team.

of *h*+ is 'to enable participants to make good sense of the Bible for themselves, in the church and in the world, through learning, practicing and mediating key hermeneutical virtues and skills' (Bible Society, 2011a).[36] The roots of *h*+ in this research are apparent in the overarching learning outcomes, which state that by the end of the course participants will have:

1. Appreciated that making good sense of the Bible is part and parcel of Christian discipleship.
2. Understood how hermeneutical virtues are significant for making good sense of the Bible, and be growing in such virtues.
3. Developed hermeneutical skills associated with reading 'behind the text', 'within the text', and 'in front of the text', and understood their relationship to the virtues.
4. Gained skills in reflecting critically on their own hermeneutical practices (individual and corporate).

h+ is designed around an 'apprenticeship model', whereby 'participants are apprenticed by the course facilitator but also by each other'. As noted above, hermeneutical apprenticeship needs to be ongoing in the life of a church, but a course such as *h*+ can act to stimulate aspects of this apprenticeship.

h+ was developed due to the lack of face-to-face resources that took the relational nature of hermeneutical apprenticeship seriously.[37] It consisted of ten sessions of 1½ hours where each session focussed on one or more hermeneutical virtues. For example, participants are invited to 'reflect *honestly* on what they bring to their reading of the Bible' through a questionnaire. Traditional understandings of the Nativity are examined, mental pictures of Jesus considered, and contrasting cultural interpretations of the Good Samaritan assessed.[38] For *faithfulness*, emphasis is placed upon appreciating the historical circumstances of Bible passages. Of Jesus' saying to 'turn the other cheek' in Matthew 5, participants looked at its historical context (including slapping role-play) to see whether a non-violent resistance interpretation makes good sense of this passage. *h*+ did not seek to align itself with particular interpretations, but rather to encourage participants to reflect on *how* we interpret – an important difference, especially since the course ran in churches across the denominations. The pedagogical task was to communicate hermeneutical ideas in an accessible format that was not simplistic.

---

[36] This and subsequent quotations are from pp. 4–5 of the Facilitator's Guide.

[37] Prototypes of *h*+ were trialled nationally in England and then developed for release in late 2011.

[38] E.g. see rejesus (2002–15), Mark Allan Powell (2001: 21–2).

h+ ran via a facilitator training model until March 2014 and is now being revised for a relaunch in the near future.[39] During this first edition phase of *h*+, over 500 facilitators were trained to run the course in England, Ireland, and the Balkans, and 1,300 copies of the participant's guide were distributed.[40] To date, as far as I am aware, that makes *h*+ the most widespread hermeneutics course for Christian communities in the UK. There are many valuable external mediators that may catalyse and enrich hermeneutical apprenticeship for congregations. The purpose of exploring *h*+ briefly here has been to outline how one such mediator may do just that.[41]

'How Do We Read?' Revisited

I began this book with the question 'How do we read?' and this is how I will finish. I have made the case that this is a critical question for the church, as the tale of two churches and other Bible research indicates. 'How do we read?' is two questions in one, requiring both descriptive and prescriptive responses for congregational hermeneutics. The resonance and dissonance between the voices responding to this two-in-one question generated much of the argument for the book. Other methodological frames have also been incorporated to nuance this simple descriptive/prescriptive understanding, namely the triangle of conversations between researcher (myself), congregations and the Christian Story; the pastoral cycle (experience, analysis, reflection, action); critical realism (ontological realism, epistemological relativism, judgemental rationality) and the four voices of theology (normative, formal, espoused, and operant). This theological ethnography has sought to discern signs of disruptive and affirmative transformation expressed in the key theological category of virtue emerging from these accounts.

---

[39]   September 2015 is the current date on the website (Bible Society, nd). A key revision is to reduce the number of sessions.

[40]   Conversation with Mike Simmonds, 5/2/15; email from Bible Society, 6/2/15.

[41]   Feedback on *h*+ from facilitators and participants has been largely positive, and in many cases, very positive. When it comes to hermeneutics, however, it is often observed that is impossible to please everyone! Bible Society funded a doctoral student to evaluate the early pilot phase of *h*+ and her internal report provides a fair and balanced analysis of participant feedback which then fed into the subsequent development of *h*+. Of the first edition of *h*+, the Anglican Communion's *Bible in the Life of the Church* project invited 'Anglicans across the world to join in the *h*+ programme', noting of participants that *h*+ had 'freed them up to ask questions' as well as 'given them the curiosity and confidence to dig deeper into the text, and re-engage passionately and intelligently with the Bible' (2012: 49; cf. Anglican Consultative Council, 2013; Cameron, 2012).

Hermeneutical practices were tangled up in the life of the churches and comprised the saying, doing, making and learning of hermeneutics. The insider heading for their diverse hermeneutical practices was 'hearing God speak through Scripture'. Many of these practices, especially fusion processes, were silently espoused, operating below the surface of congregational life. It was argued, however, that implicit does not mean non-existent, and that patterns of hermeneutical practice were evident within and across the congregations. Hermeneutical practices in the congregations were seen to be simultaneously premodern, modern and to a lesser degree postmodern, but also had their own hybrid distinctiveness. Through a substantial interaction between the hermeneutical categories of horizon and fusion and those arising from the tale of two churches, a number of key categories for congregational hermeneutics became apparent. Horizonal beliefs divided into starting points and goals for engagement with Scripture, and fusion processes were those ways in which congregants made connections between their horizon(s) and the text. Personal, small group and public horizons were evident, where the congregational horizon was at least the product of the complex interactions between these three horizons. Congregational tradition was shown to shape the congregations' hermeneutical practices and thus their engagement with Scripture. Ruled reading was evident in both churches, although the rules varied in size and in degree of self-consciousness.

Epistemology was identified as another implicit feature of congregational horizon(s) that was highly significant for hermeneutical practices. The epistemological split seen in the tale applies to more than these two churches. Operating with nearly mutually exclusive epistemologies, it is not surprising that congregations and broader ecclesial traditions struggle to understand 'how the Bible works' on the other side of the divide. Mediation was also shown to be vital for understanding congregational hermeneutics, since hermeneutical practices are shaped by how they are learned and thus by how they are mediated within churches. Associations with mediatory configurations were noted in relation to stream-down/trickle-down dynamics and homogenous/heterogeneous sets of mediators. Certain mediators appeared to be able to cross the boundaries of theological and congregational tradition, potentially able to offer limited yet disruptive transformation of horizons.

Virtue hermeneutics was initially suggested by the insider use of 'faithful' and 'radical' at Holder and Fellowship, alongside their less explicit instances of courage and honesty. It was also informed by the small virtue hermeneutics tradition largely within biblical studies. These various strands coalesced in a move that enabled me to look at the ethnographic in theological focus, broadening the prescriptive discussion beyond the two churches. The seven hermeneutical virtues identified give content to the core argument of the book, which is to call for a more intentional, corporate and virtuous hermeneutical apprenticeship.

Honesty is needed to recognise that we are actually interpreting Scripture and to be aware of what we bring of ourselves to Bible engagement. *Faithfulness* drives us to develop hermeneutical practices that create time and space for paying careful attention to the text within our contemporary context, as well as reflect on how we mediate hermeneutics. *Openness* encourages churches to be ready to hear God's unexpected voice through the text or through other hermeneutical mediators. *Courage* intensifies aspects of openness, often through being prepared to let transformative disruptive readings change things. *Humility* recognises that there may be a number of virtuous readings of Scripture, and that my/our reading is partial and provisional. However, establishing a more explicit hermeneutical tradition has the great advantage of building genuine *confidence* for handling Scripture in congregations (in tension with humility). Finally, hermeneutical practices are not primarily a solo enterprise – the virtues must be learnt and acted upon in *community*.

Appendix A
Public Bible Settings

Table A.1   Holder Public Settings

Service	Sermon	Preacher	Date	Passage	Title	Outline provided	Type
SunPM1h	1	OwenH	18/9/2005	Rev 2:2–17	Deadly compromise	As title	Text / theme
SunAM1h	2	JoeH	25/9/2005	Mk 11:1–19	Keeping up appearances	No	Text
Member's Meeting	n/a	n/a	4/10/2005	n/a	n/a	n/a	n/a
SunAM2h	3	OwenH	16/10/2005	Mk 12:41–4	Cirrhosis of the giver	No	Theme / text
SunAM3h	4	JustinH	30/10/2005	Mk 14:1–42	Facing challenges	Facing challenges	Text
SunAM4h	5	OwenH	13/11/2005	Mk 14:43–50	What is the world's greatest mystery?	As title	Theme
Anniversary Service	6	John	19/11/2005	Acts 2:36–47	-	No	Text
TuesPMh	7	JoeH	6/12/2005	Eph 2; Php 2	-	No	Theme / text
SunAM5h	8	RodneyH	18/12/2005	(Isa 9); Matt 1, 2; Lk 2	Where are you going?	No	Theme
SunAM6h	9	Theo	1/1/2006	Lk 16:20–31	-	No	Text / theme

continued

Table A.1 *concluded*

Service	Sermon	Preacher	Date	Passage	Title	Outline provided	Type
SunAM7h	10	OwenH	5/2/2006	Ezra 2	A Vision for the Future	As title	Theme / mult. Spring. / narrative
SunAM8h	11	OwenH	5/3/2006	Ezra 5:1–5; Hag 1:1–13	God still speaks	From failure to success	Text / mult. Spring.
SunAM9h	12	OwenH	26/3/2006	Matt 7:21–7	What are you putting your trust in?	No	Theme / text

Note: 13 Holder public settings in total were included in the fieldwork, including 12 sermons with a median length of 28 minutes.

Table A.2   Fellowship Public Settings

Service	Sermon	Preacher	Date	Passage	Type
SunAM1f	1	Ian	13/2/2005	Matt 5:17–20	Text / thematic
SunAM2f	2	BobF	20/2/2005	Matt 5:21–6	Text
SunAM3f	3	DerekF	27/2/2005	Matt 5:27–30	Thematic / text
SunAM4f	4	SteveF and JasonF	6/3/2005	Matt 5:13–16	Thematic / springboard
SunAM5f	5	Liz	13/3/2005	Gen 2:24	Springboard
SunAM6f	6	BillF	20/3/2005	(Mk 15:33–41)	Thematic
Church Consultation	n/a	n/a	20/3/2005	n/a	n/a
SunAM7f	7	DerekF	10/4/2005	Matt 5:33–7	Thematic / text
Metamorphis	8	Walter and Daphne	17/4/2005	Lk 4	Springboard
SunAM8f	9	Dan	8/5/2005	Matt 6:5–15	Thematic / text
SunAM9f	10	DerekF	15/5/2005	Acts 2:1–4	Thematic / text
SunAM10f	11	Joel and Joseph	22/5/2005	n/a	Testimony
SunAM11f	12	DerekF	3/7/2005	Matt 3:3–17	Text
SunAM12f	13	PeterF	10/7/2005	Matt 7:15–23	Narrative

Note: 14 Fellowship public settings in total were included in the fieldwork, including 13 sermons with a median length of 39 minutes.

Appendix B
Small Group Bible Settings

Table B.1   Holder Small Groups

Session	Date	No.	Gender	Passage	Leader
X1	18/10/2005	17	6M / 11F	Mal 1:1–5	HarryH
X2	25/10/2005	9	5M / 4F	Mal 1:6–14	HarryH
X3	15/11/2005	10	3M / 7F	Mal 2:10–17	HarryH
X4	22/11/2005	8	2M / 6F	Mal 3:1–5	JamesH
X5	29/11/2005	9	3M / 6F	Mal 3:6–12	JamesH
Y1	10/1/2006	17	6M / 11F	Mk 10:32–45	RodneyH
Y2	24/1/2006	14	5M / 9F	Job 1:1–2:10	RodneyH
Y3	31/1/2006	14	3M / 11F	Gen 20	PaulH
Y4	28/2/2006	10	3M / 7F	Gen 39	RodneyH
Y5	21/3/2006	14	5M / 9F	Jas 3:1–12	RodneyH
WedAM	29/3/2006	8	8F	Prov 31; Acts 9:32–45	LindaH

Note: 11 Holder small group settings in total were included in the fieldwork. Housegroup X used a handout sheet each time, and Housegroup Y used a BSG each time (Nystrom, 2000).

Table B.2   Fellowship Small Groups

Session	Date	No.	Gender	Passage / Theme	Leader
A1	10/3/2005	12	6M / 6F	Mk 4:35–6:6	JasonF
A2	24/3/2005	12	-	Mk 6:14–7:23	AaronF
A3	14/4/2005	12	5M / 7F	Mk 6:45–56; 7:1–30; 8:1–9; 8:22–30	JaneF
A4	25/5/2005	13	6M / 7F	Mission / Jas 2:14–17 (plus 10 others)	SteveF
B1	23/3/2005	9	-	Hell (2 Thess 1:6–9)	DamienF
B2	13/4/2005	10	3M / 7F	The Idolatry of Materialism and Narcissism / (Psa 71); Matt 16:24, 22:37–40; Jn 8:58, 10:30, 12:25; Gal 5:14	HelenF
B3	11/5/2005	9	2M / 7F	Psa 46	SarahF
B4	25/5/2005	10	4M / 7F	Christian Aid / Lev 19:13, 35; Ezek 28:5; Mi 6:8	Mark
C1	4/3/2005	8	3M / 5F	Withered fig tree / Sermon on the Mount and Plain	GordonF
C2	6/5/2005	14	-	Islam	Richard
TuesAM1	1/3/2005	8	3M / 5F	Eph 5:22–33	DerekF
TuesAM2	8/3/2005	8	3M / 5F	Eph 6:1–9	JasonF
TuesAM3	22/3/2005	7	3M / 4F	Psa 22	DerekF
TuesAM4	12/4/2005	8	4M / 4F	Php 1:1–11	DerekF
TuesAM5	19/4/2005	7	4M / 3F	Php 1:12–30	DerekF
ThursAM1	3/3/2005	4	4M	2 Cor 7:1–16	SteveF
ThursAM2	14/4/2005	8	8M	2 Cor 9	JasonF
ThursAM3	21/4/2005	6	6M	2 Cor 10	HenryF
ThursAM4	5/5/2005	5	5M	2 Cor 11	SteveF
ThursPM1	21/4/2005	27	9M / 18F	Ex 24–5	Martyn
ThursPM2	5/5/2005	11	-	Jas 1:1–11	DerekF
ThursPM3	19/5/2005	11	5M / 6F	Jas 1:1–12	DerekF

Note: 22 Fellowship small group settings in total were included in the fieldwork. Housegroups A, B, C met in congregant's homes, whereas the other small groups met at the Good News centre. Housegroup A used a BSG for sessions 1–3; Housegroup B used handout sheets for sessions 1–2; Housegroup C used a handout for session 2.

Appendix C
Holder and Fellowship Congregants

Table C.1   Holder Congregants

Person	Interview	Small Group	Service / Sermon
AngelaH	-	Y	-
AnnaH	6/4/2006	X	-
BridgetH	13/4/2006	WedAM	-
CharlotteH	-	-	SunAM2h
DeborahH	-	-	Anniv. Serv.
DennisH	27/4/2006	Y	-
DorisH	6/4/2006	n/a	-
DotH	4/4/2006	Y	-
DougH	-	-	SunAM3h, Anniv. Serv.
HarryH	9/1/2006	X (leader)	SunAM8h
IonaH	10/4/2006	-	-
JamesH	-	X (leader)	-
JoeH	13/1/2006	-	S2h, S7h, Anniv. Serv., SunAM1h
John	-	-	S6h
JustinH	2/1/2006	Organiser	S4h
KarlH	20/3/2006	X	-
KateH	-	X	-
LindaH	-	WedAM	-
LucyH	4/4/2006	Y	-
MossH	4/4/2006	Y	-
OwenH	21/11/2005	-	S1h, 3h, 5h, 10h, 11h, 12h
PatriciaH	24/3/2006	Y / WedAM	-
PaulH	-	Y (leader)	-
RodneyH	7/4/2006	Y (leader)	S8h
RubyH	-	-	SunAM5h
SiobhanH	10/4/2006	X	-
Theo	-	-	S9h
ThelmaH	-	X	-
TimH	-	-	Anniv. Serv.
TommyH	-	X	-
WendyH	3/4/2006	Y	-

Note: This table indicates which congregants had interviews. In addition, their involvement within small groups, services and sermons is also indicated, but only according to use in this book.

Table C.2   Fellowship Congregants

Person	Interview	Small Group	Service / Sermon
AaronF	-	A	-
AmyF	19/7/2005	A	
AnneF	-	-	SunAM8f
BillF	-	-	S6f
BobF	-	-	S2f, SunAM8f
BruceF	26/5/2005	ThursPM	SunAM9f
Charles	-	-	-
DamienF	-	B	-
Dan	-	-	S9f
Daphne	-	-	S8f
DerekF	18/2/2005 and 2/8/2005	TuesAM (leader), ThursAM (leader), ThursPM (leader)	S3f, S7f, S10f, S12f
FlorenceF	-	A	-
FrancisF	23/5/2005	B (leader)	-
GordonF	1/8/2005	C (leader)	SunAM1f
GrahamF	18/7/2005	A (leader)	
HelenF	-	B	-
HenryF	-	ThursAM	-
Ian	-	-	S1f
JackF	-	-	-
JaneF	-	A	-
JasonF	-	A / TuesAM / ThursAM	S4f
Joel	-	-	S11f
Joseph	-	-	S11f
Liz	-	-	S5
Mark	-	B	-
Martyn	-	ThursPM	-
MaryF	-	TuesAM	-
MattF	19/7/2005	-	-
MelissaF	-	-	Church conslt.
MichelleF	25/7/2005	B	SunAM5f
NadineF	22/7/2005	-	-
NinaF	2/6/2005	B / TuesAM / ThursPM	-
PenelopeF	27/7/2005	A (leader)	-
PeterF	-	-	S13f
ReneeF	3/8/2005	C	-

continued

Table C.2 *concluded*

Person	Interview	Small Group	Service / Sermon
Richard	-	C	-
RossF	7/6/2005	A	-
SarahF	10/6/2005	B (leader) / TuesAM	-
SteveF	9/8/2005	TuesAM / ThursAM	S4f
TheresinaF	8/6/2005	Alpha	SunAM9f
TomF	25/7/2005	C / ThursPM	-
Walter	-	-	S8f
WilliamF	-	-	SunAM11f

Note: This table indicates which congregants had interviews. In addition, their involvement within small groups, services and sermons is also indicated, but only according to use in this book.

Appendix D
Holder and Fellowship Songs

Table D.1   Holder and Fellowship Song Comparisons

Measure	Holder	Fellow.	Notes
Total distinct songs	65	62	All figures for distinct songs unless noted
Total songs	78	80	i.e. sung on more than one occasion
Median songs per service	7	7	
Shared songs	20%	21%	
Dependent	11%	10%	Hermeneutical types for songs
Quotation	17%	15%	
Reconstructive	55%	62%	
Referential	31%	21%	
None	18%	15%	
Dep or Quo or Rec	68%	77%	i.e. those that incorporate Scripture in some way
NT	62%	59%	
OT	42%	43%	
Objective	71%	46%	Ward song types
Subjective	65%	80%	
Reflexive	12%	18%	
Intimacy	15%	28%	Selected song themes
Cross	28%	21%	
Songs about the Bible	8%	6%	
Songs for Children	12%	5%	
From before 1960	15%	11%	
			NB: Ratios are all for total songs
I to We	1.74	4.09	i.e. 1.74:1 I:We; 4.09:1 I:We
God (all) to I	2.08	1.73	

continued

Table D.1 *concluded*

Measure	Holder	Fellow.	Notes
Christ to Father	8.52	12.14	Christ and all distinct equivalents (e.g. Jesus)
Christ to Spirit	89.5	14.17	
Christ to God	1.29	1	God and all distinct generic equivalents (e.g. Lord)

Appendix E
Mediator Influence Rankings

Table E.1   Holder Mediator Rankings (respondent and sample)

Rank	Items	Responses	Sample Mean	Errors
1	Sermons on Sunday	104	5.92	0
2	Christian Songs	101	4.65	1
3	Housegroup	90	4.65	0
4	My Christian Friends	90	4.36	0
5	Other Bible Studies	84	4.27	0
6	Bible Reading notes	85	4.16	0
7	Study Bible	77	3.98	0
8	Christianity Explored	82	3.72	0
9	Christian Events	76	3.58	0
10	Other Christian books	76	3.53	0
11	Bible Commentaries	73	3.45	0
12	Other Churches	68	2.49	1

Rank	Items	Resp. Mean
1	Sermons on Sunday	5.96
2	Study Bible	5.43
3	Housegroup	5.42
4	Other Bible Studies	5.33
5	Bible Reading notes	5.14
6	My Christian Friends	5.09
7	Bible Commentaries	4.96
8	Christian Events	4.95
9	Other Christian books	4.88
10	Christian Songs	4.79
11	Christianity Explored	4.77
12	Books about how to read the Bible	3.95

continued

Table E.1 concluded

Rank	Items	Responses	Sample Mean	Errors
13	My Parents	70	2.39	1
14	Books about how to read the Bible	59	2.24	1
15	My Children	63	2.09	0
16	Christian magazine / newspapers	73	2.03	0
17	My sisters / brothers	64	1.85	0
18	Training / theology courses	55	1.71	0
19	Christian websites	55	1.36	0

Rank	Items	Resp. Mean
13	Other Churches	3.81
14	My Parents	3.56
15	My Children	3.48
16	Training / theology courses	3.27
17	My sisters / brothers	3.03
18	Christian magazine / newspapers	2.92
19	Christian websites	2.60

Note: N=105. Sample mean ranks items according to the mean item score for the whole sample, including those who did not respond to items (value assumed = 0). Respondent mean ranks items according to the mean item score for only those who responded. See Chapter 7 for further explanation.

Table E.2   Fellowship Mediator Rankings (respondent and sample)

Rank	Items	Responses	Sample Mean	Errors
1	My Christian Friends	70	4.61	0
2	Sermons on Sunday	68	4.28	0
3	Housegroup	61	3.71	0
4	Christian Songs	67	3.37	0
5	Other Christian books	58	3.36	0
6	Church Bible Studies	58	3.25	0
7	Study Bible	57	3.24	0
8	Bible Reading notes	58	3.17	0
9	Commentaries	58	3.13	0
10	National Christian Events	52	2.77	0
11	Services at other Churches	56	2.77	0
12	My Parents	58	2.48	0
13	Alpha	51	2.40	0
14	Training / theology courses	45	2.25	0
15	Monthly celebration	52	2.25	0

Rank	Items	Resp. Mean
1	My Christian Friends	4.94
2	Sermons on Sunday	4.72
3	Housegroup	4.56
4	Other Christian books	4.34
5	Study Bible	4.26
6	Church Bible Studies	4.21
7	Bible Reading notes	4.10
8	Commentaries	4.05
9	National Christian Events	4.00
10	Christian Songs	3.78
11	Training / theology courses	3.76
12	Services at other Churches	3.71
13	Alpha	3.53
14	Monthly celebration	3.25
15	My Parents	3.21

continued

Table E.2 *concluded*

Rank	Items	Responses	Sample Mean	Errors
16	My sisters / brothers	56	1.76	0
17	My Children	44	1.69	0
18	Books about how to read the Bible	45	1.46	1

Rank	Items	Resp. Mean
16	My Children	2.89
17	Books about how to read the Bible	2.40
18	My sisters / brothers	2.36

Note: N=75. Some items are different due to the different congregational context. See note for Table E.1.

Appendix F
Bible Problems for Interviewees

Table F.1   Bible Problems for Interviewees

Holder Evangelical Church	City Reach Christian Fellowship
The flood (LucyH),	Creation (MattF, MichelleF, PenelopeF)
Canaanite conquest (IonaH, DotH, DennisH)	'the wars in the Old Testament' (NinaF)
Leviticus (WendyH, JustinH, MossH)	'God in the OT as a jealous God' (MichelleF)
Numbers (MossH)	'God wreaking vengeance on people' in Isaiah (ReneeF)
the lying spirit of 1 Ki 22:22 (WendyH)	suffering in Job (MattF)
Chronicles (AnnaH)	the minor prophets (SarahF)
divorcing of foreign wives in Ezr (IonaH)	the healing miracles of Jesus (NadineF)
the noble woman in Prov (IonaH)	certain sayings of Jesus (BruceF, NadineF)
Ezekiel (JustinH)	the role of women (AmyF, MattF)
prophets (PatriciaH)	predestination (AmyF)
'parts of the Bible that I thought were so cruel' (IonaH)	'the bit in Hebrews … about if someone's fallen away' (AmyF)
'most of the OT' (AnnaH, SiobhanH)	the book of Revelation (MattF, TomF).
chronology of the OT (DotH)	
discrepancies over Judas' hanging (WendyH)	
Jesus' saying about 'mothers and brothers' (DorisH)	
Jesus' saying to the Syrophoenician woman (DorisH)	
Rom 8:28 (DotH)	
the apostle Paul (DorisH)	
the book of Revelation (DorisH)	
role of women in the church today (PatriciaH)	
the second coming (JoeH, JustinH)	
heaven and hell (SiobhanH)	
tenets of Calvinism (WendyH, SiobhanH, JoeH, JustinH, RodneyH)	

Note: Problems are listed in canonical order. Interviewees were asked 'Are there any passages of the Bible you struggle to interpret / understand?'

Bibliography

Abraham, William J. (1982), *Divine Revelation and the Limits of Historical Criticism*, Oxford: Oxford University Press.

———— (2003), 'Faith, Assurance, and Conviction: An Epistemological Commentary on Hebrews 11:1', *Ex Auditu*, 19, 65–75.

Adam, A. K. M. (2004), 'Integral and Differential Hermeneutics', in Charles H. Cosgrove (ed.) *The Meanings We Choose: Hermeneutical Ethics, Indeterminacy and the Conflict of Interpretations*, London: T & T Clark, pp. 24–38.

Adams, Nicholas and Charles Elliott (2000), 'Ethnography is Dogmatics: Making Description Central to Systematic Theology', *Scottish Journal of Theology*, 53, 3, 339–64.

Affinity (2005), 'BECOMING Affinity (leaflet)', Reading: Affinity.

———— (2006), 'Belonging to Affinity', *Affinity* [Online], Available: www.affinity.org.uk [Accessed 2 December 2006].

———— (2006–07), 'Core Values: Affinity Mission Statement – Doctrinal Basis', *Affinity* [Online], Available: www.affinity.org.uk [Accessed 25 June 2007].

———— (2013), 'Affinity: Gospel Churches in Partnership', *Affinity* [Online], Available: http://www.affinity.org.uk/main/home [Accessed 24 January 2013].

Albrecht, Gloria (1995), *The Character of our Communities: Toward an Ethic of Liberation for the Church*, Nashville, TN: Abingdon.

Alter, Robert (1981), *The Art of Biblical Narrative*, New York: Basic Books.

American Bible Society (2011), 'The State of the Bible 2011: Analysis and Data Tables', *American Bible Society* [Online], Available: http://www.americanbible.org/uploads/content/2011_analysis.pdf [Accessed 11 July 2013].

———— (2012), 'The State of the Bible 2012: Analysis and Data Tables', *American Bible Society* [Online]. Available: http://www.americanbible.org/uploads/content/2012_analysis.pdf [Accessed 11 July 2013].

———— (2013a), 'The State of the Bible, 2013: A study of U.S. adults', *American Bible Society* [Online], Available: http://www.americanbible.org/uploads/content/State%20of%20the%20Bible%20Report%202013.pdf [Accessed 11 July 2013].

———— (2013b), 'Uncover The Word', Available: http://uncover.americanbible.org/proof [Accessed 11 July 2013].

———— (2014), 'The State of the Bible 2014', *American Bible Society* [Online], Available: http://www.americanbible.org/features/state-of-the-bible-research-2014 [Accessed 18 February 2015].

Ammerman, Nancy T. (1987), *Bible Believers: Fundamentalists in the Modern World*, New Brunswick, NJ: Rutgers University Press.

———— (1998), 'Culture and Identity in the Congregation', in Nancy T. Ammerman, et al. (eds), *Studying Congregations: A New Handbook*, Nashville, TN: Abingdon Press, pp. 78–104.

Anderson, Walter Truett (ed.) (1996), *The Fontana Postmodernism Reader*, London: Fontana.

Andrews, James A. (2012), *Hermeneutics and the Church: In Dialogue with Augustine*, Notre Dame, IN: University of Notre Dame Press.

Anglican Communion (2012), 'Deep Engagement, Fresh Discovery: Report of the Anglican Communion "Bible in the Life of the Church" Project', *Anglican Communion* [Online], Available: http://www.anglicancommunion.org/media/98131/Final-Report-for-the-web.pdf [Accessed 13 March 2015].

Anglican Consultative Council (2013), 'Bible course equipped lay leaders to "think for themselves"', *Anglican Communion News Service* [Online], July 1st, Available: http://www.anglicannews.org/news/2013/07/bible-course-equipped-lay-leaders-to-think-for-themselves.aspx [Accessed 11 February 2015].

Anizor, Uche (2014), *Kings and Priests: Scripture's Theological Account of its Readers*, Eugene, OR: Wipf and Stock.

Anscombe, G. E. M. (1958), 'Modern Moral Philosophy', *Philosophy*, 33, 1–19.

AnswersinGenesis (2015), 'Home', *Answers in Genesis* [Online], Available: http://answersingenesis.org/ [Accessed 10 March 2015].

Aquinas, Thomas (translated by Fathers of the English Dominican Province) (1947), 'Summa Theologica', *Christian Classics Ethereal Library* [Online], Available: http://www.ccel.org/ccel/aquinas/summa [Accessed 26 June 2014].

Archer, Margaret S., et al. (2004a), 'Introduction', in Margaret S. Archer, et al. (eds), *Transcendence: Critical Realism and God*, London: Routledge, pp. 1–23.

Archer, Margaret S., et al. (eds) (2004b), *Transcendence: Critical Realism and God*, London: Routledge.

Aristotle (translated by H. Rackham) (1934), 'Nicomachean Ethics', Available: http://data.perseus.org/catalog/urn:cts:greekLit:tlg0086.tlg010 [Accessed 2 June 2014].

Astley, Jeff (2002), *Ordinary Theology: Looking, Listening and Learning in Theology*, Aldershot: Ashgate.

———— (2013), 'The Analysis, Investigation and Application of Ordinary Theology', in Jeff Astley and Leslie J. Francis (eds), *Exploring Ordinary*

Theology: Everyday Christian Believing and the Church, Farnham: Ashgate, pp. 1–9.

Astley, Jeff and Ann Christie (2007), *Taking Ordinary Theology Seriously*, Cambridge: Grove Books.

Astley, Jeff and Leslie Francis (eds) (2013), *Exploring Ordinary Theology: Everyday Christian Believing and the Church*, Farnham: Ashgate.

Asylum (nd), 'The Fellowship', *Asylum* [Online], Available: http://www. asylumlondon.com/fellowship.html [Accessed 11 March 2015].

Augustine (translated by J. F. Shaw) (1886), '*De Doctrina Christiana*', *Christian Classics Ethereal Library* [Online], Available: http://www.ccel.org/ccel/ schaff/npnf102 [Accessed 26 June 2014].

Augustine (translated by Marcus Dods), (1886), '*De Civitatis Dei*', *Christian Classics Ethereal Library* [Online], Available: http://www.ccel.org/ccel/ schaff/npnf102 [Accessed 26 June 2014].

Augustine (translated by Richard Stothert) (1872), '*De Moribus Ecclesiae Catholicae*', *Christian Classics Ethereal Library* [Online], Available: http:// www.ccel.org/ccel/schaff/npnf104 [Accessed 27 June 2014].

Aune, Kristin (2002), *Single Women: Challenge to the Church?*, Milton Keynes: Paternoster.

Ballard, Paul H. (2006), 'The Bible as Pastor (special issue)', *Contact: Practical Theology and Pastoral Care*, 150, 1–54.

Ballard, Paul H. and Stephen R. Holmes (eds) (2005), *The Bible in Pastoral Practice: Readings in the Place and Function of Scripture in the Church*, London: Darton, Longman & Todd.

Banfield, Grant (2004), 'What's Really Wrong with Ethnography?', *International Education Journal*, 4, 4, 53–63.

Barrett, C. K. (1970), 'The Interpretation of the Old Testament in the New', in P. R. Ackroyd and C. F. Evans (eds), *The Cambridge History of the Bible: From Beginnings to Jerome*, Cambridge: Cambridge University Press, pp. 377–411.

Bartholomew, Craig G. (2000), 'Uncharted Waters: Philosophy, Theology and the Crisis in Biblical Interpretation', in Craig Bartholomew, et al. (eds), *Renewing Biblical Interpretation*, Carlisle: Paternoster, pp. 1–39.

———— (2003), 'Introduction', in Craig G. Bartholomew, et al. (eds), '*Behind the Text*': History and Biblical Interpretation, Carlisle: Paternoster, pp. 1–18.

———— (2005), 'In Front of the Text: The Quest of Hermeneutics', in Paul Ballard and Stephen R. Holmes (eds), *The Bible in Pastoral Practice: Readings in the Place and Function of Scripture in the Church*, London: Darton, Longman & Todd, pp. 135–52.

Bartkowski, J. P. (1996), 'Beyond Biblical Literalism and Inerrancy: Conservative Protestants and Hermeneutic Interpretation of Scripture', *Sociology of Religion*, 57, 259–72.

Barton, David and Mary Hamilton (1998), *Local Literacies: Reading and Writing in One Community*, London: Routledge.

Barton, John (ed.) (1998), *The Cambridge Companion to Biblical Interpretation*, Cambridge: Cambridge University Press.

Barton, John (1999), 'Virtue in the Bible', *Studies in Christian Ethics*, 12, 12, 12–22.

———— (2007a), *The Nature of Biblical Criticism*, Louisville, KT: Westminster John Knox Press.

———— (2007b), 'Reading Texts Holistically: The Foundation of Biblical Criticism', in A. Lemaire (ed.) *Congress Volume Ljubljana 2007 (VTSup 133)*, Leiden: Brill, pp. 367–80.

Bauckham, Richard (2003a), *Bible and Mission: Christian Witness in a Postmodern World*, Milton Keynes: Paternoster.

———— (2003b), 'Reading Scripture as a Coherent Story', in Ellen F. Davis and Richard B. Hays (eds), *The Art of Reading Scripture*, Grand Rapids, MI: Eerdmans, pp. 38–53.

Bauman, Zygmunt (1991), *Modernity and Ambivalence*, Ithaca, NY: Cornell University Press.

Baylor University (2007), 'The Baylor Religion Survey, Wave II (View of the Bible)', *Baylor Institute for Studies of Religion through Association of Religion Data Archives* [Online], Available: http://www.thearda.com/QuickStats/qs_107_s.asp [Accessed 18 July 2013].

Beadle, Ron and Geoff Moore (2006), 'MacIntyre on Virtue and Organization', *Organization Studies*, 27, 3, 323–40.

Bebbington, David and David Ceri Jones (2013), 'Conclusion', in David Bebbington and David Ceri Jones (eds), *Evangelicalism and Fundamentalism in the United Kingdom during the Twentieth Century*, Oxford: OUP, pp. 366–76.

Bebbington, David W. (1989), *Evangelicalism in Modern Britain: A History from the 1730s to the 1980s*, London: Unwin Hyman.

———— (1994), 'Evangelicalism in its Settings: the British and American Movements since 1940', in Mark A. Noll, et al. (eds), *Evangelicalism: Comparative Studies of Popular Protestantism in North America, the British Isles, and Beyond, 1700–1990*, Oxford: Oxford University Press, pp. 365–88.

———— (2007), 'Evangelicals and public worship, 1965 – 2005', *Evangelical Quarterly*, 79, 1, 3–22.

———— (2008), 'Evangelicalism and Cultural Diffusion', in Mark Smith (ed.) *British Evangelical Identities Past and Present (Volume 1): Aspects of the History and Sociology of Evangelicalism in Britain and Ireland*, Milton Keynes: Paternoster, pp. 18–34.

—— (2009), 'Evangelicalism and Fundamentalism in Britain project', *EFB project* [Online], Available: http://www.eauk.org/efb/downloads.cfm [Accessed 6 September 2011].

Behm, J. (1967), 'Transformed', in Geoffrey W. Bromiley (ed.) *Theological Dictionary of the New Testament*, Grand Rapids, MI: Eerdmans, pp. 742–59.

Bennett, Zoë (2013), *Using the Bible in Practical Theology: Historical and Contemporary Perspectives*, Farnham: Ashgate.

BIAPT (2012), 'BIAPT Special Interest Groups – The Bible and Practical Theology', *BIAPT* [Online], Available: https://www.ssl–id.net/biapt.org. uk/members/sigs.php [Accessed 4 February 2013].

Bible Society (2008), *Taking the Pulse: Is the Bible Alive and Well in the Church Today? A Survey of Congregation Members and Church Leaders*, Swindon: Bible Society.

—— (2011a), *h+ Making Good Sense of the Bible: Facilitator's Guide*, Swindon: Bible Society.

—— (2011b), *h+ Making Good Sense of the Bible: Participant's Handbook*, Swindon: Bible Society.

—— (nd), 'h+ Making Good Sense of the Bible', *Bible Society* [Online], Available: http://www.hplus.org.uk/ [Accessed 11 February 2015].

Bielo, James S. (ed.) (2009a), *The Social Life of Scriptures: Cross-Cultural Perspectives on Biblicism*, New Brunswick, NJ: Rutgers University Press.

Bielo, James S. (2009b), *Words upon the Word: An Ethnography of Evangelical Group Bible Study*, New York, NY: New York University Press.

—— (2011), *Emerging Evangelicals: Faith, Modernity, and the Desire for Authenticity*, New York, NY: New York University Press.

Billings, J. Todd (2010), *The Word of God for the People of God: An Entryway to the Theological Interpretation of Scripture*, Grand Rapids, MI: Eerdmans.

Blocher, Henri (1997), 'Scripture and Tradition: An Evangelical Response', *Evangelical Review of Theology*, 21, 2, 121–7.

—— (2004), 'Simon Gathercole meets Henri Blocher', *Themelios*, 29, 3, 37–42.

Bolt, Peter and Tony Payne (1997), *News of the Hour: Mark's Gospel*, New Malden: The Good Book Company (Matthias Media).

Boone, Kathleen C. (1989), *The Bible Tells Them So: The Discourse of Protestant Fundamentalism*, London: SCM.

Bosch, David (1991), *Transforming Mission: Paradigm Shifts in the Theology of Mission*, Maryknoll: Orbis.

Bray, Gerald (1996), *Biblical Interpretation: Past and Present*, Downers Grove, IL: IVP.

Brierley, Peter (2006), *Pulling Out Of The Nose Dive: A Contemporary Picture of Churchgoing: What The 2005 English Church Reveals*, Eltham, London: Christian Research.

Briggs, Richard S. (1995), 'Gnats, Camels and Aporias: Who Should Be Straining Out What? Christianity and Deconstruction', *Vox Evangelica*, 25, 17–32.

———— (2005), *Light to Live By: How to Interpret the Bible*, Bletchley: Scripture Union.

———— (2007), 'The Role of the Bible in Formation and Transformation: A Hermeneutical and Theological Analysis', *Anvil*, 24, 3, 167–82.

———— (2010), *The Virtuous Reader: Old Testament Narrative and Interpretive Virtue*, Grand Rapids, MI: Baker Books.

Briggs, Richard and Zoë Bennett (2014), 'Review Article – Using the Bible in Practical Theology: Historical and Contemporary Perspectives', *Theology and Ministry* [Online], Available: https://www.dur.ac.uk/resources/theologyandministry/TheologyandMinistry3_7.pdf [Accessed 16 February 2015].

British New Testament Society (2013), 'Seminar Groups', *BNTS* [Online], Available: http://www.bnts.org.uk/groups [Accessed 4 February 2013].

Brittain, Christopher Craig (2014), 'Why Ecclesiology Cannot Live By Doctrine Alone', *Ecclesial Practices*, 1, 5–30.

Brother Yun and Paul Hattaway (2002), *The Heavenly Man: The Remarkable True Story of Chinese Christian Brother Yun*, Oxford: Monarch.

Brown, Sally A. (2009), 'Exploring the Text-Practice Interface: Acquiring the Virtue of Hermeneutical Modesty', *Theology Today*, 66, 279–94.

———— (2011), 'Hermeneutical Theory', in Bonnie J. Miller-McLemore (ed.) *The Wiley-Blackwell Companion to Practical Theology*, Oxford: Wiley-Blackwell, pp. 112–22.

Browning, Don S. (1991), *A Fundamental Practical Theology: Descriptive and Strategic Proposals*, Minneapolis, MN: Augsburg Fortress.

Brueggemann, Walter (1993), *Texts Under Negotiation: The Bible and Postmodern Imagination*, London: SCM.

———— (2009), *Redescribing Reality: What We Do When We Read the Bible*, London: SCM.

Buckler, Guy and Jeff Astley (1992), 'Learning and Believing in an Urban Parish', in Jeff Astley and David Day (eds), *The Contours of Christian Education*, Great Wakering, Essex: McCrimmons, pp. 396–416.

Bultmann, Rudolf (1964), 'Is Exegesis without Presuppositions Possible?', in Schubert M. Ogden (ed.) *Existence and Faith: Shorter Writings of Rudolf Bultmann*, London: Collins, pp. 342–51.

Calver, Clive and Rob Warner (1996), *Together We Stand*, London: Hodder & Stoughton.

Cameron, Helen (2012), 'Reflections on the challenges of using the pastoral cycle in a faith-based organisation', *British and Irish Association of Practical Theology*

[Online], 11th July, Available: http://www.biapt.org.uk/documents/Helen CameronSS12.pdf [Accessed 11 February 2015].

Cameron, Helen, et al. (2010), *Talking about God in Practice: Theological Action Research and Practical Theology*, London: SCM.

Cameron, Helen, et al. (2012), *Theological Reflection for Human Flourishing: Pastoral Practice and Public Theology*, London: SCM.

Cameron, Helen, et al. (eds) (2005), *Studying Local Churches: A Handbook*, London: SCM.

Campbell, Alistair (2001), 'The Nature of Practical Theology', in James Woodward and Stephen Pattison (eds), *The Blackwell Reader in Pastoral and Practical Theology*, Oxford: Blackwell, pp. 77–88.

Cartledge, Mark J. (2003), *Practical Theology: Charismatic and Empirical Perspectives*, Carlisle: Paternoster.

Cassian, John (translated by Edgar C. S. Gibson) (1894), 'The Conferences of John Cassian', *Christian Classics Ethereal Library* [Online], Available: http://www.ccel.org/ccel/cassian/conferences.html [Accessed 1 March 2015].

Castells, Manuel (2000), *The Rise of the Network Society*, Oxford: Blackwell.

Catholic Biblical Federation (2008a), 'Scriptures reading (report vol. 1a): Comparison of 12 national cases in three continents – base population', *GfK Eurisko* [Online], Available: http://www.c–b–f.org/documents/survey_population_general.pdf [Accessed 18 July 2013].

——— (2008b), 'Scriptures reading (report vol. 2a): Comparison of 12 national cases in three continents – base attending church services', *GfK Eurisko* [Online], Available: http://www.c–b–f.org/documents/survey_church_goers.pdf [Accessed 18 July 2013].

Catholic Church and Baptist World Alliance (2006–10), 'The Word of God in the Life of the Church: A Report of International Conversations between The Catholic Church and the Baptist World Alliance 2006–2010', *Vatican* [Online], Available: http://www.vatican.va/roman_curia/pontifical_councils/chrstuni/Bapstist%20alliance/rc_pc_chrstuni_doc_20101213_report–2006–2010_en.html [Accessed 30 June 2014].

Center for Bible Engagement (2006), 'Bible Literacy and Spiritual Growth: Survey Results', *Center for Bible Engagement* [Online], Available: http://www.centerforbibleengagement.org/images/stories/pdf/cbe_survey_results.pdf [Accessed 11 July 2013].

Chapman, Alister, et al. (eds) (2009), *Seeing Things Their Way: Intellectual History and the Return of Religion*, Notre Dame, IN: University of Notre Dame Press.

Charry, Ellen T. (1997), *By the Renewing of Your Minds: The Pastoral Function of Christian Doctrine*, Oxford: Oxford University Press.

Christian Telegraph (1999–2015), 'Bible Society Australia seeks to lift Bible reading rates', *Christian Telegraph* [Online], Available: http://www.christian telegraph.com/issue17671.html [Accessed 18 February 2015].

Christie, Ann (2012), *Ordinary Christology: Who do you say I am? Answers from the Pews*, Farnham: Ashgate.

Clifford, J. (1986), 'Introduction: Partial Truths', in J. Clifford and G. Marcus (eds), *Writing Culture: The Poetics and Politics of Ethnography*, Berkeley: University of California Press, pp. 1–26.

Clines, David J. A. (1990), *What Does Eve Do To Help? and other readerly questions to the Old Testament*, Sheffield: Sheffield Academic Press.

——— (1995), 'Varieties of Indeterminacy', *Semeia*, 71, 1, 17–28.

——— (1997), *The Bible in the Modern World*, Sheffield: Sheffield Academic Press.

Cole, Arnold and Pamela Caudill Ovwigho (2012), 'Bible Engagement as the Key to Spiritual Growth: A Research Synthesis', *Center for Bible Engagement* [Online], Available: http://www.centerforbibleengagement.org/images/stories/pdf/Research_Synthesis_Bible_Engagement_and_Spiritual_Growth_Aug2012.pdf [Accessed 11 July 2013].

Coleman, Simon (2006), 'Textuality and Embodiment among Charismatic Christians', in Elisabeth Arweck and Peter Collins (eds), *Reading Religion in Text and Context: Reflections of Faith and Practice in Religious Materials*, Aldershot: Ashgate, pp. 157–68.

Collier, Andrew (2004), 'The Masters of Suspicion', in Margaret S. Archer, et al. (eds), *Transcendence: Critical Realism and God*, London: Routledge, pp. 82–91.

Conder, Tim and Daniel Rhodes (2009), *Free For All: Rediscovering the Bible in Community*, Grand Rapids, MI: Baker Book House.

Congar, O.P., Yves M. J. (1968), *A History of Theology*, New York: Doubleday.

Copleston, F. C. (1955), *Aquinas*, Harmondsworth: Penguin.

Cosgrove, Charles H. (2004), 'Introduction', in Charles H. Cosgrove, et al. (eds), *The Meanings We Choose: Hermeneutics, Ethics, Indeterminacy and the Conflict of Interpretations*, London: T & T Clark, pp. 1–22.

Csinos, David M. (2010), '"Come, Follow Me": Apprenticeship in Jesus' Approach to Education', *Religious Education*, 105, 1, 45–62.

Dancy, J. (1985), *Introduction to Contemporary Epistemology*, Oxford: Blackwell.

Danermark, Berth (2002), 'Interdisciplinary Research and Critical Realism: The Example of Disability Research', *Journal of Critical Realism*, 5, 1, 56–64.

Davies, Andrew (2009), 'What Does it Mean to Read the Bible as a Pentecostal?', *Journal of Pentecostal Theology*, 18, 216–29.

Davis, Ellen F. (2002), 'Preserving Virtues: Renewing the Tradition of the Sages', in William P. Brown (ed.) *Character & Scripture: Moral Formation, Community, and Biblical Interpretation*, Grand Rapids, MI: Eerdmans, pp. 183–201.

Davis, Ellen F. and Richard B. Hays (eds) (2003), *The Art of Reading Scripture*, Grand Rapids, MI: Eerdmans.

Day, Abby and Lois Lee (2013), 'Making Sense of the Census: The SocRel Response (BSA Sociology of Religion Study Group)', Available: http://socrel.org.uk/wpress/wp-content/uploads/2013/07/Day-Abby-and-Lois-Lee-2013-Making-Sense-of-the-Census-Report-FINAL-AD-LL.pdf [Accessed 10 July 2013].

DePaul, Michael and Linda Zagzebski (eds) (2003), *Intellectual Virtue: Perspectives from Ethics and Epistemology*, Oxford: OUP.

Derrida, Jacques (translated by Gayatri C. Spivak) (1976), *Of Grammatology*, Baltimore, MD: Johns Hopkins University Press.

———— (translated by J. Mehlmann and S. Weber) (1988), *Limited Inc*, Evanston, IL: Northwestern University Press.

de Wit, Hans (2004), 'Through the Eyes of Another: Objectives and Backgrounds', in Hans de Wit, et al. (eds), *Through the Eyes of Another: Intercultural Reading of the Bible*, Amsterdam: Institute of Mennonite Studies, pp. 3–53.

———— (2012), *Empirical Hermeneutics, Interculturality, and Holy Scripture*, Amsterdam: Institute of Mennonite Studies.

de Wit, Hans, et al. (eds) (2004), *Through the Eyes of Another: Intercultural Reading of the Bible*, Amsterdam: Institute of Mennonite Studies.

DeYoung, Rebecca Konyndyk (2012), 'Courage', in Michael W. Austin and R. Douglas Geivett (eds), *Being Good: Christian Virtues for Everyday Life*, Grand Rapids, MI: Eerdmans, pp. 145–65.

Dickson, Ian (2003), 'The Use of the Bible in Pastoral Practice: Research Project of Cardiff University and Bible Society 2002–2003', Available: http://www.cardiff.ac.uk/share/research/projectreports/previousprojects/biblepastoralpractice/the-use-of-the-bible-in-pastoral-practice.html [Accessed 4 February 2013].

———— (2007), 'The Bible in Pastoral Ministry: The Quest for Best Practice', *The Journal of Adult Theological Education*, 4, 1, 103–21.

Dietrich, Walter and Ulrich Luz (eds) (2002), *The Bible in a World Context: An Experiment in Contextual Hermeneutics*, Grand Rapids, MI: Eerdmans.

Digital Journal (2008), 'Survey: Bible Not Being Read As Much As Before', *Digital Journal* [Online]. Available: http://www.digitaljournal.com/article/259865 [Accessed 18 February 2015].

Dockery, David S. (1992), *Biblical Interpretation Then and Now: Contemporary Hermeneutics in the Light of the Early Church*, Grand Rapids, MI: Baker Bk House.

Dowie, Al (2002), *Interpreting Culture in a Scottish Congregation*, New York: Peter Lang.

Dretske, Fred (1995), 'Naïve Realism', in Ted Honderich (ed.) *The Oxford Companion to Philosophy*, Oxford: Oxford University Press, p. 602.

Dube, Musa W. and Gerald O. West (1996a), 'An Introduction: How we have come to "Read With"', *Semeia*, 73, 7–17.

——— (1996b), '"Reading With" : An Exploration of the Interface between Critical and Ordinary Readings of the Bible: African Overtures', *Semeia*, 73, 1–284.

Dube, Musa W. and Gerald O. West (eds) (2001), *The Bible in Africa: Transactions, Trajectories, and Trends*, Leiden: Brill.

Dunn, James D. G. (2002), 'The Bible and Scholarship: On Bridging the Gap between the Academy and the Church', *Anvil*, 19, 2, 109–18.

Dykstra, Craig and Dorothy C. Bass (2002), 'A Theological Understanding of Christian Practices', in Miroslav Volf and Dorothy C. Bass (eds), *Practicing Theology: Beliefs and Practices in Christian Life*, Grand Rapids, MI: Eerdmans, pp. 13–32.

Ecclesiology and Ethnography network (2013), 'Ecclesiology and Ethnography: Exploring Empirical and Theological Research on the Church'. Available: http://ecclesiologyandethnography.wordpress.com/ [Accessed 19 February 2013].

Ellington, Dustin W. (2011), 'Imitating Paul's Relationship to the Gospel: 1 Corinthians 8.1–11.1', *Journal for the Study of the New Testament*, 33, 3, 303–15.

Engelke, Matthew (2007), *A Problem of Presence: Beyond Scripture in an African Church*, London: University of California Press.

Erickson, Millard J. (1983), *Christian Theology*, Grand Rapids, MI: Baker Books.

Evangelical Alliance and Christian Research (2011), '21st Century Evangelicals', *Evangelical Alliance* [Online], Available: http://www.eauk.org/church/resources/snapshot/21st-century-evangelicals.cfm [Accessed 21 March 2012].

Evans, C. A. (1992), 'Midrash', in Joel B. Green, et al. (eds), *Dictionary of Jesus and the Gospels*, Leicester: IVP, pp. 544–8.

Evans, C. Stephen (2003), 'Tradition, Biblical Interpretation and Historical Truth', in Craig Bartholomew, et al. (eds), *"Behind the Text": History and Biblical Interpretation*, Grand Rapids, MI: Zondervan, pp. 320–38.

Fackre, Gabriel J. (1989), 'Evangelical Hermeneutics: Commonality and Diversity', *Interpretation*, 43, 2, 117–29.

Faith & Leadership (2009), 'William Snyder: Cultivating Communities', *Faith and Leadership* [Online], July 26, Available: http://www.faithandleadership.com/multimedia/william-snyder-cultivating-communities [Accessed 5 February 2015].

Fee, Gordon D. (1990), 'Issues in Evangelical Hermeneutics II: The Crucial Issue – Authorial Intentionality: A Proposal Regarding New Testament Imperatives', *Crux*, 26, 3, 35–42.

———— (1991), 'Exegesis and the Role of Tradition in Evangelical Hermeneutics', *Evangelical Review of Theology*, 17, 4, 421–36.

Fee, Gordon D. and Douglas Stuart (2003), *How to Read the Bible for All Its Worth*, Grand Rapids, MI: Zondervan.

Fergusson, David (2013), 'The Bible in Modernity', in Angus Paddison and Neil Messer (eds), *The Bible: Culture, Community, Society*, London: Bloomsbury T & T Clark, pp. 9–30.

Fiddes, Paul (2008), 'Learning from Others: Baptists and Receptive Ecumenism', *Louvain Studies*, 33, 1–2, 54–73.

———— (2012), 'Ecclesiology and Ethnography: Two Disciplines, Two Worlds?', in Pete Ward (ed.) *Perspectives on Ecclesiology and Ethnography*, Grand Rapids, MI: Eerdmans, pp. 13–35.

FIEC (2004a), 'Basis of Faith', *FIEC* [Online], Available: www.fiec.org.uk [Accessed 25 June 2007].

———— (2004b), 'Welcome to Prepared for Service', *FIEC* [Online], Available: www.fiec.org.uk [Accessed 22 June 2007].

———— (2007), 'Home page', *FIEC* [Online], Available: www.fiec.org.uk [Accessed 29 July 2008].

———— (2011), 'FIEC: Bible Churches Together', *FIEC* [Online], Available: www.fiec.org.uk [Accessed 21 February 2012].

Field, Clive (2012), '2011 Census – Searching for Explanations', *British Religion in Numbers* [Online], Available: http://www.brin.ac.uk/news/2012/2011-census-searching-for-explanations/ [Accessed 2 May 2013].

Field, Clive D. (2014), 'Is the Bible Becoming a Closed Book? British Opinion Poll Evidence', *Journal of Contemporary Religion*, 29, 3, 503–28.

Fiorenza, Elisabeth Schüssler (1983), *In Memory of Her: A Feminist Theological Reconstruction of Christian Origins*, London: SCM.

Fish, Stanley (1980), *Is There a Text in this Class? The Authority of Interpretative Communities*, Cambridge: Harvard University Press.

Fisher, Elizabeth, et al. (1992), 'A Survey of Bible Reading Practice and Attitudes to the Bible among Anglican Congregations', in Jeff Astley and David Day (eds), *The Contours of Christian Education*, Great Wakering: McCrimmons, pp. 382–95.

Floding, Matthew and Glenn Swier (2011), 'Legitimate Peripheral Participation: Entering a Community of Practice', *Reflective Practice: Formation and Supervision in Ministry* [Online], 31, Available: http://journals.sfu.ca/rpfs/index.php/rpfs/article/view/116/115 [Accessed 28 January 2015].

Flyvbjerg, Bent (2006), 'Five Misunderstandings about Case-Study Research', in Clive Seale, et al. (eds), *Qualitative Research Practice*, London: Sage, pp. 420–34.

Ford, David F. (2005), 'Epilogue: Twelve Theses for Christian Theology in the Twenty-first Century', in David F. Ford and Rachel Muers (eds), *The Modern*

Theologians: An Introduction to Christian Theology Since 1918, Oxford: Blackwell Publishing, pp. 760–61.

Ford, David F., et al. (eds) (2012), *The Modern Theologians Reader*, Chichester: Wiley-Blackwell.

Fowl, Stephen E. (1993), 'Imitation of Paul/Of Christ', in Gerald F. Hawthorne, et al. (eds), *Dictionary of Paul and his Letters*, Leicester: IVP, pp. 428–31.

———— (1997a), 'Introduction', in Stephen E. Fowl (ed.), *The Theological Interpretation of Scripture: Classic and Contemporary Readings*, Oxford: Blackwell, pp. xii–xxx.

———— (1997b), *The Theological Interpretation of Scripture: Classic and Contemporary Readings*, Oxford: Blackwell.

———— (1998), *Engaging Scripture: A Model for Theological Interpretation*, Oxford: Blackwell.

———— (2005), *Philippians*, Grand Rapids, MI: Eerdmans.

———— (2009), *Theological Interpretation of Scripture: A Short Introduction*, Milton Keynes: Paternoster.

Fowl, Stephen E. and L. Gregory Jones (1991), *Reading in Communion: Scripture and Ethics in the Christian Life*, London: SPCK.

Fox, Robin (1991), *Encounter with Anthropology*, New Brunswick, NJ: Transaction.

Francis, Leslie J. (2000), 'The Pews Talk Back: The Church Congregation Survey', in Jeff Astley (ed.), *Learning in the Way: Research and Reflection on Adult Christian Education*, Leominster: Gracewing, pp. 161–86.

Francis, Pope (2013), 'Apostolic Exhortation Evangelii Gaudium of the Holy Father to the Bishops, Clergy, Consecrated Persons and the Lay Faithful on the Proclamation of the Gospel in Today's World', *Vatican* [Online], Available: http://w2.vatican.va/content/francesco/en/apost_exhortations/documents/papa-francesco_esortazione-ap_20131124_evangelii-gaudium.html#_ftnref138 [Accessed 8 January 2015].

Frede, Dorothea (2013), 'The Historic Decline of Virtue Ethics', in Daniel C. Russell (ed.), *The Cambridge Companion to Virtue Ethics*, Cambridge: Cambridge University Press, pp. 124–48.

Froehlich, Karlfried (ed.) (1984), *Biblical Interpretation in the Early Church*, Philadelphia: Minneapolis.

Fulkerson, Mary McClintock (2007), *Places of Redemption: Theology for a Worldly Church*, Oxford: Oxford University Press.

Fung, R. Y. K. (1993), 'Body of Christ', in Gerald F. Hawthorne, et al. (eds), *Dictionary of Paul and his Letters*, Downers Grove, IL: IVP, pp. 76–82.

Gadamer, Hans-Georg (trans. J. C. Weinsheimer and D. G. Marshall) (2004), *Truth and Method (2nd rev. edition)*, London: Continuum.

Galli, Mark (2002), 'Why I Don't Imitate Christ', *Christianity Today*, July 8, 58.

Gathje, Peter R. (2011), 'The Cost of Virtue: What Power in the Open Door Community Might Speak to Virtue Ethics', in Christian Scharen and Aana Marie Vigen (eds), *Ethnography as Christian Theology and Ethics*, London: Continuum, pp. 207–24.

Gay, Doug (2011), *Remixing the Church*, London: SCM Press.

Geertz, Clifford (1973), *The Interpretation of Cultures*, New York: Basic Books.

Gillett, David K. (1993), *Trust and Obey: Explorations in Evangelical Spirituality*, London: Darton, Longman & Todd.

Gooder, Paula (2008a), 'In Search of the Early "Church": The New Testament and the development of Christian communities', in Gerald Mannion and Lewis S. Mudge (eds), *The Routledge Companion to the Christian Church*, Oxford: Routledge, pp. 9–27.

——— (2008b), *Searching for Meaning: An Introduction to Interpreting the New Testament*, London: SPCK.

Goodhew, David (2012), 'Conclusion: The Death and Resurrection of Christianity in Contemporary Britain', in David Goodhew (ed.), *Church Growth in Britain: 1980 to the Present*, Farnham: Ashgate, pp. 253–7.

——— (2013), 'Evangelical, But Not "Fundamentalist": A Case Study of the New Churches in York, 1980–2011', in David Bebbington and David Ceri Jones (eds), *Evangelicalism and Fundamentalism in the United Kingdom during the Twentieth Century*, Oxford: OUP, pp. 230–50.

Goodliff, Andy (2011), 'Interview with Simon Woodman and Helen Dare on Baptist Hermeneutics', *andygoodliff: church, world and the christian life* [Online], Available: http://andygoodliff.typepad.com/my_weblog/2011/06/interview-with-simon-woodman-and-helen-dare-on-baptist-hermeneutics.html [Accessed 15 January 2015].

Gramsci, Antonio (edited by Quintin Hoare and Geoffrey Nowell-Smith) (1971), *Selections from the Prison Notebooks of Antonio Gramsci*, London: Lawrence and Wishart.

Grant, Robert M. and David Tracy (1984), *A Short History of the Interpretation of the Bible*, London: SCM.

Green, Joel B. (2002), 'Scripture and Theology: Failed Experiments, Fresh Perspectives', *Interpretation*, 56, 1, 5–20.

Green, Judith and David Bloome (1997), 'Ethnography and Ethnographers of and in Education: A Situated Perspective', in James Flood, et al. (eds), *Handbook of Research on Teaching Literacy through the Communicative and Visual Arts*, New York, NY: Macmillan, pp. 181–202.

Green, Laurie (1990), *Let's Do Theology: A Pastoral Cycle Resource Book*, London: Mowbrays.

Greggs, Tom (2010), 'Introduction – Opening Evangelicalism: Towards a Post-Critical and Formative Theology', in Tom Greggs (ed.), *New Perspectives for*

Evangelical Theology: Engaging with God, Scripture and the World, London: Routledge, pp. 1–13.

Grenz, Stanley J. and John R. Franke (2001), *Beyond Foundationalism: Shaping Theology in a Postmodern Context*, Louisville, KT: Westminster John Knox Press.

Grondin, Jean (1994), *Introduction to Philosophical Hermeneutics*, New Haven, CT: Yale University Press.

Guest, Mathew, et al. (eds) (2004), *Congregational Studies in the UK: Christianity in a Post-Christian Context*, Aldershot: Ashgate.

Gumbel, Nicky (1996), *Challenging Lifestyle*, Eastbourne: Kingsway.

Habermas, Jürgen (1971), *Knowledge and Human Interests*, Boston: Beacon Press.

———— (1985), 'On Hermeneutics Claim to Universality', in Kurt Mueller-Vollmer (ed.), *The Hermeneutics Reader*, New York: Continuum, pp. 293–319.

———— (1988), *On the Logic of the Social Sciences*, Cambridge, MA: MIT Press.

Hammersley, Martyn and Paul Atkinson (1995), *Ethnography: Principles in Practice*, London: Routledge.

Hanson, R. P. C. (1970), 'Biblical Exegesis in the Early Church', in P. R. Ackroyd and C. F. Evans (eds), *The Cambridge History of the Bible: From Beginnings to Jerome*, Cambridge: Cambridge University Press, pp. 412–53.

Harmon, Steven R. (2012), 'Ecclesial Theology blog – "Congregational Hermeneutics" and the Christian scholar', Available: http://ecclesialtheology. blogspot.co.uk/2012/02/congregational-hermeneutics-and.html [Accessed 5 February 2013].

Harris, Harriet (1998), *Fundamentalism and Evangelicals*, Oxford: Oxford University Press.

———— (2001a), 'How helpful is the term "Fundamentalist"?', in Christopher Partridge (ed.), *Fundamentalisms*, Carlisle: Paternoster, pp. 3–18.

———— (2001b), 'Protestant Fundamentalism', in Christopher Partridge (ed.), *Fundamentalisms*, Carlisle: Paternoster, pp. 33–51.

———— (2002), 'Fundamentalism in a Protestant Context', in Martyn Percy and Ian Jones (eds), *Fundamentalism in Church and Society*, London: SPCK, pp. 7–24.

———— (2006), 'Fundamentalisms', in John W. Rogerson and Judith Lieu (eds), *The Oxford Handbook of Biblical Studies*, Oxford: Oxford University Press, pp. 810–40.

———— (2013), *Fundamentalism and the Bible*, London: Equinox.

Harrisville, Roy A. and Walter Sundberg (1995), *The Bible in Modern Culture: Theology and Historical-Critical Method from Spinoza to Käsemann*, Grand Rapids, MI: Eerdmans.

Hauerwas, Stanley (1974), *Vision and Virtue: Essays in Christian Theological Reflection*, Notre Dame, IN: Fides Publishers.

———— (1981), *A Community of Character: Toward a Constructive Christian Social Ethic*, Notre Dame, IN: University of Notre Dame Press.

———— (2010a), *Hannah's Child: A Theologian's Memoir*, Grand Rapids, MI: Eerdmans.

———— (2010b), 'How We Lay Bricks and Make Disciples', in Luke Bretherton and Russell Rook (eds), *Living Out Loud: Conversations about Virtue, Ethics, and Evangelicalism*, Milton Keynes: Paternoster, pp. 39–59.

Hauerwas, Stanley and Charles R. Pinches (1997), *Christians Among the Virtues: Theological Conversations with Ancient and Modern Ethics*, Notre Dame, IN: University of Notre Dame Press.

———— (2010), 'On Developing Hopeful Virtues', in Luke Bretherton and Russell Rook (eds), *Living Out Loud: Conversations about Virtue, Ethics, and Evangelicalism*, Milton Keynes: Paternoster, pp. 80–99.

Hawkins, Greg L. and Cally Parkinson (2007), *Reveal: Where are You? The Answer will transform your Church*, South Barrington, IL: Willow Creek Association.

———— (2011), *Move: What 1,000 Churches Reveal about Spiritual Growth*, Grand Rapids, MI: Zondervan.

Hays, Richard B. (1989), *Echoes of Scripture in the Letters of Paul*, New Haven: Yale University Press.

———— (1996), *The Moral Vision of the New Testament: A Contemporary Introduction to New Testament Ethics*, San Francisco, CA: Harper Collins.

Healy, Mary and Robin Parry (2007), *The Bible and Epistemology: Biblical Soundings on the Knowledge of God*, Milton Keynes: Paternoster.

Healy, Nicholas M. (2003), 'Practices and the New Ecclesiology: Misplaced Concreteness?', *International Journal of Systematic Theology*, 5, 3, 287–308.

———— (2005), 'Introduction', in Thomas G. Weinandy, et al. (eds), *Aquinas on Scripture: An Introduction to his Biblical Commentaries*, London: T & T Clark, pp. 1–20.

Herdt, Jennifer A. (2008), *Putting on Virtue: The Legacy of the Splendid Vices*, Chicago: University of Chicago Press.

Hewitt, Benita and Rob Powys-Smith (2011), *Bible Engagement in England & Wales*, Swindon: Bible Society (Christian Research).

Heythrop College (2013), 'Theology in Four Voices', *Heythrop College* [Online], Available: http://oldwww.heythrop.ac.uk/research/heythrop-institute-religion-and-society/arcs-project/theology-in-four-voices.html [Accessed 18 February 2015].

Hiebert, Paul G. (1999), *Missiological Implications of Epistemological Shifts: Affirming Truth in a Modern/Postmodern World*, Harrisburg: Trinity Press International.

Hiemstra, Rick (2013a), 'Confidence, Conversation and Community: Bible Engagement in Canada (Executive Summary), 2013', *Canadian Bible Forum*

[Online], Available: http://www.bibleengagementstudy.ca/ [Accessed 18 February 2015].

——— (2013b), 'Confidence, Conversation and Community: Bible Engagement in Canada, 2013', *Canadian Bible Forum* [Online], Available: http://www.bibleengagementstudy.ca/ [Accessed 18 February 2015].

Holmes, Stephen R. (2002), *Listening to the Past: The Place of Tradition in Theology*, Carlisle: Paternoster.

——— (2007), 'British (and European) Evangelical Theologies', in Timothy Larsen and Daniel J. Treier (eds), *The Cambridge Companion to Evangelical Theology*, Cambridge: Cambridge University Press, pp. 241–58.

——— (2009), 'Evangelical Doctrines of Scripture in Transatlantic Perspective: The 2008 Laing Lecture', *Evangelical Quarterly*, 81, 38–63.

Horrobin, Peter and Greg Leavers (1990), *Mission Praise: Combined Words Edition*, London: Marshall Pickering.

Intercultural Bible Collective (2015), 'Through the Eyes of Another: Intercultural Reading of the Bible', Available: www.bible4all.org [Accessed 28 July 2015].

International Council on Biblical Inerrancy (1978), 'The Chicago Statement on Biblical Inerrancy' [Online], Available: http://www.bible-researcher.com/chicago1.html [Accessed 30 July 2015].

——— (1982), 'The Chicago Statement on Biblical Hermeneutics' [Online], Available: www.bible-researcher.com/chicago2.html [Accessed 30 July 2015].

Iser, Wolfgang (1978), *The Act of Reading: A Theory of Aesthetic Response*, Baltimore, MD: Johns Hopkins University Press.

Jackson, Robert (1997), *Religious Education: An Interpretive Approach*, London: Hodder & Stoughton.

Jacobs, Alan (2001), *A Theology of Reading: The Hermeneutics of Love*, Boulder, CO: Westview Press.

——— (2007), 'On Charitable Teaching', *Journal of Education and Christian Belief*, 11, 2, 13–24.

Jeanrond, Werner G. (1992), 'History of Biblical Hermeneutics', in D. N. Freeman, et al. (eds), *The Anchor Bible Dictionary*, New York: Doubleday, pp. 433–43.

Jeffrey, Bob and Geoff Troman (2004), 'Time for Ethnography', *British Educational Research Journal*, 30, 4, 535–48.

Jensen, Alexander S. (2007), *Theological Hermeneutics*, London: SCM.

Jenson, Robert W. (1995), 'Hermeneutics and the Life of the Church', in Carl E. Braaten and Robert W. Jenson (eds), *Reclaiming the Bible for the Church*, Grand Rapids, MI: Eerdmans, pp. 89–105.

Johnson, R. and D. Chambers (2004), *The Practice of Cultural Studies*, London: SAGE.

Jones, L. Gregory (2003), 'Embodying Scripture in the Community of Faith', in Ellen F. Davis and Richard B. Hays (eds), *The Art of Reading Scripture*, Grand Rapids, MI: Eerdmans, pp. 143–62.

Juel, Donald H. (2003), 'Interpreting Israel's Scriptures in the New Testament', in Alan J. Hauser and Duane F. Watson (eds), *A History of Biblical Interpretation: The Ancient Period*, Grand Rapids, MI: Eerdmans, pp. 283–303.

Kay, William (2004), 'Introduction', in William Kay and Anne E. Dyer (eds), *Pentecostal and Charismatic Studies: A Reader*, London: SCM, pp. ix–xxxiii.

Kings, Graham (2003), 'Canal, River and Rapids: Contemporary Evangelicalism in the Church of England', *Anvil*, 20, 3, 167–84.

Kingsway Music (2003), *Songs of Fellowship: Combined Words Edition Volumes 1–3*, Eastbourne: Kingsway.

Klein, William W., et al. (1993), *Introduction to Biblical Interpretation*, Dallas, TX: Word.

(Jos) de Kock, A. (2012), 'Promising approaches to catechesis in church communities: towards a research framework', *International Journal of Practical Theology*, 16, 2, 176–96.

Kreitzer, Larry (1996), *2 Corinthians*, Sheffield: Sheffield Academic Press.

Kugel, J. L. and R. A. Greer (1986), *Early Biblical Interpretation*, Philadelphia, PA: Westminster John Knox Press.

Kümmel, W. G. (1973), *The New Testament: The History of the Investigation of its Problems*, London: SCM.

Labanow, Cory (2009), *Evangelicalism and the Emerging Church: A Congregational Study of a Vineyard Church*, Farnham: Ashgate.

Lakhani, Nina. (2011), 'Prayer can cure, churches tell those with HIV', *The Independent* [Online], Available: http://www.independent.co.uk/life-style/health-and-families/health-news/prayer-can-cure-churches-tell-those-with-hiv-2372511.html [Accessed 2 November 2011].

Lanser-van der Velde, Alma (2004), 'Making Things in Common: The Group Dynamics Dimension of the Hermeneutic Process', in Hans de Wit (ed.), *Through the Eyes of Another: Intercultural reading of the Bible*, Amsterdam: Institute of Mennonite Studies, pp. 288–303.

Lash, Nicholas (1986), *Theology on the Way to Emmaus*, London: SCM.

Lategan, Bernard C. (1992), 'Hermeneutics', in D. N. Freeman, et al. (eds), *The Anchor Bible Dictionary*, New York: Doubleday, pp. 149–54.

Lave, Jean and Etienne Wenger (1991), *Situated learning: Legitimate peripheral participation*, Cambridge: Cambridge University Press.

Lawrence, Louise (2009), *The Word in Place: Reading the New Testament in Contemporary Contexts*, London: SPCK.

Lewis, C. S. (1975), *Fern-seed and Elephants and Other Essays on Christianity*, Glasgow: Fount.

Lindars, Barnabus (1988), 'The New Testament', in John Rogerson, et al. (eds), *The Study and Use of the Bible*, Grand Rapids, MI: Eerdmans, pp. 229–397.

London School of Theology (1998), 'The Scriptures: Doctrinal Basis', *London School of Theology* [Online], Available: http://www.lst.ac.uk/downloads/DoctrinalBasis.pdf [Accessed 25 February 2015].

Longenecker, Richard (1975), *Biblical Exegesis in the Apostolic Period*, Grand Rapids, MI: Eerdmans.

Luther, Martin (2012), 'Disputation against Scholastic Theology', in Timothy F. Lull and William R. Russell (eds), *Martin Luther's Basic Theological Writings*, Minneapolis, MN: Fortress Press, pp. 3–7.

Luther, Martin (translated by Henry Cole) (1823), 'De Servo Arbitrio', *Christian Classics Ethereal Library* [Online], Available: http://www.ccel.org/ccel/luther/bondage [Accessed 2 March 2015].

———— (translated by C. A. Buchheim) (1883), 'To the Christian Nobility of the German Nation Respecting the Reformation of the Christian Estate', *Christian Classics Ethereal Library* [Online], Available: http://www.ccel.org/ccel/luther/first_prin [Accessed 9 July 2014].

———— (translated by Theodore C. Graebner) (1949), 'Commentary on St. Paul's Epistle to the Galatians', *Christian Classics Ethereal Library* [Online], Available: http://www.ccel.org/ccel/luther/galatians [Accessed 1 July 2014].

Lyon, Stephen (2011), 'Mind the Gap! Reflections on the "Bible in the Life of the Church" Project', *The Anglican Theological Review*, 93, 3, 451–64.

Maanen, John van (1988), *Tales of the Field: On Writing Ethnography*, Chicago: University of Chicago Press.

MacArthur, John (ed.) (2004), *MacArthur Study Bible (NKJV)*, Nashville, TN: Nelson Bibles.

MacDonald, Nathan (2009), 'Israel and the Old Testament Story in Irenaeus's Presentation of the Rule of Faith', *Journal of Theological Interpretation*, 3, 2, 281–98.

MacIntyre, Alasdair (1985), *After Virtue: A Study in Moral Theory*, London: Duckworth.

Malley, Brian (2004), *How the Bible Works: An Anthropological Study of Evangelical Biblicism*, Walnut Creek, CA: AltaMira.

Marshall, I. Howard (2004), *Beyond the Bible: Moving from Scripture to Theology*, Milton Keynes: Paternoster.

Matthias Media (2008), 'Matthias Media: Our Theology: What We Believe', *matthiasmedia* [Online], Available: www.matthiasmedia.com.au/our_theology.php [Accessed 5 January 2008].

———— (2014), 'matthiasmedia', *matthiasmedia* [Online], Available: www.matthiasmedia.com.au [Accessed 11 March 2015].

McCleod, William T. (1986), *The Collins Paperback Thesaurus in A-to-Z Form*, Glasgow: Collins.

McGrath, Alister E. (1990), 'Reformation', in R. J. Coggins and J. L. Houlden (eds), *The SCM Dictionary of Biblical Interpretation*, London: SCM, pp. 582–5.

——— (1995), *Evangelicalism and the Future of Christianity*, London: Hodder & Stoughton.

——— (2000a), 'Engaging the Great Tradition: Evangelical Theology and the Role of Tradition', in John G. Stackhouse (ed.), *Evangelical Futures: A Conversation on Theological Method*, Grand Rapids, MI: Baker Books, pp. 139–58.

——— (2000b), 'Evangelical Theological Method: The State of the Art', in John G. Stackhouse (ed.), *Evangelical Futures: A Conversation on Theological Method*, Grand Rapids, MI: Baker Books, pp. 15–38.

——— (2002a), *The Future of Christianity*, Oxford: Blackwell.

——— (2002b), *A Scientific Theology: Reality*, London: Continuum Books.

McNally, R. E. (1986), *The Bible in the Early Middle Ages*, Atlanta, GA: Scholars Press.

Meeks, Wayne (1991), 'The Man from Heaven in Paul's Letter to the Philippians', in Birger Pearson (ed.), *The Future of Early Christianity: Essays in Honor of Helmut Koester*, Minneapolis, MN: Fortress Press, pp. 329–36.

Melchert, Charles F. (1998), *Wise Teaching: Biblical Wisdom and Educational Ministry*, Harrisburg, PA: Trinity Press International.

Mesters, Carlos (1980), 'How the Bible is Interpreted in Some Basic Christian Communities in Brazil', in Hans Küng, et al. (eds), *Conflicting Ways of Interpreting the Bible*, Edinburgh: T & T Clark, pp. 41–6.

——— (1983a), 'Bible Study Centre for People's Pastoral Action (Brazil): The Use of the Bible among the Common People', *Ministry by the People*, Geneva: World Council of Churches, pp. 78–92.

——— (1983b), 'The Use of the Bible in Christian Communities of the Common People', in N. K. Gottwald (ed.), *The Bible and Liberation*, Maryknoll, NY: Orbis Books, pp. 119–33.

——— (1989), *Defenseless Flower: A New Reading of the Bible*, Maryknoll, NY: Orbis Books.

——— (1990), 'The Popular Interpretation of the Bible: History and Method', *I have heard the cry of my people*, Curitiba: Lutheran World Federation Eighth Assembly, 28/29.

Milbank, John (1990), *Theology and Social Theory: Beyond Secular Reason*, Oxford: Blackwell.

Miller-McLemore, Bonnie J. (2012a), 'Five Misunderstandings about Practical Theology', *International Journal of Practical Theology*, 16, 1, 5–26.

———— (2012b), 'Introduction: The Contributions of Practical Theology', in Bonnie J. Miller-McLemore (ed.), *The Wiley-Blackwell Companion to Practical Theology*, Oxford: Wiley-Blackwell, pp. 1–20.

Mitchell, J. (1984), 'Typicality and the Case Study', in R. F. Ellen (ed.), *Ethnographic Research: A Guide to Conduct*, New York, NY: New York Academic, pp. 238–41.

Moberly, R. W. L. (2010), '"Interpret the Bible Like Any Other Book?" Requiem for an Axiom', *Journal of Theological Interpretation*, 4, 1, 91–110.

Moore, Stephen D. (1989), *Literary Criticism and the Gospels: The Theoretical Challenge*, London: Yale University Press.

Morgan, Robert with John Barton (1988), *Biblical Interpretation*, Oxford: Oxford University Press.

Morris, L. (1993), 'Faith', in Gerald F. Hawthorne, et al. (eds), *Dictionary of Paul and his Letters*, Leicester: IVP, pp. 285–91.

Mosala, Itumeleng J. (1989), *Biblical Hermeneutics and Black Theology in South Africa*, Grand Rapids, MI: Eerdmans.

Moule, C. F. D. (1966), *The Birth of the New Testament (2nd rev. edition)*, London: Black.

Mudge, Lewis S. (1984), 'Thinking about the Church's Thinking: Toward a Theological Ethnography', *Theological Education*, 20, 2, 42–54.

Murray, Stuart (2000), *Biblical Interpretation in the Anabaptist Tradition*, Kitchener, ON: Pandora Press.

National Opinion Research Center (2010), 'General Social Survey Cross-Section and Panel Combined (View of the Bible)', *Association of Religion Data Archives* [Online], Available: http://www.thearda.com/QuickStats/QS_107.asp [Accessed 18 July 2013].

Negus, K. (1996), *Popular Music in Theory: An Introduction*, Cambridge: Polity Press.

Neil, W. (1963), 'The Criticism and Theological Use of the Bible, 1700–1950', in S. L. Greenslade (ed.), *The Cambridge History of the Bible: The West from the Reformation to the Present Day*, Cambridge: Cambridge University Press, pp. 238–93.

Neill, Stephen and Tom Wright (1988), *The Interpretation of the New Testament 1861–1986 (second edition)*, Oxford: Oxford University Press.

Newbigin, Lesslie (1989), *The Gospel in a Pluralist Society*, London: SPCK.

———— (1995), *Proper Confidence: Faith, Doubt and Certainty in Christian Discipleship*, London: SPCK.

Noll, Mark A. (2004), *Between Faith and Criticism: Evangelicals, Scholarship, and the Bible in America (second edition)*, Vancouver: Regent College Publishing.

Nouwen, Henri (1992), *The Return of the Prodigal Son: A Story of Homecoming*, London: Darton, Longman & Todd.

Nystrom, Carolyn (2000), *Integrity: Living the Truth (10 Studies for Individuals or Groups)*, Bletchley: Scripture Union.

O'Brien, P. T. (1993a), 'Church', in Gerald F. Hawthorne, et al. (eds), *Dictionary of Paul and his Letters*, Leicester: IVP, pp. 123–31.

——— (1993b), 'Fellowship, Communion, Sharing', in Gerald F. Hawthorne, et al. (eds), *Dictionary of Paul and his Letters*, Leicester: IVP, pp. 293–5.

Office for National Statistics (2013), 'What does the Census tell us about religion in 2011?', *ONS* [Online], Available: http://www.ons.gov.uk/ons/rel/census/2011-census/detailed-characteristics-for-local-authorities-in-england-and-wales/sty-religion.html [Accessed 11 July 2013].

Oliver, Gordon (2006), *Holy Bible, Human Bible: Questions Pastoral Practice Must Ask*, London: Darton, Longman & Todd.

Opie, Stephen (2008), 'Bible Engagement in New Zealand: Survey of Attitudes and Behaviour (March – June 2008)', Ignite Research for Bible Society New Zealand.

Packer, James I. (1978), *The Evangelical Anglican Identity Problem: An Analysis*, Oxford: Latimer House.

——— (1990), 'Understanding the Bible: Evangelical Hermeneutics', *Restoring the Vision*, Eastbourne: MARC, pp. 39–58.

Paddison, Angus (2009), *Scripture: A Very Theological Proposal*, London: T & T Clark.

Page, Nick (2004), *And Now Let's Move Into A Time Of Nonsense: Why Worship Songs Are Failing The Church*, Milton Keynes: Authentic.

Palmer, Richard (1969), *Hermeneutics: Interpretation Theory in Schleiermacher, Dilthey, Heidegger, and Gadamer*, Evanston, IL: Northwestern University Press.

Pardue, Stephen T. (2010), 'Athens and Jerusalem Once More: What the Turn to Virtue Means for Theological Exegesis', *Journal of Theological Interpretation*, 4, 2, 295–308.

Parris, David P. (2006), *Reading the Bible with Giants: How 2000 Years of Biblical Interpretation Can Shed New Light on Old Texts*, Milton Keynes: Paternoster.

Pattison, Stephen, et al. (2007), *Using the Bible in Christian Ministry: A Workbook*, London: Darton, Longman & Todd.

Pearsall, Judy (ed.) (1998), *The New Oxford Dictionary of English*, Oxford: Clarendon Press.

Perriman, Andrew (1998), *Speaking of Women: Interpreting Paul*, Leicester: Apollos.

Peterson, Eugene H. (2006), *Eat This Book: The Art of Spiritual Reading*, London: Hodder & Stoughton.

Pew Research Center (2011), 'Global Christianity – A Report on the Size and Distribution of the World's Christian Population', *PewResearchCenter:*

Religion & Public Life [Online], Available: http://www.pewforum. org/2011/12/19/global-christianity-movements-and-denominations/ [Accessed 19 February 2015].

Phillips, Elizabeth (2012), 'Charting the "Ethnographic Turn": Theologians and the Study of Christian Congregations', in Pete Ward (ed.), *Perspectives on Ecclesiology and Ethnography*, Grand Rapids, MI: Eerdmans, pp. 95–106.

Phillips, Pete (nd), 'CODEC – Briefing Sheet #2: National Biblical Literacy Survey 2009', Available: http://www.dur.ac.uk/resources/cblc/ BriefingSheet2.pdf [Accessed 10 July 2013].

Pinsent, Andrew (2012), 'Humility', in Michael W. Austin and R. Douglas Geivett (eds), *Being Good: Christian Virtues for Everyday Life*, Grand Rapids, MI: Eerdmans, pp. 242–64.

Piper, J. (1980), 'Historical Criticism in the Dock: Recent Developments in Germany', *Journal of the Evangelical Theological Society*, 23, 325–34.

Plantinga, Alvin (1983), 'Reason and Belief in God', in Alvin Plantinga and Nicholas Wolterstorff (eds), *Faith and Rationality*, Notre Dame, IN: University of Notre Dame Press, pp. 16–93.

———— (2003), 'Two (or More) Kinds of Scripture Scholarship', in Craig Bartholomew, et al. (eds), *"Behind" the Text: History and Biblical Interpretation*, Carlisle: Paternoster, pp. 19–57.

Pontifical Bible Commission (1993), 'The Interpretation of the Bible in the Church', *Catholic Resources* [Online], Available: http://catholic-resources. org/ChurchDocs/PBC_Interp4.htm [Accessed 8 January 2015].

Porter, Jean (2006), 'Virtue Ethics', in Robin Gill (ed.), *The Cambridge Companion to Christian Ethics*, Cambridge: Cambridge University Press, pp. 96–111.

Powell, Mark Allan (2001), *Chasing the Eastern Star: Adventures in Biblical Reader-Response Criticism*, Louisville, KT: Westminster John Knox Press.

Quicke, Michael (2005), 'The Scriptures in Preaching', in Paul Ballard and Stephen R. Holmes (eds), *The Bible in Pastoral Practice: Readings in the Place and Function of Scripture in the Church*, London: Darton, Longman & Todd, pp. 241–57.

Rae, Murray (2007), '"Incline Your Ear So That You May Live": Principles of Biblical Epistemology', in Mary Healy and Robin Parry (eds), *The Bible and Epistemology: Biblical Soundings on the Knowledge of God*, Milton Keynes: Authentic, pp. 161–80.

Randall, Ian (2005), *What a Friend We Have in Jesus: The Evangelical Tradition*, London: Darton, Longman & Todd.

Rankin, Russ (2012), 'Study: Bible Engagement in Churchgoers' Hearts, Not Always Practiced', *Lifeway Research* [Online], Available: http://www.lifeway. com/Article/research-survey-bible-engagement-churchgoers [Accessed 15 July 2013].

rejesus (2002–15), 'Faces of Jesus', *rejesus* [Online], Available: www.rejesus. co.uk/site/module/faces_of_jesus/ [Accessed 15 March 2015].

Reventlow, Henning Graf (2001), 'The Early Church', in John Rogerson (ed.), *The Oxford Illustrated History of the Bible*, Oxford: Oxford University Press, pp. 166–79.

Riches, John (2010), *What is Contextual Bible Study? A Practical Guide with Group Studies for Advent and Lent*, London: SPCK.

Ricoeur, Paul (1969), *The Symbolism of Evil*, Boston, MA: Beacon Press.

———— (1970), *Freud and Philosophy: An Essay on Interpretation*, New Haven, CT: Yale University Press.

———— (1981), *Hermeneutics and the Human Sciences*, Cambridge: Cambridge University Press.

Ricoeur, Paul and Lewis S. Mudge (eds) (1981), *Essays on Biblical Interpretation*, London: SPCK.

Rogers, Andrew P. (2007), 'Reading Scripture in Congregations: Towards an Ordinary Hermeneutics', in Luke Bretherton and Andrew Walker (eds), *Remembering Our Future: Explorations in Deep Church*, Milton Keynes: Paternoster, pp. 81–107.

———— (2009), *Ordinary Biblical Hermeneutics and the Transformation of Congregational Horizons within English Evangelicalism: A Theological Ethnographic Study*, PhD, King's College, London.

———— (2010), 'Review of The Bible and Lay People: An Empirical Approach to Ordinary Hermeneutics', *Practical Theology*, 3, 2, 253–6.

———— (2011), 'Review of The Word in Place: Reading the New Testament in Contemporary Contexts', *Practical Theology*, 4, 1, 132–4.

———— (2013a), *Being Built Together: Final Report*, London: University of Roehampton.

———— (2013b), 'Congregational Hermeneutics: A Tale of Two Churches', *Journal of Contemporary Religion*, 28, 3, 489–506.

———— (2013c), 'Congregational Hermeneutics: Towards Virtuous Apprenticeship', in Jeff Astley and Leslie Francis (eds), *Exploring Ordinary Theology: Everyday Christian Believing and the Church*, Farnham: Ashgate, pp. 117–26.

Rogers, Eugene F. (1996), 'How the Virtues of an Interpreter Presuppose and Perfect Hermeneutics: The Case of Thomas Aquinas', *The Journal of Religion*, 76, 1, 64–81.

Rogerson, John (1988), 'The Old Testament', in John Rogerson, et al. (eds), *The Study and Use of the Bible*, Basingstoke: Marshall Pickering, pp. 3–150.

———— (1992), 'History of OT Interpretation', in D. N. Freeman et al. (eds), *The Anchor Bible Dictionary*, New York: Doubleday, pp. 424–33.

Rooms, Nigel (2012), 'Paul as Practical Theologian: *Phronesis* in Philippians', *Practical Theology*, 5, 1, 81–94.

Rowland, Christopher and John Vincent (eds) (2001), *Bible and Practice (British Liberation Theology)*, Sheffield: Urban Theology Unit.

Rowland, Christopher and Mark Corner (1990), *Liberating Exegesis: The Challenge of Liberation Theology to Biblical Studies*, London: SPCK.

Ryle, Gilbert (1971), *Collected Papers, Volume 2*, London: Hutchinson.

Sawyer, John F. A. (1990), 'Interpretation, History of', in R. J. Coggins and J. L. Houlden (eds), *The SCM Dictionary of Biblical Interpretation*, London: SCM, pp. 316–20.

Sayer, Andrew (2000), *Realism and Social Science*, London: SAGE.

Scharen, Christian (2005), '"Judicious narratives", or Ethnography as Ecclesiology', *Scottish Journal of Theology*, 58, 2, 125–42.

Scharen, Christian (ed.) (2012), *Explorations in Ecclesiology and Ethnography*, Grand Rapids, MI: Eerdmans.

Scharen, Christian and Aana Marie Vigen (eds) (2011), *Ethnography as Christian Theology and Ethics*, New York, NY: Continuum.

Schindler, D. C. (2007), 'Mystery and Mastery: Philosophical Reflections on Biblical Epistemology', in Mary Healy and Robin Parry (eds), *The Bible and Epistemology: Biblical Soundings on the Knowledge of God*, Milton Keynes: Authentic, pp. 181–98.

Schleiermacher, Friedrich D. E. (1985), 'Foundations: General Theory and Art of Interpretation', in Kurt Mueller-Vollmer (ed.), *The Hermeneutics Reader: Texts of the German Tradition from the Enlightenment to the Present*, New York, NY: Continuum, pp. 72–97.

Schnackenburg, Rudolf (1991), *The Epistle to the Ephesians: A Commentary*, Edinburgh: T & T Clark.

Segovia, Fernando F. and Mary Ann Tolbert (eds) (1995a), *Reading from this Place I: Social Location and Biblical Interpretation in North America*, Minneapolis, MN: Augsburg Fortress.

——— (1995b), *Reading from this Place II: Social Location and Biblical Intepretation in Global Perspective*, Minneapolis, MN: Augsburg Fortress.

Seung, T. K. (1982), *Structuralism and Hermeneutics*, New York, NY: Columbia University Press.

Sharp, Carolyn J. (2004), 'The Formation of Godly Community: Old Testament Hermeneutics in the Presence of the Other', *The Anglican Theological Review*, 86, 4, 623–36.

Sinn, Simone (2002), *The Church as Participatory Community: On the Interrelationship of Hermeneutics, Ecclesiology and Ethics*, Dublin: Columba Press.

——— (2008), 'Hermeneutics and Ecclesiology', in Gerard Mannion and Lewis S. Mudge (eds), *The Routledge Companion to the Christian Church*, Oxford: Routledge, pp. 576–93.

Slagter, Cynthia G. (2007), 'Approaching Interpretive Virtues Through Reading Aloud', *Journal of Education and Christian Belief*, 11, 2, 95–107.

Smalley, Beryl (1983), *The Study of the Bible in the Middle Ages (3rd rev. ed.)*, Oxford: Basil Blackwell.

Smart, James D. (1970), *The Strange Silence of the Bible in the Church: A Study in Hermeneutics*, London: SCM.

Smith, Christian (2012), *The Bible Made Impossible: Why Biblicism is not a Truly Evangelical Reading of Scripture*, Grand Rapids, MI: Brazos Press.

Smith, Mark (2008), 'Introduction', in Mark Smith (ed.), *British Evangelical Identities Past and Present (Volume 1): Aspects of the History and Sociology of Evangelicalism in Britain and Ireland*, Milton Keynes: Paternoster, pp. 1–17.

Smith-Christopher, Daniel (1995), 'Introduction', in Daniel Smith-Christopher (ed.), *Text & Experience: Towards a Cultural Exegesis of the Bible*, Sheffield: Sheffield Academic Press, pp. 11–22.

Society of Biblical Literature (2013), 'Bible and Practical Theology', *SBL* [Online], Available: http://www.sbl-site.org/meetings/Congresses_CallForPaperDetails.aspx?MeetingId=21&VolunteerUnitId=478 [Accessed 4 February 2013].

——— (2015), '2015 Annual Meeting', *SBL* [Online], Available: http://www.sbl-site.org/meetings/Congresses_ProgramUnits.aspx?MeetingId=27 [Accessed 16 February 2015].

Sparks, Kenton L. (2008), *God's Word in Human Words: An Evangelical Appropriation of Critical Biblical Scholarship*, Grand Rapids, MI: Baker Academic.

Stackhouse, Ian (2004), *The Gospel-Driven Church: Retrieving Classical Ministries for Contemporary Revivalism*, Milton Keynes: Authentic.

——— (2007), 'God's Transforming Presence: Spirit Empowered Worship and Its Mediation', in Andrew Walker and Luke Bretherton (eds), *Remembering Our Future: Explorations in Deep Church*, Milton Keynes: Paternoster, pp. 150–69.

Stanley, Brian (2013), *The Global Diffusion of Evangelicalism: The Age of Billy Graham and John Stott*, Downers Grove, IL: InterVarsity Press.

Steinmetz, David C. (1997), 'The Superiority of Pre-Critical Exegesis', in Stephen Fowl (ed.), *The Theological Interpretation of Scripture*, Oxford: Blackwell, pp. 26–38.

Stendahl, Krister (1962), 'Biblical Theology, Contemporary', in George Arthur Buttrick (ed.), *The Interpreter's Dictionary of the Bible*, Nashville, TN: Abingdon, pp. 418–32.

Steven, James H. S. (2002), *Worship in the Spirit: Charismatic Worship in the Church of England*, Milton Keynes: Paternoster.

Stibbe, Mark W. G. (1998), 'This is That: Some Thoughts Concerning Charismatic Hermeneutics', *Anvil*, 15, 3, 181–93.

Stott, John R. W. (1977), *What is an Evangelical?*, London: CPAS.

———— (1984), *Understanding the Bible (revised ed.)*, Milton Keynes: Scripture Union.

———— (2003), *Evangelical Truth: A Personal Plea for Unity, Integrity and Faithfulness*, Downers Grove, IL: IVP.

Stringer, Martin (1999), *On the Perception of Worship: The Ethnography of Worship in Four Christian Congregations in Manchester*, Birmingham: University of Birmingham Press.

Stuhlmacher, Peter (1977), *Historical Criticism and the Theological Interpretation of Scripture*, London: SPCK.

Sugirtharajah, R. S. (ed.) (1991), *Voices from the Margin: Interpreting the Bible in the Third World*, London: SPCK.

———— (1999), *Vernacular Hermeneutics*, Sheffield: Sheffield Academic Press.

Swinton, John (2012), '"Where is your Church?" Moving toward a Hospitable and Sanctified Ethnography', in Pete Ward (ed.), *Perspectives on Ecclesiology and Ethnography*, Grand Rapids, MI: Eerdmans, pp. 71–94.

Swinton, John and Harriet Mowat (2006), *Practical Theology and Qualitative Research*, London: SCM Press.

Tennison, D. Allen (2005), 'Charismatic Biblical Interpretation', in Kevin J. Vanhoozer (ed.), *Dictionary for Theological Interpretation of the Bible*, Grand Rapids, MI: Baker Book House, pp. 106–9.

The Contextual Bible Study Development Group (2005), *Conversations: The Companion*, Glasgow: Scottish Bible Society.

The Good Book Company (2007), 'Explore', *thegoodbook.co.uk* [Online], Available: www.thegoodbook.co.uk [Accessed 5 January 2007].

The Scripture Project (2003), 'Nine Theses on the Interpretation of Scripture', in Ellen F. Davis and Richard B. Hays (eds), *The Art of Reading Scripture*, Grand Rapids, MI: Eerdmans, pp. 1–8.

The Ujamaa Centre (2014), 'Doing Contextual Bible Study: A Resource Manual', *University of Kwazulu-Natal* [Online], Available: http://ujamaa.ukzn.ac.za/ Libraries/manuals/Ujamaa_CBS_bible_study_Manual_part_1_2.sflb.ashx [Accessed 13 January 2015].

Thiselton, Anthony C. (1980), *The Two Horizons: New Testament Hermeneutics and Philosophical Description*, Carlisle: Paternoster Press.

———— (1992), *New Horizons in Hermeneutics: The Theory and Practice of Transforming Biblical Reading*, Grand Rapids, MI: Zondervan.

———— (1998), 'Thirty Years of Hermeneutics : Retrospect and Prospects', in J. Krašovec (ed.), *Interpretation of the Bible*, Sheffield: Sheffield Academic Press, pp. 1559–73.

———— (2007), *The Hermeneutics of Doctrine*, Grand Rapids, MI: Eerdmans.

———— (2009), *Hermeneutics: An Introduction*, Grand Rapids, MI: Eerdmans.

Tidball, Derek (1994), *Who are the Evangelicals? Tracing the Roots of Today's Movement*, London: Marshall Pickering.

——— (2005), 'The Bible in Evangelical Spirituality', in Paul Ballard and Stephen R. Holmes (eds), *The Bible in Pastoral Practice: Readings in the Place and Function of Scripture in the Church*, London: Darton, Longman & Todd, pp. 258–74.

Tisdale, Leonora Tubbs (1997), *Preaching as Local Theology and Folk Art*, Minneapolis, MN: Fortress.

Todd, Andrew J. (2013), 'The Interaction of Talk and Text: Re-contextualising Biblical Interpretation', *Practical Theology*, 6, 1, 69–85.

Tomkins, Stephen (2011), 'What would Jesus do?: The rise of a slogan', *BBC News Magazine* [Online], Available: http://www.bbc.co.uk/news/magazine-16068178 [Accessed 2 February 2015].

Tomlinson, Dave (1995), *The Post-Evangelical*, Triangle.

Treier, Daniel J. (2006), *Virtue and the Voice of God: Toward Theology as Wisdom*, Grand Rapids, MI: Eerdmans.

——— (2008), *Introducing Theological Interpretation of Scripture: Recovering a Christian Practice*, Grand Rapids, MI: Baker Academic.

Trible, Phyllis (1984), *Texts of Terror: Literary-Feminist Readings of Biblical Narratives*, Philadelphia, PA: Fortress Press.

Troeger, Thomas H. (1998), 'Hymns as Midrashim: Congregational Song as Biblical Interpretation and Theological Reconstruction', *The Hymn*, 49, 3, 13–16.

Vander Velde, Frances (2000), *Women of the Bible*, Grand Rapids, MI: Kregel.

Vanhoozer, Kevin (2006), 'Imprisoned or Free? Text, Status, and Theological Interpretation in the Master / Slave Discourse of Philemon', in A. K. M. Adam, et al. (eds), *Reading Scripture with the Church: Toward a Hermeneutic for Theological Interpretation*, Grand Rapids, MI: Baker Books, pp. 51–94.

Vanhoozer, Kevin J. (1992), 'Hyperactive Hermeneutics: Is the Bible Being Overinterpreted?', *Catalyst*, 19, 1, 3–4.

——— (1998), *Is There A Meaning In This Text? The Bible, The Reader and The Morality of Literary Knowledge*, Leicester: Apollos.

——— (2002), *First Theology: God, Scripture and Hermeneutics*, Downers Grove, IL: InterVarsity Press.

——— (2004), 'Into the Great "Beyond": A Theologian's Response to the Marshall Plan', in I. Howard Marshall (ed.), *Beyond the Bible: Moving from Scripture to Theology*, Grand Rapids, MI: Baker Books, pp. 81–95.

Vermeer, Paul (2010), 'Religious Education and Socialization', *Religious Education*, 105, 1, 103–16.

Village, Andrew (2005a), 'Assessing Belief about the Bible: A Study among Anglican Laity', *Review of Religious Research*, 46, 3, 243–54.

——— (2005b), 'Christian Belief about the Bible and the Holy Spirit in relation to Psychological Type', *Research in the Social Scientific Study of Religion*, 16, 1–16.

——— (2005c), 'Dimensions of Belief about Miraculous Healing', *Mental Health, Religion and Culture*, 8, 97–107.

——— (2005d), 'Factors Shaping Biblical Literalism: A Study Among Anglican Laity', *Journal of Beliefs and Values*, 26, 1, 29–38.

——— (2007), *The Bible and Lay People: An Empirical Approach to Ordinary Hermeneutics*, Aldershot: Ashgate.

——— (2013), 'The Bible and Ordinary Readers', in Jeff Astley and Leslie Francis (eds), *Exploring Ordinary Theology: Everyday Christian Believing and the Church*, Farnham: Ashgate, pp. 127–36.

Village, Andrew and Leslie Francis (2005), 'The Relationship of Psychological Type Preference to Biblical Interpretation', *Journal of Empirical Theology*, 18, 74–89.

Vincent, John (2001), 'Outworkings: a Gospel Practice Criticism', *Expository Times*, 113, 1, 16–18.

——— (2002), 'Outworkings: Gospel Practice Today', *Expository Times*, 113, 11, 367–71.

——— (2004), 'Theological Practice', *Theology*, CVII, 839, 343–50.

——— (2005), *Outworkings: Gospel Practice and Interpretation*, Sheffield: Urban Theology Unit.

Vincent, John (ed.) (2011), *Stilling the Storm: Contemporary Responses to Mark 4:35 – 5:1*, Blandford Forum: Deo Publishing.

Volf, Miroslav (2010), *Captive to the Word of God: Engaging the Scriptures for Contemporary Theological Reflection*, Grand Rapids, MI: Eerdmans.

Waggoner, Brad J. (2008), *The Shape of Faith to Come: Spiritual Formation and the Future of Discipleship*, Nashville, TN: Broadman & Holman Publishers.

Walker, Andrew (2007a), 'Deep Church as *Paradosis*: On Relating Scripture and Tradition', in Luke Bretherton and Andrew Walker (eds), *Remembering Our Future: Explorations in Deep Church*, Milton Keynes: Paternoster, pp. 59–80.

——— (2007b), 'Recovering Deep Church: Theological and Spiritual Renewal', in Andrew Walker and Luke Bretherton (eds), *Remembering Our Future: Explorations in Deep Church*, Milton Keynes: Paternoster, pp. 1–29.

Wall, Robert W. (2000), 'Reading the Bible from within our Traditions: The "Rule of Faith" in Theological Hermeneutics', in J. B. Green and M. Turner (eds), *Between Two Horizons: Spanning New Testament Studies and Systematic Theology*, Grand Rapids, MI: Eerdmans, pp. 88–107.

Walls, Andrew (2002), *The Cross-Cultural Process in Christian History*, Maryknoll, New York, NY: Orbis Books.

Walton, Roger (2003), 'Using the Bible and Christian Tradition in Theological Reflection', *British Journal of Theological Education*, 13, 2, 133–51.

——— (2011), 'Disciples Together: The Small Group as a Vehicle for Discipleship Formation', *Journal of Adult Theological Education*, 8, 2, 99–114.

——— (2014), *Disciples Together: Discipleship, Formation and Small Groups*, London: SCM.

Ward, Frances (2004), 'The Messiness of Studying Congregations using Ethnographic Methods', in Mathew Guest, et al. (eds), *Congregational Studies in the UK: Christianity in a Post-Christian Context*, Farnham: Ashgate, pp. 125–37.

Ward, Peter (2002), *Liquid Church*, Carlisle: Paternoster.

——— (2005), *Selling Worship: How What We Sing Has Changed The Church*, Milton Keynes: Paternoster.

——— (2008), *Participation and Mediation: A Practical Theology for the Liquid Church*, London: SCM.

——— (2012a), 'Introduction', in Pete Ward (ed.), *Perspectives on Ecclesiology and Ethnography*, Grand Rapids, MI: Eerdmans, pp. 1–10.

Ward, Pete (ed.) (2012b), *Perspectives on Ecclesiology and Ethnography*, Grand Rapids, MI: Eerdmans.

Ward, Pete and Sarah Dunlop (2011), 'Practical Theology and the Ordinary: Visual Research among Migrant Polish Catholic Young People', *Practical Theology*, 4, 3, 295–313.

Warner, Rob (2007), *Reinventing English Evangelicalism, 1966–2001: A Theological and Sociological Study*, Milton Keynes: Paternoster.

——— (2013), 'Evangelical Bases of Faith and Fundamentalizing Tendencies', in David Bebbington and David Ceri Jones (eds), *Evangelicalism and Fundamentalism in the United Kingdom in the Twentieth Century*, Oxford: OUP, pp. 328–47.

Warren, Rick (2003), *The Purpose-Driven Life: What On Earth Am I Here For?*, Grand Rapids, MI: Zondervan.

Watson, Francis (1994), *Text, Church and World: Biblical Interpretation in Theological Perspective*, Edinburgh: T & T Clark.

——— (2010), 'Hermeneutics and the Doctrine of Scripture: Why They Need Each Other', *International Journal of Systematic Theology*, 12, 2, 118–43.

Webster, John (2003), *Holy Scripture: A Dogmatic Sketch*, Cambridge: Cambridge University Press.

——— (2006), *Word and Church: Essays in Church Dogmatics*, London: Continuum.

——— (2012), '"In the Society of God": Some Principles of Ecclesiology', in Pete Ward (ed.), *Perspectives on Ecclesiology and Ethnography*, Grand Rapids, MI: Eerdmans, pp. 200–222.

Wenger, Etienne (1998), *Communities of Practice: Learning, Meaning, and Identity*, New York: Cambridge University Press.

———— (nd), 'Introduction to Communities of Practice: A Brief Overview of the Concept and its Uses', *Wenger–Trayner* [Online], Available: http://wenger-trayner.com/introduction-to-communities-of-practice/ [Accessed 13 March 2015].

West, Gerald O. (1991), *Biblical Hermeneutics of Liberation: Modes of Reading the Bible in the South African Context*, Pietermaritzburg: Cluster Publications.

———— (1993), *Contextual Bible Study*, Pietermaritzburg: Cluster Publications.

———— (1999), *The Academy of the Poor: Towards a Dialogical Reading of the Bible*, Sheffield: Sheffield Academic Press.

———— (2007a), 'Introduction', in Gerald O. West (ed.), *Reading Other-Wise: Socially Engaged Biblical Scholars Reading with Their Local Communities*, Atlanta, GA: Society of Biblical Literature, pp. 1–5.

West, Gerald O. (ed.) (2007b), *Reading Other-Wise: Socially Engaged Biblical Scholars Reading with Their Local Communities*, Atlanta, GA: Society of Biblical Literature.

Wetzel, James (2004), 'Splendid Vices and Secular Virtues: Variations on Milbank's Augustine', *Journal of Religious Ethics*, 32, 2, 271–300.

Whipp, Margaret (2012), 'Lucky Lections: On Using the Bible in Practical Theology', *Practical Theology*, 5, 3, 341–4.

Wiles, M. F. (1970), 'Theodore of Mopsuestia as Representative of the Antiochene School', in P. R. Ackroyd and C. A. Evans (eds), *The Cambridge History of the Bible: From the Beginnings to Jerome*, Cambridge: Cambridge University Press, pp. 489–509.

Williams, D. H. (1999), *Retrieving the Tradition & Renewing Evangelicalism: A Primer for Suspicious Protestants*, Grand Rapids, MI: Eerdmans.

———— (2005), *Evangelicals and Tradition: The Formative Influences of the Early Church*, Milton Keynes: Paternoster.

Williams, Stuart Murray (2008), 'Anabaptist Hermeneutics: A Summary', Available: http://www.anabaptistnetwork.com/node/247 [Accessed 5 February 2013].

Willis, Paul (2000), *The Ethnographic Imagination*, Cambridge: Polity Press.

Willis, Paul and Mats Trondman (2001), 'Manifesto', *Ethnography*, 1, 1.

Wimbush, Vincent (ed.) (2008), *Theorizing Scriptures: New Critical Orientations to a Cultural Phenomenon*, New Brunswick, NJ: Rutgers University Press.

Wink, Walter (1973), *The Bible in Human Transformation*, Philadelphia, PA: Fortress.

———— (2003), *Jesus and Nonviolence: A Third Way*, Minneapolis, MN: Fortress Press.

Wm. B. Eerdmans Publishing Company (2015a), 'The Two Horizons New Testament Commentary', *Wm. B. Eerdmans Publishing Co.* [Online], Available: http://www.eerdmans.com/Products/CategoryCenter.aspx?CategoryId=SE!THNTC [Accessed 25 February 2015].

———— (2015b), 'The Two Horizons Old Testament Commentary', *Wm. B. Eerdmans Publishing Co.* [Online], Available: http://www.eerdmans.com/Products/CategoryCenter.aspx?CategoryId=SE!THOTC [Accessed 25 Feburary 2015].

Wolfhart Pannenberg (trans. George H. Kehm) (1970), *Basic Questions in Theology, Vol. 1*, London: SCM Press Ltd.

Wolters, Al (2000), 'Confessional Criticism and the Night Visions of Zechariah', in Craig G. Bartholomew, et al. (eds), *Renewing Biblical Interpretation*, Carlisle: Paternoster, pp. 90–117.

Wolterstorff, Nicholas (1984), *Reason within the Bounds of Religion*, Grand Rapids, MI: Eerdmans.

Wood, Charles M. (2000), *The Formation of Christian Understanding: Theological Hermeneutics*, Eugene, OR: Wipf and Stock.

Wood, W. Jay (1998), *Epistemology: Becoming Intellectually Virtuous*, Downers Grove, IL: IVP.

Wooden, Cindy (2008), 'Not an easy read: Survey indicates Bible hard to understand', *Catholic News Service* [Online], Available: http://www.catholicnews.com/data/stories/cns/0802435.htm [Accessed 18 July 2013].

Workshop (nd), 'Statements of Faith', *Workshop* [Online], Available: www.workshop.org.uk/statementsoffaith [Accessed 11 March 2015].

World Council of Churches (1998), 'A Treasure in Earthen Vessels: An Instrument for an Ecumenical Reflection on Hermeneutics', *World Council of Churches* [Online], Available: http://www.oikoumene.org/en/resources/documents/commissions/faith-and-order/iv-interpretation-the-meaning-of-our-words-and-symbols/a-treasure-in-earthen-vessels [Accessed 6 November 2014].

Wright, N. T. (1992), *The New Testament and the People of God*, Minneapolis, MN: Augsburg Fortress.

———— (2013), *Paul and the Faithfulness of God (Parts III and IV)*, London: SPCK.

Wright, Tom (2010), *Virtue Reborn*, London: SPCK.

Wuthnow, Robert (ed.) (1994a), *"I Come Away Stronger": How Small Groups Are Shaping American Religion*, Grand Rapids, MI: Eerdmans.

Wuthnow, Robert (1994b), *Sharing the Journey: Support Groups and America's New Quest for Community*, New York, NY: Free Press.

Wyld, Richard Michael (2014), *The Hermeneutics of Hope: The Significance of a Doctrine of Christian Hope for the Theological Interpretation of the Bible*, Durham theses, Durham University: Available at Durham E-Theses Online: http://etheses.dur.ac.uk/10648/.

Yin, Robert (1989), *Case Study Research: Design and Methods*, London: Sage.

Young, Frances (1990), 'Alexandrian Interpretation', in R. J. Coggins and J. L. Houlden (eds), *The SCM Dictionary of Biblical Interpretation*, London: SCM, pp. 10–12.

————— (2003), 'Alexandrian and Antiochene Exegesis', in Alan J. Hauser and Duane F. Watson (eds), *A History of Biblical Interpretation: The Ancient Period*, Grand Rapids, MI: Eerdmans, pp. 334–54.

Zagzebski, Linda Trinkhaus (1996), *Virtues of the Mind: An Inquiry into the Nature of Virtue and the Ethical Foundations of Knowledge*, Cambridge: Cambridge University Press.

Subject and Name Index

References to footnotes consist of the page number followed by the letter 'n' followed by the number of the footnote, e.g. 138n42 refers to footnote 42 on page 138. References to figures are shown in *italics*. References to tables are shown in **bold**.

Scripture Index

References to footnotes consist of the page number followed by the letter 'n' followed by the number of the footnote, e.g. 188n29 refers to footnote 29 on page 188.

OLD TESTAMENT

NEW TESTAMENT